This book is dedicated to my grandparents who had the courage to settle in a strange and often hostile country, to my parents whose lives were drastically altered by the internment and relocation, and to sansei, such as myself, who struggled to seek acceptance and find a place in Canadian society.

T0243615

GAMAN

PERSEVERANCE

ALSO BY ART MIKI

The Japanese Canadian Redress Legacy: A Community Revitalized

Shaku of Wondrous Grace: Through the Garden of Yoshimaru Abe
(with Henry Kojima and Sylvia Jansen)

GAMAN

PERSEVERANCE

Japanese Canadians' Journey to Justice

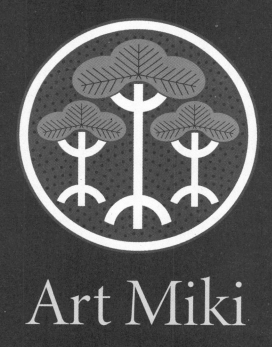

Art Miki

Foreword by Phil Fontaine

TALONBOOKS

Talonbooks
9259 Shaughnessy Street, Vancouver, British Columbia, Canada V6P 6R4
talonbooks.com

Talonbooks is located on xʷməθkʷəy̓əm, Sḵwx̱wú7mesh, and səlilwətaɬ Lands.

First printing: 2023

Typeset in Arno
Printed and bound in Canada on 100% post-consumer recycled paper

Miki family crest used on the cover stylized by Jesse Miki. The image of three trees comes from the Miki surname, 三 mi meaning "three" and 木 ki meaning "trees."

All photographs from the Art Miki collection unless otherwise noted
Cover and interior design by Leslie Smith

Talonbooks acknowledges the financial support of the Canada Council for the Arts, the Government of Canada through the Canada Book Fund, and the Province of British Columbia through the British Columbia Arts Council and the Book Publishing Tax Credit.

LIBRARY AND ARCHIVES CANADA CATALOGUING IN PUBLICATION

Title: Gaman – perseverance : Japanese Canadians' journey to justice / by Arthur K. Miki ; foreword by Phil Fontaine.
Names: Miki, Arthur K., author.
Description: Includes bibliographical references and index.
Identifiers: Canadiana 2023054861X | ISBN 9781772015416 (softcover)
Subjects: LCSH: Miki, Arthur K. | LCSH: Japanese—Canada—Biography. | LCSH: Japanese—Reparations—Canada. | LCSH: Reparations for historical injustices—Canada. | CSH: Japanese Canadians—Biography. | CSH: Japanese Canadians—Forced relocation and internment, 1941-1949. | LCGFT: Auto-biographies.
Classification: LCC FC106.J3 M55 2023 | DDC 971/.0049560092—dc23

by Phil Fontaine

I am honoured to provide this contribution to Art Miki's book because I consider him a dear friend and as someone that not only recognized injustice but did something about it. Born Arthur Kazumi Miki in Vancouver, British Columbia, in 1936, Art was forced, along with his family, to relocate from their fruit farm near Vancouver to a sugar-beet farm in Ste. Agathe, Manitoba, when he was five years old.

Following the attack on Pearl Harbor in December 1941 during World War II, the Canadian government wrongly confiscated the homes and businesses of Canadians of Japanese descent. Many were also sent to internment camps due to unfounded suspicions of potential Japanese espionage. This unjust practice occurred in both the United States and Canada. The Miki family decided to accept the move to Manitoba rather than risk having the family separated in an internment camp.

Art later became an educator, serving for many years, first as a teacher and then as vice-principal and principal of schools in Manitoba. In 1984, Art started his tenure as President of the National Association of Japanese Canadians (NAJC), and he led the group through a negotiated process with the Canadian government that resulted in the Japanese Canadian Redress Settlement in September 1988. The settlement provided compensation to Japanese Canadians who suffered because of the confiscation of property and their internment experience in the 1940s. Art's strong leadership and negotiating and bridge-building skills were critical throughout the negotiation process.

When I was National Chief of the Assembly of First Nations (AFN), we worked for many years to negotiate the Indian Residential Schools Settlement Agreement, which was eventually completed and implemented in September 2007. The Japanese Canadian Redress Settlement provided us with an important blueprint that helped guide the First Nations' collective effort, and Art was a valuable source of advice and encouragement for me personally throughout what was a long and challenging process.

I am so pleased to contribute to this book in a small way and I know that readers will be enriched by learning about Japanese Canadians and their experiences in Canada. All Canadians, regardless of ancestry, will benefit by learning about Art and about an important part of Canadian history that may not be widely known.

Anything Is Possible

The Japanese word *gaman* 我慢 has its origin in Zen Buddhism and, as a verb, means "to endure the seemingly unbearable with patience and dignity." Gaman was a belief held by many Japanese Canadians who were placed in traumatic and unpredictable situations during World War II. They faced hardship and humiliation as "enemy aliens." Despite losing their homes and livelihoods, interned and forced to disperse across Canada, Japanese Canadians rebuilt their lives after the war with determination and perseverance. Gaman was reflected during the redress movement when dedicated community leaders and supporters who sought justice for past wrongs were subjected to harassment and criticism from their own community members. The credibility of the National Association of Japanese Canadians (NAJC) as a national representative was questioned along with the legitimacy of roadblocks and frustrations that often confronted us during the redress journey. The redress campaign was a lesson in perseverance for all of us.

The main theme of my memoir, which can be summarized by the formula "Anything is possible," is my personal belief that has guided me in my life's journey, a road well travelled, filled with hardships, unexpected diversions and challenges, but also hope, successes, celebrations, and fulfillment. It is this journey that *Gaman* explores: my early years through my family's history (whose traits will no doubt be familiar to many Japanese Canadians), growing up in a climate of uncertainty and hardship following World War II, integrating into

Canadian society as an educator and community leader, and finding new challenges during the post-redress era.

The success of the redress settlement led me on different paths that I had never envisioned were possible, and those experiences have enhanced my life to the fullest. Even though this book found its genesis back in the early 1990s, as I became older I was able to incorporate further life experiences that have made my life fulfilling and gratifying.

This journey that I embarked upon was guided by beliefs and teachings that I applied when faced with challenges. I have always tried to maintain a positive outlook whenever faced with troublesome situations. One thing I learned from my aunt Kome Nagasaki, my father's eldest sister, is that a positive view of life and people is always infectious. She claimed that she was the luckiest person alive, despite being a victim of abuses during World War II. She lived to ninety-nine years of age. I attribute her long years to the positive attitude she carried all her life. Even when situations seem hopeless and untenable, one should try to look for some positive aspect that gives hope. My philosophy of overcoming adversity is based on a conviction that anything is achievable. I, for one, have never shied away from challenges but would rather face them head-on, with the confidence that I would be able to overcome obstacles and meet my goals.

I strongly feel that in facing challenges, one must take risks and not be afraid of failure. In my school office, I had a saying posted on the wall: "If you don't make mistakes, you are not learning." There is a Chinese proverb that says: "Failure is not the opposite of success; it's part of success." Setbacks and failure are great learning tools that will be an asset later on. I found that people sometimes saw potential in me that I had not envisioned. For instance, it was another principal whose confidence in my ability gave me the impetus to become an elementary school principal.

In my personal journey, I have often felt that destiny, fate, or chance happenings have greatly influenced my life. I would like to think that it all *was* predetermined. There were many chance happenings that changed my life's direction or created a new path.

The most challenging action I faced during my journey was as president of the NAJC and spokesperson for the Japanese Canadian community in the struggle to seek redress from the Canadian government. In 1942, the Canadian government, using the power of the War

Measures Act, enacted unjust policies that deprived Japanese Canadians of their basic rights and destroyed vibrant Japanese Canadian communities in British Columbia. This memoir details the struggles to seek redemption and acknowledgment from the Canadian government. The repercussions of the historic redress agreement would have a tremendous impact on my life, as they did for other Japanese Canadians and for Canadian society as a whole.

The redress settlement has had many positive implications, not only for Japanese Canadians but for Canadian society. It has heightened Canadians' awareness of the historical injustices inflicted by our own government, not only on Canadians of Japanese ancestry but on other minority groups as well, and has established a precedent for other groups to seek redress. The settlement has been a catalyst for the revitalization of a community that was dispersed and was reluctant to talk about the past. For me, the government's actions to redress the past injustices was an expression of Canada's commitment to the preservation of human rights, and especially of the rights of minorities. I am confident that legislation such as the Canadian Charter of Rights and Freedoms, the Emergencies Act, and the Multiculturalism Act will ensure in the future that the unjust treatment of Japanese Canadians will not be repeated.

This book is an opportunity for me to document the inner workings of the NAJC and negotiations with the Canadian government. For Japanese Canadians who received redress, this book details the complexities of the redress struggle for our community and provides a better understanding of the purpose and processes that led to a successful resolution. For future generations, it can act as a study of a minority group's struggle to overcome the political process and system.

The most gratifying personal reward of the redress struggle was the genuine interest and involvement of dedicated Japanese Canadians who took up the challenge and succeeded in finally achieving redemption for a community whose rights were so unmercifully violated by their own government. What began as a "voice in the wilderness" became a story of national prominence and a truly Canadian issue. The early cynicism and antagonistic reactions that I encountered from individuals within the Japanese Canadian community gradually evolved into hope as powerful voices emerged saying that redress might be achievable in their lifetime. This was reinforced by

Canadians from all walks of life who joined the National Coalition in support of a just and meaningful resolution and the tremendous influence of the media in educating Canadians and urging the government to negotiate redress.

Gaman also includes an abridged narrative of my life's journey. I want to share that the redress experience had a tremendous impact on the rest of my life. It has accorded me opportunities and challenges that I would not have envisioned possible. Being engaged in the political process and forming contacts with politicians and bureaucrats became a motivation for me to run in the 1993 federal election. As a Member of the Order of Canada, I was given the opportunity to become a Canadian citizenship judge in 1998, an experience I will forever cherish. I received tremendous satisfaction in welcoming new citizens to Canada.

I use Japanese words to describe the various sectors of the Japanese Canadian community. *Issei* is a term used to describe the first generation of Japanese immigrants living in a foreign country. My grandparents, who were born in Japan and immigrated to Canada, were issei. *Nisei* refers to the second generation or children of issei. My parents, who were both born in Canada, were nisei. I am a *sansei*, a third-generation; *yonsei* is fourth-generation, and my grandchildren are *gosei*, fifth-generation. Another term used in the Japanese Canadian community is *nikkei*, which refers to people of Japanese ancestry living abroad as citizens of another country. *Nikkei* is often used in organizational names or events.

CHAPTER 1

Rough Beginnings

i settle inside the
hide she cleaned

scraping downward
as her arms ache

she slides inside
the wounded skin

wound up as a doll
moves legs along

the train as cattle
car with her kids

her pregnant body
in so many borders

lines of field grass
flitting by the window

& she was going to ask
for a scene change?

river flow of family
afloat a drift of snow

diamonds in the rough
angels on the ground

a race to erase so long
we said so long so long

in the bye by lingual of
falling from the pear tree

—ROY MIKI
from "era sure," *Random Access File* (1995, reprinted with permission)

Once there was a berry-and-fruit farm of seven acres in Haney, British Columbia, that belonged to Tokusaburo and Yoshi Ooto. They lived in a modest one-and-a-half-storey house with a veranda that stretched across the front. A cherry tree grew in front of the house, its branches reaching out over the yard.

Behind the Ootos' home was a smaller house where Tokusaburo and Yoshi's daughter Shizuko and her family lived. Their little boys played in their grandfather's orchard, a beautiful place with a creek running through it. Often, the boys picked apples and pears to take a few bites, only to leave the rest to rot on the ground. In the fall, Tokusaburo walked with his grandson a half mile every day to go to kindergarten.

Or so I'm told.

I only have a few memories of living in British Columbia, things like the evening my family was at my maternal grandparents' house and someone noticed that the chimney on our house was on fire. My grandfather and father ran out with buckets of water to put it out. Luckily, the trouble was caught quickly, and the damage was minor.

Most recollections of my early life have been forged in my mind by looking at old black-and-white photographs that my mother kept but threatened to throw out because "They take up too much room, and besides, who wants them anyhow?" Pictures are my connection to the past. When I see a picture of myself as a small child, dressed up in my best tam and short-pants suit, sitting on my mother's lap on the steps leading up to my grandparents' front veranda, I wonder if the picture was taken on a special occasion, and who took it.

In 1987, the images from the old photographs became clearer when my mother, my brother Roy, my wife Keiko, and I visited Haney and the houses where my grandparents and parents had lived.

Of course, many things had changed.

The land had been subdivided, other homes built on the property. The fruit trees were all gone except for the cherry tree, and it was certainly not as big as I remembered. Only a dried-up gully marked where the creek had been.

The original houses were still being used. The house that I had lived in had been renovated, as my mother pointed out: "The living room used to be the garage." In contrast, my grandparents' house had not changed at all. Even the front veranda and the steps were the originals, and the cupboards that my grandfather built in the dining room were still there. The current owner told us that when he had started digging beside the house, he had found layers of tiles, which could have been placed there for drainage. "Somebody went to a lot of trouble to prepare this," he commented. This is where my grandfather had planted the raspberry and strawberry bushes.

While attending my niece's wedding in Vancouver in September 1992, Keiko and I took our three children out to Haney to visit their great-grandparents' former homestead. Although they had never been to Haney, they had seen old photographs of the farm. For them it was an excursion into the past. We found that the house that I lived in was boarded up, windows broken, ready to be demolished. What was more disheartening was that the small creek that I remembered as a four-year-old child was no longer there. The developers had filled the creek and levelled it to make way for a cul-de-sac and more new houses.

Fortunately, my grandparents' house was still occupied by the owner I had met previously. He allowed us to walk through it and described all the things that were part of the original house, such as the veranda, which was now in a state of disrepair. The owner was feeling pressured by the developers to sell his property – to be replaced by more new homes. With an offer of $850,000 for the land and house, the owner didn't think he would hold out much longer. A year later, when I visited Haney, my grandparents' house was empty

ABOVE: Art's grandparents' house in Haney, BC, circa 1940. From left to right: Art, Kunio, and Art's mother, Shizuko, holding Joan

All photographs are from the Art Miki collection unless otherwise noted.

BELOW: The same house in Haney, BC, 1992, with Art's children Tani, Jonathan, and Geoffrey standing on the porch

and boarded up. Sadly, I realized that the next time I returned, whatever remnants of the past that had existed for my family would only be memories.

It was in May 1903 that Grandfather Ooto and his wife, both from Fukuoka Prefecture in southwest Japan, left Yokohama and landed in Victoria, BC. Initially, Grandfather Ooto worked in mines and sawmills. Confident that the Skeena area in northern BC could be a prosperous fishing centre, he and his wife moved there, worked the fishing season, and he found a job at Cunningham Sawmills nearby. My grandfather won an agreement with the Skeena River Commercial Co. Cannery to act as an employment broker and supply Japanese cannery workers to the area. They lived in Port Essington across the bay from Prince Rupert at a fish cannery where many Japanese women worked. My mother, Shizuko, was born in Port Essington and lived there with her parents and two brothers, Tameo and Takeo. Realizing when the children were school-aged that Port Essington was not a suitable environment to raise a family, my grandparents decided to move the family south where they believed the schools would be better.

Then, in 1918, almost two decades after immigrating to Canada, Grandfather Ooto bought fourteen acres of land in Port Haney and moved there with his family to establish the berry-and-fruit farm. The stability of this permanent home ensured that his children would be able to attend school regularly. Later, he sold seven acres of his property to the Mitani family, who were friends.

My paternal grandparents were also from Fukuoka, but they settled in Canada in quite a different way. My aunt, Kome Nagasaki, is my father's oldest sister. She told me that her father, Yukutaro Shintani, came to Canada with his first wife in 1892 and started as a sawmill worker at the Hastings Mill in Vancouver. When his wife passed away in 1897, my grandfather, unable to care for his daughter, took her back to Japan, where she unexpectedly died. He then decided to return to Canada as a single man and became a naturalized Canadian as a Shintani. He returned to Japan to marry Kiyo Miki through an arrangement. Both the Shintani and Miki families were from Karita in Fukuoka Prefecture. On marriage Yukutaro changed his name to Miki because there were no Miki male heirs. To ensure the continuation of a family name, it was a common practice at the time for Japanese husbands to take their wife's name if she had no brothers.

After remarrying, Yukutaro Miki wanted to return to Canada but lacked the finances to do so. In 1899, the Mikis were able to arrange free passage to Hawai'i in return for working on a sugar-cane plantation for at least a year, earning $13 a month. With enough money saved, they migrated to Vancouver rather than the mainland United States because Yukutaro was familiar with British Columbia. So in 1900, Yukutaro and Kiyo Miki returned to Canada to live in Tynehead, BC, a logging camp near New Westminster.

My father, Kazuo Miki, was born on June 22, 1907, in Tynehead. His father, Yukutaro, later became a fisherman on the Fraser River and along the West Coast of BC, fishing for salmon during the summer and shrimp in the winter. Later, he became a full-time shrimp fisherman. Yukutaro was known to be a heavy drinker and developed a bad stomach. He passed away in 1922, leaving behind a young family, forcing Kiyo to care for her seven children by running a rooming house. My aunt, Kome Nagasaki, the eldest daughter, recalls that after her father's death, Kiyo took the two youngest daughters to Japan to be raised by her sister and returned to Canada to support the four remaining children, including my father. I remember my father sending money to Japan during my youth and found out later that he was helping support his remaining sister. One sister died in 1926 and the other in 1946, after the war had ended. Unfortunately, after my father passed away in 1969, there was no contact with his family. Her children remember Kiyo as a strong independent leader for the family. Kiyo succeeded in caring for her remaining children herself, worked her whole life, and lived to the modest age of ninety-three. She was born a tiger on the Japanese zodiac, and with her intelligence and perception took charge of her unforeseen situation. Apparently, she loved to gamble at hanafuda (a Japanese card game) and blackjack, which her peers deemed unladylike behaviour. She didn't drink, but she smoked. I remember when my grandmother came for my father's funeral: each morning I would see her at the kitchen table with a tin of tobacco and paper rolling her cigarettes for the day. She was a feisty and determined woman.

I was born in Haney on September 1, 1936, followed by my brother Kunio (Leslie) and sister Joan. My birth wasn't registered until my parents were living in Vancouver and so my birth certificate states that I was born in Vancouver. My mother told me that she named me Arthur after a minister she knew because she hoped that one day I would become a minister. My middle name is Kazumi, which means "harmony."

My parents were married in March 1935 and moved to Alexander Street in Vancouver. When I was two years old, my father found work as a truck driver for Canal Logging Company, owned by Kahei Kamimura, and so the family lived at the logging camp in the mountains just north of Mission, BC. Mr. Kamimura started a number of sawmills in British Columbia in the 1920s; before the war he owned sawmills all over the province and hired Japanese Canadians as workers.

Most Japanese Canadians of my father's generation were wage labourers, working in the fishing, farming, mining, or lumber industries. Without the right to vote, Japanese Canadians were restricted from a number of professions and from employment in the civil service. British Columbia passed legislation in 1895 that made it illegal to put the name of a Japanese Canadian or Chinese Canadian on the voters' list.

Back in the spring of 1940, my parents, younger brother Kunio, and sister Joan lived at the Canal Lake camp site with the other workers' families. One day in May, my father was driving a logging truck past our house when it got a flat tire. Just on the other side of the road, which sloped down because of the hilly terrain, my brother and I were playing with a neighbour, unaware of the problem. Without warning, the flat caused the back of the truck to tilt, freeing the huge logs to roll off the flatbed and down the slope to the area where we were playing.

My friend was the luckiest of the three of us and escaped unharmed, but my brother and I were not so fortunate. One of the huge logs rolled over Kunio's leg and broke it. A branch protruding from one of the rolling logs caught the side of my face, ripping open my left cheek, leaving half my face hanging from my jaw. It happened so quickly I didn't know in the moment what had occurred. My mother, who was with my baby sister Joan, saw the accident and quickly called for my father to get a towel to cover my face. For a moment he was unaware that we were injured. When he noticed what had happened, he was too shocked to respond. When my mother saw the blood, she ran into the house to get a clean towel with which to

OPPOSITE LEFT: Art's baby photo, Vancouver, BC, 1936

OPPOSITE RIGHT: Art at two years old with his mother Shizuko Miki, Vancouver, 1938

OPPOSITE BOTTOM: Four-year-old Art, one-year-old sister Joan sitting on Shizuko's lap, and three-year-old brother Kunio at Canal Lake logging camp, 1940

ABOVE: Five-year-old Art with his kindergarten class in Haney, BC

hold the portion of my face that was torn and hanging. She called to my father, who refused even to come close to me. "Go and get a driver," she said. "Get someone with a car to take Art to the hospital."

Frank Araki, who was on the campsite that day, recalls that we were fortunate that Mr. Mori, one of the workers, returned to the campsite with his car shortly after the accident occurred. The truck with the flat tire blocked the road and prevented the use of other cars in the area to take me into Mission. Mr. Sato quickly turned around and drove my mother and me to Mission Hospital. There, my mother told the doctor that she wanted me taken to a hospital in Vancouver. The doctor disagreed: "No, he might die before you get to Vancouver, so you better not take him." The wound was hastily closed with about thirty stitches, as it was feared that I would die from the loss of blood and the extent of the damage. The accident left a noticeable, permanent scar on the left side of my face. As my mother had to return to the logging camp to be with my sister Joan, Grandmother Miki came from Vancouver and stayed with me at the hospital for five days until I was able to go home. My brother went to live with Grandmother Ooto to recuperate from his broken leg. About seven years later, I needed surgery to correct the alignment of scar tissue around my mouth and to facilitate speech.

During the summer of 1941, my parents moved to my grand-parents' farm in Haney because the logging company closed down, forcing my father out of work; also, it was time for me to start going to school. We lived in my grandparents' home while my father con-verted a garage on the property into a home for us. My mother recalls that they had just had the living room done and had bought new fur-niture when they were forced to leave. "We never even sat in it," she lamented. By fall, we moved in and I began attending kindergarten classes. My father found another job driving for a logging company out of town and only came home on weekends. Grandfather Ooto used to walk me to school until a neighbour's daughter attending school agreed to walk with me.

Then Japanese Canadians were given orders to leave their homes and move away from coastal areas. My mother was hopeful and thought that Canadian-born and naturalized Canadians, like her father and mother, would be spared the drastic measures limiting their freedoms. But shortly after, she found out that was not the case. Responding to the threat of war with Japan, Canada invoked the War Measures Act, giving the Cabinet sweeping powers to govern by Order-in-Council without the approval of Parliament. On February 24, 1942, Cabinet passed Order-in-Council PC 1486, which authorized the removal of all persons of Japanese ancestry from within one hundred miles of BC's west coast. Furthermore, it assigned the RCMP the power to search without warrant, enforce a dusk-to-dawn curfew, and to confiscate cars, radios, cameras, and firearms. When my mother was told that everybody, even those born in Canada, had to move, she was infuriated.

Japanese Canadians who lived on Vancouver Island and along the mainland coast were the first to be removed. Because of the shortage of farmworkers, the Manitoba Sugar Beet Growers sent representatives to the Haney area to recruit workers for the sugar-beet farms in southern Manitoba. At the time, my mother was pregnant and was told by government officials that she should go to an internment camp because there were doctors there; if she went to the Prairies, there wouldn't be any doctors. But she refused to go because she wanted to stay with her parents, who did not want to go to a camp. My mother said, "We wanted to keep our family together, so that's why we wanted to go to Manitoba. If I was separated from my parents, I would be sent to Greenwood with my husband's mother and sister." My grandparents and parents decided that the move to Manitoba was the best alternative. This was a cruel policy at the time, splitting up families if they chose to move to the BC Interior and sending husbands and fathers to road camps, away from their wives and children. This policy didn't last long, but the uprooting process had begun.

One of the many dilemmas that faced Japanese Canadians, including my grandfather, was what to do with their property. Although government officials assured people that their property would be held in trust by the Custodian of Enemy Property, many were skeptical. There was an uneasy feeling that the government wanted to get rid of all people of Japanese origin on the West Coast.

An Anglo-Canadian minister visiting the United Church in Haney, who stayed at Grandfather Ooto's home, suggested to my grandfather, "You should sell your place. The war will last four or five years." Thinking that something was better than nothing, many farmers sold their farms to real estate opportunists for very low prices, as there was no time to put their properties on the market. Rather than having his property confiscated, Grandfather Ooto received only $2,500 for his home and business. Today, the same property is worth several million dollars.

One of Grandfather Ooto's friends, Kunesaburo Hayakawa, was among the first Japanese Canadians to be affected by Order-in-Council PC 1486. Japanese Canadians who lived in coastal villages such as Prince Rupert were the first to be removed from their homes and brought to Vancouver.

Mr. Hayakawa was sent to a road camp with other Japanese nationals; Grandfather Ooto brought Mr. Hayakawa's two grown children, Nori and Joe, to stay with him in Haney rather than be taken to Hastings Park, where barns and buildings had been hastily designated as makeshift holding tanks for displaced Japanese Canadians. When the first "evacuees" had arrived, there were still traces of manure on the floor, and the stench of the former residents lingered strongly.

In May 1942, Mr. Hayakawa was released from the road camp. Arriving in Haney to retrieve his children, he was informed that the Ooto and Miki families would be leaving by train in a few days for the sugar-beet fields. Knowing that they had nowhere else to go, Grandfather Ooto suggested that the Hayakawas join my family for the trek to Manitoba.

On May 22, 1942, during the Victoria Day weekend, the Ootos, the Mikis, and the Hayakawas all arrived in Winnipeg and were taken to the Immigration Hall adjacent to the Canadian Pacific Railway station. My mother recalls that the train passengers were from Haney and Hammond, with one family from Mission. Each person received two dollars for food, and the trip took three days and two nights in cramped day coaches. Japanese Canadians were held at Immigration Hall until arrangements were made to go with farmers. Each day farmers would come down to the Hall to look at the families and to decide which Japanese Canadian families they wanted to take back to their sugar-beet farms. Harold Hirose, one of the leaders of the Japanese Canadian community during this period, recalls that the selection process was akin to that of a slave market. Families with several able-bodied adults were usually the first to be selected. Some families with young children and an adult or two that were able to work remained at the Immigration Hall for several months before being placed. Those families were not considered a priority by the authorities. We were the second group out of three that came that year, bringing 1,075 Japanese Canadians to Manitoba.

After staying overnight in Winnipeg, our family and the Hayakawas were transported by an old farm truck to Les Lemoine's farm near Ste. Agathe, a small French Canadian community forty kilometres south of Winnipeg on Highway 75. We were taken to a four-room, abandoned structure that was to become the home for seven adults and four young children. My mother did the cooking while all the other adults worked in the fields. At this time my mother was pregnant; she was expecting in the fall. In order for her to deliver her child, she had to write a letter to the government requesting permission to travel to the Winnipeg Health Centre to give birth. At that time, Japanese Canadians were restricted from visiting or travelling beyond ten miles and barred from living in Winnipeg. As a result, permission from the Royal Canadian Mounted Police (RCMP) through the British Columbia Securities Commission (BCSC) was required. She travelled to Winnipeg alone by bus under these dire conditions to the Women's Pavilion, where my brother Roy was born on October 10, 1942.

While there was no overt hostility expressed towards us by the Ste. Agathe residents, this was little comfort for the families who had been forcibly displaced from the thriving greenery of the orchards and strawberry patches of British Columbia to the seemingly desolate and endless prairie fields of Manitoba. Growing and harvesting sugar beets proved to be difficult and tedious work compared to what we were accustomed to. For their laborious efforts, my family was paid twenty-five cents an hour so as not to exceed the lowest wage paid to a soldier in the Canadian army.

Our house, a dilapidated shack, was situated in a field unsheltered from the cold harsh winter winds and blowing snow. The house was poorly insulated, lacked running water or electricity, and provided minimal shelter. There was no water on the property; my father had to borrow the farmer's truck and haul water in barrels from a well. My grandfather built a wooden "ofuro," or Japanese bath, in a shack so that the adults would be able to bathe. The kids had their baths in a large round galvanized container about fifteen inches deep that sat in the middle of the kitchen.

I began attending Ste. Agathe School, which was run by the Roman Catholic Church, in September 1942 and was taught in French by the

First Christmas in Manitoba for Art, Kunio, and Joan

nuns. As a six-year-old child, the sudden thrust into an unfamiliar school environment was made even more traumatic because of my unfamiliarity with the French language. Although I spoke Japanese and some English at home, my first two years of education were in French. Because I was not Catholic, I was excused from the regular religious services that were incorporated into the secular program.

My recollection of these school experiences is very limited, but my mother remembers that I walked about a half mile to get to school every day. She recalls that when the weather began to get cold, I often came home with frozen cheeks from the long walk. Although lacking experience of just how cold Manitoba winters could get, my parents quickly realized that the jackets worn in British Columbia were not adequate here, and so they went out and bought a "jacket with a hood" for me.

After the first winter, my grandparents and parents rented a house in Ste. Agathe. The Hayakawas found accommodations in an apartment in town. The French Canadian townspeople were helpful and friendly. They were also curious about us, because many had never seen Japanese people before.

My father worked on the sugar-beet farm for two summers, and in the fall of 1943, he received permission from the BCSC to work in Winnipeg. He lived in a rooming house on Smith Street in downtown Winnipeg while we remained in Ste. Agathe for the winter. Separation of Japanese Canadian families was quite common at the time, as the fathers or other adult family members had to find jobs elsewhere in factories or at logging camps in Northern Ontario in order to survive. The sugar-beet farming wages were simply not sufficient to carry a family through the idle winters.

My father found permanent employment as a machinist at Monarch Machinery in the west end of Winnipeg. Japanese Canadians who wished to live within the city limits had to have approval from the BCSC. Such moves were discouraged, as men were needed on the farms due to the war shortage of labourers. I'm not sure how my father was able to arrange to keep his job in Winnipeg, especially in our early days in Manitoba. People like Harold and Florence Hirose, who settled within Winnipeg in 1943, found that only a few people were willing to rent housing to Japanese Canadians; all they could find was substandard housing that no one else would take.

Because my father had a job in Winnipeg, he received permission from the BCSC for the family to leave the farm and move near the city. In the summer of 1944, we rented a small three-room house for the family and grandparents in North Kildonan, which was then located on the outskirts of Winnipeg; we did not require permission to reside there. By 1944, a few Japanese Canadian families had moved into North Kildonan. The community was of predominantly Mennonite background and was very accepting of Japanese Canadians. Accommodations for Japanese Canadian families were much more readily available there than in Winnipeg, and we were invited by the

GAMAN — PERSEVERANCE

OPPOSITE ABOVE: Working in the field. Kunio and Art stand in front. Behind them from left to right are grandfather Tokusaburo Ooto, father Kazuo Miki, Takao Ooto, friends Kunesaburo Hayakawa and Nori Hayakawa, and grandmother Yoshi Ooto, 1942

ABOVE: Sugar-beet house in Ste. Agathe, MB, 1942

OPPOSITE BELOW: Art and Kunio with their French Canadian friends

LEFT: Family in Ste. Agathe, MB: Kunio, Uncle Takao Ooto, Joan, and Art

Mennonites to attend their Sunday schools and even summer classes for Bible study. I remember spending several summer holidays in Bible classes.

But not all municipalities were as hospitable. St. Andrews Council, just north of North Kildonan, petitioned the BCSC and the provincial government to remove Japanese Canadians who, they said, were living in their municipality against the wishes of the local residents. Connie Matsuo and her family were placed on a sugar-beet farm at Lockport in the St. Andrews municipality. In her memoir, she recalled:

> It turned out to be a nightmare. The shack was sixteen by twenty feet sitting in an open field. Between the lumber there were cracks [through which you could] see daylight. Six adults and two children had to share the house. Strangers came to see "what kind of face has the Japs got, we don't want them around here." The community was terrible to us because many families in the area sent their sons to war in Hong Kong. They belonged to the Winnipeg Grenadiers. People came in groups to see what kind of creatures Japs were and finally they kicked us out of Lockport. We were there for one month.[1]

Although this might be an isolated case, such open hostility and racism are difficult to endure, especially when people are made to feel defenceless in a strange environment.

For myself, the move to a new school, Lord Kitchener School in North Kildonan, was an extremely traumatic event. Having completed grades one and two in Ste. Agathe, I was placed in a grade-three classroom. On the very first day, I was handed a reading book and asked to read part of a story, "The Fox and the Crow." All the words were meaningless, and I couldn't pronounce or read any of them. The teacher then realized I couldn't read English. I was taken out of the class and placed in a grade-two room by the school principal. Although there were several Japanese Canadian students in the school, I was taunted by other students (especially at the beginning) and recall getting into several fights. The principal once strapped me

---

1   From Connie's memoir of her family's experiences in the relocation and settlement in Manitoba, which she privately shared with me. The document is now located in the Japanese Cultural Association of Manitoba's historical archives in Winnipeg.

Art and his grade-four teacher, Mrs. Keith, formerly Miss Burton, 2018

for defending myself in a fight after being harassed. Being new to the school, there were students who often called us names because, as they said, "You look different." But as time passed, the teasing and the name-calling ceased. We became accepted and developed both Japanese Canadian and non–Japanese Canadian friends.

I remember a pretty young teacher at the school who would sometimes walk with us on her way to catch the bus home. It was her first year of teaching and she was called Miss Burton. Although there might have been some negative attitudes towards the Japanese from teachers, I never sensed that from her. One day in the 1980s, I was at the Polo Park mall in Winnipeg when an older woman stopped me. She had remembered me because of the media attention I'd received following my involvement with the redress campaign and told me that she was my grade-four teacher at Lord Kitchener. I looked at her and said, "You must be Miss Burton." She looked surprised that I had remembered her name. I was curious and asked what she recalled about me as a student. She told me that I had beautiful handwriting and that I was her favourite student. She was now Mrs. Keith and was accompanied by her husband, whom I met on the same occasion. Many years after that encounter, I met Mrs. Keith again at an apartment I was visiting, and we had a short conversation. In the interim, her husband had passed away. Strangely, Koji Sato, a member of the

Horizons Club at the Japanese Cultural Centre, had told me excitedly that he had met someone who lived in their building and who had been my teacher. It turned out that it was Mrs. Keith, formerly Miss Burton. I made it a point to visit her at her assisted living complex and reminisced about her teaching days. It was then she told me how proud she was to have taught me. What a memorable, heartfelt encounter I had with my grade-four teacher – seventy years later!

Both my parents had to work for pay in order to care for four young children and their aging grandparents. As long as I can remember, Grandmother Ooto cared for the children in her non-verbal manner and was confined to house chores, while my parents struggled working long hours outside our home.

My mother found a job at Dominion Tanners on Dufferin Avenue in the north end of Winnipeg. She went to work there because a woman at the BCSC told her that several Japanese Canadians were working there. It was owned by a German man who was willing to hire Japanese Canadian workers. Every day, she was up before five in the morning to walk about a mile from our home on Edison Avenue to the end of the bus line to catch a ride to work. She returned late each night, ending the day with that long walk home, where more work usually awaited her. Here was a woman, unaccustomed to such deprivation in British Columbia, now suddenly forced to alter her lifestyle to face the hardships and terrible conditions resulting from expulsion from the West Coast. As a child, I didn't question the reasons for the move from BC; today, we recognize that there was no justifiable reason why people such as my parents and grandparents should have had to endure such pain and suffering.

Working at Dominion Tanners, my mother revealed a side that I was unaware of as a child. She easily developed friendships with the white workers and possessed this wonderful, warm-hearted ability to freely interact with others. She established a close relationship with one of the workers, Adam Lambert, who would become a lifelong friend of the family. Adam eventually married Sally Eyemoto, who was a family relative through marriage. My mother later attended night school to learn bookkeeping, which would become her life's work. Again she developed close rapport with any of the bosses or owners she worked under and became close friends with their families. My father, on the other hand, was quiet and reserved, quite opposite to my mother, but what impressed me was his handiwork, as he created and sewed Mom's dresses for special occasions.

Although my parents were fortunate to find employment in Winnipeg to support the family, there were ongoing efforts to prevent Japanese Canadians from earning a livelihood. In 1942, the Imperial Order Daughters of the Empire (IODE), a Canadian women's charitable organization founded in 1900, sent a letter to then Manitoba Premier Erick Willis that requested: "BE IT Resolved that the Provincial Charter in Session DO PETITION the Provincial Government not to permit the Japanese to enter any business, or fill any position, keeping in mind the necessity of placing our returned men of the Services when the present conflict ended."[2] In Saint-Boniface, on April 19, 1944, Mayor George McLean and council rejected a request to employ Japanese Canadians for packing plants. The mayor told the *Winnipeg Free Press* "that the entire council is prepared to do anything in its power to see that the employment of Japanese in St. Boniface does not happen."[3] It was never clear to me as a child why such negative reactions existed, and this reaction from the St. Boniface mayor is an example of needless racism. What were they afraid of? Such discriminatory attitudes were prevalent in employers, and most Japanese Canadians eventually found employment with companies that were owned by Jews or Germans.

Grandfather Ooto was seventy-six years old when he passed away at our home, at 211 Edison Avenue in North Kildonan, six years after the move to Manitoba. The relocation was a nightmare for him and had taken its toll. Like most issei, he had toiled for a lifetime, only to lose all he had established with a stroke of Prime Minister Mackenzie King's pen as the government ordered the expulsion of Japanese Canadians from the coast.

I remember Tokusaburo Ooto as a proud person. I think he must have felt that he lost much more than just property in the relocation, but he never once expressed a desire to return to Japan. He had been a leader in Haney, and when the Canadian government began

---

2   Letter from the Imperial Order Daughters of the Empire and Children of the Empire to the Honourable Erick Willis, PM of Manitoba, May 18, 1942.

3   "St. Boniface Would Ban Jap Workers [...]," *Winnipeg Free Press*, April 20, 1944, 3, archives. winnipegfreepress.com/winnipeg-free-press/1944-04-20/page-3/. [Editor's note: URLs for newspaper articles are provided in this book whenever they could be located. Some web pages may require a paid subscription or institutional membership.]

Art's grandparents and Uncle Tak Ooto with Joan, Kunio, and Art in North Kildonan, Winnipeg, 1946

pressuring Japanese Canadians to "repatriate" to Japan, he tried to talk people out of it. "You can't kid yourself. It's going to be worse there," he'd tell them. There was one family in particular that he tried to convince, and failed. Within a few years of returning to Japan, both parents had died, and the children returned to Canada one by one as soon as it was financially possible.

In retrospect, I can see that the forced move to Manitoba and the loss of his farm had a devastating effect on my grandfather. At an age when he should have been retiring and enjoying the benefits of his hard work, he was forced to move to unfamiliar surroundings where working on the beet farm was demanding and strenuous. I don't recall my grandfather ever being happy in Manitoba. On his deathbed, he distributed small personal mementos to all of his grandchildren, but he was clearly bothered that he had so little to give.

In 1948, Japanese Canadians were finally allowed to reside in Winnipeg, but had difficulty finding suitable accommodations, clearly because of racism and discrimination. I think my parents found it easier to buy a house in a poorer section or the inner city of Winnipeg, which they could barely afford. They were fortunate to have a friend in Adam Lambert, who lent them money for the down payment. The house they purchased was located at 631 Alexander Avenue, near Logan Avenue and Sherbrook Street in Winnipeg. The name Alexander, and perhaps even the address number, may have appealed to them because they had once lived at 621 Alexander Street in Vancouver, before the war. Although there were three adults and four children living in the house, my parents rented out part of the upstairs to another family to help pay the mortgage. I continued my elementary education at Victoria-Albert School, moved on to junior high at Hugh John Macdonald, and completed my high school education at Daniel McIntyre Collegiate.

For my parents, dealing with the uprooting was painful and they were extremely disappointed with the Canadian government's actions towards them. Like most internees, they felt a sense of betrayal and shame in being marked as "enemy aliens." When I reflect back on the early days in Winnipeg, despite the hardships I am astounded by my parent's resilience and fortitude in re-establishing their life, having to work long hours to make ends meet while living in crowded conditions. The pattern is similar to what new immigrants face today, usually living in the core area of a city where accommodations are cheaper and then moving to preferable residential areas once they have accumulated financial stability.

The people I grew up with in this neighbourhood were poor. Many of their parents were of Polish, Ukrainian, or Métis descent, and most worked as labourers. At the time, we didn't realize that we were disadvantaged, but most of us held one or more part-time jobs during the school year to support our own needs.

In our community there were no established sports programs, so we had to take the initiative to organize baseball, hockey, and football activities and coach teams without any adult involvement or supervision. As a fifteen-year-old, I was coaching a hockey team composed of boys aged ten, eleven, and twelve. Unfortunately, many of the parents couldn't even afford to pay for things like hockey sticks and team uniforms, so we decided to raise funds by going door to door in the area, asking people for donations. Within a couple of weeks, we managed to collect several hundred dollars. When the City Parks officials, who were responsible for the playground hockey league, discovered what we were doing, they confronted us and demanded that we return all the money we had collected. The players who went out

TOP: Grade-six hockey team at Victoria-Albert School, 1949, with Art far left

BOTTOM: Some of the grade-seven class at Victoria-Albert School, 1952, ranked in order of "smartness" (clockwise right to left)

soliciting were disappointed and upset. The bureaucracy had asserted their power and attempted to deny these young players from having the necessary equipment that the other teams had.

Someone suggested that we take our case to the mayor. The popular Mayor Stephen Juba was a down-to-earth politician who lived in the area and was easy to talk to. We had canvassed him, and he had already contributed funds to our cause. Every kid in the area knew that if they went to the Jubas' house on William Avenue on Halloween, they would receive a dollar. So a friend and I, two fifteen-year-old teenagers, arranged to meet the mayor at his City Hall office on Main Street to discuss the problem. We explained the situation to Mayor Juba and the effect the lack of funds would have on the team. He willingly listened to our concerns and was sympathetic to the dilemma that we faced. I felt that he appreciated the initiative we had taken to provide kids with hockey equipment that most parents couldn't afford. Not only did Mayor Juba assure us that we would not have to return the money, but he generously offered more money if we needed to purchase hockey sweaters, socks, and sticks for each player.

It was around this time that I was shown two samurai dolls that Grandmother Ooto had given me when I was born. One was a standing figure, the other sat on a horse; both were in armour and set on wooden bases. It was customary in Japan and among Japanese Canadians before the relocation to give dolls to newborn babies – samurai dolls for boys, and dancer dolls or dolls representing the imperial court for girls – as it was hoped that the dolls would attract misfortune to themselves, away from the children who owned them.

With little time for packing and the limited luggage people could take as they were removed from their homes, Grandmother Ooto had carefully stored these dolls to bring to Manitoba. I was taken aback when these were discovered in the bottom of the trunk five years after our arrival. For me, the dolls are the symbol of the importance my grandmother placed on preserving her values and culture despite being forcibly removed and limited to taking the essentials. These dolls were used in an exhibit at the National Library of Canada in Ottawa when my experience as a Japanese Canadian during the internment was profiled. The dolls raised the question of priorities when people were being dislocated. For my grandmother, my being the first-born meant the dolls were an important figure to safeguard and protect.

The forced removal from the West Coast, the internment, and the dispersal across Canada had a lasting detrimental effect on Japanese Canadian communities and families. At the time of World War II, Japanese Canadians lacked the language, education, and political knowledge to fight blatant government oppression. Japanese Canadian parents impressed upon their children the importance of getting a good education, because they believed that education would be the vehicle that would lead them to better jobs, more successful careers, and acceptance in the Canadian community. Most parents worked long hours at low-paying jobs and sacrificed their own needs to ensure that their children received the benefits of higher education. Education was, in fact, overemphasized, and today Japanese Canadians accrue the benefits of their forebears' persistence and sacrifice, as we have one of the highest proportions of university graduates among all so-called ethnic groups.

During the dispersal period, government encouraged Japanese Canadians to assimilate into the larger Canadian society, and care was taken not to have clusters of Japanese Canadians living near each other. As a result, my generation grew up knowing very few other Japanese Canadians. This lack of association with others from within the community resulted in many marriages outside our ethnic background. Today, Japanese Canadians are one of the most "assimilated" groups in Canada, with intermarriage rates of over 95 percent among our young people. It is ironic that one of the negative reactions expressed by a BC politician against the Japanese in early British Columbia was that "they could not be assimilated." In order to be more like mainstream Canadians, many Japanese Canadians have sacrificed their Japanese heritage and cast aside their language. Their children did not learn the Japanese language, nor did they participate in cultural activities.

Fortunately, there is a revival of interest within the present generation, who seem to value the importance of maintaining their identity and heritage.

CHAPTER 2

Adolescence to Adulthood

In order to make ends meet, my parents had to work long hours and were away from the home until late at night. As in the case of most Japanese Canadian families, our grandparents lived with us. After the death of my grandfather, it was my grandmother who looked after us while our parents worked. Because my grandmother spoke only Japanese, she had very little verbal communication with the kids and we pretty much had control of what we wanted to do.

When I was eight or nine, a friend and I skipped school to catch a muskrat – there was a creek running through the edge of my friend's neighbourhood. We managed to catch the muskrat, kill it, and skin it, intending to sell the fur and make money. We hung the skin up to dry, but it smelled so horrible that after a few days we had to throw the pelt away.

Another time, three classmates and I decided to skip school and go to the home of one of the guys whose parents were both away at work, and so we had the house to ourselves, where we played and smoked cigarettes. Each day we pretended to go to school but went to the friend's house and went home when school was over. After two days of absence from school, the principal finally became suspicious; we were caught and all the parents were notified. I don't remember my parents being visibly angry, but I did have to promise not to do it again. I wondered whether my parents might have been more lenient and at times overlooked negative behaviours because they had faced overt and systemic racism all their lives and wanted their kids to be accepted by other kids.

My brothers weren't exactly model students either, and whenever we got into trouble, my mother would have to contact the principal to discuss the problem. Although she was upset with us, she would listen to our side before she acted. There were many times she had to take time off work to go to our school, and she wouldn't hesitate to express her feelings if the matter appeared trivial to her. A few times she gave the school principal or teacher hell for picking on her kids. She stuck up for us.

This is a story I have never told anyone. When I was eleven years old, I went to the Hudson's Bay Store in downtown Winnipeg, where I spotted a pair of hockey gloves that I wanted. I took them. As I stepped outside the store, a security person stopped me, saw the gloves, and took me back inside. I was taken to a small dingy room in the basement where the security person called my parents. He explained to my mother what I had done and told her that I would not be released until she came to the store. At that time we didn't have a car, so my mother had to take the bus downtown to the Bay. As I was leaving, the security warned me that I was barred from the Bay for three years. When we returned home, Mother didn't get angry or scold me. She knew that I was embarrassed and humiliated enough. She made me a cup of cocoa, put her hands on my shoulder, and said, "You know, Art, if you wanted the gloves badly, we would have found a way to pay for them." For three years I avoided the Bay, fearing that I might be recognized.

By the time I was in grade six or seven, I was a fairly good student, and none of us were malicious troublemakers. I remember when my youngest brother Roy was in grade five, he yelled at the teacher who was making extraordinary demands of a physically challenged student and told the teacher to leave the student alone. By standing up for the student, Roy got expelled from school. The principal called my mother and told her that Roy would not be allowed to return to school unless she met with the principal. She did, but she defended Roy. Even then, as later on, Roy was questioning authority, ready to fight for what he believed in.

When my brother Kunio was fourteen years old and in junior high school, he had extremely long hair when all the boys wore their hair short. Kunio was something of a rebel and wanted to be different from the other guys. The principal, unhappy with his long hair, called him to the office and gave him ten dollars to get a haircut. When the principal found out that Kunio didn't get his hair cut but spent the money on something else, he was upset and called my mother to the school. The principal told her about the ten dollars and that Kunio didn't go to the barber. After listening, Mother responded from her perspective: "Isn't it silly to think that you can give a fourteen-year-old ten dollars and expect him to get a haircut?" I don't think she offered to pay back the money.

I recall another incident involving Kunio, who was then a grade-ten student at Daniel McIntyre Collegiate, the same school I had attended. It happened Kunio was working full-time for the Canadian National Railway at night and missed a lot of days. Whenever he missed classes, I would write an excuse note for him so that my parents didn't know. This amounted to many days in the first three months of school. One day, a gentleman came to the house, walked in the door and into the room where Kunio was sleeping. It was the principal of the high school, who woke Kunio up and took him to school. My grandmother, who spoke no English, was dumbfounded and had a hard time explaining to my mother what had happened. Mother was summoned by the principal to discuss Kunio's absences. During the meeting, the principal showed my mother stacks of notes allegedly signed by her but actually signed by me. My mother was shocked and embarrassed. When she asked why she had not been notified sooner, the principal said he thought that Kunio was on the football team and so he had left it. I felt sorry for her for being placed in such an awkward situation. When she came home, I thought she would be extremely angry with me, but to my surprise all she said was: "You know that was wrong." I really respected the way she handled the situation. She knew how badly I felt and that being angry at me would not accomplish anything.

My mother was the person who influenced us most. She was a high-school graduate at a time when very few females completed high school. She was very articulate and related to other people, especially non-Japanese, with ease and sincerity. Unlike women of her nisei generation who were more complacent and reticent to speak out, my mother would not hesitate to speak her mind when necessary and was not intimidated by authorities if she felt she had been wronged or when defending her children. Her assertive attitude eventually

Art and friend Len Sanderson as teenagers

influenced Roy and me to become engaged in the redress movement. She was extremely supportive of our involvement and kept reminding us what Japanese Canadians had lost. Some of her closest friends became strong advocates for redress. She was my role model.

The need to be accepted by our peer group seemed far more important than many other considerations when we were young. There was pressure to be like your friends and have the same material things they had, like clothes and even cars. We all had part-time jobs to fulfill those needs because our parents were so poor. Most of my friends dropped out of high school to get full-time employment.

My first job was as a *Winnipeg Free Press* newspaper boy near my home. The people in my area were extremely poor, and I had difficulty collecting payments. Some wouldn't pay for several months and then would move without notice. As a paperboy, I had to absorb the loss. At the age of eleven, I began to set pins in a downtown bowling alley, working from five to seven o'clock after school (I was too young to work later in the evening). While I was in high school, I was fortunate to get a prestigious paper route which catered to businesses on Carlton Street, the same street as Winnipeg's Free Press Building. As a result, I was the first to receive my papers, so that my customers would have the paper "hot off the press." I was able to deliver papers and set pins throughout my high-school years. During and after high school, I managed a pool hall in the evening for the owner, Ed Audet, who was also a barber and became a good friend. He entrusted me to run his business, which helped me supplement my income. All my years in junior and senior high school, I had a part-time job and even worked during the summer holidays and yet found time to play sports. It sounds as if I didn't have much time for my studies, which was true. My grades were nothing to brag about.

After graduating from Daniel McIntyre Collegiate, I worked as an office clerk at the Board of Grain Commissioners, a job I did not find challenging in the least. One day in my third year on the job, my boss Allan Melrose, who was in his sixties and looking forward to retirement, called me over and said, "I'd like to give you some advice, Art. I think you're much too smart to be working at a job like this. Do you want to end up like me?" It was constructive comments from individuals such as Allan who had a sincere interest in my potential that prompted me to assess my future and spurred me on to make better use of my abilities. With the advice he had given me, I decided to go to university and further my education.

After resigning from the Board, I enrolled at the Faculty of Engineering at the University of Manitoba in 1959. At that time, French or another second language was a requirement for entry into the Faculties of Science or Arts, and thus limited my choice of faculties. I decided that engineering was my best option, because it did not require a second language and the education and training allowed for direct entry into employment. Of all the friends from my neighbourhood, I was the first to go to university. After failing a few courses and realizing that I may have made the wrong choice, I decided to take a year off to reassess whether to return to engineering or consider a new path.

In the summer of 1961, by chance I ran into Ralph Prior, a high-school friend, whom I had not seen since we graduated. He had been working as a travelling salesperson in British Columbia and had decided to return to Manitoba to train as a teacher. Ralph invited me along, since he was on his way to enroll at the Manitoba Teachers' College. There we met Mr. Brisbin, the principal, who outlined the subsidies that the province was offering to students to attend the college because of the shortage of teachers in Manitoba. I sat listening and thinking that this was a great deal. The cost of attending the Teachers' College was far less than that of engineering. Also, it was a one-year program. The lower cost for tuition and the strong job prospects after graduation appealed to me and convinced me to register with Ralph. In September 1961, I was on my way to becoming a teacher.

Although I had very little knowledge of what to expect, I enjoyed the thought of my newly aquired vocation. I had always been interested in sports and working with young people and felt that I could make a contribution in education. Recalling my own school experiences, I knew that I had some ideas about how to make learning interesting, relevant, and fun, and to create an environment where students would enjoy learning. My interest in going into education was naturally a surprise to most of my friends, who had little respect for teachers and considered school a waste of time.

My first teaching position after graduating in 1962 was at Cross Lake, approximately 650 kilometres north of Winnipeg. Ralph and I applied to teach together for the then Department of Indian Affairs. We were assigned to a two-room school on the Cross Lake Indian Reservation (today the Cross Lake First Nation, or ᐱᒥᒋᑲᒫᐠ ᓂᐦᐃᖬᐄᐧ pimicikamâk nîhithawî) in Northern Manitoba, where we had to fly in by seaplane. My students were all Treaty Indian and ranged in age from five to twelve, kindergarten to grade four. This was the first time I experienced watching students board the plane to be taken to what I would eventually learn was a residential school. There was no high school at Cross Lake. I noticed that some students were reluctant to leave and pleaded with their parents not to go, but there was no

TOP: Art at Cross Lake School, fall, 1962

BOTTOM: Art's students at Cross Lake School, ranging from kindergarten to grade four

choice. It was years later I learned about the Canadian Indian residential school system and the impact it had upon Indigenous students and their parents.

At the time, I assumed that because there was no high school on the reserve, it was customary for students to go to other outside schools to continue their education. Being young and naive, I was completely unaware of how the residential school experience and the government's rationale for its existence would affect the lives of those students. While I was up north at Cross Lake, I don't recall anyone ever telling me about any feelings, negative or otherwise, towards residential schools. Like most Canadians, I was completely unaware at the time of the abusive treatment towards the students or of the cultural genocide against Indigenous Peoples that was occurring in Canada. I surmised that most parents likely received their education at on-reserve schools like the one that I was at. These schools went up to grade eight. In communities where local schools did not exist, these students would have attended residential schools. When I was first assigned to this teaching position, I was warned that a number of students would be missing from school, as some families would go to the traplines for several months at a time. At that time many Indigenous families relied on their traditional way of life.

I enjoyed the experience up north and felt that I had developed a positive rapport with the students and parents. Teachers were instructed to have students speak only English while in the classroom or on the playground and not the variety of Cree mostly spoken in and around Cross Lake, which is Wood Cree, or ᓄᐦᐃᖬᐁᐃᐅ Nîhithawîwin. This was my introduction to how the government attempted to eradicate Indigenous cultures and languages. The teaching materials and textbooks were oriented towards the experiences of white middle-class societies and were meaningless to my students' everyday lives. For example, one textbook told a story of white children going up an escalator in a large department store. The only store these students ever saw was the one-storey Hudson's Bay store, and the concept of an escalator was far removed from their experiences in Cross Lake.

The informal school setting and the independence we were given resulted in a great learning experience for me. We were able to try different instructional approaches and had fun running the school. Teaching was only one aspect of our job. The teacherage that Ralph and I shared was adjacent to the school and was heated with a wooden stove. We used water from the Nelson River for drinking, washing, and cooking. There was no plumbing, and so we had to use an outhouse. Also, the school was old and heated by a wood furnace. The caretaker would come early to start the fire, but by mid-October I often interrupted my teaching to run down and stoke the furnace. Another non-teaching responsibility was, each day, to mix milk powder with water to make the milk that was given to the students during recess break and lunch. This was part of the government's program to ensure that students received calcium in their diet.

I remember that, a few years ago, a couple sat beside my wife Keiko and me at a Costco store in Winnipeg as we were having a hot dog. The fellow looked at me and asked if I was Art Miki. The couple told me that their niece had been in my classroom in Cross Lake in 1961 and that they recognized me from a photograph they had. I looked at his wife and recognized her as a young clerk at the Hudson's Bay store. We had a wonderful chat and it was gratifying for me to hear that their niece was married, living in Saskatchewan, and had a son playing junior hockey. It was surreal to think they would recognize me and remember my name.

However, unable to cope with the isolation and the crude living conditions, I decided to leave Cross Lake after only four months and not complete the school year. Shortly after returning to Winnipeg, I was hired to teach a grade-four class at Sargent Park School in the Winnipeg School Division No. 1, the largest school division in Manitoba. The students' reaction to having a Japanese Canadian teacher was noticeably different. In Cross Lake, students never questioned my ancestry. They may have thought that I was Indigenous. But students in the city, aware of my differences in skin colour and facial features, were also curious about my lifestyle, such as how I lived, what foods I ate, and the language I spoke at home. Most were surprised that my lifestyle was not much different from their own. Going through this exploration of self, my culture and heritage, I became more comfortable with my own identity.

The following school year, I was transferred to Luxton School in Winnipeg's north end, where I had a class of twenty-two grade-six students, sixteen of them repeating the grade. There were only five girls in the class. I had been taking judo for a few years, reinforcing the stereotype about Asians and martial arts. The students' knowledge of my martial arts background helped me get through those

Wedding photo, December 1963. From left to right: best man Roy, bridesmaid Ei Sakai, Keiko, and Art

first months of teaching, since teaching judo during physical education classes turned out to be a great way to connect with the tough boys. Although they were a difficult group, I was able to make positive connections and really enjoyed teaching these students. I started teaching judo classes as an extracurricular activity in several schools. It was a popular activity, especially with the boys.

As interest in my Japanese background increased, I felt that as a teacher and role model I should become more involved in the Japanese Canadian community. Previously, I had joined the bowling league in 1961, and in 1962 the youth group, called the Young Buddhist Association (YBA). I wasn't a Buddhist but was asked to join the group to help organize activities for younger Japanese Canadians.

At one of the youth dances we had organized, I met Keiko Nishikihama, who at the time was a nursing student at Misericordia General Hospital in Winnipeg. Keiko graduated as a registered nurse in 1963, the same year we were married. Keiko's parents had lived in

Vancouver in 1942; her father worked at the Codfish Cooperative in Steveston, south of Vancouver. Because of the impending internment orders, the family hastily moved to live with relatives in Steveston on February 28, and Keiko was born on March 1 at the Japanese Fishermen's Hospital. Forty days later, the family relocated to Minto, a self-supporting internment camp in the BC Interior. After two years in Minto, they moved to Middlechurch to work and live on Ed Mancer's market-gardening farm, north of Winnipeg, an arrangement similar to those on sugar-beet farms. Following the harvest, Mr. Nishikihama travelled to Whitemouth, Manitoba, to work for a moss-gathering company. In Middlechurch, Keiko's sister, Eiko, only eleven years old, had to take on adult responsibilities, looking after her three younger siblings, as both parents worked in the fields, and acting as the family interpreter when communications with non-Japanese people were necessary. As an adult she would later express anger that she had been deprived of her childhood. This was not uncommon for many youths who were thrust into adult roles because of family circumstances. In 1950, the Nishikihama family moved to Winnipeg, on Isabel Street, not far from my parents' home. Winnipeg was not new for Mr. Nishikihama, as he had worked at Royal Alexandra Hotel before the war.

In 1963, in my second year of teaching, I decided to join the executive of the Manitoba Japanese Canadian Citizens' Association (MJCCA). Meetings were held in both Japanese and English, so I often had difficulty following the drift of the Japanese parts of discussions. As the group's issei, who were born in Japan, dropped out of the executive, the meetings were conducted more and more in English.

After four years of teaching in three Winnipeg schools, I decided to return to university to finish the science degree that I had been working on during the evenings and summers while I was teaching. Considering my earlier indifferent efforts as a student in high school, I surprised myself, enjoying university and doing well in my classes.

Since I had taken a two-year leave of absence in 1966 from the Winnipeg School Division, Keiko became the sole supporter of our family, working as a registered nurse at Misericordia Hospital. By this time our first son, Geoffrey, was two years old. After graduating with a Bachelor of Science degree from the University of Winnipeg in 1968, majoring in mathematics, I continued to work on my degree

Graduation from the University of Winnipeg, 1968

in education, receiving a Bachelor of Education degree in 1969 from the University of Manitoba. My interest in continuing with university heightened, and after returning to full-time teaching, I entered the master's program, specializing in the mathematics curriculum, by attending classes in the evening and summers. In the spring of 1975, I received a Master of Education degree from the University of Manitoba.

It was destiny again that resulted in me leaving the Winnipeg School Division to go to another division. When my leave of absence was over in 1968, I reported back to the Winnipeg School Division for placement as a teacher for the fall of 1968. After the university sessions were over in the spring, I worked as a substitute teacher until the end of the school year. In early July, I discussed with the Superintendent of Secondary Education the possibility of teaching junior high, rather than remaining at the elementary level. Although placement to a specific grade was not confirmed, I was assured that I would be assigned a teaching position at either the elementary or junior-high level for September.

Meanwhile, Keiko was working at the hospital, and I studied at university for most of the summer; we had planned to go to British Columbia for holidays. We would not be returning home until the day before school opened. The day before we were to leave, I still hadn't received confirmation of a position, so I called the superintendent and discovered that my file had been misplaced. I had not been assigned.

I began to panic. The superintendent assured me that I would be kept as a supply teacher until a teaching position became available. Although I would be guaranteed a job, I was dismayed at the bureaucratic bungling that had taken place. Late that afternoon I quickly scanned the "Teachers Wanted" column in the *Winnipeg Free Press*. An elementary teaching position was advertised for the Transcona-Springfield School Division No. 12. I called them immediately.

Mrs. Thelma Call, the assistant superintendent, asked if I could come down at once for an interview. By the time I reached Transcona, which is located in the east end of Winnipeg, it was five o'clock in the afternoon. Most of the office staff had gone home, but Mrs. Call was waiting for me. After the interview, she offered me a grade-six teaching position. I signed the contract on the spot.

The next day, Keiko, Geoffrey, and I left for Vancouver.

On our return to Winnipeg, I found a copy of a teaching contract in the mail from the Winnipeg School Division and my placement there announced in the *Winnipeg Free Press*. Immediately, I contacted the principal of the school, whom I knew, and explained that I had signed with another school division because of the earlier mix-up that had occurred. He assured me that he would look after the matter and said not to worry.

Again, when I look back at my teaching career, that accidental mix-up that resulted in my changing school divisions was the best move for me career-wise. Transcona-Springfield, a growing school division, offered many opportunities for young teachers back then. In 1969, my second year at Central School, I became a teacher for a grade-six Major Work program designed for gifted students – a program I thoroughly enjoyed. As a student in graduate studies at the University of Manitoba, I took the opportunity to experiment with some innovative strategies in teaching mathematics and conducted research on activity-based learning. This method of learning had already been established in Great Britain, but in North America it was still new. Implementing this unique teaching technique required some special mathematical equipment and, therefore, funds were needed to purchase the materials.

Mr. Reeven Cramer became the new Superintendent of Education for the Transcona-Springfield School Division that year. He was a gruff, outspoken person, somewhat dictatorial, and not well liked by teachers or principals. The first time he addressed a large gathering of school division staff, he made disparaging remarks about the division's principals and teachers and their ethics. The school staff were unimpressed. The teachers were extremely upset at the lack of empathy or support he displayed. He projected himself as a tyrant who was ready to "change the world." At the end of his discouraging comments, he invited any staff member who had proposals that might improve the school system or its programs to make an appointment with him to share their ideas.

In March 1970, I wrote him a letter requesting to meet with him regarding the mathematics project I wanted to implement. Mr. Cramer, a short, stocky man who had a pipe to his mouth even if it wasn't lit, wasn't as intimidating as I thought. When I met him face to face, his first comment was about the high mark I received in the calculus course on my university transcript. Obviously, he had gone over my academic record before meeting with me.

When I described my project and indicated the financial support that I would require, he said, "After six months in this school division, you're the first teacher to take me up on my invitation." After discussing how the program would stimulate interest and active participation in mathematics learning, he agreed to provide me with whatever materials were required. He said, "Prepare a list of all the things you require, and we'll purchase it and send it to your classroom." Taking a risk creates advantages and opportunities.

In 1970, when a vice-principal position became available at Central School, Barry Kramble, the then principal, and some staff members encouraged me to apply. I had never considered becoming a school administrator; rather I thought I would prefer to be a mathematics consultant because of my interest in the field and academic training. However, such possibilities didn't exist in this school division. Thinking "Why not?" I applied for the vice-principal's position and was interviewed. A few weeks later I received a call from Mr. Cramer, telling me that I was now the new vice-principal at Central School. Then, in 1972, I was appointed vice-principal at Wayoata Elementary School. Taking that big step into a leadership role helped me develop more confidence in my abilities and increased my knowledge of curriculum implementation, school organization, and teacher welfare.

That same year of 1970, I was elected vice-president of the Transcona-Springfield Teachers' Association, the voice for the four hundred teachers in the school division. The following year, I became the Association's president, just as it was becoming embroiled in a bitter controversy regarding the reassignment of a number of principals that upset teaching staff and parents. There were protests from teachers and parent groups, who wanted the school board to reverse their decision on the arbitrary transfer of a large number of administrators without logical explanation, resulting in divisive conflicts between senior administration and school staff. The parents at board meetings reacted strongly against the board's actions and supported the teachers.

This educational issue generated extensive media coverage, and as president, I was asked to speak to the media on a number of occasions. Vice-President George Heshka and I spent many hours drafting position papers on behalf of teachers for presentation to school-board members. I found the role exhausting. The dispute with the school board carried on for several months, but I gained first-hand experience in dealing with political conflicts, elected officials, and the media, which would later be a valuable asset during the redress movement.

The school division expanded as housing developments grew, and a new school was being planned for the east end of Transcona. That meant a principal would be required. Although I had limited administrative experience, my experience with the teacher organization and knowledge of the school division's operations were sufficient reasons for me to consider applying for the position. The schools where I had been a student were so rigid and operated like prisons. At Hugh John MacDonald School, as junior-high students, we had to walk single file in one direction as we moved from one classroom to another in a two-storey building. For library we had to wash our hands before we were allowed to touch a book, and if a student turned a page too loudly or talked, they were reprimanded. I vowed that if I had the opportunity to create a school structure, I would implement a different approach where learning would be enjoyable and students encouraged to interact and learn from each other. When the position was advertised, I submitted my résumé and application for the newly planned Harold Hatcher School. This was my chance to put some of my ideas into practice and develop a comprehensive, innovative plan concerning the organization, operation, and programming for the new school. By now I had cultivated a definite educational philosophy – that students learn and progress at different rates and benefit by learning from children of other ages in more informal classroom settings, which I considered would be an improvement to the traditional schooling concept where students of the same age are expected to learn the same materials despite individual differences.

When Mr. Cramer moved to Winnipeg School Division No. 1, Mrs. Vera Derenchuk became the Superintendent of Education. She had very progressive educational ideas and planned the building of the new school with a specific philosophy in mind. My ideas must have been compatible with Mrs. Derenchuk's vision, because in 1974 I was appointed the first principal of Harold Hatcher School. This gave me the opportunity to design a different kind of school structure. A non-graded school based on the team-teaching concept was introduced. I believe that we were the only school in Manitoba to

Principal Art reading to kindergarten students

incorporate a non-graded structure at that time. I was able to select and hire teachers who would be able to develop programs and teaching materials for the students. It was an exciting time for all of us.

Several meetings were held with parents to describe the school organization, elicit their support, and address their concerns. We made sure that parents were involved in the process and in the school. I believe the collaborative spirit that we created with parents was instrumental in the positive support we received.

As a principal of a school, I was in a position to influence change, to improve the quality of learning, and to make learning exciting. Each year in setting our annual school goals, I had the staff undertake specific projects or themes, such as "the environment," "Canada," "multiculturalism," or "racism," in which the entire school staff and students participated. One of the projects we held at Harold Hatcher was a mini Folklorama. Folklorama, an annual event started in Winnipeg in 1970, is now the world's largest multicultural festival. When school staff adopted the theme "multiculturalism," the parents decided on the mini Folklorama idea and volunteered to make food and bring artifacts to the school. Harold Hatcher was opened to the community, and His Worship Bill Norrie, mayor of Winnipeg, and the Honourable Pearl McGonigal, Lieutenant-Governor of Manitoba, attended. The event was an overwhelming success, and as a reward, the Lieutenant Governor decreed that the students be given a half-day holiday from school. Not to be outdone, Vera Derenchuk announced that the teachers would be given a half-day off as well. The staff used that time for a great staff get-together.

After twelve years at Harold Hatcher, I was transferred as principal to Regent Park School, in preparation for students moving in two years to a new facility, Joseph Teres School, that was under construction. I was given the opportunity again to establish a new school, including monitoring the construction of the building and purchasing the furnishings and equipment. The school opened in 1984 and allowed me to continue to work on innovative teaching techniques and creative extracurricular programming. One concept that I promoted was student responsibility. I felt that if students had ownership of a school happening, they would be more respectful of the school environment. I attended a workshop on conflict resolution to develop skills on how to resolve disagreements and thought that these skills would be valuable for teachers and students. I presented a proposal to staff that we train a group of students on conflict management skills and have them as proctors on the playground during recess to resolve student conflicts instead of teachers intervening. Two teachers volunteered to organize the project. I arranged for them to receive training and then teach a group of grade-five students, who volunteered as conflict managers, skills such a listening, communication, and involving the conflicted students to find solutions. Their role was to help monitor the playground and try to resolve any disputes that arose there. Most often they were successful and there was no need to involve the adults on duty. I found that this approach was effective, as students felt freer to work out solutions with the conflict manager rather than having an adult intervene. The teachers supported the program because the students were taking responsibility for helping each other.

The one area I found was difficult to teach students was about racism. How does one become sensitized to the hurt and trauma that victims of racism feel? I knew that many teachers felt uncomfortable broaching the subject, and so I explored ways to do so. In 1985 while I was president of NAJC, I was also on the board of Prairie Theatre Exchange (PTE), a theatre company in Winnipeg that promotes Canadian content. They presented *Enemy Graces*, a play by Sharon Stearns, which tells the story of a Japanese Canadian family in an internment camp in Sandon, BC, in 1942 who comes to terms with the struggle and imprisonment and uprooting they face. Because the NAJC was in the early stages of the redress campaign at that time, the showing of the play was timely, as the internment story of the internment was not known by most Canadians. It exposed the audience to the restrictions and harsh treatments that Japanese Canadian citizens endured. I thought that mounting a production such as *Enemy Graces* before a diverse audience was an effective and non-threatening approach to dealing with racism in Canada's history.

As principal at Joseph Teres School, I developed a proposal called Actors Against Racism, incorporating the theatre concept and involving elementary-school students. I discussed this idea with Judy Sutton, a creative music teacher on staff, and asked whether such a project would be feasible. She was extremely excited and volunteered to create a production using the students' ideas and voices and incorporating music and song. However, to proceed, I would need financial support to pay for a substitute teacher so Judy Sutton would be free to work with the students without disrupting the school's music program. I had previous contacts at the Multiculturalism Branch of the Department of Canadian Heritage and approached the program officer about possible funding. Although the Branch generally supported community organizations and not educational institutions, an exception was made because of the project's unique approach to teaching about racism. I received a grant in 1992 to cover the cost of a substitute during the time Judy Sutton was developing the presentation, as well as the cost for bussing, since we wanted the students to perform their musical production at other schools.

Thirty grade-five and grade-six students were selected by their teachers to write the story outline and lyrics and perform their work to an audience of students, parents, and teachers. The project was developed in two phases. The initial phase was an intensive three-and-a-half-day workshop exploring various aspects of being different and looking at historical aspects of oppression. Among the group were students from Chinese, Black, Filipino, Indigenous, and South Asian backgrounds. The school population of 465 students was predominantly white. Most students were not aware of the project's expectations except that it had something to do with racism. As students arrived for the first session, Ms. Sutton handed each student a balloon and asked them to blow it up. All the balloons were red except for one green balloon. The students were instructed to hit the balloon in the air and catch any balloon. This was done several times and at the end the student who initially received the green balloon ended up with the same one. This was a springboard for the teacher to begin exploring differences. When the students were asked why they did not catch the green balloon, several students replied that it was because the green balloon was different. The students were amazed that most of them had unconsciously avoided the balloon that was different from the rest.

As students were exposed to different topics, such as differences and stereotypes, they engaged in group and partner discussions, shared views and ideas with each other, and wrote a skit, poetry, or just thoughts. I spoke to the group about the racism experienced by Japanese Canadians in the past. The discussion on the history of racism was a powerful experience for the teacher and students. Mrs. Sutton assembled these materials and shaped them into a musical production using Lennon and Ono's "Imagine" as the theme. In working with students from different ethnic and cultural backgrounds, her approach was to guide the sharing process gradually, allowing students to become comfortable and open. "This was a valuable experience for the kids involved and I hope that that it will be for the audiences," she stated. Self-disclosures by students who had experienced racism had a tremendous impact on their peers.

Graeme, a Black student, shared this story: "When I was five, I would go out for recess. I was in kindergarten and the school went up to grade seven. These grade seveners kept coming up to me calling me the N-word over and over. They kept coming on every recess. I didn't know what it meant then, but now it hurts."

Warren, a Filipino student, told this story to the group: "I went to Ontario last year to meet my pen pals. When I was coming back from lunch, a kid called me a racist name, I tried to ignore it but it was hard. Other kids began to do the same. I never encountered this before."

Some comments from the students after hearing their stories were the following:

"I felt sorry for them."

"It was hard to understand why someone who never saw the person before, out of the blue, would say racist names."

"It's hard to believe that it can happen in our school, but it does. You just don't realize it."

The second phase of the project was preparation for the performance, entitled *Forever Together*. During the week of intensive rehearsals, performers readjusted the script that Ms. Sutton had written and suggested format alterations, determined appropriate costumes, and practised the songs and dialogue. What made this project unique was that the words of the presentation were the words of the students themselves.

Actors Against Racism's initial performance of *Forever Together* was at Joseph Teres School in front of students, parents, and teachers and received extremely favourable and emotional responses from all. The group performed at eight elementary schools within the school division and three schools outside it. The cohesiveness and co-operation among the performers enabled them to project a forceful message that racism was not acceptable. The dramatic approach was a meaningful way to get students talking about racism. One participant commented, "It's serious because you're teaching a lesson in a different way. It's more interesting to watch. You get more out of it than by reading a book." Nevertheless, a student discussion guide was also provided for teachers whose classes attended the performance. The guide included song lyrics, key elements of the presentation, and questions to stimulate further discussion.

The impact on the actors of *Forever Together* was startling, yielding comments such as: "We learned to be friends; we didn't know each other before the play" and "We put ourselves in their [victims of racism's] shoes and [imagined] how they would feel." Graeme, the same student quoted above, also shared: "Before I was racist towards Indigenous people, but not anymore."

The actors agreed that adults, including their parents, would benefit from their message. Here are some insightful comments they made:

"Some parents are racist and kids do what their parents do."

"Some people claim they're not racist and yet they call Black people the N-word. My dad calls Blacks the N-word. I haven't said anything to him yet."

The audience of younger children benefitted also. Here are some messages from grade-four students:

"Let's stop racism. We all have to work together. We should all be friends, accept them how they are and not how you would like them to be."

"I think that racism is an uncool thing. 'Cool' is being friends with different people."

I attended all the performances, and each time I was deeply moved by the audience reaction, which showed me this was a great way for students and adults to understand and appreciate the effects of racism. The performers unanimously agreed that the experience of learning, creating, and performing would be beneficial to all students in understanding and combating racism. As they become adults, will they speak against racism? Will they develop positive social and professional relationships with people from diverse cultural and ethnic backgrounds? These were measures from which we could assess the success of this project. In my discussions with the students, I sensed that the positive attitudes, understanding, and appreciation resulting from *Forever Together* indicated that their interactions with others had been altered forever.

The funders attended one of the shows and were very impressed and willing to fund the project again. Unfortunately, I retired from education at the end of the school year. I think the Chinese proverb "I hear and I forget; I see and I remember; I do and I understand" best describes the process that was undertaken to develop the Actors Against Racism project. I was impressed with the enthusiasm and insights the actor-students demonstrated in dealing with sensitive and personal encounters with racism. The Canadian Teachers' Federation included an essay of mine on the project in their publication *Racism and Education: Different Perspectives and Experiences* in October 1992 as a resource for their members.[1]

As a school principal, I was extremely fortunate to have worked under Vera Derenchuk, Transcona-Springfield's educational leader, who was passionately committed to having school administrators develop leadership and communication skills. Attending many workshops and conferences helped me expand my communication and presentation skills as a workshop leader and speaker at both divisional and provincial educational events. As a mathematics specialist at the elementary-school level, I had created a number of games and activities to interest students in the beauty of numbers. I conducted a mathematics workshop across the province; it was a popular request from school divisions. I also created several card games to reinforce

---

1   Arthur Miki, "Actors Against Racism (A.A.R.) Forever Together," in Canadian Teachers'
     Federation / Fédération canadienne des enseignantes et des enseignants, *Racism and
     Education: Different Perspectives and Experiences / Le racisme et l'éducation: Perspectives
     et expériences diverses*, October 1992, 65–72, files.eric.ed.gov/fulltext/ED394873.pdf.

the understanding of numerical concepts such as ones, tens, hundreds, etc., and strengthen multiplication skills. I also spoke at many conferences on topics such as student evaluation, student responsibility, and educational goal setting. All of these opportunities improved my ability to work with others and communicate more effectively, while helping me develop skills in decision-making, conflict management, and leadership. Naturally, these skills proved invaluable in my role as president of the NAJC. As a gesture of my appreciation for Ms. Derenchuk's support during the redress campaign, I gifted her with the lithograph *Watari Dori* by Linda Ohama, which the NAJC commissioned as a fundraising tool. Whenever I met her after retirement, she would tell me that the picture was a cherished reminder of my success and our extraordinary relationship.

During my years in education, I was actively involved in Japanese Canadian organizations, both locally and nationally. I felt an obligation as a person of Japanese ancestry, as an educator, and as a person proud of his heritage to contribute to the strengthening and betterment of our community organizations. I was president of the Manitoba Japanese Canadian Citizens' Association (MJCCA) for three terms, coordinator of the Japanese pavilion in Folklorama several times, mayor of the pavilion there, and on the board of the more recently established Manitoba Japanese Canadian Cultural Centre (MJCCC). I represented Manitoba on the National Japanese Canadian Centennial Society board and formed a local committee to undertake the centennial projects during 1977; I also participated with the National Japanese Canadian Citizens' Association (NJCCA), the political body responsible for issues of national concern such as redress.

To balance my community involvement, I also participated in several ethnic and multicultural organizations and advisory groups outside the Japanese Canadian community. I was on the federal advisory board for Multiculturalism in the early 1980s for the minister of multiculturalism, and later on the Manitoba Intercultural Council, an advisory body to the Province of Manitoba. For a number of years, I was on the board of the Canadian Ethnocultural Council, representing national ethnic organizations, and later I was with the National Visibility Council on Labour Force Development; both groups were located in Ottawa. My volunteer involvement included being on the board of the Winnipeg Chinese Cultural and Community Centre and serving as the Alumni Representative on the Board of Regents for the University of Winnipeg. I found that these diverse roles gave me a broader perspective on what Canadian society is all about, and on the benefits of volunteerism. These experiences benefitted me immensely in developing as a person, an educator, and a leader.

CHAPTER 3

Redress: A Vision

Much of the detail of the early history of Japanese Canadians began to surface in the 1970s. Toyo Takata, the author of *Nikkei Legacy: The Story of Japanese Canadians from Settlement to Today*, wrote in his 1983 book that the first recorded Japanese immigrant to Canada was Manzo Nagano, whose arrival in Victoria on May 14, 1877, paved the way for others.[1] Nagano had stowed away on a British ship that docked in Yokohama harbour and was put ashore on Vancouver Island. Toyo's research was the springboard for launching the Japanese Canadian Centennial celebrations in 1977. Naomi Krasovec (née Kuwada) and I represented Manitoba on the Japanese Canadian Centennial Board and helped organize various activities for the Manitoba Japanese Canadian community. The Centennial provided an opportunity for Canadians of all origins to pause and reflect on Canada's past and to recognize the people whose courage, sacrifice, perseverance, patience, and industry enabled them to overcome great obstacles in order to establish homes in Canada for their families and descendants. For many young people, the stories of their parents' pre- and postwar ordeals were a shocking exposé. The people who were most affected by these experiences had not shared their appalling history with their children. Parents had blotted out the past – especially the shattering forced relocation from the coast.

As part of the Japanese Canadian Centennial celebrations, a

---

1   Toyo Takata, *Nikkei Legacy: The Story of Japanese Canadians from Settlement to Today* (Chapel Hill, NC: University of North Carolina Press, 1983), 9.

photographic exhibit of Tamio Wakayama's works, entitled *The Japanese Canadians, 1877–1977*, toured across Canada and brought to light for many Canadians and even Japanese Canadians a history of hostility, discrimination, and frustration. This exhibit resulted from a collective effort of individuals in Vancouver and from different generations under the name of the Japanese Canadian Centennial Project.[2]

When I saw the exhibit, I was moved by the hardships and discrimination that my grandparents and my parents had encountered and was awed by the tenacity and courage it must have taken to survive in Canada during that period. This was the first time I was so thoroughly exposed to vivid descriptions of the pre-war and wartime experiences my family endured. Ken Adachi's book *The Enemy That Never Was: A History of the Japanese Canadians*, which was finally published in 1976, added to the broadening of my knowledge of the unjust actions of the Canadian government towards Japanese Canadians, whose lives were disrupted and forever altered.

While researching her 1981 book *The Politics of Racism: The Uprooting of Japanese Canadians during the Second World War*, Ann Gomer Sunahara used documents in the Canadian archives that were finally opened to the public in the late 1970s to tell the real story of the internment and forced relocation of Japanese Canadians. The documented reports, letters, and files that Ann located reaffirmed the notion held by many Japanese Canadians that the actions of the Canadian government were not for national security reasons, as it professed. They were the result of racist attitudes towards the Japanese in British Columbia.

The revelation of this aspect of our history, in particular the period during and after World War II, and that it had never been officially addressed, let alone resolved, aroused feelings of bitterness and frustration in many Japanese Canadians. The Liberal government of Mackenzie King had stripped Canadians of Japanese ancestry of their legal and human rights by confiscating their property, removing them from their homes, and forcibly relocating them to internment and prisoner-of-war camps or to sugar-beet farms. Prime Minister Lester

---

2   The exhibit was adapted and recorded into a book: Japanese Canadian Centennial Project, *A Dream of Riches: The Japanese Canadians, 1877–1977* / 千金の夢：日系カナダ人百年史 / *Un rêve de richesses: Les Japonais au Canada, 1877–1977* (Vancouver: Japanese Canadian Centennial Project, 1978).

GAMAN — PERSEVERANCE

B. Pearson once commented that this was a "black mark against Canada's traditional fairness." The injustice remained unresolved.

The Japanese Canadian Reparations Committee was formed by the National Japanese Canadian Citizens' Association (NJCCA) in 1976 and began the long, arduous task of researching and developing proposals for compensation. In the early days, the term "reparations" was used but was later changed to "redress." Some activists, such as Roger Obata, emphatically stated that the handling of property claims through the Bird Commission, a Royal Commission that had been established in April 1947 with Justice Henry Bird as its commissioner, was the forerunner to redress. The Commission's mandate was to hold hearings across Canada on Japanese Canadians' wartime property losses and to recommend to the federal government what compensation should be paid to qualified claimants.

For Roger, the Bird Commission's limited terms of reference, which covered only a small proportion of claims, was completely unsatisfactory. Millions of dollars in property and possession losses were not eligible because of the narrowness of the terms of reference. Only differences between the sale price of properties and their "fair market value" were considered, and it was up to the claimant to prove the market value. Many refused to participate in what they called a charade, because they argued that it was a cosmetic solution to a wound of much greater proportions. In the end the claimants received something in the order of eight cents on the dollar in compensation.

What irked Roger even further was that the claimants' own legal counsel advocated that they sign waivers stating that once they received compensation, they would not make any further claims to the government regarding property. Roger said, "I was totally against that and so was Kunio Hidaka and I resigned from the Co-operative Committee." The Co-operative Committee's role was to oversee the Bird Commission's responsibilities. The issue of the signing of waivers never surfaced during any of the redress discussions with government ministers or officials. This matter was either overlooked in their research or it was considered inadvisable to highlight past decisions as a justification for saying that the matter of redress had already been resolved.

The Bird Commission hearings terminated on March 3, 1950, but the results were by most accounts a complete failure, not at all resolving one of the worst civil rights violations in Canadian history. As a reflection of the dissatisfaction felt by the Japanese Canadian community, only 1,434 claims were submitted. The stringent requirements placed on potential claimants discouraged many from applying. The monetary settlement fell far short of what could be considered minimally acceptable. But far worse, the commission failed to consider losses that were not monetary but were equally as devastating. No consideration was given for the psychological, social, cultural, and familial destruction caused by the upheaval. And so efforts to gain reparations or redress – whichever term you preferred – proved fruitless.

In 1978, the NJCCA Reparations Committee began examining precedents that might be used to justify seeking monetary considerations as part of a more comprehensive reparations package. In 1971, the United States government had awarded nearly a billion dollars to Indigenous Alaskans after twelve hundred of them were arrested during a demonstration on the steps of the United States Capitol. In its verdict, which resulted in part in the Alaska Native Claims Settlement Act (ANCSA), the courts had said that claimants had been unjustly arrested and should be awarded $10,000 each. Although Japanese Canadians were not placed under arrest, government authorities had confined them for an extended period of time.

Another precedent known in the international courts is the post–WW II principle of *Wiedergutmachung*, which is the German word for "restitution, reparation," literally "the fact of making good again." Under the program begun in 1952, West Germany paid out billions of dollars in compensation to victims of the nazi regime. In 1979, the funds were increased and, more recently, more monies were made available to Holocaust victims. Although the treatment of Japanese Canadians cannot be equated with the degree of suffering endured by the Jewish people under the nazi regime, it can nevertheless be said that Japanese Canadians were unjustly deprived of their rights and freedoms in their own country and driven from their homes to be placed in internment camps.

In Canada, the issue of compensation has irrefutable precedents. Under what is known as "comprehensive claims," Canadian governments has approved Indigenous Land claims amounting to hundreds of millions of dollars, and I believe will likely continue to do so in the future. These cases, and others still under negotiation, are based on the argument that Indigenous Peoples did not sign formal treaties when their Lands were seized. Other "specific claims," involving abrogation of existing treaties and obligations, are also in various stages of submission or negotiations. Like the Indigenous groups who are fighting to retain Lands that they consider rightfully theirs, Japanese Canadians believed that they should seek compensation for the federal government's irresponsible handling of their property and possessions.

At its 1980 National Conference, the NJCCA's Reparations Committee reported that a nationwide survey of the Japanese Canadian community concluded that the establishment of a foundation would best achieve our goals and objectives. The funds from the foundation would be used to support seniors and educational and cultural activities in the Japanese Canadian community. However, the NJCCA council members were never given access to the results of the survey so that they could have validated the legitimacy of the so-called national survey. It was not clear how this survey was conducted and who was asked to respond, as council members were unaware that it had even occurred. Council members felt that it was premature for the committee to ask for opinions on what form of redress was appropriate when most people in the community had little or no understanding of the redress issue – at this time, the issue had not penetrated the consciousness of most Japanese Canadians. Nevertheless, the committee suggested that the proposal of a foundation made the issue of redress "politically acceptable" to the government. They maintained that any mention of other forms of compensation, such as individual payments, would not get the ear of the government and hope for redress would be lost. Political feasibility seemed to override the considerations of the victims of the injustice. It was political manoeuvring on the part of the committee to "psyche" the internment victims into thinking that the most viable solution for redress was the proposal of a foundation.

At the 1980 meeting in Vancouver, the National Council of the NJCCA requested that the committee conduct further discussions with the community regarding redress options. The Reparations Committee, renamed the Redress Committee during the meeting, was asked to study the results of grassroots input and submit a report to the National Executive Committee, who then would make recommendations to the National Council. As a strategic move, the name of the NJCCA was also changed to the National Association of Japanese Canadians (NAJC). It was hoped that the name change would encourage some local Japanese Canadian organizations that had broken away from the NJCCA because of disputes in the past to join the newly named NAJC and strengthen its national voice.

When the redress campaign first began, it was basically a crusade for the Japanese Canadian community. Our contacts were limited to a few sympathetic supporters within the political system, and we lacked the know-how to effectively lobby politicians. We learned quickly and realized that political action such as the redress campaign required not only commitment and support from the Japanese Canadian community, but depended heavily on support from other groups and individuals within the Canadian community.

In Canada, Japanese Canadians lacked political influence or political skills. We had never had an elected Japanese Canadian Member of Parliament who might have been able to raise the redress issue in the House or advocate on behalf of the community. By contrast, in the United States, Japanese American politicians such as Senator Daniel Inouye, Congressman Norman Mineta, and others were instrumental in influencing Congress to establish a commission to conduct hearings on the wartime experiences of Japanese Americans. These politicians personally shared their experiences with their colleagues and helped to educate and persuade other elected and governmental officials to support reparations in the United States. It was the commission's recommendations in 1982 that would eventually become the basis for the US settlement and have implications for the Japanese Canadian redress agreement, six years later.

The US commission's hearings and recommendations received publicity in Canada, and Japanese Canadians who had had similar experiences during the war began to discuss the possibility of seeking redress from the Canadian government. Attempting to capitalize on the coverage on the US recommendation, in 1983 Japanese Canadian leaders such as George Imai initiated discussions with Minister of Multiculturalism James Fleming on the possibilities for redress. I believe that Imai may have given the minister and government officials the impression that a minimal symbolic gesture would be all that was necessary to satisfy the Japanese Canadian community.

During the early '80s, newspaper articles in Canada suggested that Japanese Canadians were considering pressing the government of Canada for some form of compensation to redress wartime injustices. I found that newspaper articles and editorials were an excellent vehicle for providing readers insights into the progress of the redress movement from an outside perspective; I began to rely heavily on using media as a reference. These media comments were spurred by the hearings that were being held in the United States by the Congressional Commission on Wartime Relocation and Internment of Civilians (CWRIC). An editorial of September 11, 1981, in the *Vancouver Sun* stated that "It would be much better, in any event, if the government of Canada didn't wait to be asked, but acted for all Canadians, of whatever ethnic origin, to erase any lingering doubts about the kind of society we aspire to be." It also suggested the compensation "they have in mind is modest – either a cultural centre or an extended care home for senior citizens of Japanese heritage."[3]

Because the actions of the Liberal government in the 1940s against Canadians of Japanese ancestry were legal at the time, the redress movement had to be pursued as a moral and political question. Past litigation by Japanese Canadian owners through the courts involving property claims resulting from the confiscation of properties under the War Measures Act were not successful because the actions of the government were considered legal, though not morally right. It would not be up to the courts to decide the legitimacy of redress, but up to the politicians and Parliament to determine whether "redress" was definable. Therefore, seeking the ear of politicians on redress was the initial priority. Although some politicians were aware of the treatment accorded to Japanese Canadians during wartime, many were ignorant of that part of Canadian history. Individual Japanese Canadians contacted Members of Parliament and other politicians to enlighten them of the hardships and trauma experienced during World War II.

Although no official position had yet been determined, the perception in the media was that the Japanese Canadian community was dragging its feet in comparison with Japanese Americans. A July 1982 *Globe and Mail* article entitled "Japanese-Canadians Seek Relocation Redress" stated that community leaders were hoping to reach a consensus of Japanese Canadians across the country that upcoming fall before approaching the federal government with a plan for restitution. NAJC President Gordon Kadota said, "The Japanese

---

3 "Looking Back," *Vancouver Sun*, September 11, 1981, 4, www.newspapers.com/article /the-vancouver-sun/133552973/.

community has waited so long to seek redress because that's how long it has taken society to recognize that an injustice was committed."[4]

Even before the NAJC had officially embarked on the redress campaign, early editorials in Canadian media were positive about acknowledging that a grave injustice had been inflicted upon citizens of Japanese ancestry in Canada. A *Province* editorial from Vancouver on August 3, 1982, entitled "Canada's Shame," stated: "It would be very healthy for Canada to tackle the issue. And to work out the most appropriate way to compensate these sorely wronged people for their losses."[5] A *Vancouver Sun* editorial on September 22, 1983, was more forceful in its statement and urged the government to "Erase the Black Mark."[6] It was five years to the day when that black mark would finally be erased. In August 1982, Keith Spicer, a Vancouver-based columnist, wrote in the *Vancouver Sun* that Japanese Canadians were "victims of a vengeful paranoia" and that "Japanese Canadians deserve support in asking for redress."[7]

The difficulty in establishing a consensus about what appropriate redress would be lingered on. In the spring of 1983, the Redress Committee of the NAJC decided to conduct telephone surveys across the country to determine the community's preferred form of compensation. However, plans for a comprehensive national survey did not evolve, as many of the centres who were asked to participate felt uneasy about the process, especially when most respondents would not have sufficient knowledge and understanding of the issue. At the community level, there was a scarcity of information on redress; most people were unfamiliar with the concept and what it meant. In Toronto, approximately four hundred responses from a telephone survey were received, and this became the basis for the National Redress Committee's position. According to the results of this limited survey, the Redress Committee reported that the form of community

---

4   "Japanese-Canadians Seek Relocation Redress," *Globe and Mail*, July 30, 1982, 8, www .proquest.com/historical-newspapers/japanese-canadians-seek-relocation-redress /docview/1238748403/se-2.

5   "Canada's Shame," *Province*, August 3, 1982, 9, www.newspapers.com/article/the-province /133552737/.

6   "Erase the Black Mark," *Vancouver Sun*, September 22, 1983, A4, www.newspapers.com /article/the-vancouver-sun/133552834/.

7   Keith Spicer, "Victims of a Vengeful Paranoia," *Vancouver Sun*, August 4, 1982, 5, www .newspapers.com/article/the-vancouver-sun/133553106/.

compensation that would be most appropriate was the establishment of a foundation or trust fund. The validity of the questionnaire used to solicit the telephone responses was questioned. Criticisms indicated that the responses were skewed towards community compensation because of the way the questions were phrased and asked, forcing respondents to choose between either individual or group compensation but not allowing for the combination of the two ideas.

The National Redress Committee's proposal that the Japanese Canadian community was seeking redress in the form of a foundation was hotly debated at the September 1983 meeting of the NAJC in Toronto. Groups within the Japanese Canadian community, the Sodan Kai group in Toronto and the Japanese Canadian Centennial Project (JCCP) in Vancouver, advocated the inclusion of individual compensation and opposed the position taken by the National Redress Committee chaired by George Imai. The report of the Commission on Wartime Relocation and Internment of Civilians in the United States in 1982 recommended compensations of $20,000 for each of the approximately sixty thousand surviving internees. Proponents of individual compensation stated that the US recommendation was a clear precedent and that Japanese Canadians should not ask for anything less.

A bitter battle raged over the differing views on compensation. George Imai hoped to receive the endorsement of the committee's recommendation to establish a foundation and announce that a community consensus on redress had been reached. But the delegates representing centres across the country were not prepared to make a decision on what form of redress to seek. Too many questions were left unanswered. Many wondered, considering how much time had already passed, why there was such a pressing need by the committee to reach a consensus. These criticisms resulted in the committee's resignation. However, on the following day, the committee was reinstated. This conflict was disturbing to National Council members, and George Imai was persuaded to resume his position as chair of the Redress Committee.

Unusual, unexplained occurrences left many of the delegates scratching their heads at times. The granting of government funds to the National Redress Committee under George Imai without the knowledge of the NAJC President, Gordon Kadota, was considered an unusual procedure. It is customary that applications for funding be signed by the president rather than the chairperson of the committee. These funds were to be used to conduct telephone surveys and facilitate consultation meetings such as the one held in September 1983 to arrive at a community consensus on redress. When I became president of the NAJC, I met with multiculturalism officials to discuss the funds that were given to the Committee. I was told by one of the program directors that the application had bypassed the normal procedures and was approved directly by the minister of multiculturalism.

Another anomaly was the insistence by George Imai that the committee's position had to be endorsed at the September meeting. It seemed odd that the committee could not wait until further input from the Japanese Canadian community had been sought. The telephone survey did not reflect a representative sample and could not be legitimately construed as a national opinion. Why was there such a demand for a decision when our community had waited over forty years, while the US recommendation had just been put forward? Accepting the committee's position would eliminate any possibility for individual compensation, even though this was advocated in the United States. It seemed strange that there was such urgency to bring forward a recommendation. What was the underlying motivation?

In June 1983, a *Toronto Star* article suggested that the government was considering compensating Japanese Canadians. "The government is generally looking at the matter," confirmed Justice Minister Mark MacGuigan. "There has been an exchange of letters between Ottawa and Japanese Canadian officials but no formal discussions have been held." In the same article, Multiculturalism Minister Jim Fleming said that he recently had discussed the issue "as a matter of goodwill" with George Imai. "We should be considering the possibility of compensation, but Cabinet has not yet discussed the matter," Fleming said. "At first, there should be some recognition of the wrongness [of the detention and seizure of Japanese Canadians] and then look at what is practical and reasonable." George Imai, in the same article, said, "The association favours a trust fund or foundation."[8] According to a multiculturalism official I talked to, George Imai had sent a letter to the minister which was supposedly a request for a settlement, with the understanding that a community consensus would be reached.

8   "Japanese-Canadians May Get Compensation," *Toronto Star,* June 1, 1983, A1, www.proquest
    .com/newspapers/japanese-canadians-may-get-compensation/docview/435772090/se-2.

Although there was no unanimous support to disregard individual compensation, the National Redress Committee was unwilling to reconsider other alternatives and was insistent that the National Council adopt their recommendation. The National Council was not prepared to endorse the committee's position and asked that further work with the community be done.

The September 1983 meeting was the beginning of an intensive effort to make Japanese Canadians more aware and involved in the redress process. Gordon Kadota travelled to each of the centres to motivate local organizations to take a more active role in educating their communities and the public about the Japanese Canadian experience during and after World War II. It was necessary to develop a base of information for the Japanese Canadian community about the inhumane treatment of its members and the government's premeditated role in stripping its citizens of their rights.

The difficulty encountered in determining a consensus is partially attributable to differences in views held by the various generations in the Japanese Canadian community. Issei were the pioneers from Japan who chose Canada as their home; most Japanese men immigrated between 1877 and 1907 and most women came after 1908. Nisei were Canadian-born children of issei. Sansei were born largely during the 1940s and 1950s. These three generations were directly affected by the government's actions, but in different ways.

There are specific attributes that seem to dominate a particular generation which makes them unique compared to other generations. Although generalizations can be made regarding the characteristics associated with each generation, they must of course be taken with a grain of salt. Within one generation there can be large differences in ages. For example, I am considered an older sansei because the median age for sansei is ten to fifteen years younger than I am. Many people my age are nisei. How different would my attitude be compared to a sansei who is a generation younger? Through my travels across Canada, meeting with various Japanese Canadian communities, I noticed that there were definite attitudes that could be associated with specific generations, especially when discussing redress. My analysis is not based on any sociological study but on my casual observations and contact with community members.

The issei's road was an especially difficult one. Most were poor and limited in education. They encountered personal and social discrimination and faced undue hardships socially and economically because, in addition to being unfamiliar with the mainstream Canadian way of life, discrimination against them was enforced through government legislation. They endured anti-Japanese sentiments and prejudice with a feeling of helplessness. Unable to assimilate entirely into Canadian society, they found solace in their own community neighbourhoods, where a common language existed. Their knowledge of Canadian society and politics was limited, making them extremely vulnerable to the will of the Canadian majority. This was shown dramatically by their lack of resistance to the government's actions in 1942. In fact, issei often simply complied and encouraged nisei to do the same. They reasoned that if they obeyed the government's orders, they were demonstrating good citizenship.

Issei made the best of a difficult situation and displayed the traditional Japanese virtues of perseverance, ambition, and industriousness in overcoming the hardships they encountered as immigrants. They sacrificed much for their children, although they could not adjust to the Canadian outlook of nisei.

Many issei came to Canada seeking financial gain and eventually hoped to return to Japan. They maintained a strong allegiance to their homeland and, during World War II, had difficulty determining where their loyalties lay. During repatriation some chose to return to Japan, but their motivations varied. Some may have felt a strong bond with Japan, others may have been frustrated by the actions of the Canadian government. Others, especially nisei, wanted to remain in Canada but respected their parent's wishes to go to Japan. I remember my mother telling me that her father believed Japan would win the war.

During the war, Japanese Canadians sensed the racist motives behind the government's orders, but they could only accept and obey. Many issei were not legally Canadian citizens. Most issei learned to live with their property losses and held limited interest in civil rights. Their political position was neutral.

What issei contributed to the redress cause was a living example of people who had overcome extremely difficult obstacles. Issei were an important source of emotional support for younger Japanese Canadians. They may have sensed the futility of the effort and feared that the prejudice of the past would resurface. They were reluctant to fight the government that allowed them to stay in Canada despite the sufferings they encountered. They were the group who professed the "shigata ga nai" or "it can't be helped" attitude. It is understandable why this group would be more comfortable supporting community compensation, as they did not want to appear selfish, nor did they feel that they deserved individual compensation.

Born and raised in a Canadian culture, nisei were outwardly reserved, demonstrated obedience to authority, had pride in education, and showed qualities of determination and diligence. These were familiar Japanese traits inculcated by issei influences. In general, nisei were children of immigrant parents of low socio-economic status, constantly facing discrimination from government and society at large. Many nisei were politically complacent during the war. Realizing the power of the government and negative public opinion, they felt compelled to accept the internment orders. One group of dissident nisei was the exception: they were the Nisei Mass Evacuation Group, who opposed the BC Security Commission move to split families up, sending the males off to road camps and placing women, children, and the elderly in internment camps.

During the postwar period, nisei turned their attention to educational success and perseverance as a means of seeking middle-class status. Nisei today speak proudly of their financial successes and have built themselves a reputation of being one of the most thriving minority groups in Canada.

The nisei generation is, however, marked by psychological scars from their past. Many have abandoned their cultural ties and have assimilated into the dominant society. Some harbour feelings of insecurity and bitterness, in some cases directed at their issei parents. The Japanese Canadian Centennial activities and the redress movement may be responsible for the revival of their self-awareness and self-acceptance. Many of them are, after decades, finally learning to accept their Japanese identity.

The reactions of nisei towards redress were mixed. Those who had begun the process of self-awareness recognized the grave injustice that had been inflicted upon them, their parents, and their children and took an active role in supporting the redress movement. Others who felt "assimilated" tended to view the relocation and internment as a godsend that took them out of the ghetto and allowed them the opportunity to achieve financial and social success.

Many nisei maintained that it was futile to pursue monetary compensation from the government; after forty years they considered it a lost cause. "Why dig up the past?" Some went so far as to say: "That's the best thing that happened to us." There was widespread fear that if the issue of compensation was raised publicly, Japanese Canadians would immediately be labelled as "materialistic" or "money-grabbing" by the wider Canadian public. Perhaps it was this insecurity, coupled with the desire to avoid negative reactions, that caused many to avoid the issue.

To other nisei, an apology from the prime minister would not be adequate. They felt that the government must recognize the true extent of the wrong and demonstrate this through monetary compensation. To foster acceptance of the concept of compensation, nisei saw that education about the redress issue among Japanese Canadians was a necessary priority. Nisei played a dominant role in the redress movement. Their past experience, their knowledge of the community, and their interest in the political process would prove to be invaluable contributions to the success of the redress campaign.

I am a sansei and was born into an entirely different social and economic milieu than my parents and grandparents. Having been brought up in a Canadian environment, sansei are generally more vocal, aggressive, confident, and more adapted to mainstream Canadian life.

The government's relocation policy forced families to disperse, resulting in very little contact with other Japanese Canadian families. The only time I encountered other Japanese Canadian kids was at a picnic that our parents attended or at family gatherings. In my case, all my cousins reside in other provinces, so contact with them throughout my life has been limited or non-existent. Many sansei have indicated that they were often the only Japanese Canadian in their school. In my case there were a few, but we were never close as friends. I found parents of sansei avoided exposing them to Japanese culture and language, unlike issei, who before the war compelled their children to attend Japanese language classes. This may also be the reason that no coherent Japanese community – or even cultural centres – existed before redress in areas where Japanese Canadians lived. Unfortunately, deprived of most of their Japanese heritage during their upbringing, sansei struggled with their identity. The common analogy was comparing us to a banana, "yellow on the outside but white in the inside." In my early twenties, I became involved with the local community organization and was exposed to

Japanese traditions and cultural activities adopted from the previous generations. However, this was not the case for a majority of sansei. The issue of identity – "Who am I?" – still persists among sansei. They grew up during the era of multiculturalism when learning about your family's roots and identity was surging and remarkable growth in technological advances was being made by Japan. As the status of Japan became highly respected, this had a positive impact on the sansei psyche. They exhibited more self-confidence and a positive self-concept. The Japanese Canadian Centennial in 1977 created in sansei an awareness of their history – a history that was not shared by their parents. With the educational opportunities often provided through the sacrifices made by their parents, sansei have had the freedom to choose among many career options. Their diversity of interests and talents allowed them to penetrate almost all areas of Canadian society, whether in professions such as medicine, architecture, the media, education, the arts, or athletics.

This experience with freedom of choice facilitated sansei participation within the Japanese Canadian community. Those who developed a strong attachment to their cultural heritage were more likely to become actively involved in Japanese Canadian community activities, while others may have only had a passing interest.

Despite the confidence of this generation, the majority of sansei were ambivalent towards past injustices and were content not to be involved. Others simply considered this not to be their problem. There was a lack of empathy for the previous generations, because their stories had not been told or were not understood. Some sansei indicated that no amount of monetary compensation would be sufficient for the psychological damages suffered by the victims, and there was still fear that the redress issue would produce negative publicity for the community.

It was the few politically inclined and intellectually committed sansei able to identify the treatment of Japanese Canadians as a violation of fundamental human and civil rights who became involved in the redress movement. It was sansei who were enthusiastic, well educated, and had the professional experience vital to the movement who provided the needed skills and leadership for Japanese Canadians to pursue redress. And pursue it they did.

CHAPTER 4

Struggle Within

The latter part of 1983 was a crucial period for the NAJC, especially for the redress campaign. Within the national organization there appeared to be a power struggle between George Imai of Toronto, the chairperson of the National Redress Committee, and the president, Gordon Kadota of Vancouver. Until 1979, the NAJC headquarters had been located in the city where the president resided. When Gordon was elected president in 1980, the NAJC headquarters were moved to Vancouver, while the NAJC National Redress Committee was centred in Toronto. In a way, the struggle was a clash of opinions between Vancouver and Toronto powers – a classic Canadian east-versus-west conflict.

The annual general meeting of the NAJC was called for January 1984 in Winnipeg. At this meeting, it was hoped that the NAJC would establish an official redress position and elect a new NAJC president, since Gordon Kadota was stepping down.

I was asked by representatives from the smaller centres to run as a candidate for the presidency. Some conference delegates felt that a president from a neutral centre such as Winnipeg would help counteract the Vancouver/Toronto tension. In considering the nomination, I asked several members of the Manitoba community if they would assist and advise me if the national headquarters were to be moved to Winnipeg. Confident that I had their support, I accepted the nomination. Jack Oki from Toronto was also nominated as a candidate in an effort for Toronto to regain the national office, so that the president would work closely with the National Redress Committee.

Extensive lobbying was done for both candidates. The election of Oki would ensure that Imai and the National Redress Committee would have the president's ear and receive unquestioned, carte-blanche support. On the other hand, many non-Toronto members feared isolation if the headquarters returned to Toronto. Many council members felt that a National Executive Committee assisting the president from Winnipeg would be more inclined to communicate with the rest of the centres than would one from Toronto. Many expected that a more objective approach in seeking consensus on a redress position would emerge from an NAJC executive based in Winnipeg. Imai, past president of the NJCCA, and his supporters from past years backed Oki. The vote was close, and I was successful by a very slim margin.

When I became the president in 1984, my house became the NAJC headquarters, and so boxes of files were moved into my basement. My home address and phone number were listed as the organization's national office on the NAJC letterhead, and meetings were held around our dining room table. The official correspondences for the NAJC were often printed out on an $89 printer hooked up to an Atari computer. I must say that our organization lacked the funds to have a sophisticated operation, relying on our own resources for meetings and communications, but it was bolstered by the enthusiasm and dedication of the volunteers assisting me.

After I was elected, the National Executive Committee, established in Winnipeg, was formed with Harold Hirose as treasurer, Carol Matsumoto as secretary, and Henry Kojima, Lucy Yamashita, Alan Yoshino, Fred Kaita, and Joy Ooto as members-at-large. They assisted with the day-to-day responsibilities such as organizing national meetings and communication with the centres, as well as maintaining the financial records. It was a long four-year commitment; each volunteer served faithfully and diligently until the redress settlement was reached in 1988.

At the time I became president, I did not realize that I was becoming involved in what would prove to be a long struggle, not only with the redress movement but also with the internal conflicts within the Japanese Canadian community. New in my role, I was

President's Committee, 1984. Front row from left to right: Joy Ooto, Art, and Carol Matsumoto. Back row from left to right: Henry Kojima, Harold Hirose, Lucy Yamashita, and Alan Yoshino. Missing: Fred Kaita

not aware of what had transpired between Imai, his redress committee, and Gordon Kadota during his term in office. However, that blissful ignorance was short-lived. Essentially, I spent the first two years dealing with internal controversy within the community – my introduction to Japanese Canadian politics!

After the January 1984 meeting, I made a statement to the media regarding the motions adopted at the AGM that outlined the NAJC's official resolution regarding our redress position. Subsequently, Imai sent me a threatening telegram suggesting that my comment (quoted as "full compensation") "may have closed the door" to any further approaches to the federal government, "at least for the foreseeable future."

His reaction shocked me, and I was taken aback by his comments.

I didn't know what he was talking about at first. I'm not sure why Imai was so concerned with the phrase "full compensation" and the effect it might have. Although I didn't know for the longest time why he reacted in that manner, I surmised that it might have something to do with a prior commitment or agreement he might have made with the government. The term "full compensation" might have contradicted the position he had discussed with government officials earlier. His reference to "closing the doors" suggested to me that discussions on redress were being held with the government without the knowledge of the NAJC National Council. I began to wonder whether or not we were all playing for the same team and with the same objectives.

I believe that the statement I made to the press contained the council's intent about redress motions. I said that the NAJC was seeking "acknowledgment from the Canadian government of the injustices committed against Japanese Canadians during and after World War II and that NAJC seek redress in the form of monetary compensation."[1] George Imai accused me of changing the intent of the motions. I sensed that he wanted the interpretation of the motions to suggest that the NAJC seek the acknowledgment first and compensation later. But I felt strongly that this approach would have weakened the NAJC position. Without any commitment to negotiate, the decision to discuss compensation would be at the whim of the government.

Having made the decision to officially seek redress from the government, initial contact was made through the minister of multiculturalism and the prime minister. On February 18, 1984, Ministry of Multiculturalism staff members Kerry Johnston, Eric Lugtijheld, and Laura Ruzzier met with Tony Nabata of the Ottawa chapter and me in Ottawa to discuss funding for the administration of the process and the progress of the redress program. A few weeks earlier, I had informally met the Honourable David Collenette, minister for multiculturalism, who expressed concern that there was no monetary figure for compensation in the position put forward by the Japanese Canadian community.

The government officials again raised this matter of a compensa-

---

1   National Association of Japanese Canadians (NAJC), *Democracy Betrayed: The Case for Redress; A Submission to the Government of Canada on the Violation of Rights and Freedoms of Japanese Canadians during and after World War II* (Winnipeg: National Association of Japanese Canadians, 1984), 72.

tion figure. They seemed intent on finding out what we were thinking. I indicated that more time was required to establish an appropriate figure and that the community had not reached a consensus. The officials suggested that establishing a compensation figure would enhance our position for negotiations. We were skeptical, fearing that this was a ploy by the government to get us to reveal how much compensation we were seeking. If the request were substantial, the government would reject the amount as being outlandish and attempt to turn public opinion against the NAJC.

Since I had limited knowledge of the political process, Kerry Johnston offered his insights as to what would happen to the NAJC redress brief once it was presented to government. He suggested that the brief should be submitted through the Honourable Serge Joyal, secretary of state, to David Collenette and the Honourable Mark MacGuigan, minister of justice. One of the departments would then prepare a document that would be presented to Cabinet by the three ministers. Cabinet would discuss the proposal and either approve it or prepare a counterproposal that would be sent back to the NAJC. "This process," said Kerry Johnston, "would continue until an agreement was reached." With this approach, the NAJC would be negotiating with Cabinet.

Meanwhile, Imai was continuing to make allegations that I had taken unilateral action and committed the NAJC to a complete compensation settlement. He wanted the NAJC Council to reprimand me. I couldn't understand how my statements could have jeopardized discussions with the government when in my mind we had not established what was considered appropriate redress. To clarify Imai's concerns, the National Executive Committee suggested that Imai and Oki be invited to a meeting with the committee to clear up the confusion. The invitation was offered but both refused to attend, and the matter was left for discussion at the April council meeting in Vancouver.

In the meantime, the National Redress Committee (NRC) held its meeting in Toronto on March 17, 1984, to develop redress options for the upcoming April meeting. Strangely, I was not directly notified of the NRC meeting, but I decided to attend although I felt unwelcome.

At the meeting, a special letter to Prime Minister Pierre Trudeau was drafted by the committee to be delivered in person by the president. Oki and Imai insisted that the letter requesting "the

Government of Canada to officially acknowledge the injustices and agree to negotiate compensation" be sent immediately without consultation with the National Council. Imai thought the wording would allow the government enough latitude to move on the acknowledgment and their form of compensation. I personally thought that "the agreement to negotiate compensation" after the acknowledgment of wrongdoings by the government would place us in a weak negotiating position. Having issued the acknowledgment and accompanying apology, the government would have lost any motivation to negotiate and would, in essence, delay the completion of the process.

I decided that since we could not get responses from all centres regarding the content, we should wait until the April 8 National Council meeting to discuss the letter and receive input directly from council members. Again, I was naive as to why this delay irked both Oki and Imai, and why they felt such urgency for the prime minister to have this letter. When I reflected on various events and actions, I began to suspect that Imai and Oki (and possibly other members of the National Redress Committee) had already conceived a plan, one they felt the government would be favourable to in redressing the Japanese Canadian community.

On March 28, 1984, the government report *Equality Now!*, produced by an all-party Special Committee on the Participation of Visible Minorities in Canadian Society, was released to the public. The report included two key recommendations (33 and 34) related to Japanese Canadian experience. The first was "that the Parliament of Canada should officially acknowledge the mistreatment accorded to Japanese in Canada during and after World War II and the Government of Canada should undertake negotiations to redress these wrongs." The second was that "Justice Canada should review the War Measures Act with the view to proposing the safeguards necessary to prevent a recurrence of the kind of mistreatment suffered by the Japanese in Canada during and after World War II."[2] The release of the *Equality Now!* report would have been a public-relations-perfect

2   Government of Canada, House of Commons, Special Committee on the Participation of Visible Minorities in Canadian Society / Comité spécial sur la participation des minorités visibles à la société canadienne, *Equality Now! Report of the Special Committee on Visible Minorities in Canadian Society* (Ottawa: Queen's Printer for Canada, 1984; online: Library of Parliament, Canadian Parliamentary Historical Resources), 62, parl.canadiana.ca/view /oop.com_HOC_3202_15_2.

moment for the government to respond to the community's claims for redress.

Although Imai had never shared the possibility that the government was contemplating some form of redress with the NAJC Council or the National Executive Committee, his actions and reactions suggested it. I believe now that if the letter to the prime minister had been sent prior to the release of *Equality Now!*, there might have been an announcement coinciding with the release of the report stating that the government was already in the process of discussing redress with the Japanese Canadian community. Furthermore, the statement in the report insinuated that the government would acknowledge the wrong first and then enter into redress negotiation, which is contrary to the position that the NAJC Council had adopted. It was frustrating to us that the NRC was constantly attempting to manipulate the NAJC's redress objectives to a point of view that the government would find acceptable.

A *Winnipeg Free Press* headline of March 29, 1984, read: "Ottawa to Defer Wartime Apology." It indicated that Cabinet was waiting for a consensus to develop within the Japanese Canadian community before reaching a decision. Minister Collenette stated that there had been in-fighting for years among the country's forty-four thousand Japanese Canadians as to whether compensation should be sought. "Some people are afraid of reopening old wounds and creating a backlash," he was quoted as saying.[3] The language that Collenette used was similar to Imai's. Collenette's further comment that "the government wants any form of apology and compensation to be universal enough to include other repressed groups" strongly suggested that a symbolic gesture was being considered to recognize the injustices, and so individual redress for Japanese Canadians would be out of the realm of possibility.

Such a solution would not have been favourable or satisfactory to the Japanese Canadian community, nor would it have been contemplated by the NAJC. It seems that the government wanted to use the acknowledgment to demonstrate to Canadians how seriously they were treating the *Equality Now!* report. Newspaper articles following the report's release captured Trudeau and Collenette's views. The prime minister, in a *Winnipeg Sun* article, was quoted as saying that

---

3   "Ottawa to Defer Wartime Apology," *Winnipeg Free Press*, March 29, 1984, 37, archives .winnipegfreepress.com/winnipeg-free-press/1984-03-29/page-37/.

he didn't believe in attempting to rewrite history.[4] I responded to the prime minister's statement by stating, "Trudeau's being hypocritical. That's not what he says when he's talking about French rights. For a country that says it prides itself on its treatment of minorities, I think it's a pretty sorry statement for Trudeau to make."[5]

The Canadian government has a moral obligation to redress the wrongs it commits. What Trudeau was saying is that once a wrong has been committed, it is best left in the past. He revealed his ignorance of the history of the issue by stating that the government should "give jobs with the money to the people who are unemployed now rather than trying to use that money to compensate people whose ancestors in some way have been deprived."[6]

"We're not trying to get compensation for the ancestors of the victims, but we are asking for compensation for people who are alive today and were directly affected – those who lost personal possessions, homes, and businesses in the name of national security," I responded.[7]

I suspect the prime minister was more than a little leery of discussing redress, not just because of his vision of the consequences, but because of his past blunders with the issue. In 1976, while visiting Japan, Trudeau had made an impromptu apology to the Japanese for Canada's wartime mistreatment of Japanese Canadians, publicly demonstrating his ignorance of the history, and causing all kinds of stress for the diplomatic corps and the prime minister's advisors. A strong condemnation of Trudeau's comments about "not rewriting history" and having no sympathy for the NAJC position was expressed in the *Winnipeg Free Press* editorial of April 4, 1984, entitled "Redress Should Be Made":

> They [Japanese Canadians] are asking that a dark period in Canada's history be finally acknowledged by the government. They are not asking that the government of today redress all ancient wrongs against groups that have occurred throughout

---

4   Heidi Graham, "PM Lashed for 'Ignorant' View," *Winnipeg Sun*, April 4, 1984, 8, www
    .newspapers.com/article/the-winnipeg-sun/133497158/.

5   Ibid.

6   Ibid.

7   Ibid.

Canada's history. They are suggesting that the government of today make some effort to acknowledge and make amends for a wrong that was done, within recent memory, to a specific group of people, many of whom are living today. They are not making outrageous demands that would deprive the unemployed of work. They should enter into negotiations with the government of Canada about how redress might be made. But an acknowledgment of the injustice and some attempt at least at redress would be helpful to those who suffered and healthy for all Canadian society.[8]

When Collenette was asked how the government would respond to the recommendation on Japanese Canadian redress in the *Equality Now!* report, he said he would join the prime minister in opposing the call for financial compensation for Japanese Canadians interned during World War II: "Compensation would set a precedent for other minority groups whose human rights also were breached in past years."[9] It was clear from Collenette's responses that the government would not contemplate any form of compensation to individuals. Consequently, the proposal to negotiate redress after the acknowledgment would be meaningless when this specific option had already been ruled out.

At the January 1984 NAJC meeting, when Imai was reaffirmed for a new term as chairperson of the National Redress Committee, he was specifically instructed that the NRC was accountable to the National Executive Committee because, in the past, the NRC had seemed to work independently of the NAJC. This instruction was reiterated at the National Council meeting in April, and the Council further adopted a motion that the NAJC president would be the only spokesperson for the organization. It was made clear to George Imai that he was no longer the spokesperson on the redress file with government officials.

I was asked by the executive to meet with Imai and the NRC in Toronto to get assurances that there would be open and direct

---

8   "Redress Should Be Made," *Winnipeg Free Press*, April 4, 1984, 9, archives.winnipegfree press.com/winnipeg-free-press/1984-04-04/page-9/.

9   "Moderate Approach on Minorities Hinted," *Winnipeg Free Press*, April 6, 1984, 15, www.proquest.com/newspapers/moderate-approach-on-minorities-hinted-commons /docview/753075919/se-2.

communications between the president and Imai's committee. At this meeting, some of Toronto's Japanese Canadians let it be known by their snide comments that they thought they were the only ones who had the necessary political "smarts" and connections. One member of the committee even made snobbish remarks to me, saying that I lived in the "boondocks," and wondered why I would even question them. I felt embarrassed by that outrageously rude comment. I guess, in that person's eyes, Canada revolved around Toronto and the rest of us were nonentities. This "we know best" attitude was evident throughout the early stages of the redress campaign. It was that kind of arrogance that had precipitated the antagonism between Toronto and Vancouver.

Imai refused to give me any commitment for open communications, and his responses indicated an unwillingness to co-operate. He even threatened that he might consider negotiating with the government himself, should he be contacted with a proposal. At the time, I didn't realize that the NAJC being left out of the process was a distinct possibility.

I received correspondence from Minister of Multiculturalism Collenette asking the NAJC to support the government's initiative of an acknowledgment and the establishment of a $5-million foundation. Imai and the NRC gave their blessing to the government's proposal and wanted the NAJC endorsement. Imai used the Toronto issei to justify the speedy redress solution of a foundation, implying that the first-generation Japanese Canadians feared backlash and that they were dying off.

In a letter to me from April 13, 1984, Collenette made it clear that the government had ruled out individual compensation. The letter stated: "Though the Prime Minister and I are both inclined to argue against individual compensation for regrettable acts by past governments, if unlawfully taken, we have in no way ruled out redress for Canadians of Japanese origin as a community." In a letter to Collenette on April 18, I responded to his statement in these terms: "We strongly feel that individual compensation should not be ruled out as a possibility because consensus on this issue has not been reached within our community."

Personal accounts by Japanese Canadian individuals that appeared in newspaper and magazine articles were a powerful tool for creating awareness and understanding in Canadians about the effects of the internment. First-hand descriptions of the trauma experienced by victims who had been forced to leave their homes and placed in camps or sugar-beet fields were most meaningful to readers, evoking a sense of realism about internment experiences.

A stirring account from Masumi Mitsui appeared in the *Toronto Star* on April 11, 1984 (and later in *Maclean's* magazine).[10] Mitsui was a sergeant in the Canadian army in World War I who took part in the April 1917 Battle of Vimy Ridge and received the Military Medal for bravery. Shortly after the bombing of Pearl Harbor, Mitsui sent a letter dated December 9, 1941, on behalf of the Japanese branch of the Royal Canadian Legion, of which he was president, and offered to serve again in the Canadian Armed Forces. He was refused. The day after, the RCMP took Mitsui away, forcing him to act as an interpreter at the barbed-wire compound in Hastings Park where Japanese Canadians were being interned. Masumi Mitsui was so enraged that when he entered the office of the captain in charge of West Coast security, he threw his medals of bravery down on the table in front of the captain, swearing at him in anger. The officer mumbled that he had his orders and got down on his knees to pick up the medals that had scattered on the floor. Mitsui's farm and possessions were sold; he and his family were shipped to the little town of Greenwood in south-central BC. Having demonstrated his loyalty to Canada by serving in the army with remarkable bravery, he was nevertheless labelled an "enemy alien" during World War II. Mitsui died in 1987 at the age of ninety-nine as the last Japanese Canadian World War I veteran.

In Parliament several politicians publicly spoke in support of redress for Japanese Canadians. Lynn McDonald, the New Democratic Member of Parliament for the Broadview–Greenwood riding in Toronto, asked Prime Minister Trudeau in the House on April 2, 1984, whether he would introduce a resolution to acknowledge the wrongdoings of the former Liberal government, re-examine the War Measures Act, and begin negotiations with Japanese Canadian community representatives. The prime minister's response was that he had already personally expressed regret but was not "inclined to envision questions of compensation for acts which have

---

10   "Masumi Mitsui Has a Right to Be Angry: Canadian Hero at Vimy Ridge, an Internee in World War II," *Toronto Star*, April 11, 1984, A17, www.proquest.com/newspapers/masumi-mitsui-has-right-be-angry-canadian-hero-at/docview/752381980/se-2.

perhaps discoloured our history in the past."[11] Rebuffed, McDonald decided to introduce a private member's bill asking Parliament to acknowledge the many injustices committed against Canadians of Japanese ancestry and to enter into negotiations for compensation. She called me as president of the NAJC to support her initiative. Although we supported the intent of the bill, the NAJC decided not to formally endorse Lynn McDonald's proposal because a rejection in the House might have thwarted our attempts for redress in the future. We wanted to keep our options open. On April 12, 1984, the motion was tabled in the House but was not seconded and died on the Order Paper when Parliament was dissolved on July 9, 1984, in order to have elections under a new leader. Pierre Trudeau had announced his resignation as prime minister in March 1, 1984, but remained on until John Turner was chosen at a national convention.

In his first speech to the Senate on May 8, 1984, rookie Liberal Senator Jerry Grafstein introduced a motion that the federal government deliver a formal apology to Japanese Canadians for wartime injustices. He suggested that a Special Claims Commissioner be appointed to pay partial compensation for claims resulting from the incarceration and loss of properties and businesses. He recommended that a fund of $50 million be set aside for claims and the balance returned to the government after the commission had completed its responsibilities. Grafstein delivered an extensive discourse on the experiences of Japanese Canadians and the results of the Bird Commission, presenting many facts and compelling arguments that had influenced him to support redress. He challenged the senators with these fiery words: "Pay today. Calculate a fair formula for these living Canadians – perhaps an annuity. Pay we must. Pay we should."[12]

On April 26, 1984, I received a letter from Shirley Yamada, president of the NAJC's Toronto chapter, expressing clearly the feelings

---

11 John Gray, "PM Cool to Compensating Interned Japanese," *Globe and Mail*, April 3, 1984, 1, www.proquest.com/historical-newspapers/pm-cool-compensating-interned-japanese /docview/1400711037/se-2.

12 See the Honourable Jerahmiel [Jerry] S. Grafstein, "Maiden Speech in the Senate on Compensation and Apology to Japanese Canadians (May 8, 1984)," in Jerry S. Grafstein, *Parade: A Tribute to Remarkable Contemporaries* (Oakville, ON: Mosaic Press, 2017), books.google.ca/books?id=SrRJDwAAQBAJ&newbks=1&newbks_redir=0&lpg= PP1&hl=fr&pg=PT47#v=onepage&q&f=false, and Senate of Canada, *Debates of the Senate: Official Report (Hansard)* (Ottawa: Queen's Printer, 1983), 530.

of many people who felt that redress was being pushed ahead too quickly. She wrote:

> I'm of the opinion that the government can wait until our community has carefully thought out the options. More time spent on educating the public and indeed, our own people, as witness the young woman [Japanese Canadian] who didn't seem to realize the redress issue had been discussed heatedly over the past year and the MPs who'll be voting on this issue would not be wasted time. If our claims are just (and I see no one arguing the point), then they will be valid for [the] several more months, if need be, that we may take to form a consensus. If we rush, we'll probably be forced, yet again, to accept another token sum. We've been that route before. This time the government must show its sincerity by putting its money where its mouth is.

On May 16, 1984, Richard Cleroux reported in the *Globe and Mail* that Conservative leader Brian Mulroney was in favour of compensation for the Japanese Canadians who had been unfairly interned during World War II. Mulroney said that Japanese Canadians "are not looking for overwhelming compensation ... They're looking for symbolism and reassurance."[13] Mulroney added that he disagreed with Trudeau's stand that to compensate Japanese Canadians would mean that the government would have to compensate other groups. "The fact of the matter is, it was 30 years ago and Canadian citizens were arbitrarily deprived of their rights and this should not happen. If there was a Conservative government I can assure you we would be compensating Japanese Canadians."[14] Mulroney's words were music to our ears. His statement would be quoted many times over by the NAJC and the media during the redress campaign, and it became an albatross around Mulroney's neck during his time as prime minister.

Upon return from my June 9, 1984, meeting in Toronto with Imai,

---

13   Richard Cleroux, "Compensate Internees for Unfair Treatment, Mulroney Urges PM," *Globe and Mail*, May 16, 1984, 5, www.proquest.com/historical-newspapers/compensate-internees-unfair-treatment-mulroney/docview/1237488633/se-2. Also quoted in Roy Miki and Cassandra Kobayashi, *Justice in Our Time: The Japanese Canadian Redress Settlement* (Vancouver: Talonbooks; Winnipeg: National Association of Japanese Canadians, 1991), 73.

14   Ibid.

a member of the NAJC Council informed me that Imai had invited him to go to Ottawa for an announcement regarding redress. This was a surprise to me! During my meeting with Imai, he must have been aware that Collenette would be bringing forth a proposal responding to the Japanese Canadian redress issue and the *Equality Now!* report in the House of Commons, and yet he had not shared a word of this possibility.

Clearly, Imai was prepared to accept the government's proposal on behalf of the NAJC without the latter's approval. No wonder he wasn't prepared to make a commitment to communicate with the NAJC. After calls to other centres such as those of Lethbridge, Calgary, Hamilton, and Montréal, we had confirmation that a select group of people were contacted, especially supporters of Imai, and those council members were requested to invite issei members of the community to go to Ottawa.

The government was planning to make an announcement on Japanese Canadian redress. Had the delegation of council members and issei attended the presentation, it would have conveyed the impression to the government, media, and the general Canadian public that the proposal was endorsed and accepted by the Japanese Canadian community. I'm not sure whether the government fully absorbed the implications of bypassing the NAJC; perhaps they were given assurances that Imai had the community's support.

Whatever the case, we had to respond quickly. Henry Kojima and I met with the Honourable Lloyd Axworthy of the Liberal Cabinet at his Winnipeg office to make it known that Imai did not represent the views of the NAJC, nor did he have the mandate to endorse the government's proposal. We asked that Axworthy share this information with Cabinet. We stressed that if the announcement were to go ahead, the government would receive harsh criticism from the Japanese Canadian community, and their actions would not be seen as an honourable gesture. The proposed redress announcement did not materialize on the date planned.

A telephone conference of NAJC Council was quickly convened on June 17, 1984, to discuss the aborted governmental announcement. Later, in my contacts with government officials in multiculturalism, I was informed that they were in almost "daily contact" with members of our organization. They must have been talking with Imai, as my contact with government officials was very limited.

Imai's attempt to assemble, without authorization, a delegation to attend the redress announcement in Ottawa was the last straw. The NAJC Council saw no alternative but to dissolve the National Redress Committee. Imai knew the rules of the game, and he had overstepped his authority by entering into discussions with federal government officials before a community consensus could be reached.

The Issei-bu of Toronto, an organization representing the first generation of Japanese Canadians, sent a strongly worded letter to me rejecting the council's action and asking for the reinstatement of the NRC. They did not "agree to accept our reasoning that Mr. Imai's behaviour disturbed the unity of the national body." They further claimed that "the Executive of the NAJC has taken actions by listening to one side of the story and ignoring our isseis' wishes and opinions."

The decision to dissolve the NRC was made by the NAJC Council. There was no turning back. The council felt that there was now a lack of trust and confidence in the NRC and directed me to become the only spokesperson for the NAJC on redress. To reinforce this directive, a telegram was sent on June 19, 1984, to Collenette from renowned author Joy Kogawa, writer Ken Adachi, former Deputy Finance Minister Thomas Shoyama, and environmentalist David Suzuki underscoring that I, as president, was the only official spokesperson for the NAJC. "We're trying to get Mr. Collenette to listen to the whole community, not just listen to George Imai. His mandate was not to negotiate with the federal government," Adachi wrote.

I can only speculate on the motives behind Imai and Oki's urgency to have the redress issue resolved. I believe Imai wanted to be known for achieving redress for the Japanese Canadian community. In the early years, Imai was that "voice in the wilderness" calling for redress. As more people began to take interest in the redress campaign, Imai sensed that he would lose control of the movement unless he could develop a compensation proposal acceptable to the government and have the government quickly apologize. I believe the issue became one of expediency rather than of the importance of determining a process that would reflect the needs and expectations of the community. The difficulty for the Japanese Canadian community was that their understanding of the significance of redress was at an early learning stage, and to make a significant decision such as an acceptance of a government offer was premature. The National Council members expressed the need for more time for dialogue and involvement from the communities across Canada to determine an appropriate resolution.

It seems clear to me that the process of awareness and eventual participation in determining appropriate redress was the necessary step to enable Japanese Canadians to come to terms with the harsh realities of the internment experience and to begin the healing process. Had the efforts of Imai and Oki been successful, redress would have been completed in 1984. This would have resulted in a tremendous resentment on the part of Japanese Canadians towards the NAJC when later on the US redress bill passed giving Japanese Americans individual compensation. I was happy that we stood our ground and delayed the process. It would have been extremely difficult, likely impossible, to get the government to renegotiate after an agreement had been accepted; nor would the Canadian public have had any sympathy for Japanese Canadians. In hindsight, these delays were the best course of action for the redress movement.

After the dissolution of the NRC, Collenette asked me to respond to the government's proposal of an apology and the establishment of a $5 million fund to acknowledge injustices against all victims of racism in Canada, a proposal which the NRC had endorsed. A telegram was sent to Collenette on June 19, 1984, stating that I admired the explanation for the government's official position, but was opposed to it for fear that the government's official position might be viewed as being linked to the NAJC redress submission. We would not endorse the Liberal government's offer.

Newspaper editorials across Canada consistently commented on the progress of redress, often urging the government to take positive action. The *Winnipeg Free Press*'s editorial headline on April 4, 1984, read: "Redress Should Be Made."[15] The *Globe and Mail*, in response to Multiculturalism Minister David Collenette's refusal to apologize to Japanese Canadians, published an editorial on June 26, 1984, headlined "Still Unenlightened,"[16] which criticized the government for their inaction.

Shortly after this, an NAJC supporter from the North York chapter sent me an interesting article from the June 29, 1984, edition

---

15   "Redress Should Be Made," *Winnipeg Free Press*, April 4, 1984, 9, archives.winnipegfree press.com/winnipeg-free-press/1984-04-04/page-9/.

16   "Still Unenlightened," *Globe and Mail*, June 26, 1984, 6, www.proquest.com/historical -newspapers/still-unenlightened/docview/1313818135/se-2.

of the *Canada Times*, a nikkei newspaper in Toronto. This was an interview with Mr. Collenette printed in Japanese but not in English. The letter writer had kindly retranslated the article and sent it to me. "[Asked to comment on redress, Mr. Collenette said:] Opinions are divided in the Japanese community; moreover, the NAJC Council and President Miki have, for a one-sided reason, dissolved the National Redress Committee which has been talking (not negotiating) with multiculturalism officials for the past year and a half. In addition, they have notified me to the effect that they have decided on President Miki alone as the representative to negotiate with the government." Collenette then indicated that he would refuse the NAJC's advice: "There are many outstanding people in the Japanese Canadian community, and we should certainly listen to the older persons who experienced the insulting treatment and injustices because of war ... not just to the opinions of Mr. Miki. Mr. Miki, like myself, is still young; viewed in another way, an unfinished [or half-baked] product of the postwar. Before reaching a general conclusion, he should lend an ear to the opinions of all. I am talking angrily because I am angry."[17] Obviously, the minister was frustrated and desired to move on the government's agenda without full input from the community. In Imai and Oki, the government had found strong allies. They had both began to think like the government and lost perspective on their responsibility to the community.

On June 20, 1984, despite not having the endorsement of the Japanese Canadian community, Collenette delivered a hollow expression of regret in the House of Commons. He said that the government "regrets that at times throughout our history, Canadians representing minority communities have been victims of discrimination and intolerance." Furthermore, it regretted "the deprivation and hardships suffered by most members of the Japanese-Canadian community during the Second World War and its immediate aftermath and takes pride that the Charter of Rights and Freedoms ... now affords members of minority communities protection against the recurrences of such treatment."[18]

---

17 *Canada Times*, June 19, 1984 (translated from the Japanese).

18 See Roy Miki, *Redress: Inside the Japanese Canadian Call for Justice (Vancouver: Raincoast Books, 2004)*, 317–318, or Government of Canada, House of Commons, Special Committee on Participation of Visible Minorities in Canadian Society, *Response of the Government of Canada to Equality Now! The Report of the Special Parliamentary Committee on Visible Minorities in Canadian Society* (Ottawa: Minister of Supply and Services Canada, 1984), 14.

The media questioned Senator Grafstein concerning his defence of the prime minister's response to the Japanese Canadian redress request. The Senator acknowledged that there were serious divisions in Cabinet and responded: "I understand the political process sufficiently to say that I'm not sure there is a huge consensus in this country for measures that would take it [apology and redress] to the extent I think is appropriate."[19] Grafstein had previously contradicted Prime Minister Trudeau's position that you can't rewrite history when he said: "Good old Canadian common sense knows it is never too late to correct a wrong. Canadians believe in affirmative action."[20]

Grafstein continued to raise the redress issue in the Senate, asking Senate leader Duff Roblin on several occasions when the government intended to apologize to Japanese Canadians and what form of compensation was being considered. Grafstein was one of the earliest supporters of monetary compensation. In my telephone discussion with him regarding his proposal for financing the redress claims, he suggested that the government funds be used as partial compensation for property claims that were never adequately settled. I indicated that the NAJC was looking at broader parameters than just property losses.

The NAJC did not agree that the Charter of Rights and Freedoms would now protect minority groups from the violation of rights that were imposed upon Japanese Canadians. The "notwithstanding clause" in section 33 of the Charter[21] would allow Parliament or Provincial Legislatures to override equality rights such as freedom from discrimination on the basis of racial ancestry by simply declaring this intention in the legislation. For example, the Québec legislature invoked section 33 of the Charter to pass a secularism law, Bill 21, on June 16, 2019, which bans public employees including teachers and police officers from wearing "religious symbols" at work (although a cross hangs prominently in the National Assembly).

And there was no question that an expression of "regret" was a poor substitute for an apology. No apology was intended by

---

19 Ann Silversides, "Japanese Canadians Disturbed over Refusal to Apologize," *Globe and Mail*, June 29, 1984, M4, www.proquest.com/historical-newspapers/japanese-canadians-disturbed-over-refusal/docview/1237540871/se-2.

20 Grafstein, "Maiden Speech in the Senate"; Senate of Canada, *Debates of the Senate*, 531.

21 Government of Canada, *The Canadian Charter of Rights and Freedoms*, section 33, "Notwithstanding Clause," last modified April 14, 2022, www.justice.gc.ca/eng/csj-sjc/rfc-dlc/ccrf-ccdl/check/art33.html.

Collenette's words; he later explained to reporters that an apology would mean that something wrong had happened, and the actions of the King government in 1942, as regrettable as they had been, were "legitimate." Whatever the government intended, this expression of "regret" was a further insult to Japanese Canadians.

The expression of regret was coupled with the announcement of a $5 million endowment to launch a charitable foundation to promote racial harmony and to "serve as a continuing and dynamic memorial to the courage and perseverance of the issei generation of the Japanese-Canadian community."[22] Imai's influence was apparent in the wording.

In addition, Collenette told the press that I sent him a telegram indicating that the NAJC favoured the acknowledgment of past injustices but wanted to negotiate redress with the government. The minister was aware before he made the announcement that the government did not have the support of the NAJC. I indicated to him that I was opposed to his decision to table the government's response to the *Equality Now!* report and would take my chances with the Honourable John Turner, who was the strongest leadership contender to succeed Trudeau (who had announced his resignation on February 29, 1984). The government's response was wholly inadequate, and the NAJC would continue to press for direct financial compensation.

Luckily, with only seven sitting days remaining before Parliament recessed, the bill had very little chance of passing. Gordon Fairweather, chairman of the Canadian Human Rights Commission, said that it would have been better for the federal government to have done nothing rather than to respond the way it did.

In the final day of the parliamentary session, the Honourable Brian Mulroney, leader of the Opposition, questioned Prime Minister Trudeau: "Would the Prime Minister grasp the moment to right an historic wrong that has been inflicted on Canadians of Japanese origin? Will the Prime Minister, on this special day, take time to convey, either on behalf of the Government or on behalf of the Parliament of Canada, a formal apology to Canadian citizens whose rights were trampled upon in the war years?"[23] After Trudeau skirted around

---

22 See Miki, *Redress*, 318; Government of Canada, *Response of the Government of Canada to Equality Now!*, 14.

23 Government of Canada, House of Commons, *House of Commons Debates: Official Report*, vol. 4 (Ottawa: E. Cloutier, Queen's Printer and Controller of Stationery, 1984), 5306.

the question, refusing to address it specifically, Mulroney posed a supplementary one: "There is a world of difference between a regret and a formal apology. All I am asking the prime minister today is to acknowledge the fact that this country, this Government, this Parliament, was wrong, and to convey our deep and genuine apologies to the Japanese Canadians."[24]

After much prodding by the leader of the Opposition, Trudeau finally responded: "I do not see how I can apologize for some historic event to which we or these people in the House were not a party. We can regret that it happened."[25] The apology was not forthcoming. The House recessed on June 29, 1984, and the bill died. Trudeau was no longer prime minister.

The NAJC immediately requested a meeting with Prime Minister John Turner, placed in power the following day, in the hope that he would take a more enlightened approach than his predecessor. In a letter to me, Turner indicated that he would "like to see some recognition of the wrong to which the Japanese Canadians were subjected." He told reporters that he favoured some sort of "symbolic" compensation and would be willing to meet personally with NAJC representatives.

I made telephone calls and sent telegrams to the prime minister's office requesting a meeting with the prime minister in early August 1984, during the school summer recess. After I had returned to my role as school principal, I finally received a call from Turner's office saying that a meeting had been scheduled for August 27 in Vancouver. Unfortunately, I was scheduled to attend an important administrative meeting with the superintendent of education on the same day. This was an annual planning meeting, the one that Vera Derenchuk called the most important meeting of the year: "So you better not miss it." My immediate response to the prime minister's secretary was that I might have difficulty with the date and that I would have to get permission from the superintendent to absent myself. Apparently, the secretary was shocked with my reply, saying: "My god! This is the prime minister who wants to meet with you." I ended up calling Vera Derenchuk to let her know that I would have to miss her meeting, and why. She was flattered that I considered asking the prime minister's office to change the date so that I wouldn't miss

24 Ibid.

25 Ibid.

her meeting. Jokingly, she repeated this story to others, especially to the school board members, suggesting that I felt that meeting with the superintendent of education was more important than meeting with the prime minister.

On August 27 my brother Roy Miki, who was chair of the Greater Vancouver Redress Committee, Don Rosenbloom, our legal counsel, and I met Turner and his political staff in his room at the lavish Four Seasons Hotel in downtown Vancouver. This was my first formal meeting with the prime minister of Canada. The security was unbelievable. There was an abundance of RCMP officers as we were escorted from the hotel lobby to elevators specially reserved for the prime minister's staff. We were escorted to the prime minister's room, not knowing what to expect. Being invited to the meeting and having read about Turner's more flexible attitude in the press, we sensed that the Liberal leader was willing to take a different approach than Trudeau. I was somewhat optimistic but not convinced that there would be change in the Liberal strategy.

Entering the room, we were introduced to the prime minister by one of his staff as we shook hands. I thanked him for this opportunity to meet, and then we sat down to serious business. Roy and I explained the NAJC position to Turner and expressed the importance of having the redress issue resolved in a manner satisfactory to the Japanese Canadian community. We also conveyed our dissatisfaction with the manner in which the Liberal government had bypassed the community to express regret rather than working with it to reach an amicable solution. Should the Liberal government be re-elected, we requested that the prime minister and the government give an official acknowledgment of the wrong and a commitment to negotiate a just settlement. In this regard, Turner appeared most reluctant to agree to "negotiations," since he kept hedging away from the word, but he did go so far as to say he would read the brief and then discuss it with the NAJC. On the question of compensation, the prime minister again used the adjective "symbolic." If, after the federal election, the Liberals were to become the official opposition, Turner agreed to support an all-party resolution but was vague on its substance. When asked whether he would support a resolution that acknowledged the wrong and committed the government to the process of negotiations, he said he wanted to read the brief before making such a commitment.

Following the meeting, a press conference had been arranged in the downstairs lobby of the Four Seasons Hotel. John Turner and I made statements regarding our meeting to the assembled press. Mr. Turner stated that he favoured an all-party attempt to redress Japanese Canadians. He was ready to receive the NAJC brief after the election and would meet with the NAJC representatives to discuss the contents of the brief so his government could determine the terms of reference for the all-party resolution.

In June 1984 Keith Spicer, a columnist for the *Vancouver Sun*, wrote an article suggesting that John Turner should take the opportunity to use "the old injustice to make a new image" for himself by promising to actively deal with the Japanese Canadian redress issue.[26] Turner would not make such a commitment.

As it turned out, the Liberals were not re-elected, and so the NAJC turned its attention towards the newly elected Conservative government.

---

26 Keith Spicer, "An Old Injustice Offers Opportunity," *Vancouver Sun*, June 28, 1984, 5, www.newspapers.com/article/the-vancouver-sun/133500036/.

CHAPTER 5

Optimism

Anyone who was passionately involved in the redress movement will tell you that it was a campaign of highs and lows, hopes and disappointments. Having heard the words spoken by Brian Mulroney in the House in 1984, elated Japanese Canadians anticipated that the issue of redress would be quickly resolved. We would soon realize that these were false hopes, and that the struggle for redress would continue for several more years.

When the Conservatives assumed power in September 1984, the Right Honourable Brian Mulroney, now prime minister, was reminded of his public commitment to sincerely address the redress question: "If there were a Conservative government, I can assure you we would be compensating Japanese Canadians."

Anticipating that Jack Murta would become the minister of multiculturalism, Henry Kojima and I met with him before the September 4 election while he was still a candidate for Manitoba's Lisgar riding. Moments following his swearing-in as the minister for multiculturalism, the Honourable Jack Murta indicated to reporters that his party was on record as favouring a public apology to Japanese Canadians. He said he was considering establishing a committee of two or three people to do some research into what "the compensation" would include.

In the period following the election, the NAJC established a positive relationship with the two opposition critics for multiculturalism, Liberal Sergio Marchi and New Democrat Ernie Epp. Both became strong advocates for the NAJC and were members of the Standing Committee on Multiculturalism, raising the redress issue with members of the committee at opportune times. They monitored the progress of the redress negotiations by keeping in touch with me. The role of the opposition critics was to press the government to live up to their obligations. Whenever the opportunity arose in Question Period to raise the redress issue with the minister or prime minister, I would be contacted by either Marchi or Epp to see if there was a specific question that they should ask on our behalf. Both opposition critics constantly reminded the prime minister that he had made a promise to compensate Japanese Canadians. Their continued questioning in the House stimulated inquiries from the media asking me for responses to the reactions from the minister or the prime minister. In this way, the redress issue had continual exposure in the media, which helped keep the issue present in the minds of Canadians.

I first met Sergio Marchi after the Conservatives took power in 1984, when he was elected as a Liberal MP for Toronto's York West riding. He was a young, enthusiastic, articulate MP of Italian descent and became the multiculturalism critic for the Honourable John Turner. After the Liberals assumed power in the fall of 1993, I conducted an interview with Marchi, who was appointed Minister of Immigration, asking him to reflect on his role in the Japanese Canadian redress process.

Marchi admitted that when he first became the multiculturalism critic he lacked an understanding of the redress issue, and so he immersed himself in the topic by talking to Japanese Canadians across the country, including me. Marchi was very aware of Pierre Trudeau's position, but nevertheless recommended to John Turner, his leader, that he reconsider the Liberal position. After discussing it with the caucus and recognizing the injustice, John Turner decided that the Liberals should alter their position. Marchi claimed that it was an important thing to do because he believed that what we do today counts so much for the kind of future we want to build.

At times it appeared that the struggle for redress was futile, but Marchi said that he was motivated to continue on because, "When I get a letter or I'd meet them [elderly members of the Japanese Canadian community] in Vancouver or Winnipeg, it always reminded me ... that they were the individuals who were impacted the most and we knew that because of their age – people were passing on without ever seeing this thing [redress]."[1] When Marchi eventually heard the prime minister's announcement about redress, he recalled: "Those images of the people came back. That made me feel really, really good."

Facing the prospect of negotiating with the government, the NAJC decided at our April 1984 meeting to compile a brief that would outline the rationale for redress in a historical context. A committee chaired by Tony Nabata and consisting of Randy Enomoto, George Imai, Elmer Hara, Gordon Kadota, Roy Miki, Tamio Wakayama, and Allan Hoyano deliberated on the main elements of the brief. With the help of others, including lawyer Don Rosenbloom, the committee was given the tedious task of developing a draft report for the June Council meeting in Winnipeg. The draft was reviewed by the NAJC National Council and revised for release following the federal election.

This brief, which outlined the NAJC claim for redress, was entitled *Democracy Betrayed: The Case for Redress*.[2] Its content was based on findings from government archival documents and research that had been conducted by Ann Gomer Sunahara for her 1981 book *The Politics of Racism*. The report did not make specific monetary demands other than a commitment from the government to discuss the issue of appropriate compensation. Copies were delivered to Jack Murta the day before it was released. The NAJC desired to meet with Prime Minister Brian Mulroney to present him with a copy of the brief, but a meeting could not be arranged because "he was too busy."

On November 20, 1984, a day prior to the NAJC's scheduled press conference in Ottawa to release the report, I was with some fellow members from Toronto and Ottawa in the Centre Block of the Parliament Buildings to deliver *Democracy Betrayed* to the prime minister's office. As we were standing in the main rotunda, Maryka Omatsu, member of the NAJC team, noticed by chance the prime minister coming down the hallway with hordes of reporters following

---

1   Sergio Marchi, in discussion with the author, December 10, 1993, in Ottawa.

2   National Association of Japanese Canadians (NAJC), *Democracy Betrayed: The Case for Redress; A Submission to the Government of Canada on the Violation of Rights and Freedoms of Japanese Canadians during and after World War II* (Winnipeg: National Association of Japanese Canadians, 1984). A Japanese translation was also produced: *Uragirareta Minshushugi: Hosho mondai no tame ni* 裏切られた民主主義：補償問題のために. See the Nikkei National Museum Library Collection, nikkeimuseum.org/www.item_detail.php?art_id=A21553.

him. He skirted past us and then stopped to speak with the crowd of reporters. Maryka turned to me and said, "Art, why don't you give the prime minister the brief right now?" I thought about it for a moment and replied, "Why not?" I inched in beside the reporters and when the scrum began to break up I approached Prime Minister Mulroney directly. I introduced myself as the president of the National Association of Japanese Canadians, said, "I want to give you this brief from the National Association," and handed him a brown envelope with two copies of *Democracy Betrayed*. He thanked me and then headed for his caucus meeting.

The following day, at the NAJC press conference in the basement of the Centre Block, *Democracy Betrayed* was released to the media. In Vancouver, another press conference was being held simultaneously by the Vancouver Redress Committee to introduce the brief to the media there. We wanted to ensure that the media at both ends of the country received the long-awaited document at the same time. This was a precious historic moment for all Canadians of Japanese ancestry, because it was the first time since the wartime years that Japanese Canadians, as a community, officially called upon the government of Canada to act with honour and in good faith to redress the wrongs the community had suffered. Up to that day, the government had yet to acknowledge formally that Canadians, because of their Japanese ancestry, were innocent victims of policies and actions that stripped them of their democratic rights.

The information contained in the brief stressed that the internment of Japanese Canadians by the federal government in 1942 was motivated by "racism and political opportunism," and not by threats to national security. The wartime government of Mackenzie King announced on February 25, 1942, that the compulsory removal of all Japanese Canadians was necessary "to safeguard the defences of the Pacific Coast of Canada."[3] The government claimed that "the denial of civil and human rights of these Canadians was necessary to ensure Canada's security," the brief stated. "Today, the government documents show the claim to be completely false." No Japanese Canadian was ever convicted of a crime involving a breach of security.

Democracy Betrayed called for the federal government to "acknowledge its responsibilities to compensate Japanese Canadians" and to

---

3   NAJC, *Democracy Betrayed*, 12.

commit itself to initiate a process of negotiations towards "a just and honourable settlement of the claim." This recommendation was similar to the one proposed by the all-party Commons Committee report *Equality Now!* in March that was rejected by the former Liberal leader Pierre Trudeau.

Jack Murta promptly responded to the NAJC claim for redress by revealing that he favoured some form of parliamentary apology to Japanese Canadians and suggested establishing a committee to investigate the possibility of compensation. In another press statement, Murta suggested that the government was contemplating unilateral action on redress. In response to the minister's latter comment, I quickly wrote him a letter on November 23, 1984, which stressed: "Let it be clearly understood by the Government that any settlement of our claim without consultation and negotiations with the NAJC is completely unacceptable. A unilateral declaration of a settlement by the Federal Government will be met with disapproval by our community."

Later, Murta was quoted in the *Globe and Mail* as saying: "The older Japanese Canadians, the ones who were actually involved in the uprooting for the most part, don't want compensation."[4] Obviously, he had been talking to issei members of the community orchestrated by George Imai and the Toronto Japanese Canadian Citizens' Association or receiving information from other sources. I responded in writing to his comments with the following message: "The fact that you unearthed some elders in our community who have expressed disinterest in compensation is not meaningful. However, as duly elected representatives of our community, I can assure you that the majority opinion is that compensation is one component of our settlement."

Finally, Murta requested a meeting with the NAJC. Being from Manitoba, he was frequently in Winnipeg, and meetings were held with short notice. On November 24, 1984, members of the National Executive Committee with Elmer Hara, Gordon Hirabayashi, and Roy Miki met with Murta and two members of his staff, Elizabeth Willcock and Stacey Newton. Murta indicated that the government wanted a quick resolution, and that a proposal for Cabinet was being

---

4   "Murta Says Internees Likely to Get Apology," *Globe and Mail*, November 22, 1984, 12, www.proquest.com/historical-newspapers/murta-says-internees-likely-get-apology /docview/1237603365/se-2.

prepared even without our input. He pointed out that the compensation package they were proposing might avoid direct compensation to the victims. We were told that parameters had already been predetermined, and we felt Murta was trying to feel us out for our reaction. We made it clear to him that the only satisfactory response was a commitment by the government to honour the negotiation process.

Murta requested that his staff meet with the National Council of the NAJC to begin discussions on how to arrive at a redress settlement. The National Council members were summoned to Winnipeg for meetings on December 14 and 15, 1984, to meet with delegation head Doug Bowie, the assistant deputy minister for Secretary of State; Orest Kruhlak, regional director for Secretary of State, Pacific Region; and Anne Scotton, member of the Corporate Policy Group representing the minister. At a private pre-meeting caucus on December 14, the National Council members agreed that we should get the government to acknowledge the NAJC as the legitimate voice of Japanese Canadians, and that they should deal exclusively with the NAJC to reach a redress solution. We also expressed our desire to participate in the writing of the acknowledgment. Murta had previously indicated interest in having government officials visit local centres to hold public redress meetings. Council members were uncomfortable with this prospect and felt that it would not be in our best interest for this to occur. The council members feared that government officials would talk only to people they knew opposed the NAJC and then announce that the government had consulted with the community.

The following day, the meeting with the government officials was held on the top floor of the Westin Hotel located at Winnipeg's historic junction of Portage and Main. The NAJC emphasized the importance of having a commitment from the government to accept the negotiation process. If the government insisted on holding meetings in the local communities, the council felt that these should be held once negotiations were underway. We knew that we could not prevent officials from meeting the Japanese Canadian community.

It was interesting to note that during our discussions, even the government officials agreed that asking for the acknowledgment first and working on the compensation portion later would be a disadvantage to the NAJC. Once the acknowledgment was issued, pressure from the opposition and media might lessen and the compensation portion would no longer remain important to the government. After discussing issues such as funding for the redress program, acknowledgment wording, and the form and nature of compensation, a news release was developed between the government and NAJC.

The council members were elated and could not believe that redress might become a reality as the government officials and NAJC representatives outlined the contents of the news release at a press conference on December 15, 1984. The joint release was a public demonstration that the government was committed to enter into serious discussions with the NAJC to establish a negotiation process. The key statement in the release was that "a full and frank discussion was undertaken establishing a negotiation process between the NAJC and the Federal Government." This included the time frame for the process of negotiations, wording and content of the acknowledgment, and the amount and nature of compensation. It was a tremendous step forward, and the NAJC Council eagerly anticipated a quick settlement.

After redress I talked to Anne Scotton, who had attended the December 15 meeting as the minister's representative, and asked her what they hoped from meeting with the NAJC council. Anne indicated, "I think the objective of the exercise from the government's point of view was to establish what the parameters for 'discussions' would be and to establish what the position of the NAJC was or would be at that time without offering anything on the part of the government formally." The meeting became derailed when the NAJC insisted that use of the word "negotiation" be stated in the press release. The government officials, including Minister Murta, agreed that they wanted to use "discussions" and had no mandate to use the term "negotiate" because that was not their intention. After rewriting the press release four or five times, Anne concurred that the term "negotiation" was inserted in order to appease the demands from the NAJC representatives, but in the mindset of the government officials they were thinking "discussions." That change in the wording was precipitated by Doug Bowie, the assistant deputy minister, who had a personal interest in the redress issue and commitment to it. Doug had grown up in the Lethbridge area in southern Alberta, where a large number of Japanese Canadians had been placed on sugar-beet farms, and was knowledgeable of what the internees had experienced. He may have pushed for the use of the word "negotiation." A month later, Doug Bowie was relieved of his position. This information from Anne explains the frustration we encountered at the January meetings. A negotiation team was quickly established by the NAJC Council consisting of Elmer Hara, Roy Miki, Ritsuko Inouye, Harold Hirose, and myself. Roger Obata was named as an alternate with two legal advisors, Don Rosenbloom and Maryka Omatsu. Meeting dates were established and negotiations began on January 4, 1985.

At the first so-called negotiations meeting, government officials Kruhlak and Scotton surprised us with the government's intentions. Kruhlak informed us that a deadline of January 29 had been decided, by which time all substantive issues would need to be resolved in our talks. We were told that discussions beyond that date would only deal with matters regarding the implementation of the settlement. The NAJC negotiation team expressed its dissatisfaction with the imposed deadline and reminded the government officials of Bowie's assurances given at the December 15, 1984, meeting that the time frame for negotiations would be flexible.

At the second negotiations session on January 12, we were informed that the deadline would still be imposed but extended by three weeks until February 20. We were also advised that this inflexible approach on the part of the government was a political decision, and that non-compliance could lead the government either to act unilaterally or to shelve the issue for good.

Mr. Murta was quoted in the *Winnipeg Free Press* on January 14 as saying that he "hopes that a formal apology to Japanese Canadians would be issued during a one-day debate in the Commons this month."[5] Following his comments, contacts with other ethnic groups suggested to us that the government was unilaterally planning an announcement on redress around the deadline date that was first mentioned at the January 4 meeting. Mr. Murta's proposal received approval at the cabinet's social planning committee on January 23, and the following day, as the final step, it was to be taken to the inner planning and priorities committee. It was clear after two meetings that he was going ahead with the proposal.

We urged Mr. Murta not to proceed until the NAJC Council had the opportunity to consider the proposal. Roy Miki told Dan Turner of the *Ottawa Citizen* that the current government's unilateral action

---

5   "Talks Move Slowly," *Winnipeg Free Press*, January 14, 1985, 15, archives.winnipegfreepress
    .com/winnipeg-free-press/1985-01-14/page-15/.

reminded him of the government's attitude towards the Japanese before the internment: "They're saying, 'You've got three weeks to agree to this.' It's like: 'You've got 24 hours to pack your bags and leave the coast. We're doing it for your own good.'"[6]

In a letter to Murta on January 18, 1985, outlining the NAJC's aversion to the enormous pressure placed upon our negotiation team to reach a redress settlement immediately, we indicated our rejection of the imposed deadline. A flexible timeline was necessary in order for our community to contribute to the process and benefit from it. We explained to Mr. Murta on many occasions the importance of a process to negotiate a redress resolution that was satisfactory to the Japanese Canadian community. We were hard-pressed to see any justification whatsoever for the imposition of an inflexible deadline. After so many years during which the issue had been neglected, why had it suddenly become so important to resolve the issue immediately?

When I reflect back on the days leading up to the threat of an imposed settlement, I think government officials thought that by endorsing the negotiations process with the NAJC, they could accelerate acceptance by agreeing to meet but not discussing any substantive concerns that we put forward. It seemed ludicrous that after two meetings a deadline would be imposed. To consider the meetings as a negotiation process was a pretence and a way to put pressure on the NAJC to succumb to the government's predetermined position. It was frustrating and a disappointment for me to think that we had been deceived into thinking that there would be a legitimate process.

As for compensation, Kruhlak informed us that the government was prepared to consider only "symbolic compensation," and that the monetary amount would bear no relationship to the actual losses incurred by our community. He indicated the government was prepared to offer a $6–$10 million foundation, although he was unable to explain how the government arrived at this "symbolic figure."

We reminded Murta in our letter that the government's decision to predetermine the amount and form of compensation was an about-face from the agreement made at the December 15, 1984, meeting. We clearly stated that the NAJC position was that the

---

6   Dan Turner, "Talks with Japanese Canadians Deadlocked," *Ottawa Citizen*, January 21, 1985, 1, www.newspapers.com/article/the-ottawa-citizen/133498855/.

monetary figure of settlement could only be arrived at by examining the losses suffered by our community and how those losses affected the victims. When the question of the government's disregard for the negotiation process was raised, Kruhlak surprisingly intimated that the government did not approach the meetings as negotiations. Yet the press release issued jointly by the NAJC and the government, and endorsed by Murta, stated clearly that the government was undertaking a negotiation process with the NAJC. We strongly underscored to Murta that a meaningful resolution to redress had to be a product of direct and substantial negotiations with the NAJC.

A week later, at a face-to-face meeting in Vancouver with NAJC representatives Roy Miki, Cassandra Kobayashi, and Don Rosenbloom, Murta reaffirmed that he did not intend to negotiate with the NAJC. He said that the government was willing to offer an acknowledgment and a $6 million educational fund. Although the offer was not presented to us in writing, he admitted that the fund would not be in the control of the Japanese Canadian community. After great anticipation we found that the government's position was not really much different from that of the previous Liberal government. We requested that Murta facilitate a meeting with Prime Minister Mulroney, a meeting that never materialized. The NAJC Council agreed through a telephone conference on January 24 that the NAJC should reject any unilateral action and should press for the continuation of the negotiation process.

On Friday afternoon, January 18, 1985, I received a phone call from Elizabeth Willcock, Murta's Chief of Staff, asking me to attend a meeting in Toronto the following day. She said that airline tickets were waiting for me at the airport. Murta had planned to meet with a number of Japanese Canadians from the Toronto and Hamilton areas, including George Imai and his supporters. Intuition told me that Murta was arranging a confrontation between the NAJC and the Japanese Canadian opposition. I refused to attend the meeting.

That same evening, at about eight o'clock, I received a call from Murta himself asking me to attend the meeting in Toronto. I indicated that it was not in the best interest of the NAJC for me to attend this meeting and mentioned my concerns that Japanese Canadians were being played off each other and that the NAJC was being set up. I expressed my disappointment that he had gone back on his word about agreeing to negotiate. His blunt response indicated that he had no intention of negotiating, but rather of "consulting." In discussing the government's imposed deadlines, he would not accept my request that we needed time for our community to provide input regarding the redress settlement. Several times during our conversation, he made arrogant remarks reminding me that "HE WAS THE MINIS-TER." At one point, he threatened to visit each Japanese Canadian centre to personally get feedback on the government's offer. He said he could arrange for the use of a government jet and visit the centres within a few days. I suggested that he try that, but we would not be party to such actions. He calmed down, sensing that he could not convince me to attend the Toronto meeting. That phone call lasted about three hours. I was becoming frustrated with the pressure to relent, but it strengthened my resolve and reinforced my conviction that my decision not to attend was the right one.

I sensed a feeling of desperation from Jack Murta with his use of threats to entice me to attend the Toronto meeting. Even though I thought that the NAJC was the recognized representative organiza-tion for the Japanese Canadian community, it became obvious that Murta's officials had been in contact with NAJC's opponents, who had likely assured the government that its offer would be acceptable to them. Having me attend the Toronto meeting would have given credence to the government's declaration that the community had been consulted in time to meet the deadline of the announcement, set for February 1985. I abhorred the attempted manipulation by the minister's office, but I guess that was to be expected given how recklessly they wanted to attain their goal.

Seeing that the meetings with the NAJC were not working out as government officials had planned, I realized the minister was taking advantage of the support George Imai and his group showed for his compensation plan. Mr. Murta wanted my attendance at the Toronto meeting to show the Canadian public that he had consulted with Japanese Canadians, and that Japanese Canadians supported the gov-ernment's proposal. I suspect that Mr. Murta was implying that the NAJC did not speak for all Japanese Canadians and that there was a group in our community who supported the government's proposal. It was the "divide and conquer" tactic. With the support expressed in Toronto, he was ready to move ahead with the redress announcement despite opposition from the NAJC.

By this time, George Imai was calling his group the Japanese

Canadian National Redress Committee, which claimed to represent the survivors. Imai told the media that his group was satisfied with the government's plan to apologize and establish a universal fund. He attacked the NAJC by saying that the group consists of "mainly young people who are asking for an exorbitant amount of money."[7]

In anticipation of possible unilateral action, the NAJC's strategy team, along with some members of the Ottawa community, hastily converged in Ottawa from January 28 to 30, 1985, to meet with members of the Opposition parties. A press conference was scheduled in the Centre Block's basement to stress our opposition to the government's plans to push their proposal through the House without the NAJC's agreement. We requested a meeting with Mr. Murta before the press conference, but a telegram response from his office indicated that he was not available.

Once we were in Ottawa, however, after our dissatisfaction with the negotiation process was publicized, Murta decided to meet with the NAJC delegation. No substantive progress was made. He indicated to the press that he hoped the party House leaders would agree to an all-party resolution that week. After the meeting, Murta told reporters: "We are not and we never have been negotiating." Reporters justly pointed out to him that his remarks conflicted sharply with the wording of the joint press release from the NAJC and his department that verified both sides agreed to "establishing a negotiation process."

A press conference was held on January 28 in Ottawa, where the NAJC informed the media of its objections to the government's intention to move unilaterally with a redress announcement in the House. The NAJC continually stressed how important the negotiation process was to the Japanese Canadian community; only direct and substantial negotiations could produce a meaningful settlement. We saw the process of negotiation as an opportunity for Japanese Canadians to come to terms with the injustices of the past and to begin to heal.

At an early meeting in January, Minister Murta had raised interesting questions: "What did your community lose?" and "Can you quantify it?" To be honest, we didn't have the data and knew that none was available, so we could not respond to the question of

---

7   "Opposition Spurns Plan to Compensate Japanese," *Winnipeg Free Press*, January 29, 1985, 4, archives.winnipegfreepress.com/winnipeg-free-press/1985-01-29/.

monetary losses suffered by the community. Realizing that a study on actual socio-economic losses was necessary, the NAJC approached a reputable national accounting firm, Price Waterhouse, who quoted that the cost to undertake the study would be in the range of $150,000. It was impossible for the NAJC to fund such a study, so we requested financial support from the government through the minister's officials.

Although Murta indicated that he appreciated the value of the study, we were told that the government had decided to reject the NAJC request. He explained that the government used the term "compensation," but that they had never intended direct compensation to Japanese Canadians and felt that supporting a socio-economic study might commit them to taking that direction.

One of Murta's officials commented, "Why would the government fund a study that will be used against us?" We were perplexed by this response, because there were clear precedents in which the government had funded studies and even paid legal fees for groups opposed to government policies. Indigenous groups, for example, have received funding to conduct studies related to their Land claims. I guessed from the government's perspective that if the NAJC was unable to arrange for the study on economic losses, the NAJC's demand for compensation would be weakened.

Although the NAJC was not seeking dollar-for-dollar compensation, we believed that the settlement should bear some relationship to the losses suffered by Japanese Canadians. Unable to receive financial support from the government, the NAJC announced that we would finance the study through community fundraising. However, the community response was poor, as many were skeptical whether redress was even possible. The NAJC raised approximately $40,000, far short of the amount needed.

But as it turns out, the Price Waterhouse story is another example of happenstance or good fortune. In the discussions regarding the importance of the study, then Price Waterhouse President Phil Barter was reminded of his father's words. He recalled that his father had been president during the wartime era, was extremely upset at how Japanese Canadians were being treated, and regretted that he didn't do anything about it. As a result, Phil Barter felt that he could honour his father's memory and promised to do the study, provided that the NAJC was willing to pay for the upfront costs such as sending researchers to the Public Archives of Canada to collect and assess the data. This was manageable for the NAJC. Price Waterhouse would prepare the report. They were hired to undertake the study, which was to examine losses through confiscation of properties, loss of income, disruption of education, loss of life-insurance policies and pension benefits, and loss of community facilities. The NAJC agreed that if there was a redress settlement, the remainder of the fees would be paid. In retrospect, the strength of the Price Waterhouse study results became a benchmark for the final redress settlement and had significant influence on the media.

On January 29, 1985, the NAJC representatives met with the Honourable John Turner and the Liberal caucus, as well as with the Honourable Ed Broadbent and the NDP caucus, receiving assurances from both parties that they would not support any resolution unless it had the consent of the NAJC. Following the meeting between the NAJC and the Liberals, John Turner told reporters: "At this stage, we will resist any effort by the Government of Canada to achieve unanimity in the House of Commons until we are satisfied that the [negotiation] process has been continued in a meaningful way."[8]

During our discussions with Ed Broadbent and his colleagues, Broadbent received a memo from one of his staff asking the House leaders to meet the next morning regarding the announcement of the acknowledgment and the Japanese Canadian redress settlement. Mr. Broadbent asked me, "Are you aware that the government is planning to make a redress announcement tomorrow?" I replied, "No, this is news to us. We have not reached an agreement, nor are we satisfied with the present negotiation progress."

When Mr. Broadbent showed us the wording of the acknowledgment, we were shocked. During an earlier negotiation meeting and after much discussion, we had agreed upon the acknowledgment's exact wording. The version that Mr. Broadbent showed us was not the same wording that the NAJC and the government officials had worked on. It was the original resolution that was first brought forward to us by the government, without the substantive changes we had agreed upon.

Recognizing our dissatisfaction with the government's position

---

8   "Japanese Accuse Ottawa of Forcing Compensation Deal," *Toronto Star*, January 29, 1985, A3, www.proquest.com/newspapers/japanese-accuse-ottawa-forcing-compensation-deal /docview/752871853/se-2.

and actions on redress, Mr. Broadbent quickly told Ian Deans, the party House leader, to block the government's plan to force a resolution. Earlier in the day, John Turner also rejected the government's intent to introduce the bill without full negotiation with the NAJC. Unable to obtain all-party support, Jack Murta announced that he was suspending action for the time being.

Recognizing that our organization's negotiations and strategy team consisted mainly of individuals who were either very young or not born during the internment period, we consciously invited victims who were young adults at the time to give personal perspectives on the effects of the forced relocation on them and their families. Whenever we met in Toronto or Ottawa, Norm Oikawa from Hamilton was always willing to join us at meetings with government officials. I first met Norm at a meeting in Toronto, and we became good friends after I found out that he had known my dad in Mission, BC, before the war. He shared stories of my dad and what he was like in the early days – apparently he drove a motorcycle and was an excellent mechanic. To support the NAJC's fundraising campaign, Norm went house to house visiting Japanese Canadian families in southwestern Ontario getting their support for redress and selling Watari Dori prints. He was a tireless advocate and inspiration to me because of his compassion and belief in democracy. If the meeting was in Ottawa, we could count on Amy Yamazaki or Harry and Yoshi Ashimoto to be there as living victims who could eloquently share the feelings of hardships and frustrations they had experienced.

In Winnipeg, I always called upon Harold Hirose, a World War II vet, a founding member of our national organization, and an early leader in Winnipeg. During the redress campaign, I looked to Harold as part of the President's Committee for advice and support because of his wealth of experience in the Japanese Canadian community and his strong propensity for human rights. Harold was a close friend of my parents and so whenever I was able, I would listen to stories of his exploits. He was born in Cumberland on Vancouver Island. After high school, he had gone alone to Vancouver to attend business school despite opposition from his parents. In 1934, his parents moved to Surrey, BC, and purchased a fifteen-acre place. He worked for the Surrey Berry Grower's Cooperative Association until war broke out. He married Florence Omoto just before being moved from the West Coast and jokingly tells people that the government paid for his honeymoon. Although many of the farmers from Surrey went to sugar-beet farms in Alberta, Harold, his family, and new bride decided to go to Manitoba to a farm at St. Jean Baptiste. After a few months there, in July 1942, Harold and his family were the first Japanese Canadians to receive special permission from the BC Security Commission to live in Winnipeg.

Finding a place to live in Winnipeg was a challenge for Harold. Hearing "Sorry, we've rented the room" so often was frustrating, knowing as he did that the denial was due to racism and his being Japanese. He decided to use a different tactic and called the prospective landlord, saying, "I am a Japanese Canadian. I am married; I have no children. I have no dog or any pets. I am seeking accommodations." Finally, a woman on Dominion Street, after a moment's hesitation, said, "That's okay." Excited and relieved, Harold broke the good news to Florence, stuffed their measly belongings into bags, and took a taxi to Dominion Street. When the woman answered the door, she said, "I'm sorry, I've talked to the other roomers, and they have threatened to leave if I take you." Finally, he found a guardian angel in Mrs. McCracken. When he called her and said, "I'm a Japanese Canadian," she replied abruptly, "Why would you say that?" Harold, surprised by her response, then heard her say, "It's not much of a place. If it's okay with you, I would be glad to rent it to you." The house, located near Winnipeg's Knox United Church, became their first home. It was from there that Harold was later able to assist other Japanese Canadians to find accommodations and jobs and even put them up if they needed a temporary place to stay. Harold also established the first organization that assisted Japanese Canadian with their relocation to Manitoba or dealing with unfair treatment on the sugar-beet farms.

To support his family, Harold wanted to enlist in the Canadian army but was rejected on several occasions. However, when he heard that a special battalion of Japanese Canadians was being established, he volunteered without hesitation and in April 1945 was sworn in along with eight other nisei in Winnipeg as a Japanese-language interpreter. After joining other nisei training with the invasion force in Mumbai (Bombay at the time), Harold was attached to the 34th Indian Infantry Division to translate Japanese documents. Harold felt that if you wanted to live as a full-fledged citizen, you were obligated

Harold Hirose at the 1988 Ottawa rally
PHOTO: Gordon King

to do everything in your power to demonstrate your loyalty to Canada, such as volunteering for wartime service.

After his return from the war, Harold applied to purchase property through the Veterans' Land Act, which the government had established for returning veterans. He was rejected because government officials claimed that he was Japanese and not eligible. His status as a veteran was nullified because of his ancestry. He told me about receiving a letter from the government with a payment of a mere $36 for his confiscated five-acre property in Surrey, BC. What irked Harold most was that the government deducted a fee for looking after their property, a fee for the sale of the property, and then a charge for internment travel and food costs. With such stories of inequality, his presence at meetings had a profound impact on politicians and bureaucrats, reminding them of the atrocity of the government's actions.

As the year 1985 progressed, Opposition critics Sergio Marchi of the Liberals and Ernie Epp of the NDP urged the minister to be more flexible in his talks with the Japanese Canadians. Marchi remarked that the imposition of a settlement was akin to the imposition of the policies of dispossession, dispersal, and incarceration on Japanese Canadians during the war, and my brother Roy reminded me that it was history repeating itself. Ernie Epp said that two meetings were simply not enough to negotiate a settlement, and that it seemed "unjust not to consider whether some persons don't deserve individual compensation – people whose lives were really ruined."[9] Epp's observations summed up the crux of the impasse, because the government, in their proposal, had refused even to look at the possibility of individual compensation – exactly what the NAJC believed to be what most internees wanted.

To fulfill the commitment the prime minister made while in Opposition, Murta looked for an expeditious solution with strict deadlines – a solution that would be of political benefit to the government. However, this was not to be.

Doug Bowie was instrumental in orchestrating the agreement to negotiate and received the endorsement of the minister. In my discussions with Bowie after he left government, he indicated that he

9   Dan Turner, "Turner Opposes Government's Offer of Redress to Japanese Canadians," *Ottawa Citizen*, January 29, 1985, A3, www.newspapers.com/article/the-ottawa-citizen /133499010/.

was blamed for placing the government in an untenable position by using the term "negotiations" when the government's intent was not to negotiate. I believe that Bowie was forced to leave the government because of what they considered to be bad advice.

The agreement of December 15, 1984, became a powerful tool for the NAJC in their discussions with Opposition politicians and the media, especially when the government attempted to renege on their promise. A *Globe and Mail* editorial dated February 2, 1985, stated, "The Government should accept the principle of individual compensation now and undertake an economic losses study to assess the dollar value as did the US Commission on Wartime Relocation and Internment of Civilians, established in 1980. The study's findings could then serve as the basis for negotiations between Ottawa and the NAJC."[10] We welcomed the mention of individual compensation in the press, as the government had steadfastly refused to consider it. Now individual compensation became a consideration for the general public.

Some of the stories that individuals shared at the National Council meetings had a powerful impact on us all. I was moved by the intensity of internees' words and their feelings of sorrow, which convinced council members of the necessity of including individual recognition if a redress outcome was to be meaningful for the victims.

At the NAJC Council meeting in Calgary in February 1985, I recall that a Japanese Canadian gentleman drove in from Taber, Alberta, specifically to meet me, bringing with him a scrapbook containing photographs of the homestead he owned prior to internment. He tearfully told me that he had once owned five hundred acres in the Fraser Valley, which had been confiscated by the government in 1942. He showed me the letter from the government that indicated he would receive $4,500 for his property. The sad part of his story was that five years prior, he had been driving through the Fraser Valley when he approached the property that once belonged to him and noticed a sign that read, "One-Acre Lots for Sale." Curiously thinking that it might be memorable to purchase part of his original homestead, he stopped and inquired about the price. The owner wanted $23,000 an acre. Shocked, he thought to himself, "I used to own five hundred acres. What would it be worth today?" Weighing what he

---

10   "Versions of Redress," *Globe and Mail*, February 2, 1985, 6, www.proquest.com/historical
      -newspapers/versions-redress/docview/1151624011/se-2.

had lost, the gentleman from Taber said, "You know, I still feel bitter. Had the government not taken the land and sold it, maybe life would have been different. But they told us that they would not sell it. They told us they would keep it in trust for us. Then I found out that the government sold it. If they had kept it, I would not feel so bitter." It doesn't take a mathematician to figure out the tremendous financial loss he suffered as a result of the government expropriation of his property. For this reason, he attended the subsequent meetings of the NAJC Council, expressing his unconditional support for the NAJC in demanding redress from the Canadian government.

After returning home to Winnipeg from the Calgary meeting, I received a long-distance call early one Sunday morning from a woman in Calgary. She had heard on television that the NAJC was seeking redress on behalf of Japanese Canadians who were interned and deprived of their rights. She said to me, "You don't know me, but I am a Japanese Canadian and have wanted to talk to you. I want to share this experience with you. When my family was moved to an internment camp, my mother took it so hard, because my father was taken away to a road camp. This was the first time my family was separated. I guess my mother was not the type of person who was able to cope with it and she became mentally ill. She died before we left the camp." The woman who called me was about fourteen years old at that time and the burden of looking after her sisters fell to her, because her father was not there. She was wholly supportive of redress because of the unforgettable and devastating effect relocation had for her mother, how it destroyed the family and altered her life forever. There must have been many untold tragic events that affected Japanese Canadians because of the government's insensitive punitive policies.

At one of the NAJC Council meetings, Jerry Hisaoka, a representative from Lethbridge, related a story from his teenage years to me. Jerry was a member of the army cadet corps in Vancouver before the war. When he attended the cadet gathering shortly after the bombing of Pearl Harbor, he was told by the commanding officer that he could no longer be a cadet because he was Japanese. This devastated Jerry, who was fourteen years old at the time and had difficulty accepting the reason given, because he always considered himself to be a Canadian. "This was a shock to me and I couldn't believe that they thought that I was now the enemy," recalled Jerry.

Hearing these stories made it more essential that the NAJC persevere in the fight for justice.

Having reached a critical stage in the redress campaign, the NAJC held a National Council meeting in Calgary on February 2 and 3, 1985, to assess the government's actions. A crucial decision was made "to continue to pursue acknowledgment, non-monetary and monetary compensation as one package." We considered this bargaining position to be a stronger and more secure approach in the long run. The NAJC negotiation team would no longer be able to accept acknowledgment first and then negotiate compensation later. The council adopted other proposals for redress, such as citizenship for exiled or deported Japanese Canadians and pardons for people convicted under the War Measures Act.

I was asked to send a letter to the prime minister requesting a meeting with him and appealing for his intervention. We also expressed our willingness to carry on the bilateral talks with the government as long as they agreed that any proposed settlement required the approval of the NAJC and that discussions on compensation be deferred until the economic losses study had been completed.

Even though Jack Murta indicated that talks were suspended, his comments in the media suggested that he would continue discussions if we requested a meeting. We met in Winnipeg on March 30. During the meeting, Murta explained that the proposed $6–$10 million educational trust fund should be understood not as a form of compensation, but as a "memorialization" of the wartime treatment of Canadians of Japanese ancestry. I reported to Murta that in community meetings across Canada, the government's redress package was considered unacceptable as a meaningful settlement. Instead, I reported, there was strong interest in compensation based on a socio-economic study that set out, in an objective and professional manner, a record of losses.

Although there continued to be other meetings with Jack Murta, nothing substantive was gained in our encounters. After meeting on June 4 with the Japanese Canadian National Redress Association of Survivors led by George Imai and Jack Oki, Murta asked our opinion on inviting representatives of the newly formed group to participate in future discussions. He implied in his letter to me that perhaps the NAJC did not represent the interests of the survivors.

On July 27, 1985, I responded in writing, indicating that the NAJC objected to his suggestion to include representatives from the

Survivors group in future redress discussions and that the NAJC "has always placed the survivors' concerns foremost" in our negotiations. We felt that the inclusion of other groups in redress discussions would legitimize those individuals as representatives of our community. Both opposition critics, Sergio Marchi and Ernie Epp, met with the same group and refused to give them recognition as a rightful representative of our community. Furthermore, the NDP issued a press release reaffirming their support for the process of negotiations pursued by the NAJC. The media recognized that the government was using devious methods to "railroad" the NAJC into accepting their offer and wrote favourable articles and editorials supporting the NAJC's affirmation that compensation should be based on the results of a socio-economic study.

Lacking ministerial experience, Jack Murta relied heavily on his staff for direction and advice. The negotiation meetings were conducted by his department's bureaucrats, who kept him apprised of the progress of our deliberations. Having heeded the advice of his staff, the minister was placed in a vulnerable position when exposed nationally to media, especially on one edition of the CBC News program *The National*. Shortly after meetings in Ottawa with the Opposition parties in February 1985, I was asked to appear on the program with Murta. Host Barbara Frum first asked about my understanding of the negotiation's agreement and then questioned Murta's integrity when he admitted that he had endorsed the negotiation process in the joint press release. Mr. Murta's admission that the government "really didn't intend to negotiate" but rather intended "to consult" raised a credibility issue. Using the term "negotiate" in the press release with a deliberate intention to ignore the process agreed upon placed the government's motives in doubt. Because of his questionable actions and his inability to reach closure, it appeared that Jack Murta's days as minister of multiculturalism were numbered. In August 1985, the Honourable Jack Murta was indeed replaced as minister of multiculturalism by the Honourable Otto Jelinek.

In retrospect, it appears that Mr. Murta was placed in an untenable position by the prime minister, who expected that the Japanese Canadian redress issue would be resolved quickly. Jack Murta was a junior minister who lacked the power at the cabinet table to influence other ministers to support a more exorbitant redress package than the one he offered to the NAJC.

I met Jack Murta on several occasions after he moved from multiculturalism to other areas. In my discussions with him, I found that he sincerely believed he might have been able to reach a settlement if given more time and more latitude. He shared with me that he had gained an appreciation and a much deeper understanding of the hardships endured by Japanese Canadians. He harboured no hard feelings towards the NAJC or me, but he was disappointed that he had not delivered the Japanese Canadian redress settlement during his time as minister.

CHAPTER 6

Stalemate

The replacement of Jack Murta with Otto Jelinek was the first of many changes that the NAJC faced during the four years of redress negotiations with Mulroney's Conservative government. It became a revolving-door syndrome: each time a minister reached an impasse with the NAJC, a new minister appeared on the scene who required an orientation period on the Japanese Canadian experience and redress, and so the entire process had to be restarted, again.

When Jelinek was appointed minister of multiculturalism, he kept his post as minister of sports and fitness. He was far more knowledge-able in the latter area and was assigned to our issue in the midst of planning for the Winter Olympics in Calgary. Thus, our relationship with Jelinek started on the wrong foot. The first meeting was hastily held at Winnipeg International Airport on September 15, 1985, between connecting flights from Calgary to Ottawa. I arrived at the airport and was to look for Kim Tam from Jelinek's staff. When Mr. Tam recognized me, he came over to me and said, "Hi, Mr. Oki." I looked at him, somewhat stunned, and then said, "I'm Art Miki, president of the NAJC." I could see that Tam was extremely embar-rassed; he apologized to me profusely. Clearly, George Imai and Jack Oki had made contact with the minister and his staff even before the minister met with the NAJC. At this point, I became quite skep-tical as to the progress we would make with Mr. Jelinek, but I still wanted to try.

We were rushed off to a quiet, sterile meeting room at the airport where the NAJC delegation, consisting of Harold Hirose, Henry Kojima, Lucy Yamashita, and myself, met with Otto Jelinek, Doug Bowie, and Kim Tam. After all the niceties, Mr. Jelinek opened the meeting by saying to us, "I really understand your situation. You see, I'm an immigrant." Harold Hirose, a nisei, quickly retorted in disgust, "You don't understand our situation: you see, we aren't immigrants. Most of us were born in Canada." Judging by his initial comment, Jelinek must have assumed that because we were not white, we were immigrants from Japan. Faced with this uninformed stereotype, we deliberately stressed that the NAJC was fighting for Canadians who had been mistreated by their own government. Dismayed by Jelinek's lack of sensitivity and understanding of the redress issue, I told the former Olympic figure skater that he was skating on thin ice.

Jelinek informed us that he wanted to know more about the national organization, its community components, progress to date with the government, and the socio-economic losses study. We talked about the dissenters in Toronto, as he hinted several times about community differences on redress. He assured us that he would continue to discuss redress with the NAJC, especially the non-monetary components, until the Price Waterhouse study was released. Then, immediately going back on his word, he demanded a compensation figure from the NAJC before the Price Waterhouse study was completed.

Jelinek then made the rather unusual request that we not involve the media while discussions were underway unless there was a breakdown in communications. It would have seemed that he wanted to keep the issue low profile, except for the fact that Jelinek himself used the media a number of times to discredit the NAJC's efforts and the organization while refusing to communicate with us.

As a follow-up to the initial meeting, the NAJC negotiation team, composed of Roy Miki, Maryka Omatsu, Harold Hirose, Roger Obata, Kay Shimizu, and myself, met with Jelinek, Doug Bowie, and Kim Tam on October 21, 1985, in Ottawa. Jelinek emphasized that "input must come from a broad spectrum," a statement he repeated throughout the meeting. When we asked Jelinek whether he considered the NAJC as the official representative organization for the Japanese Canadian community, he said that he was demonstrating his trust and respect by meeting us first. "What numbers of Japanese Canadians are associated with the NAJC?" he asked, implying, "Who do you represent?" Obviously, Jelinek didn't consider the NAJC as the official community organization. He was insistent that he would be consulting groups outside the Japanese Canadian community.

When questioned about his role, Jelinek said that he had been asked "to bring recommendations to Cabinet and it would be Cabinet's ultimate responsibility to make a decision." He also explained that his current "position was one of flexibility," contradicting his initial position, in which he refused to consider any alternatives. On the question of individual compensation, he said, "Individual compensation should be set aside as an option," and used the term "symbolic redress." He said, "There was not enough money in the world to compensate." He wouldn't accept "compensation" to Japanese Canadians as a form of redress. When I asked whether the Japanese Canadian community would have "control" over any compensation, Mr. Jelinek said Japanese Canadians "would play a leading role," but "there would be representatives from other communities involved in the decision-making process." Jelinek's response was similar to Murta's, but now he added that he would be seeking input from outside the Japanese Canadian community. I wonder whether he had the Canadian Multicultural Council, his appointed advisory body, in mind.

We then discussed some of the non-monetary aspects of the redress package. The minister assured us that the changing of the War Measures Act was now under review, and funds had already been allocated to permit minority groups to challenge the Canadian Charter of Rights and Freedoms. He pointed out that these actions were the direct result of redress efforts by the NAJC. After looking at the merged drafts of the acknowledgment from the NAJC and government officials, he agreed that it was acceptable, and he would wait for comments from the Justice Department.

Jelinek's approach to the redress issue was narrow and predetermined. He didn't appear to have the mandate to act on his own, and he seemed quite insensitive to minority rights, let alone redress. All his talk about what the "majority of Canadians" wanted out of redress and the "burden on the taxpayer" was disheartening to us.

In looking for Canadian precedents that would support individual claims for redress based on the violation of rights by the government, the NAJC came across this interesting story. I received an intriguing letter from Penny Simpson of Tatla Lake, BC, who was one of 497 people who had been detained by the police during the 1970 October Crisis in Québec. The October Crisis was sparked by the actions of Front de libération du Québec (FLQ), the most radical among Québécois separatist groups of the time, and their kidnapping of James Cross, a British trade commissioner. The FLQ's actions were (and are still) highly controversial in Québec, including in sovereigntist ranks. The threat of violence and panic in the streets resulted in Primer Minister Pierre Trudeau invoking the War Measures Act, the same act that was used against Japanese Canadians. At the time, Penny Simpson was an activist and a leading voice for the League for Socialist Action / Ligue socialiste ouvrière, a Trotskyist organization. They organized public protests and distributed information in resistance to the use of War Measures Act and called for the end of attacks on civil liberties and freedom for political prisoners. Cassandra Kobayashi, a member of the NAJC's legal team, had told us that some FLQ members received compensation for being detained under the War Measures Act. Cassandra had contacted Penny Simpson and asked her to provide us with further details. Penny explained that she "was detained under the War Measures Act on October 16, 1970, fifteen minutes before its imposition at 5 a.m. that day." She and her friend were taken into custody, and the police came to remove several boxes of documents but found nothing incriminating. Penny was released from the Tanguay prison for women one week later. She was interrogated once but was not charged with any offence under the War Measures Act or otherwise.

After her release from prison, Penny flew to Toronto, where she gave a speech and was interviewed on national television. She was one of the very first people to speak in English Canada about the FLQ crisis and her incarceration. Because of her newly acquired notoriety, she was forced to leave her job at Q.E. McIntyre in Montréal. The president of the firm wanted a letter of resignation but Penny refused to comply. The president threatened to withhold her separation pay. Penny's story was published in the Montréal sovereigntist newspaper *Le Devoir*, causing a scandal which resulted in Penny receiving her separation pay. As a penalty, she was docked six weeks of Employment Insurance Commission (EIC) benefits for quitting the job. In trying to find a new job, she found that employers would check her criminal background. Unable to find employment in Montréal, she moved to Toronto. Meanwhile, *Le Devoir* assembled a large file on the victims of the War Measures Act and published their stories regularly.

These articles were the main source of information when the campaign for compensation began, about six months after the imposition of the War Measures Act in October 1970. Penny was convinced that the Québec government was held up as the main force behind the imposition of the War Measures. It was they who supposedly "apprehended" an "insurrection" and requested the imposition. The police involved were provincial and municipal. The RCMP appeared at interrogations only. When we began to assemble our demands for compensation, we were obliged to direct our demands to the provincial government. In the end, Penny was offered $600, which she accepted. She had to sign a disclaimer stating that she would not sue the Québec government for further damages in the future and that the government was not responsible for any injuries that she may have suffered. The $600 was the exact dollar equivalent for the six weeks of lost EIC payments. She was refused compensation for the loss of her job or for having to move to Toronto on the grounds that she "was English Canadian, so that was no hardship." The financial responsibility was borne by the Québec government, because the federal government insisted that the Québec government had wanted the War Measures Act implemented.

Penny was willing to assist us not because of her personal experience or because her sister-in-law is sansei, but because of her mother's memories of 1939. During a telephone conversation, Penny indicated that "her mother worked at Union College, UBC, and watched in horror as Japanese Canadian theology students were seized and taken away, never to be seen again. The shame chokes us all. We are all determined to raise the only grandchildren of the family to be proud of their Japanese heritage."

Although the compensation to the FLQ victims was not precedent-setting for Japanese Canadians, Penny's experiences reinforced the necessity of repealing the War Measures Act, which the government had used, without evidence, to detain twenty-two thousand Japanese Canadians on suspicion of being a threat to national security.

In November 1985, a newspaper reporter followed up on our allegation that compensation had been paid to FLQ members who had been jailed. There had never been any reports of federal compensation to FLQ members. The Québec Justice Department, however, did pay undisclosed amounts to people whose homes had been damaged in the police raids and to non-FLQ members who had been held but not charged with any offences.

The scenario that Jelinek projected at the Standing Committee on Multiculturalism meeting in November 1985 was that Japanese Canadians would have to wait until the government had consulted "all Canadians before deciding compensation." He said he had made it clear to the NAJC "that they shall not be the only ones that I will be looking for input from." It made sense, he said, that advice should be sought from related organizations such as the Japanese Canadian National Redress Association of Survivors.

I accused Ottawa of "working around us" by consulting organizations with no direct connection to the internment and property losses suffered by Japanese Canadians. "Other Canadians do not understand the issue. We understand the issue. We were directly affected and we should be the only ones the government is dealing with on this issue. Mr. Jelinek's action goes directly against the concept of negotiations and makes a sham out of the agreement that was forged on December 15, 1984, with Mr. Murta."[1] Although Jelinek refused to meet with the NAJC after two meetings, he continued to use the press to attack our efforts and criticize the organization. In one article, he said that the federal government would not insult Japanese Canadians by offering money, when he knew very well that financial compensation was one of the key areas of disagreement. Instead, he indicated, he would present a redress package in January or February 1986 that would cover a "much broader range" than the $6 million offer made earlier.

In Victoria, Jelinek made a statement to the press that the NAJC was not truly representative of all Japanese Canadians, that he was not negotiating, and that there had never been any intention to provide individual reparations. Jelinek's "tough stance" approach may have appealed to right-wingers. His insensitivity and lack of compassion for one of Canada's ethnic minorities were ironic when, as a minister of multiculturalism, he should have been an advocate for all ethnic minorities; he appeared to us as the enemy.

Jelinek regularly uttered inane comments such as "there isn't enough money in Canada to compensate Japanese Canadians" in

---

1   "Compensation on Hold for Japanese Canadians," *Toronto Star*, November 27, 1985, A1, www.proquest.com/newspapers/compensation-on-hold-japanese-canadians/docview /435371401/se-2.

an effort to generate negative reactions to any negotiations and to portray his position as conciliatory. He used the divisions within the Japanese Canadian community, in particular the differing positions of the NAJC and the Japanese Canadian National Redress Association of Survivors, to justify the "need" for wider consultation and to avoid the negotiation process altogether.

Jelinek was adept at using groups to defend his position and actions. In November 1985, his own advisory council, the Canadian Multicultural Council (CMC), publicly backed the government's position and recommended a similar redress package, without conferring with the NAJC. Since the CMC was composed of individuals from various ethnic backgrounds, their proposal left the impression that many ethnic groups sided with the government against the NAJC.

When the minister appeared before the Standing Committee on Multiculturalism on November 26, 1985, Gus Mitges, chairperson and a member of the Conservative caucus, stated, "I have some serious reservations, while the government is discussing the issue and hopefully negotiating with the Japanese community, about his advisory council going public and saying the compensation is incorrect in terms of a solution to this problem. Obviously, that has set off a series of discussions in the Japanese community, and also obviously they are upset that before they can get to the table, the major advisory council is already putting out a position."[2]

The minister's response, in his disregard for the negotiation process, was that he was looking for input from other groups, including the Survivors group led by George Imai, and the provincial governments: "It only makes sense that the Canadian Multicultural Council has input into these discussions; and I see nothing wrong with them going public."[3] From my previous dialogues with the minister, I think that he was capable of encouraging the CMC to take the position it did.

On December 5, 1985, Otto Jelinek was the guest on a CBC Toronto *Radio Noon* hosted by David Schatzky, who invited callers to give their opinion on these questions: "Is it an insult to pay Japanese Canadians for what they suffered during World War II? Is it, as Mr.

---

2   House of Commons (Hansard), *Minutes of the Proceedings and Evidence of the Standing Committee on Multiculturalism*, issue 2, November 26, 1985, 15.

3   Ibid.

Jelinek says, too expensive? Do they deserve more than an apology?" David Suzuki was the first to make an introductory comment: "In terms of an insult, I hope that he [Jelinek] has consulted a lot of Japanese Canadians so that he understands what would and what would not insult Japanese Canadians. My own feeling is, that's for us to decide, not for him; and the fact that a large part of the Japanese Canadian community has in fact been seeking compensation would suggest to me that they wouldn't feel insulted at all were the government to decide to give financial compensation."[4]

The callers to the program favoured compensation by two to one. Japanese Canadians had the opportunity to air their feelings. A nisei from Oakville related a sad tale of his family's destruction as a result of her father's incarceration and the loss of a business. "The suffering still goes on," she said. Another caller was George Imai, former chairperson of the National Redress Committee that opposed the NAJC and who endorsed Mr. Jelinek's offer of a $10 million foundation and rejected the negotiation process. The minister's response to Imai was, "I'm certainly delighted to hear that gentleman is supportive of what we are trying to do."

In February 1986, a letter in the *Globe and Mail* with the headline "Ottawa Plan for Redress for War Victims Praised" from the leadership of the Canadian Multicultural Council (CMC) further escalated attacks on the NAJC by alleging that the NAJC did not represent the victims of the injustices, and argued against individual compensation.[5] The CMC is a federally appointed advisory body reporting to the minister for multiculturalism. Later, CMC President Louis Melosky, a prominent Winnipeg Conservative Party supporter, endorsed Jelinek's view that any apology to Japanese Canadians should be part of an apology to other ethnic groups. The Council's timely intervention in the negotiation process between the government and the NAJC was blatant partisanship, giving endorsement to the minister's stance. Their statements received quick condemnation from the NAJC and the Canadian Ethnocultural Council (CEC), a coalition of national ethnocultural organizations based in Ottawa. In a March 20, 1986, letter to the editor of the *Globe and Mail* titled

4   CBC *Radio Noon*, hosted by David Schatzky, December 5, 1985.

5   Louis C. Melosky, Orest Rudzik, and Peter McCreath, "Ottawa Plan for Redress for War Victims Praised," *Globe and Mail*, February 19, 1986, A7, www.proquest.com/historical -newspapers/ottawa-plan-redress-war-victims-praised/docview/1143806426/se-2.

"Compensating Victims," Roy Miki and Cassandra Kobayashi, members of the Vancouver Redress Committee, responded to the CEC's statement: "It is appalling that they should attack the National Association of Japanese Canadians, which is attempting to encourage dialogue within the Japanese Canadian community. At the very least, they could have the courtesy to first ask the NAJC for answers to their rhetorical questions."[6] In another letter to the *Globe and Mail* editor published in the same issue, Navin M. Parekh, president of the CEC, expressed his concern: "It is unfortunate that prominent members of the CMC – which is appointed by the minister of state for multiculturalism to act as an advisory body for Canada's ethnic communities – should publicly take sides in an already painful debate within the Japanese Canadian community over the issue of redress ... It undermines the council's credibility and damages the ethnic community as a whole for an organization such as [the] NAJC to be subjected to public attack."[7]

We requested a meeting with the leaders of the Canadian Multicultural Council. This council, which should have been employing democratic processes, had not consulted with the NAJC when deciding what constituted appropriate redress for the Japanese Canadian community. Several Japanese Canadian seniors from Winnipeg who had been directly affected by the government's wartime actions attended the CMC meeting with me to personally explain the impact of the internment and forced relocation on their disrupted lives.

From the beginning of 1986, the threat of unilateral action by Otto Jelinek became more evident in his comments to the press. The NAJC negotiation team again travelled to Ottawa on January 27 to protest. Prior to the meeting with the minister, a small NAJC strategy team met with Keith Spicer, who was now the editor of the *Ottawa Citizen*, to discuss the NAJC's response to Jelinek's proposal of a $10 million fund. Although Spicer supported the principle of redress, he believed that the government's offer was generous and that we should accept it gracefully. He praised the efforts of the Mulroney government to resolve the issue. We agreed on that score; but we

---

6   Roy Miki and Cassandra Kobayashi, "Compensating Victims," *Globe and Mail*, March 20, 1986, A6, www.proquest.com/historical-newspapers/compensating-victims/docview/1151441839/se-2.

7   Navin M. Parekh, letter to the editor, *Globe and Mail*, March 20, 1986, A6, www.proquest.com/historical-newspapers/letter-editor-1-no-title/docview/1151430178/se-2.

underlined the importance of the NAJC having direct involvement in the process and stressed that a meaningful settlement was one that must be acceptable to the NAJC. When we talked about individual compensation, we could tell by Spicer's reaction that he was not supportive. An unsigned *Ottawa Citizen* editorial published in January 21, 1985, realistically written by Spicer, clearly accentuated the writer's personal support for the government's position when it stated that "This [offer] represents a worthy and intelligent start for settling a dishonourable episode in Canada's history. Mulroney and Multiculturalism Minister Jack Murta deserve credit for devising a package which tries to be both imaginative and realistic."[8]

Later in the day, after driving in a terrible snowstorm from the *Ottawa Citizen* office to the Multiculturalism office in Hull, we met with Jelinek in an effort to open meaningful dialogue. Before the meeting began, the minister asked whether the press could sit in on our discussions. We refused. He then asked if I would join him for the press conference that was to follow our meeting. Being suspicious of his intentions, we declined to participate in his press conference. We had already planned to hold our own press conference the following day. The meeting did not have positive results. Jelinek refused to recognize the NAJC as the representative organization, saying that other groups such as the Survivors groups would be approached.

As reported in Richard Cleroux's article in the *Globe and Mail* on January 28, 1986, titled "Japanese Canadians Get Deadline," Jelinek told reporters at the press conference on January 27 that he was growing impatient with lagging discussions on the financial figure and used strong language in threatening to bypass the NAJC if we did not come up with a dollar figure "within one month." He said that if the NAJC was going to "drag their feet" for much longer, "I think the government will have to listen to other groups, legitimate Japanese Canadian organizations which are concerned that this is dragging on too long." Furthermore, he said, "Real survivors will tell you, 'Give us an apology, an acknowledgment, something to hang our honour and dignity on. We're not looking for individual compensation.'"[9]

---

8   "Justice Delayed, but No Longer Denied," *Ottawa Citizen*, January 21, 1985, 8, www .newspapers.com/article/the-ottawa-citizen/133573456/.

9   Richard Cleroux, "Japanese Canadians Get Deadline," *Globe and Mail*, January 28, 1986, A4, www.proquest.com/historical-newspapers/japanese-canadians-get-deadline/docview /1151419670/se-2.

The minister gave the names of several groups within the Japanese Canadian community, including the Japanese Canadian Redress Association of Survivors, which he said supported the government's position. He had invited me to join in his press conference so that he could expose the names of the groups he said opposed the NAJC position and place us in a defensive mode in front of the media. His manipulative attempt to embarrass and discredit the NAJC was brutal and without conscience.

Jelinek indicated that the Price Waterhouse report would not be a basis for a monetary settlement, stating that the NAJC wanted "full and individual compensation" in "billions of dollars." I can't imagine how he arrived at this figure. By continually talking about billions of dollars, Jelinek actually helped our claim by setting a higher standard in the public's mind. Certainly, the final compensation was nowhere near billions of dollars.

With the Price Waterhouse report completed, the NAJC was better positioned to make a firm proposal. A *Vancouver Sun* editorial of January 30, 1986, commented critically on Jelinek's handling of the redress issue: "Jelinek has been quoted as saying he has been 'trying to figure out what use the Price Waterhouse report would be at all.' If he can't figure that out himself, he is in the wrong job."[10] Editorials across the country urged Jelinek to wait until the Price Waterhouse report was completed to determine what would be appropriate redress.

We responded to Jelinek's comments at our own press conference the next day. Reporters wanted to know how we felt about the minister's statement that a number of organizations opposed the NAJC. It was unfortunate for Jelinek that he wasn't paying closer attention to what was going on in the redress movement. Previously, George Imai and Jack Oki had opposed a grant that the City of Toronto had given to the NAJC to help defray the cost of the Price Waterhouse study. They presented the city council with a list of organizations opposed to the NAJC. Suspicious of the names on the list, members of the Toronto chapter of the NAJC contacted the leaders of each organization to determine whether they had been contacted to have their name on the list, and whether they had endorsed a specific redress position. Of the organizations that actually still existed, none

10 "Where's the Fire?," *Vancouver Sun*, January 30, 1986, A4, www.newspapers.com/article/the-vancouver-sun/133662208/.

realized that their names were being used or had ever expressed a position on redress.

I reported to the media that Jelinek had shared the same list of organizations that Imai and Oki had presented to Toronto City Council. Jelinek, or his staff, in their haste and eagerness to criticize the NAJC, had not checked the list's accuracy. The press was not impressed. In the *Globe and Mail* article "Comments by Jelinek Are Found Baffling," I was asked for my reaction to Jelinek's claim that "real survivors don't want compensation."[11] Again, I explained that Jelinek lacked understanding of our cultural mores and the traits of the Japanese. When older Japanese Canadian issei or even nisei survivors are asked directly if they want compensation, their initial reaction would be a polite "No." They don't want to appear greedy in the public eye or even to their friends and will hesitate to show their true feelings. I have attended many social functions in the Japanese community and noticed the same pattern. If a senior is offered tea or treats, their first response is a shake of the head signifying "no," although I'm sure in their mind they would like to say "yes." If you don't ask again, they might feel offended. By the second or third time, they will accept. This reaction is their reticence to appear eager or selfish. In Japanese this is referred to as *enryo* 遠慮. In communicating with older Japanese Canadians, you need to be aware and understand certain cultural traits. It was obvious to us that Jelinek misread the reactions of seniors.

I simply told the media that an apology would not be enough. What we wanted was symbolic compensation – the same fixed-amount payment to all Japanese Canadians who had been mistreated. The payment should adequately reflect the loss of basic rights that Japanese Canadians endured.

The press recognized that Jelinek was using high-handed, aggressive, threatening tactics with the NAJC. His attitude and schemes made us more determined to fight. The more Jelinek personally attacked the NAJC and employed intimidation tactics, the stronger our support base became in the media and with the general public. Roy MacGregor's January 30, 1986, article in the *Ottawa Citizen* aptly characterized Mr. Jelinek as playing Rambo in this affair. MacGregor

---

11   Richard Cleroux, "Comments by Jelinek Are Found Baffling," *Globe and Mail*, January 29, 1986, A5, www.proquest.com/historical-newspapers/comments-jelinek-are-found-baffling/docview/1143871914/se-2.

wrote, "[Jelinek] used more words than Rambo would, but essentially the same message."[12] The *Globe and Mail* editorial of January 29, titled "Mr. Jelinek's Haste," commented on Jelinek's dealings with the NAJC: "This is the man Prime Minister Mulroney entrusted with redressing what Mulroney has rightly called 'an historic injustice.' Can he not find someone with sympathy for the job?"[13] The *Toronto Star* editorial of January 30 was very blunt, suggesting: "It's time the Prime Minister, a man with proven skills as a negotiator, put an end to Jelinek's bullying tactics. Mulroney should take over the issue himself, and deliver an honourable settlement. That would be an act of leadership."[14]

Jelinek's statement in the March 7, 1986, *Globe and Mail* article "No Money, Just Apology, Jelinek Says"[15] showed that he had backtracked from his initial position. Japanese Canadians would get an apology from the government, he said, though it might be part of an overall apology to Jewish Canadians, Ukrainian Canadians, and Chinese Canadians who had also suffered at the hands of the government in the past. "If you do something strictly for the Japanese Canadian community, it could set a precedent," Jelinek was quoted as saying. This comment echoed those of Prime Minister Trudeau during the last days of the Liberal reign. Jelinek added: "I think it would be irresponsible for Canadian taxpayers to consider compensation forty-three years later to the tune of billions of dollars. We can't afford it ... [Compensation] is not the issue. [The Price Waterhouse study] will have no bearing on what the monetary figure is going to be."[16]

On the same day, March 7, that these remarks appeared in print, I was attending the National Conference for Mathematics Teachers

12 Roy MacGregor, "Jelinek Acting like Rambo in Compensation Wrangle," *Ottawa Citizen*, January 30, 1986, A3, www.proquest.com/newspapers/jelinek-acting-like-rambo-compensation-wrangle/docview/238906939/se-2.

13 "Mr. Jelinek's Haste," *Globe and Mail*, January 29, 1986, A6, www.proquest.com/newspapers/mr-jelineks-haste/docview/386213914/se-2.

14 "Time for PM to Intervene," *Toronto Star*, January 30, 1986, A14, www.proquest.com/newspapers/time-pm-intervene/docview/435372440/se-2.

15 Richard Cleroux, "No Money, Just Apology, Jelinek Says," *Globe and Mail*, March 7, 1986, A1, www.proquest.com/historical-newspapers/no-money-just-apology-jelinek-says/docview/1151428817/se-2.

16 Ibid.

at the Sheraton Hotel in Winnipeg. In the early afternoon, just as I had finished introducing the speaker in the session I was attending, two men came into the session, interrupting the speaker, and asked if Art Miki was in the audience. I introduced myself and asked what they wanted. One of the men said they had to talk to me right away because it was urgent. I didn't know who they were, but I went out into the hall, where one of them said that Mr. Jelinek needed to meet with me immediately. I replied I could not leave right away because I had a CBC radio interview scheduled at 4 p.m., right after the conference. They more or less demanded that I meet with the minister and told me that they would have a cab ready at CBC after the interview to take me to the Fort Garry Hotel. I called Harold Hirose, a member of the National Executive, and asked him to meet me at the Fort Garry Hotel for an urgent meeting with Jelinek. He assured me he would be there.

After the CBC interview, I went directly to the hotel where Jelinek and Harold Hirose were waiting for me. At the meeting, Jelinek reaffirmed his intention of taking all the proposals he had received to Cabinet but would not disclose to us who the proposals were from, or what they suggested. He did not say anything new that would warrant this emergency meeting. Six weeks earlier, Jelinek had promised to show the NAJC all recommendations before submitting them to Cabinet. Jelinek said that I still had time to submit a proposal for Cabinet as well. But why would we send a proposal to Cabinet when it was the minister's responsibility to negotiate the terms for redress? We refused to partake in this unusual suggestion. Jelinek was attempting to intimidate us into putting forward a proposal before the Price Waterhouse report was completed. Shortly after we sat down to meet, Jelinek excused himself and returned ten minutes later to continue our dialogue. It was a strange meeting! After Harold and I left, perplexed, we were baffled as to what the urgency was. I had a nagging feeling that something was happening behind the scenes and that maybe we were being manipulated by Jelinek.

When I talked to my brother Roy on the phone that evening, Jelinek's actions all became clear. I called Roy in Vancouver to tell him about the hastily arranged meetings with Jelinek. Roy had attended a press conference with the prime minister on the Friday afternoon, March 7, 2016, where the question about the government's intentions on redress was raised. The prime minister had responded by saying that the NAJC and Minister Jelinek were continuing to meet to resolve the issue. In fact, he said: "At this very moment, Mr. Jelinek is discussing a redress proposal with Mr. Miki in Winnipeg." When I told Roy what happened on Friday afternoon, it began to make sense. In preparation for the prime minister's press conference in Vancouver, expecting that the issue of redress for Japanese Canadians would surely be raised, Jelinek and his staff had orchestrated the meeting. When Jelinek stepped out of our meeting for a few minutes, he must have called Vancouver to inform the prime minister's staff that I was there. Having the prime minister indicate that a meeting was taking place at that very moment would help defuse any criticism.

During Jelinek's term as multiculturalism minister, the Japanese Canadian grassroots community became more involved in the redress process. The NAJC needed funds to pay for the Price Waterhouse study, and the generosity of the Japanese Canadian community came to its aid. Municipal governments of Toronto, Vancouver, and Lethbridge contributed as well. Multiple times, Japanese Canadians came to the defence of the NAJC against attacks from Jelinek and from within the community.

The much-anticipated release of the Price Waterhouse study on May 8, 2016, in Toronto and Vancouver is a great example of how newspaper editorials can influence the government's intentions and actions. When the NAJC announced that a study on the economic losses of Japanese Canadians during and after World War II was to be undertaken, government representatives indicated that the results would have no bearing on the government's plans. The *Globe and Mail*'s editorial of January 22, 1986, titled "Wholesome Redress" was concerned that Otto Jelinek might ignore the study and impose a settlement prior to the release of the Price Waterhouse report. "Ottawa should assess its obligation after reading the Price Waterhouse report and negotiating further with the NAJC. To deny that such obligations exist would be to say that Canada feels no moral obligation to pay back those wronged by a previous government," the editorial stated.[17] The *Montreal Gazette* editorial of January 30, "Don't Impose the Deal," supported the other editorials by stating that "[the government] should wait for the Price Waterhouse report

---

17 "Wholesome Redress," *Globe and Mail*, January 22, 1986, A6, www.proquest.com/news papers/wholesome-redress/docview/386199338/se-2.

and then negotiate an arrangement acceptable to all."[18] Although Otto Jelinek threatened several times to ignore the report and impose a settlement, it soon became apparent that this action was no longer politically feasible. Finally, he would acknowledge to the press that he would wait for the release of the Price Waterhouse study.

By the spring of 1986, the NAJC seemed to be constantly reacting to Jelinek's threat of an imposed settlement without any hope that the negotiation process would be honoured. In April, Jelinek indicated that Cabinet was considering a new option, a larger fund of up to $10 million that would be administered by the Japanese Canadian community rather than by the government. This after we had consistently reminded Jelinek and the press that the NAJC would not be satisfied with any offer made arbitrarily.

Whenever the NAJC delegation met with the NDP caucus and their leader, the Honourable Ed Broadbent, we were assured of their support and that questions regarding redress would be raised during Question Period. When Otto Jelinek refused to negotiate with the NAJC in 1986, the opposition parties were furious at the government's behaviour. The press referred to Jelinek's refusal to negotiate as one of Brian Mulroney's biggest blunders. NDP multiculturalism critic Ernie Epp accused Mulroney of losing "his 'personal honour' … if he [didn't] end the growing battle over compensation by finding someone to hammer out an agreement with the National Association of Japanese Canadians."[19] Timely statements from the Opposition critics to the media kept the redress issue alive in the public sphere and helped refocus government representatives on the commitment that the prime minister had made to the Japanese Canadian community.

Ernie Epp wrote to each subsequent minister of multiculturalism, urging them to resolve the redress issue. I was impressed by his sincere interest in seeing the issue settled in an honourable manner. I had a positive relationship with Epp and met him on several occasions when he passed through Winnipeg to discuss not only our progress with redress but other issues pertaining to Canadian multiculturalism as well. Once the NAJC made clear the importance of

18 "Don't Impose the Deal," *Montreal Gazette*, January 30, 1986, B2, www.proquest.com /newspapers/dont-impose-deal/docview/431296162/se-2.

19 "Mulroney Prodded on Internment Issue," *Winnipeg Free Press*, May 29, 1986, 26, archives .winnipegfreepress.com/winnipeg-free-press/1986-05-29/page-26/.

individual compensation to the government, the NDP also adopted the same position. Epp wrote personally to over a thousand groups and individuals throughout Canada, urging them to express their support for a fair redress settlement to the government.

By May 1986, the NAJC had completed two major projects, the Price Waterhouse report, titled *Economic Losses of Japanese Canadians after 1941*,[20] and a national survey of the Japanese Canadian community on the forms of compensation they favoured. The Price Waterhouse report estimated that at least $443 million, calculated in 1986 dollars, had been lost by Japanese Canadians during the internment. This was based on a minimum of $333 million in lost income and $110 million in lost property. The study did not include a figure for pain and suffering – the humiliation of being branded "enemy alien," the emotional trauma of the uprooting, the breakup of families, and the harsh living conditions endured. Nor were the violation of rights, destruction of the community, or expulsion from Canada included in the monetary figure. The *Globe and Mail* editorial of May 26, "To Offset a Wrong," took the Price Waterhouse report into account and indicated that "if the redress is to be more than a meaningless token, the Government should think of it in those terms, and make the compensation bear a direct relation to the losses the community suffered at its country's – this country's – hands."[21] Besides, the total loss of $443 million was far less than the "billions of dollars" Jelinek had predicted. As for the results of the NAJC's "Questionnaire on Forms of Compensation," they were released in April 1986. They showed strong support for financial compensation, disputing Jelinek's claim that elderly Japanese Canadians did not want compensation. Most of those directly affected favoured individual compensation over community compensation or combined individual and community compensation. The results provided conclusive evidence that refuted the charges by government and the Survivors group that Japanese Canadians did not support individual compensation.

---

20 National Association of Japanese Canadians with Price Waterhouse, *Economic Losses of Japanese Canadians after 1941: A Study* (Winnipeg: National Association of Japanese Canadians, 1986), landscapesofinjustice.uvic.ca/archive/media/TINA/facsimile/ubc-rbsc_roy_miki_box_65_file_7.pdf.

21 "To Offset a Wrong," *Globe and Mail*, May 26, 1986, A6, www.proquest.com/newspapers/offset-wrong/docview/386129151/se-2.

These two studies formed the basis for the NAJC's redress proposals established at the May 17–19 meeting in Winnipeg. This was the first time that the NAJC had clearly articulated the specific redress demands that the community was seeking from the federal government. With intensifying support within the Japanese Canadian community and an increasingly positive attitude of other Canadians towards redress, the National Council decided to "lay the cards on the table." It adopted a comprehensive redress proposal that included individual compensation of $25,000 to Japanese Canadians directly affected by the government's measures and a community fund of $50 million. The resolution also called for the establishment of a Japanese Canadian Human Rights Foundation, restoration of citizenship, clearing of criminal records, and amendments to the War Measures Act to ensure that similar injustices would not occur again.

The biggest fear I had once we put forward our demands in a very concrete way was how the media and the general population would react. Up to now, the NAJC had guarded the specifics but asked support for a negotiated settlement, a principle that politicians, organizations, and the public could sanction. Once demands are quantified, reactions are unpredictable. Will public support turn against us? I was not as concerned with the government's response to the redress proposal because I anticipated a negative counteraction as a matter of process. Until this point, the reaction from the media and public was one of encouragement and validation. Would this continue? The possible rejection of the proposal by the media and public was at stake.

It was a tense moment for me as the details of the NAJC redress proposals were presented to the media. It would have been easy for the tide of media sympathy and public opinion to shift negatively, facing discussion of real dollars and cents and not just an abstract principle of justice. At the press conference that followed, reporters asked us what chance the redress package had of being accepted by the government. I replied, "If we were to follow the past track record, it may not be extremely likely."[22] I was anxious to see the articles in

22   "Redress for Internment Set at $25,000 Each by Japanese Group," Globe and Mail, May 20, 1986, A5, www.proquest.com/historical-newspapers/redress-internment-set-at-25-000 -each-japanese/docview/1143874390/se-2.

the press the following day and how the announcement was received by the media and in the editorials.

The media seemed relieved that the details of our request to the government were finally out in the open. The next day, a letter and a copy of our official position were submitted to the prime minister. Jelinek had previously accused the NAJC of not putting forward a proposal, but now he had one.

I was invited by CBC to appear on a phone-in show the next afternoon to discuss the question, "Do you think that Japanese Canadians should be compensated according to their proposal?" The responses would hopefully be an accurate gauge of how Canadians might feel towards the demand for individual compensation. The first five calls were extremely negative. One person, a former veteran who had been at the Battle of Hong Kong during World War II, said, "Look at what your country did to us. We should be getting compensation from Japan." This comment was not uncommon from veterans and their families. Again, I tried to explain to the caller that many Japanese Canadians were born here, our country is Canada, and the abusive treatment was at the hands of our own government. Another caller, a Japanese Canadian woman said, "Aren't you a Christian? We should be forgiving and forgetting and not ask for compensation." I pointed out to her that several national church organizations, such as the United Church of Canada and the Lutheran Church, supported redress for Japanese Canadians.

After the fifth caller, there was an interesting shift in attitude. The next twenty callers were either quite supportive of the position we adopted or asked clarification questions and hoped for our success. Out of the twenty-five callers, nineteen approved the compensation proposal – 75 percent. I was pleased with the responses, which reassured us that Canadians were becoming more knowledgeable about the wartime experiences of Japanese Canadians. I commented on this change in the frame of mind of the callers to the host, Jim Rae. He said, "This is the pattern we often see with phone-in programs, because the ones who are most negative are waiting to express their personal opinion right away and not willing to listen to other comments." I was overwhelmed by the positive reactions; the experience gave us hope that a redress settlement was possibly imminent. All in all, although I was faced with antagonistic attitudes from some of the callers, I enjoyed the challenge and found that the phone-in format was an effective way to converse with the general Canadian public. It afforded the opportunity to educate them on the tragic events that affected Japanese Canadians, especially during wartime, but also to hear their personal feelings on redressing the past injustice. There was a marked contrast in the attitudes expressed by callers in the early days of the campaign as compared to the period after the NAJC put forward their redress proposal in May 1986. The majority of callers in the earlier stages were quite hostile to the notion of compensation and even to an apology.

The callers opposed to redress could be categorized into four areas: those who compared the treatment of captured Canadian soldiers by the Japanese military during World War II to the treatment of Japanese civilians in Canada; those who saw Japanese Canadians as immigrants who should be happy that they were allowed to remain in Canada; those who felt that our present taxes should not pay for the past wrongs of other governments; and those who felt that the government had been justified in taking strong measures during wartime for the protection of Canada. In contrast, the callers who were supportive of redress distinguished the difference between treatment of prisoners-of-war by an enemy country and the treatment of Japanese Canadians by their own Canadian government. They saw the two issues as being distinctly different. Others saw the contradiction between Canada's willingness to assist other countries in need and its ignoring of the plights of Indigenous Peoples or Japanese Canadian within its own borders. These people felt that Canada had an obligation to get their "house in order" first by compensating Japanese Canadians.

One radio talk show I was on from Regina demonstrated to me the value of having several hours to discuss the redress issue on the air. This program was aired after the NAJC had publicly released their redress proposal calling for individual and group compensation. The questions that were put to listeners were whether Japanese Canadians should receive compensation, and what was adequate compensation. I found initial callers to be quite belligerent towards any notion of compensation. However, when questioned by the host as to why they thought that way, it became apparent that their knowledge of the issue was very shallow. My presence on the program provided an opportunity to respond and share facts and rationale for our position. The more information was divulged, the more sympathetic the callers became. I noticed that subsequent callers followed up on ideas and statements that I had made earlier. Dialogue was an excellent medium for educating the public. Although not all callers could be swayed to support compensation, I felt that there was sincerity in their decision and that they were capable of expressing valid reasons for supporting or opposing compensation.

At times, we did get callers who made irrational statements to support their views. One caller from Regina claimed that she worked with Japanese Canadians who received more money than she did for the same job and didn't have any taxes deducted from their paycheque. Therefore, she totally disagreed that compensation should be given to Japanese Canadians. She concluded by saying, "What happened, happened. No one else is crying for money to be paid for their losses. None of this should be given to them. They're no better than we are. If they're Canadian, then [they should] stay quiet."

The callers who were most difficult to reason with were the patronizing ones. I remember one caller saying to the host, "Canadians let them into Canada. We were nice enough to let them in." The caller questioned why we were pressing for compensation when Canadians were so good to us. The assumption that Japanese Canadians were immigrants was prevalent. Another caller, who recognized the difference, remarked, "These people are Canadians. Why can't people understand that?"

When a caller disagreed on the principle of compensation, the host strategically asked them to put themselves in Japanese Canadians' shoes. She asked, "What would you do if the government took away your property? Wouldn't you want something done?" In most cases, the callers agreed that they would want something to be done. Of all the media venues I was involved with, I found talk shows to be the most challenging, the most enlightening, and the most enjoyable. The direct interaction with callers facilitated changes of opinions. In the Regina talk show, there was an equal split between the people who opposed redress and those who supported an apology and some form of compensation.

No one was surprised when Jelinek dismissed the report on the losses incurred by Japanese Canadians during the period of 1942 to 1949. He was quoted as saying, "I just don't understand how a study that shows $400 million or $500 million or $600 million has a direct effect on what our solution is going to be. You know that it's not going to be anywhere close to $455 million or whatever the Price Waterhouse report says. Nowhere close."[23]

In late May 1986, I met with Jelinek to discuss the NAJC redress proposals that had been developed during the May Council meeting of the NAJC in Winnipeg. Although he had continually threatened unilateral action from the beginning, he never followed through on his threat. He was now asked to present the various proposals to Cabinet so that they could decide what should be done. Jelinek indicated that the NAJC compensation request had been handed over to Cabinet. To the press, Jelinek commented that the NAJC request was "excessive" and that we had time to get another proposal to Cabinet. It was difficult to know what he was thinking, as his statements were often contradictory.

As far as Jelinek was concerned, there would be no negotiations with the NAJC. "It's not a question of negotiating with one organization, because there's more than one organization in Canada," he told the press after our May meeting. Jelinek consistently used the issue of a "split" in the community to reject the negotiation process. Each time the minister put forward the government's redress plan, the Survivors group in the Japanese Canadian community expressed their support, endorsing whatever position the government put forward. The timing of their responses made me suspect that there was a close working relationship between the minister's office and the Survivors group.

An inside source told me that supporters of the Survivors group were encouraged with funding from Jelinek's office to hold press conferences in order to denounce the NAJC as the community's representative and support the government's plan. I asked Jelinek at a face-to-face meeting in Ottawa whether he had talked to "people inside" about holding a press conference. His response to me was not a direct answer: "Art, you can't believe everything that reporters say." I asked him again, and again he would not answer yes or no but gave a rambling statement that did not respond to the question. Why wouldn't he just say no if that was the honest answer? In the end, I never got an adequate response, but his reluctance to answer led me to believe that there was some truth in my allegation. This tactic of

23   "Jelinek Rejects Report on Internees' Losses," *Globe and Mail*, May 14, 1986, A11, www.proquest.com/historical-newspapers/jelinek-rejects-report-on-internees-losses /docview/1143879163/se-2.

"divide and conquer" was a continuing strategy Jelinek used to avoid the negotiation process.

I remember that I was upset with Jelinek's comment that there would be no compromise because, in his opinion, the Japanese Canadian community was split. I said to him, "The split isn't there. You've made it out to be a split." Frustrated, I revealed to the press that Japanese Canadians would rather see the federal government abandon plans for compensation than to have a unilateral settlement imposed upon us. I consistently stressed the NAJC position that the process of arriving at a resolution was as important as the end itself, and that no compensation package would be acceptable if it were imposed rather than negotiated. This is the principle that both Opposition parties supported; both the NDP and Liberal critics, having the responsibility to scrutinize the policies and actions of the multiculturalism minister, urged the prime minister to instruct Jelinek to enter into negotiations with the NAJC. However, those urgings fell on deaf ears.

I felt that Dalton Camp's two articles on redress, which appeared in the *Toronto Star* in 1986, were timely and enlightening and would have positive consequences for the NAJC. Camp, a political columnist later to become Brian Mulroney's chief advisor, stressed in his first of two *Star* columns on redress, "Time for the Apology," that the government should do "what is right ... in order to redress a grievous wrong." Recognizing the concern expressed by Japanese Canadians that the government might attempt to settle the issue without further negotiations, Camp cautioned, "In the end, one would hope the government would [act] honourably – as no previous government has seen fit to do – that its apology to our fellow citizens will be unequivocal and its intentions to negotiate a settlement of claim will be free of cavil. Nothing could so ennoble the Canadian system of governance than that this government willingly offer to redress the wrong of one of its predecessors."[24] Such admirable statements coming from the former president of the Progressive Conservative Party elevated the credibility of the redress process.

In his second *Star* column, "The PM's Honour Is at Stake," Camp had an interesting perspective on the redress struggle. He speculated that the reason Jelinek never followed through on his threat to move

---

24 Dalton Camp, "Time for the Apology," *Toronto Star*, January 16, 1986, A19, www.news papers.com/article/the-toronto-star/133499630/.

unilaterally was that the prime minister imposed restraint on his minister from "giving further offence to Canadian citizens already grievously offended." Camp believed that Mulroney's promise of a direct apology and compensation was sincere. He wrote: "If now he will do what he said he would do, not everyone will agree. But it will, in the end, reflect some honourable distinction upon all Canadians and, as well, upon himself."[25] Camp's words implied that Otto Jelinek's lack of sensitivity in dealing with Japanese Canadians had put the prime minister's honour in peril. He may have had an influence in having Jelinek replaced as minister of multiculturalism.

Jelinek failed to convince the prime minister that he was capable of honourably settling the redress issue with Japanese Canadians, and his approach drew all kinds of fire from the media. "Imposing a settlement – even a generous one – without proper consultation won't do, either. The process of arriving at a just solution is every bit as important as the solution itself. Only sensitive negotiations can heal the wounds inflicted on a group of Canadian citizens" stated a *Toronto Star* editorial of June 3, 1986. "What was intended as redress may turn into further insult: an apology and compensation that many Japanese Canadians won't accept."[26]

A federal cabinet shuffle on June 30, 1986, saw the removal of Jelinek from multiculturalism and the appointment of the Honourable David Crombie to secretary of state and multiculturalism. Of all the multiculturalism ministers I encountered during the redress struggle, I was the least impressed with Otto Jelinek, who clearly seemed to lack sensitivity or empathy towards what Canadians now recognized as the blatant violation of human dignity undergone by Japanese Canadians.

25   Dalton Camp, "The PM's Honor Is at Stake," *Toronto Star*, May 27, 1986, A15, www .proquest.com/newspapers/pms-honor-is-at-stake/docview/435429885/se-2.

26   "Pay War Internees for Property Losses," *Toronto Star*, June 3, 1986, A14, www.newspapers .com/article/the-toronto-star/133575149/.

CHAPTER 7

Allies and Adversaries

The most significant role that the media played during the redress campaign was to educate Canadians about our history. We provided the stories and they provided the venue – a powerful combination.

—Art Miki

Although the Japanese Canadian community has existed in Canada for almost a century and a half, with the arrival of the first known immigrant from Japan, Manzo Nagano, in 1877, population statistics show that it is one of the smallest Asian Canadian groups in the country. According to the 2016 census, there are approximately 121,000 persons of Japanese ancestry in Canada, 53 percent of whom are of mixed origin, that is, of Japanese and other ethnic origins. In the last fifty years, other Asian groups have grown extensively in number because of major amendments during the 1960s to Canada's immigration policy, which removed many racial and national restrictions. The growth of the Japanese Canadian population in Canada has been minimal and makes up less than 0.5 percent of present overall population numbers. Once World War II was over, the internees were dispersed across Canada and no electoral riding had sufficient numbers of Japanese Canadian voters to meaningfully affect election results; this was unlike the influence that other larger ethnic groups would have in voting for a specific candidate. Recognizing our lack of significant political clout or contacts, we knew we would have to find allies within the political system as we embarked on the negotiations process with the federal government.

A surprising early expression of outside support came from churchman and educator Frank H. Epp on behalf of the Mennonite Central Committee Canada on October 30, 1984, in Winnipeg, when he delivered a heartfelt apology to Canadians of Japanese ancestry who had been interned and suffered property loss. Mr. Epp stated, "We believe that a profound and meaningful expression of regret is owed by Canadians through the Canadian Government. We, too, have a debt to pay as both Canadians and Mennonites."[1] This action was precipitated by a resolution to the Mennonite Central Committee Board by the political-science professor and author John H. Redekop, which stated the following: "Whereas many of the properties were confiscated by government authorities to be held in trust but then sold in violation of that trust and whereas some of these properties, especially in the Lower Fraser Valley, were subsequently purchased by Mennonites, at times unknowingly, Mennonite Central Committee Canada therefore deeply regrets these injustices and apologizes to these people of Japanese descent for the mistreatment and exploitation to which they were subjected."[2] In commemoration of the apology, the Mennonite Central Committee of Canada and the NAJC established a joint Canadian Japanese–Mennonite Scholarship fund that would be awarded annually to graduate students doing research in the protection of minorities and human rights.[3] The timing of the apology was appreciated and appropriate, as the NAJC was attempting to initiate discussions on redress with the government. The NAJC National Council met with the ministry of multiculturalism's officials shortly after the apology, when we officially arrived at a negotiations process in December 1984.

To avoid the contentious issue of the monetary figure or to deflect emphasis on the monetary aspect of compensation, the NAJC

---

1   "Mennonites Apologize to Japanese Canadians," *Manitoba NDP*, November 1984.

2   Ibid.

3   For more information, see the relevant web pages of the National Association of Japanese Canadians and Mennonite Central Committee Canada: najc.ca/funds-and-awards /canadian-japanese-mennonite-scholarship/ and mcccanada.ca/get-involved/scholar ships/cjms, respectively.

deliberately asked political parties to support a negotiated agreement, focusing on the process. We sensed that many politicians would have difficulty with the concept of individual compensation, especially in the '80s when such precedent did not exist in Canada, and that some would speak against redress if we pushed that position. A negotiated settlement would appear more politically acceptable and would involve the NAJC in working towards a resolution that would be seen as meaningful and fair.

During the early negotiation meetings with the Honourable Jack Murta and his officials, the topic of individual compensation appeared to be the government's main stumbling block, so we sought support from the Opposition parties. Although individual compensation was essential for a settlement, we were reluctant to ask politicians to endorse that position for fear we would not receive their support.

Years later, I ask Sergio Marchi how the Liberal Party might have responded if we had originally asked the Liberal caucus for unconditional support for individual compensation. Personally, Marchi was not a proponent of individual compensation and thought that caucus would have had a difficult time accepting that principle. When I interviewed him on December 10, 1993, in Ottawa, he said, "I'm a believer that while individuals suffered in the past, it was done on behalf of a community and a nation." Believing that a negotiated settlement was defensible, Marchi added, "I clearly thought that it was a perfect right for a community who was representing those individuals to sit down on the other side of the table and have the ability to go back and forth rather than be told what is good for them, because I think that adds insult to injury." Marchi admitted that he had had some doubts about whether he would ever see a redress settlement: "I suppose that if I speak cynically, I think the election and the publicity surrounding the issue probably acted as a catalyst to make it happen. But notwithstanding the political motivations, it was the right thing for the community. It was good for the community and good for the country when you look back at what we did. That was clearly one of the highlights of that Parliament."

The New Democratic Party appointed Ernie Epp, a member of the clergy from the then Thunder Bay–Nipigon riding, as their multiculturalism critic. He and other NDP MPs strongly resisted the government's Murta-led attempt to force a settlement in early 1985. In June 1985, the NDP caucus, according to Epp, issued a press release that reaffirmed their stance on redress and adopted the position that there must be a process of negotiations with the NAJC to arrive at a redress settlement, and that a proper redress settlement will be one that has been accepted by the Japanese Canadian community through its national organization.

This statement was extremely important to the NAJC, because the government was backing down on their commitment to negotiate and had attempted to discredit the NAJC as the legitimate representative for the community. Ernie Epp issued a statement in the House indicating that he had received petitions from residents in Alberta and British Columbia "who assert that the NAJC is the only elected national organization across the country." He further explained to the members of the House the NAJC's efforts to hold public meetings and use a national questionnaire to obtain grassroots advice in formulating our redress position, thus validating the NAJC as the legitimate representative for the Japanese Canadian community.

Other NDP members in the House, such as Dan Heap of Toronto and Margaret Mitchell of Vancouver, were strong advocates for the Japanese Canadian community and backed the NAJC in their redress efforts. They attended various community redress meetings and events, giving us encouragement and support. Dan Heap, who was familiar with the role that George Imai played in Toronto in dividing the Japanese Canadian community, stated, "We must speak out to declare the legitimacy of the NAJC and the falsity of many of Imai's credentials."

Although much of the dialogue on redress was with individual politicians, NAJC representatives appeared before influential parliamentary committees to lobby for changes to the War Measures Act, the Canadian Multiculturalism Act, and the Canadian Race Relations Foundation Act. One such committee was the Standing Committee on Multiculturalism, consisting of members from all political parties and the Senate. This committee made recommendations to the Cabinet and was not accountable to the minister of multiculturalism. On May 27, 1986, NAJC Vice-President Roger Obata and I were invited to appear before this Standing Committee to present the NAJC redress proposal, which had been adopted by the NAJC Council earlier in the month.[4] Several members of the all-party committee,

---

4   House of Commons (Hansard), *Minutes of Proceedings and Evidence of the Standing Committee on Multiculturalism*, May 27, 1986.

such as Sergio Marchi and Ernie Epp, had been apprised of the status of negotiations and were supportive of the NAJC. The chair, Gus Mitges, and Andrew Witer, both Conservative MPs, were also sympathetic to the NAJC's efforts. As mentioned previously, when the Honourable Otto Jelinek appeared before this same committee, Mitges questioned the minister's integrity in not honouring the process of negotiation as stated in the government press release.

Roger Obata and I were able to review the history of the redress movement, relating examples of hardships and pain Japanese Canadians had suffered and providing an in-depth historical background of the NAJC and its administrative structure. I felt that this was necessary because we suspected that our status as a truly representative organization for the community would yet again be challenged. During the question session that followed our presentation to the committee, Conservative MP and committee Vice-Chair Bill Lesick questioned the grants we had received of over $150,000 (which included the funds that had been given to George Imai for the September 1983 Council meeting) and raised the issue of NAJC representation. He then read a telegram that had been sent to the minister of multiculturalism from the Japanese Canadian National Redress Association of Survivors indicating that "compensation in the form of pension supplement will be the most acceptable to the majority of Japanese Canadian families." The telegram was signed by Alfred Arakawa, Shirley Kakutani, Ken Matsune, Katsuyoshi Morita, and Steve Sasaki. Lesick suggested that this organization represented 40 to 60 percent of Japanese Canadians, thereby attempting to disqualify the NAJC as the sole representative organization for Japanese Canadians. I rebutted his comments by indicating that the Association of Survivors had never held a public meeting to receive feedback, and so how could they conclude that the majority of Japanese Canadians favoured pension supplements? Their idea was not based on collective data from the people they purported to represent but on the group's view, one they felt would be more acceptable to taxpayers. I pointed out that the NAJC was considering pension supplements as one of the options for individual compensation – if the minister would honour the negotiation process. I sensed that this was a planned attempt by Lesick, with the possible collaboration of the minister, to discredit the NAJC. However, our appearance before the Standing Committee had positive consequences, as the majority of committee members displayed interest in the redress cause and sympathy for it. This incident also revealed the extent to which the Association of Survivors would pursue actions to vilify the NAJC and inflame discord within the community.

Realizing that there was very little chance of achieving redress through the time-consuming legal process, the NAJC turned to elected representatives, hoping their moral and ethical understanding would right the wrongs of the past. This meant that redress would only be possible if the prime minister and Cabinet were convinced that it was the right thing to do. The most challenging aspect of the redress campaign was to meet as many politicians as we could, exposing them to the history and experiences of citizens of Japanese ancestry, especially from during the wartime period. It was important for politicians to know the long-term effect of the government's drastic actions, which had deprived Japanese Canadians of their basic rights. Although we may have lacked close political contacts, many individual politicians were extremely moved when we made them aware of the sufferings inflicted upon Japanese Canadians; they demonstrated their support for redress by raising questions in the House or by making encouraging comments to the media.

THE POWER OF THE MEDIA

Throughout this memoir I make reference to newspaper articles, editorials, radio talk shows, interviews, and television programs that brought forward the perspectives of the wider Canadian public. The media has, or had at that time, a tremendous influence on how people perceive an issue since they generally communicate a sense of authenticity that people adhere to and believe. With the Japanese Canadian redress crusade, the manner in which the media presented the issue could either have been detrimental or generated support and sympathy for the correction of a historic injustice. In short, the media had the power either to promote or to destroy the redress effort. I thought the most significant role that the media played during the redress campaign was to educate Canadians about our history.

Following the heated exchange during the last days of Parliament in June 1984 between Pierre Trudeau and Brian Mulroney, the issue of compensation became a topic for open discussion in different media forums. The first radio show I participated in was CBC's *Cross Country Checkup*, a call-in program (still on air today) where authorities are asked to provide their comments on a specific topic, in combination with comments from regular listeners.[5] The show I was part of aired in 1984 shortly after the Liberal Multiculturalism Minister David Collenette expressed regret in the House for the grave injustices suffered by Japanese Canadians during and after World War II. On the program, a number of participants were asked to make statements related to the question "Should there be compensation for Japanese Canadians interned during the Second World War?" I stressed that the NAJC sought a commitment from the government to enter into negotiations. Japanese Canadians wanted an acknowledgment of the injustices suffered but had not reached consensus on what form compensation should take. If an agreement to negotiate was achieved, then the NAJC felt that with the government they could explore the many compensation options available. Ken Adachi, the author of *The Enemy That Never Was*, talked about his family being split up and his mother dying in a camp. He described the heartless treatment forced upon Japanese Canadians without any evidence that Canada's security was at risk from them. Reference was made to the United States Congressional hearing recommendation of $20,000 compensation to individual Japanese American victims, which Ken Adachi indicated was "fair enough" for Canadians as well. When asked who should receive compensation, he replied that survivors and their descendants should be entitled to compensation. Desmond Morton, a guest historian on the program to assist the host, clarified or supplemented information so that listeners would get an unbiased historical account of the treatment of Japanese Canadians.

To give perspective to the government's action at the time, Glen McPherson, a lawyer and counsel for the Custodian of Enemy Property, was invited to present his view on the program. He explained what he felt was the military climate following the bombing of Pearl

---

5   The full transcript and recording of the radio program were shared with the NAJC by the CBC and are now part of the NAJC's archives at the UBC Library's Rare Books and Special Collections (Fonds RBSC-ARC-1791, file 46-17, "CCB [*sic*: CBC] Cross Country on Japanese Redress, Checkup, no date, [possibly with war vets]," rbscarchives.library.ubc.ca/ccb-cross-country-on-japanese-redress-checkup-no-date-possibly-with-war-vets).

Harbor. With Japan moving into Southeast Asia and occupying part of the Aleutian Islands (Unangam Tanangin) off mainland Alaska, there was fear of a Japanese attack on the West Coast. He claimed that Japanese fishing boats had charts and radios and that their fishing camps and salteries appeared to be established in strategic areas. Among the twenty-two thousand Japanese Canadians living within the restricted zone on the coast, McPherson felt that there had to be enemy agents. Reflecting on what he felt were the general population's attitudes towards Japanese Canadians, he claimed our community was never fully "accepted" by other Canadians and that our presence on the West Coast was resented by a large proportion of the Vancouver population. According to McPherson, most "Japanese" (never "Japanese *Canadians*" in his mouth) were concentrated in the mainland, Steveston, and the Fraser Valley, and when they were forced to leave their homes, other Canadians who "didn't like them" took advantage of their circumstances and vandalized their properties. When program host Dennis Trudeau suggested to McPherson that, surely, there were strong arguments for compensation now given Japanese Canadians' peaceful conduct during and after World War II, he still firmly opposed the idea. But McPherson's reasoning was irrational: forcibly moving Japanese Canadians out of their homes had been "first of all for their own protection," given the danger of the situation after Pearl Harbor. He added, somewhat elliptically, that he remembered hearing "rumours" at the time that Japanese Canadians were sending the cremated ashes of their dead to Japan so they could "be with their ancestors," and that Japanese Canadian children had been "sent to Japan for military training." Was he implying that Japanese Canadians felt a stronger allegiance to Japan than to Canada and therefore weren't worthy of compensation? In which case, one could have asked how the topic of potential allegiance in the 1940s was relevant to the contemporary issue of compensation.

It was obvious to me that McPherson was attempting to justify the government's past actions on the bases of untruths and chauvinism. When the host mentioned the confiscation of Japanese Canadians' properties, and whether that alone didn't justify compensation, McPherson denied that Japanese Canadian properties had in fact been confiscated in the first place. To the host's incredulous counter – "Someone took their property and sold [it] and that's not confiscation?" – McPherson justified his claim by saying that

Japanese Canadians eventually "got the money back" and were able to seek further indemnities in 1947 and 1948 through the Bird Commission. This was of course misguided, as the Bird Commission (officially the Royal Commission on Japanese Claims), with its restrictive mandate, did not adequately repay Japanese Canadians whose properties had been confiscated. McPherson's insistence that "confiscation" didn't apply because some Japanese Canadians had received monies was a disingenuous play on semantics. It remained clear that the confiscation of Japanese Canadian properties during the war was wrong, regardless of how it was termed.

Then, questioned on why the custodian had sold off the properties that were held in trust for Japanese Canadians, McPherson gave the reason that authorities didn't know when the war might end. He said:

> The custodian's major problem was to find out where the property was located and to protect it. This was made more difficult because some Japanese [sic] didn't want to give an inventory of the property. Our problem was to protect the property. We had stores to run and had no customers, we had farms to operate and had no farmers. We had hundreds of cars at Hastings Park that were sitting in the rain and salt air rusting away. Worst of all, we didn't know when the war was going to be over. The custodian had almost an impossible job. Then he was given the power to sell the property and assets. He was to hold the money for the Japanese. He was instructed to get fair market price.[6]

Since Japanese Canadians were told that their property would be held in trust, why was it sold? McPherson indicated that the fishing boats were sold by the Japanese Fishing Vessels Committee in order "to get them back into production if [they] could" (as with sawmills, for example). But since these businesses had been run solely by Japanese Canadians who followed their own methods, the government, according to McPherson, had difficulty calling for tenders, selling the assets, and getting them up and running.

McPherson was allowed to discuss another topic on the program. The farming units seized in the Fraser Valley in the 1940s were mainly berry farms, where Japanese Canadian farmers were experts. McPherson said that these stolen plots of land were put aside for soldiers

---

6   Ibid.

returning after the war. When they were tasked with selling the properties, the Veterans' Land Act people started valuing the farms. McPherson argued that the evaluation was made by an independent body and yielded a "very handsome" value.

In retrospect, McPherson concluded by saying he believed the evacuation had been "justified and essential from a military point of view." He didn't know where enemy agents had been operating, but was convinced of their existence. With the war waging in the Far East, as far as he was concerned, it had been "in the best interest" of Japanese Canadians to be evacuated rather than to remain concentrated in the Vancouver region. Had Japanese Canadians not been moved, and with the news of atrocities suffered by Canadian troops in Hong Kong, McPherson felt there would have been "major problems in the Powell Street area." Needless to say, much of McPherson's "logic" was in fact illogical. Protecting people by interning them is not a justifiable course of action, nor does it explain why the dispossession, exile, and dispersal of Japanese Canadians by its own government were judged necessary at the time. Hearing McPherson's perspective gave me an insight into the negative attitudes and fear-mongering that existed in the minds of some Canadians.

All in all, radio talk shows like this one were an effective medium for analyzing the issues confronting the redress question. If CBC's *Cross Country Checkup* was any potent gauge of public opinion, support for Japanese Canadians had been confirmed: approximately 60 percent of the callers from across Canada were favouring compensation.

• • •

In November 1986, I received an unexpected phone call from Mr. G. Murchison of Ontario concerning his father's role in the disposal of Japanese Canadian properties during the war. His diary provides a glimpse into the workings of bureaucracy in the dispossession of Japanese properties. He offered to send me an excerpt from his father's diary that we could utilize if the information would strengthen our case with the government. He was kind enough to send me photocopied pages from the diary and an old newspaper article about his father. Mr. G. Murchison had noticed a reference in the *Globe and Mail* to old files that were discovered in the Veteran Land

Administration offices in Charlottetown, PEI, on lands that had been seized during World War II. His father, Gordon Murchison, had been the director of the Veterans' Land Act as well as of the Soldier Settlement Board during World War II, and he was "very closely involved in the valuation and ultimate disposal of lands" that were seized from Japanese Canadians by the Canadian government. The handwritten pages of his accounts, never published before, give a precious glimpse into the thinking of the time:

> All [Japanese Canadians'] fishing boats, some 2,500 of them, used in salmon fishing trade were seized, together with all industrial, commercial and residential property worth many millions of dollars. These seizures included no less than 1,100 small specialized farms in the Fraser Valley and on the Gulf Islands. Tremendous problems of administration arose for the staff of the Custodian of Enemy Property. This problem was particularly acute with respect to the farmlands. Their Japanese [Canadian] owners had no time or opportunity to dispose of their household effects or to make any farm arrangements for the upkeep and operations of the farms during their absence as internees. It's certain that [neither] the public nor the government weren't in any mood to be timorous about such things. The official custodian lacked the staff and the know-how to deal effectively with these farmlands. The only available and competent agency to deal with this problem was the Director of Soldier Settlement and his staff. The Hon. Ian Mackenzie, minister of veteran affairs, represented Vancouver South in Parliament and was insistent that the Japanese people would never return to the coastal areas as long as he could prevent it. My minister at the time was Hon. T.A. Crerar, but as a member of the Canadian War Cabinet he was a mighty busy man. Mackenzie held strong views that these Japanese lands should be taken over by the government and held for the re-establishment of Canadian veterans of World War II. It seemed natural, therefore, that the Director of Soldier Settlement was the logical agency to take over and administer these lands and thus an Order-in-Council was passed to that effect. The good Lord knew, if no one else, that I was a very busy fellow without this new assignment, but knowing a good deal about these Jap [sic] farms as a result of

the four years I spent in BC, I recognized an opportunity to do something for the Canadian veterans when the war ended.

The first problem confronting us was the setting up of a precise inventory of these lands by legal description and an on-the-spot examination of every parcel of land concerned. I called in my District Supt. for BC for a close discussion of the problems ahead and ways and means to deal with them. We decided on the names of the field inspectors to be chosen for the surveys and appraisals required, along with an indication of parcels that were potentially suitable for resettlement by Canadian Veterans. We had to decide in advance on the factors that should govern the basis of appraisal. Here we were confronted with a set of inescapable facts. The farms were now all vacant. There was no labour force available to keep these lands in a good state of productivity. The specialized type of farming such as small fruits, vegetables, flower bulbs, poultry keeping, and greenhouses was bound to deteriorate very rapidly, [and] there were annual taxes of the order of $40,000 to be provided for. The war was at a very critical stage and none of us had any idea how many more years it would last or what the final outcome would be. In summary, it was no time to be optimistic about the present or future value of these farm properties. Logically our approach to the value of these farms, so far as the Japanese owners were concerned, was to err on the side of conservative figures. It couldn't be otherwise in the circumstances.

It was found under detailed inspection that the rate of deterioration exceeded even our pessimistic fears. It was out of the question to find tenants willing or able to operate them, and thus we had to assume that these farms would, in a great many cases, inevitably run to grass and weeds. It was also found that approximately 400 parcels would not be suitable for settlement of Canadian veterans. They were either too large and expensive, such as greenhouses with up to 10,000 sq. feet of glass, or large hatcheries, or very small and isolated parcels of very low agricultural value. The Official Custodian was going ahead with the liquidation of all the commercial, industrial, and urban residential property owned by Japanese, and I recommended to the minister that I do likewise with the farms. This was agreed to but it placed me in a position full of potential embarrassments. That is to say I couldn't very well reconcile my official status of custodian of the Japanese farms and at the same time be in the market to buy these lands for resettlement purposes in my position as Director of the Veterans' Land Act 1942. I, therefore, requested and government agreed to bring to an end my position as custodian but it nevertheless behoved me and all my staff to proceed with the utmost caution and circumspection in bargaining for the purchase of these lands. I had no dealings with the absentee Jap [sic] owners. Any deal I could promulgate had to be with the Secretary of State and Official Custodian of Enemy Property. I could see some trouble ahead if things went wrong, but we were living in a state of war. If it happened that the Allies would lose the war or be forced into a more or less degrading peace, nothing mattered a damn. On the other hand, if all went well, there could be some future adjustments based on equity and fair play. All I could do[,] all my staff could do – was to exercise our best judgments at all times. There was some political dynamite in the whole situation, but that was something beyond my control.

Thus it came to pass that I submitted an offer to the Secretary of State to buy some 700 of these farms units in a bulk purchase offer. The local committee at Vancouver acting in an advisory capacity to the Minister held that my offer was too low. Sure it was on the low side, but there was no competition in the market. We reviewed our prices and increased the offer by a few hundred thousand dollars which was accepted, and in due course the Director, Veterans Land Act became the outright owner in fee simple. These lands were promptly put on the shelf pending the conclusion of the war and the parcels we didn't buy reverted to the administration of the Official Receiver, who proceeded to sell them to the best advantage as and when he could. The rest of my account of the Japanese lands will be recorded later on and at a time when the politicians tried their damnedest to make me the sacrificial goat. By that time the great majority of the lands had been allocated to Canadian veterans under firm contracts at the prices I had paid for them, so there wasn't much the political people could do about it.[7]

First, Mr. Murchison's diary entries are consistent with the views offered by Glen McPherson on the *Cross Country Checkup* radio program in 1984 and present an accurate account of the actions taken by government officials to deal with the confiscated properties. What the diary further reveals was the confirmation of Ian Mackenzie's persistent role in ensuring that Japanese Canadians would not return to British Columbia after the war and the manipulation within government so that it would be able to purchase the confiscated Japanese Canadian properties for veterans. It's obvious that Gordon Murchison, who was responsible for evaluating the properties and was then later asked to purchase the properties for the government, was in a conflict of interest. The memoirs express some fear that there could possibly be repercussions for him later. Although it is not clear what concerns the politicians had, Murchison suggested that the arrangements had gone too far and that decisions could not be reversed. We were thankful that people like Mr. Murchison would be willing to share his father's unpublished private documents in the hopes of assisting our cause. By doing so, Mr. Murchison shed light on the role his father had played in the disposal of properties confiscated from Japanese Canadians. He wrote in his letter to me, "I can recall discussing this subject with my father, and it was his view that the Japanese Canadian owners had not received fair treatment in this matter."

• • •

My first major media exposure was as a headline guest on CBC's panel game *Front Page Challenge* in January 1985, shortly after the government and the NAJC had agreed to a negotiation process. The taping of the program was held in Duncan, BC (on Vancouver Island, about fifty kilometres north of Victoria). Lorraine Thompson, CBC program coordinator, invited me to be on the show and arranged for my trip.

It was interesting to meet the different guests for the show. I had a fascinating discussion with an older gentleman named Stuart

---

7 Shared in personal correspondence with the author.

Hodgson, who was a former RCMP officer. On each show the panel covered three headlines. The headline that Hodgson represented was the story of the RCMP vessel *St. Roch*. In the 1940s, he had been a crew member on the boat, which had the distinction of being "the first vessel to traverse the Northwest Passage from west to east (1940–1942), the first to complete the passage in one season (1944), and the first to circumnavigate North America."[8] The trip from Vancouver to Halifax via the Northwest Passage took two years, in part because the ship became frozen in the ice near Herschel Island (Qikiqtaruk), in the Beaufort Sea. When I told him why I was on the program, he revealed to me that he had been one of the RCMP officers responsible for towing in confiscated Japanese Canadian fishing boats shortly after the bombing of Pearl Harbor. He indicated that he did not agree with the government's action, but he had a job to do. He said that some of the boats were severely damaged as they were bound together for the tow-in. Later, when I became a citizenship judge, Stuart Hodgson was also appointed as a judge for the Surrey office in British Columbia and recalled that we appeared on the same program.

The headline for the story I represented on *Front Page Challenge* was "Government to Apologize to Japanese Internees." The expression "Japanese internees" suggested that the victims were Japanese nationals rather than Japanese Canadians. Although I didn't make an issue out of it at that time, these subtle misrepresentations, which I believe weren't deliberate, nonetheless conveyed a false message. We became more sensitive to such images and headlines and called the source of the information on a number of occasions to have it corrected for future broadcasts. The media appreciated our concern and quickly corrected what seemed to have been an error or misunderstanding.

When my turn to appear on the show came, I stood behind the panellists so they couldn't see me as I answered their questions. It took about a minute and a half before writer, journalist, and broadcaster Pierre Berton identified the headline. A discussion with host Fred Davis and the panellists followed after a short commercial break. Berton stressed that not all people in 1942 favoured the government's actions against Japanese Canadians. He said that the

8   "Climb aboard the St. Roch – Virtually!," St. Roch National Historic Site (website), vanmaritime.com/st-roch-3/.

Vancouver Province and the *News Herald*, the latter of which he had been editor, strongly opposed the internment. The *Vancouver Sun*, Berton claimed, was a racist newspaper at that time and led the attack against Japanese Canadians fuelled by comments from Ian Mackenzie, the then Liberal Cabinet minister, thereby creating unnecessary hysteria throughout BC and the country.

I felt that the show's researchers gave a fair and thorough portrayal of the redress issue. Betty Kennedy asked what amount of compensation were we seeking from the Canadian government. It was fortunate that my appearance on *Front Page Challenge* coincided with the negotiations meetings with the government and so I could avoid a direct response. I indicated that I was not at liberty to reveal any details that were under discussions with the government. The questions that were asked by all the panellists, including Jack Webster and Allan Fotheringham, permitted me to give a broad overview of the historical background and redress issues involved, including a comparison of the Canadian experience to the Japanese American situation. The show presented the case for Japanese Canadian redress in a positive manner and was an invaluable educational opportunity. After the tapings, I attended a reception hosted by the program and met many audience members, including Japanese Canadians who came from Victoria and the surrounding areas. People were generally interested in our cause and expressed wishes for a successful conclusion.

On the drive back to the Victoria airport, I rode with Pierre Berton and Laurier LaPierre, who was a guest panellist on a different *Front Page Challenge* show that had been taped. (LaPierre was appointed to the Senate by Prime Minister Jean Chrétien in 2001.) Berton related a story of how the *Vancouver Sun* had worked to create deliberate hysteria. He told a story about a Japanese Canadian who stopped his car at a fork in the road to decide which way to go. As he was looking at a road map placed on the hood of the car, an RCMP car pulled up. He may have looked suspicious to the RCMP officer and was taken in. The next day, the *Vancouver Sun* ran a headline implying that a "Jap traitor" had been caught.

Berton told me of another incident. This was about a Japanese Canadian milkman who was out making his deliveries before dawn. Apparently unaware that curfew had been imposed, he went out and was stopped by the RCMP, who detained him for violating the government's Order-in-Council. He was eventually shipped off to a prisoner-of-war camp in Ontario, without his family having any knowledge of his whereabouts. These stories bore witness to the mistreatment and trauma suffered by Japanese Canadians and the justification for carrying on the fight for redress.

We were fortunate that the media saw the struggle of a small ethnic-minority community against the dominant establishment, the Canadian government, as a "David and Goliath"-type story. I believe that the media turned their support and empathy towards Japanese Canadians in good part because we were perceived to be the "underdogs," victims of the government's abusive and unchallenged powers. The majority of editors, reporters, commentators, and writers presented an informed view of the issue and furnished the historical context necessary for readers and listeners to understand the present-day concerns of the Japanese Canadian community. Throughout the redress campaign, the media's many avenues amplified our voice, telling our story to Canadians.

In the early days of the campaign in 1984, there was very little support from the Japanese Canadian community even to pursue redress. At a meeting with Jack Murta, he revealed to us that the government had conducted a poll on the redress question and found that there was only about 20 percent support from Canadians. This was understandable, as at that time very few Canadians were even aware of what happened to the Japanese Canadians during and after the war. As the redress campaign took hold, the media helped educate Canadians and altered public opinion. With increasing support from the Canadian public, the attitudes within the Japanese Canadian community began to change. Reassurances that Japanese Canadians were not alone in the struggle helped enhance our collective self-esteem and confidence.

From the initial stages of the redress movement and until redress was finally achieved, I noticed a tremendous transformation in the general public's comprehension of the unjust treatment of Japanese Canadians during and after World War II. In my early travels across Canada, I would explain to people I met that I was involved with the National Association of Japanese Canadians in seeking remedy for the past injustices inflicted upon our community during wartime by the Liberal government of the time. Very few people had any knowledge of what had happened to Japanese Canadians – the loss of civil liberties, the confiscation of properties, and the forced removal from the country's West Coast. This part of Canadian history, as with so many aspects of Indigenous Peoples' history, was non-existent in school textbooks. Why would most Canadians have any knowledge of these events unless they knew someone who had been directly touched?

Editorials in the major newspapers were scrutinized closely by politicians and government bureaucrats, because editorial comments were observed to reflect the views of Canadians. The *Toronto Star*'s editorial of February 4, 1985, "Wartime Wrongs Need Airing," offered the government a possible solution as to what would be an appropriate settlement for the Japanese Canadian community. The editorial stated that "it should consider appointing a joint parliamentary committee of MPs and senators to begin redressing the wrongs. The all-party group could travel across Canada and hear directly from people who had been stripped of their possessions and forcibly relocated to internment camps. Expeditious public hearings would promote a healing process among Japanese Canadians and better inform all Canadians about this shameful episode – an episode far too many young people know nothing about. They would also prepare the way for a more acceptable settlement."[9] The ideas expressed in the editorial were the result of meetings of the Toronto representatives of the NAJC strategy team, Roger Obata and Maryka Omatsu, with the *Toronto Star*'s editorial board. These face-to-face contacts were extremely helpful not only in providing the board with relevant facts, but also in offering suggestions on ways that the process might be advanced more quickly. The Toronto group met with the *Globe and Mail* editorial staff as well to share the NAJC's position and discuss the issue openly. Meetings with editorial boards were an extremely effective lobbying technique, as the editorials that followed the meetings would often be a commentary on the concerns echoed and ideas expressed by the NAJC.

Reporters who were sensitive and supportive and had developed an understanding of the redress issue were quick to contact me whenever the topic was raised by politicians, whether by a member of the Opposition or on the government side. Reporters such as Richard Cleroux of the *Globe and Mail*, Joe O'Donnell and William Walker

---

9   "Wartime Wrongs Need Airing," *Toronto Star*, February 4, 1985, A10, www.newspapers
    .com/article/the-toronto-star/133553282/.

of the *Toronto Star*, Dan Turner of the *Ottawa Citizen*, and Nancy Knickerbocker of the *Vancouver Sun* were a few of the reporters with whom I had close contact. These journalists had followed the issue for several years and were cognizant of the historical facts, writing thoughtful articles that helped Canadians learn about the wartime history of Japanese Canadians.

One of the ways that the media was extremely effective was in keeping the redress issue alive. Anytime a statement was made in the House or an interview was held with the minister on Japanese Canadian redress, reporters would call me for a comment. I was not always available because of my responsibilities as a school principal, so messages would be left with my assistant, Ann Hruda, who ensured I received them. I returned each reporter's call as soon as possible, as I viewed them as an opportunity to promote the NAJC's cause. During periods when very little appeared to be happening, if a minister made a statement it provided an opportunity for a response in the media and kept the issue alive in the public's mind.

The amount of media coverage we received was stunning. Whenever the NAJC arranged a press conference following a National Council meeting or in Ottawa during visits to meet with politicians, we received national exposure through the press, radio, and television. We couldn't have afforded that kind of publicity. I remember one press conference that we held in the basement of the Centre Block on Parliament Hill. I had just finished making statements on behalf of the NAJC, and Sergio Marchi had begun to speak in support of our organization, when suddenly the reporters and camera operators picked up their equipment and quickly exited the room in droves. We wondered what the problem was. This had never happened before at any of our press conferences. Reporters usually stayed behind to ask many questions. We found out later that at the very moment we were holding our conference, NASA's Space Shuttle *Challenger* had exploded during takeoff, killing all its crew members. Naturally, this became the story of the day.

Some reporters developed a closer relationship with us because of their interest in our community's experiences and insight into them. One such person was a young journalist from the *Winnipeg Free Press*, Larry Hill, who was sympathetic to our cause. He told me that his father, Daniel Hill, had written a book on Black history in Canada and was well known nationally for his human-rights efforts. Later,

Larry became the Ottawa correspondent for the *Winnipeg Free Press* and was stationed there, where I met him on several occasions. A number of years later I picked up his first novel, *Some Great Thing*, which deals with the issue of belonging.

Lawrence (Larry) Hill went on to become an acclaimed Canadian author. His novel *The Book of Negroes* attracted worldwide attention and was made into a CBC miniseries. His following novel, *The Illegal*, won CBC's *Canada Reads* in 2016. When Lawrence was in Winnipeg for his book signing in 2016 at McNally Robinson Booksellers, I had the chance to meet and talk with him. He recalled that as a young reporter, he told his editor that he wanted to do a story on the Japanese Canadian redress campaign. Lawrence was told not to bother because the story would "have no traction." He ignored his editor's advice and contacted me to do his article – and look what happened!

In early 1985, I met Brian Yasui, a young sansei from Toronto who was working as a reporter and interviewer for a private television news company on Parliament Hill. Brian admitted that his knowledge of the wartime treatment of Japanese Canadians was limited and that covering the redress campaign was a genuine learning experience for him. A year later, he arrived as a reporter and announcer for CBC Winnipeg, where we renewed acquaintances. He had developed into a high-profile reporter and went on to have a successful broadcasting career. Brian was the first Japanese Canadian media worker I met during the campaign, and he represented the many sansei Japanese Canadians who had very little knowledge of their families' experiences. Through his work, he was able to gain that understanding.

Along with media reports, another method of determining public opinion is polling. When we first began negotiation discussions with the Honourable Jack Murta in late 1984, he attempted to persuade us to accept the government's offer because, "according to public opinion polls, less than 20 percent of Canadians support redress." He implied that the Canadian public would be hostile if we asked for large financial compensation. However, with extensive media coverage, we believed that Canadians had become more exposed to the Japanese Canadian wartime experience and, therefore, more aware of the meaning of the negotiation process.

A national poll was conducted in March 1986 by Environics Research Group in Toronto and the results were reported in the

Globe and Mail on April 11.[10] The report found that 63 percent of the respondents favoured redress, and out of that number, 71 percent said each individual who had been unfairly treated should receive financial compensation, 25 percent thought there should be no compensation, and 10 percent had no opinion. It was interesting to note that according to party affiliation, 43 percent of Progressive Conservative, 42 percent of Liberal, and 52 percent of New Democratic Party supporters favoured individual compensation. The strongest support for individual compensation was among the university-educated (49 percent), those in professional and managerial positions (53 percent), Canadians between thirty and fifty-nine years of age (49 percent), non-British immigrants in general (52 percent), and non-European immigrants in particular (56 percent). This remarkable shift in attitude could be attributed to Jelinek's abrasive approach, the overwhelming media coverage, and the NAJC's educational campaign. The results of the polls were timely and influenced the National Council of the NAJC to formulate their comprehensive redress position in May 1986.

The poll was paid for by the multi-ethnic, Toronto-based Ad Hoc Committee for Japanese Canadian Redress, with money raised initially for a national advertising campaign, whose main caption read: "In 1942 Canada sent a lot of kids to camp." An ad placed on page 3 of the *Globe and Mail's* March 6, 1986, issue with a picture of Japanese Canadian children playing in an internment camp and text explaining why the children were in the camp aimed to heighten awareness among the general Canadian public about the redress campaign.[11] The ad asked Canadians to support the NAJC's push for a negotiated settlement, a formal acknowledgment, a just formula for compensation, and appropriate legislation to ensure that no future Canadian government could similarly mistreat another minority.

There were a few humorous incidents involving the media. One happened in Ottawa. A CBC radio reporter contacted me, wanting an interview on the progress of the redress meeting with the minister.

---

10 Deborah Wilson, "Compensation for Japanese Canadians: Poll Indicates Ottawa, Public at Odds," *Globe and Mail*, April 11, 1986, 14, www.proquest.com/historical-newspapers /poll-indicates-ottawa-public-at-odds/docview/1151455816/se-2.

11 "In 1942 Canada sent a lot of kids to camp," advertisement, *Globe and Mail*, March 6, 1986, 3, www.proquest.com/historical-newspapers/classified-ad-1-no-title/docview/1143879755 /se-2.

We arranged to meet in the lobby of the former Holiday Inn (now the Radisson Hotel Ottawa Parliament Hill) at noon on a Sunday, just before I was to return to Winnipeg; it was quite noisy because of the number of people milling around. I knew I still had the key to my hotel room, even though I had checked out. I suggested we go to the room to hold the interview. We took the elevator to the fifth floor. As I walked into the room with the female reporter following me, the chambermaid was fixing the bed. As she looked up, she appeared somewhat startled. I said to her, "Do you think I could use the room for a few minutes?" She looked at me with her mouth agape and didn't say a word. Then I said to her, "Look, I'll make it quick!" She appeared stunned, stopped what she was doing, and just stared at me. I realized at that moment what she might have been thinking. I quickly turned to the reporter and pointed at her tape recorder saying, "She's a reporter and she wants to interview me. Do you think that's okay?" A smile came over her face and she nodded her head, giving us consent to do the interview.

As an elementary school principal, my students would often say to me that they saw me on television or saw my picture in the paper. When a *Maclean's* article on me appeared, several students brought the magazine to school to show me my picture. Although most did not understand my involvement with the redress issue, they saw me in the news. One day, after an extensively covered NAJC meeting, one of the kindergarten students at the school, who must have seen the press conference, saw me walking across the parking lot and started running towards me, calling, "Mr. Miki! Mr. Miki!" I stopped, and he approached me and said, "I saw you on television last night. You're a great actor!"

When I look back at the media coverage we received, I am overwhelmed. The articles, the editorials, the human-interest stories on members of the Japanese Canadian community, the magazine articles, the radio programs, and the television coverage – all contributed immensely to increasing awareness and understanding of the Japanese Canadian experience. Thanks to the sympathetic and supportive media, we were able to put forward our message and emphasize the principles driving the redress movement.

But not all media personnel fell into that category. There were the detractors who painted negative images about Japanese Canadians and used confusing and inaccurate statements to deter the government from listening or talking to the NAJC. On January 26, 1985, Charles Lynch, a prominent writer, proposed in the *Ottawa Citizen* that the government of Japan should contribute to compensation for Japanese Canadians. His premise was that "by edict of the Japanese government, all overseas Japanese retained their native citizenship. If Japanese forces invaded the Canadian and US west coasts, the Japanese would expect co-operation from their countrymen." He gave the impression that the majority of Japanese Canadians were born in Japan and thereby had strong allegiances to it. He didn't mention that 60 percent of the victims had been born in Canada with little or no loyalty to Japan. He concluded, "But if there must be amends made to Japanese Canadians, then let the homeland that inflicted the original horrors take a hand."[12]

When we undertook the redress movement, we certainly expected opposition from various sectors of the Canadian population. We had anticipated negative reactions from those within the Japanese Canadian community who did not want the past revived or feared a backlash similar to what they had encountered in the 1940s. Others felt that challenging the government was futile, convinced that redress would be impossible. There were some Canadians who complained that our tax dollars should not be spent on compensating Japanese Canadians for events that had occurred over forty years ago, especially considering that the present government wasn't responsible for those actions. "Let Japanese bygones be bygones," wrote a Chinese Canadian veteran in a letter to the editor in the *Globe and Mail*.[13] Indeed, the most concerted effort to discredit the Japanese Canadian redress movement came from veterans or their relatives, especially those who had experienced harsh and brutal treatment by the Japanese as prisoners of war in Hong Kong. "Every day of your life you, Mr. Miki, you should get down on your knees and thank your God that you were born a Japanese rather than being born Canadian. If you were born a Canadian then, like my friend, you might have been captured at Hong Kong and forced to boil boot leather

---

12   Charles Lynch, "Maybe Japan Should Help," *Ottawa Citizen*, January 26, 1985, 24, www.newspapers.com/article/the-ottawa-citizen/133552406/.

13   "Let Japanese Bygones Be Bygones, Reader Says," letter to the editor, *Globe and Mail*, May 22, 1984, 7, www.proquest.com/historical-newspapers/let-japanese-bygones-be-reader-says/docview/1237564338/se-2.

and eat coal dust in order to survive," commented a Canadian in a letter to me.

Stories on the Japanese Canadians' quest for redress were regularly run in national magazines such as *Maclean's* and *Saturday Night*. One article that agitated Japanese Canadians was "The Enemy Within?" by J.L. Granatstein, a history professor at York University in Toronto, printed in the November 1986 issue of *Saturday Night*.[14] Granatstein attempted to cast doubt on our understanding of what occurred to Japanese Canadians historically and implied that the internment and removal of Japanese Canadians from the West Coast was justified. Much of his analysis was based on speculation and personal interpretation, rather than on fact. Ramsay Cook, a colleague of Granatstein's at York, detailed his disagreement with statements attributed to Granatstein in a letter to the Canadian academic ex-mayor of Toronto David Crombie in December 1986. He wrote, "Mr. Granatstein contends that a small number of security officers assigned to the surveillance of the Japanese Canadian community and the weak knowledge of Japanese at the command of those officers cast doubt upon the accuracy of the official reports which indicated that the Japanese Canadian community represented no threat to national security. That is pure speculation, not a historic argument." Granatstein further suggested that the Japanese consulate in Vancouver had influenced Japanese Canadians to assist in Japan's war efforts by distributing literature and participating in the consulate's activities. But he offered no concrete evidence to show that Japanese Canadians were actually recruited by the consulate.

Granatstein also assumed that because many Japanese Canadians held "dual citizenship," they could be disloyal to Canada. In *The Enemy That Never Was*, Ken Adachi explained that Japanese Canadians held dual citizenship for a specific reason: Japanese inheritance laws made it necessary for Japanese Canadians who wished to inherit family legacies from Japanese relatives to register their children as dual citizens; it had nothing to do with loyalty.[15] In sum, articles such as Granatstein's attempted to discredit the NAJC's efforts and inflamed resistance towards compensating Japanese Canadians.

---

14 J.L. Granatstein, "The Enemy Within?," *Saturday Night* 101, no. 11 (November 1986): 32–34 and 39–42, www.proquest.com/magazines/enemy-within-expulsion-japanese-bc/docview/222411251/se-2.

15 Adachi, *The Enemy That Never Was*, 175–176.

The perception that most Japanese Canadians were Japanese nationals is a common theme in letters where the writer opposes compensation and therefore advocates that the NAJC should be seeking compensation directly from Japan. In 1942, 60 percent of those interned had been born in Canada and 75 percent were Canadian citizens. Throughout the campaign, the NAJC stressed that they were seeking redress on behalf of Canadians of Japanese ancestry whose rights as Canadian citizens had been stripped. This deliberate emphasis on Canadian citizenship was to counteract false perceptions from critics who would say, "Look at what your country did to our soldiers in Hong Kong!"

Usually after some media coverage such as a press conference, I would receive phone calls from individual Canadians who were critical of the NAJC quest for redress. Most often they were people who had served overseas. The conversation often began with rude, irate comments with emphasis on how "my people" treated the soldiers, and if I didn't like what Canadians did, I should go back "where I came from." These emotional, racist comments, often made out of ignorance, required clarification. A distinction had not been made between being a citizen of Japan and a citizen of Canada. If the caller were willing to give me a chance to speak, I would point out that Japanese Canadians are Canadian citizens and not people from Japan. I would use myself as an example. I was born in Canada and so were my parents; it was my grandparents who came from Japan, so our family today is in its fifth generation in Canada. The second point that I would clarify is that the treatment of civilians, especially by their own government, is not the same as the treatment of prisoners of war by an enemy country. I agreed that both parties suffered during wartime, but I stressed that a government's responsibility is to protect its citizens and not to violate their rights by removing them from their homes, confiscating their properties, and interning them without legal cause simply because they belonged to a particular minority group.

I found that talking with these individuals, explaining the government's actions, and then placing the callers in my shoes helped. I remember receiving one phone call from a veteran, who chastised me and hurled racist comments at me. He was angry. After listening to him, I asked him coolly whether he would listen to me. I asked him what he would do if the RCMP came to his house without notice and told him that his family was being forced to leave, without any explanation, and then found out later that his house had been sold without his permission. "Would you not be angry? Would you expect the government to protect you? Would you take action?" His response was, "I would be so angry that I would do something about it." My response to him was, "This is what we're doing." At the end of our conversation, the veteran said, "I support what you are doing." Placing him in my shoes helped defuse his anger and maybe better understand the experience of Japanese Canadians. Most callers agreed with me after having heard my explanation of our cause's justification and thanked me for taking the time to explain the situation. Very rarely did the caller refuse to listen to my side. These encounters suggested to me that if we were able to talk to Canadians directly, they would gain a greater understanding and awareness of the redress issue. It certainly convinced me that a strong educational program was needed if we were to change attitudes of many Canadians and even veterans.

It is important to understand why some veterans reacted negatively when they heard that Japanese Canadians were seeking redress. John Stroud, president of the Ontario branch of the Hong Kong Veterans Commemorative Association of Canada, was one of the first prisoners of war captured by the Japanese army at the Battle of Hong Kong. Just weeks after arriving in Hong Kong, Canadian troops were defeated; Stroud spent the rest of the war in a Japanese POW camp, where living conditions were infernal. In one interview, Stroud provided this gruesome account of the parasitic infestation that reigned on site: "I have witnessed people with worms coming out of their mouths like spaghetti ... Some actually choked to death."[16] The horrid treatment by the Japanese soldiers had left emotional scars on the Canadian veterans, bitter reminders of their wartime experience.

The question of loyalty towards Japan in Japanese Canadians who lived on the West Coast arose in many letters to the editor in newspapers that I read during the redress campaign. One person, who felt that the potential for a Japanese attack of the West Coast had been real, wrote, "The Canadian government had that possibility in mind, it also had in mind, 'birds of feather flock together.' Action of the Canadian government in those days was based on fear." Although

---

16   Dave McIntosh, *Hell on Earth: Aging Faster, Dying Sooner; Canadian Prisoners of the Japanese during World War II* (Whitby, ON: McGraw-Hill Ryerson, 1997), 25.

this writer acknowledged that "they suffered disrupted lives and financial losses," he wrote that Japanese Canadians "should consider themselves lucky: they were not thrown into the ocean or gas chambers. They all survived. Tens of millions more unfortunate perished in battle lines, in concentration camps, in gas chambers." He further indicated that Canadian taxpayers should not pay compensation. "It should be paid by the aggressive Japanese empire, the creator of that problem."[17] This individual didn't understand that we were Canadians and not the enemy that Canada was fighting. This type of misconception was prevalent.

In several letters reference was made to "the Kamloops Kid," who was used as an example of disloyalty by Japanese Canadians. In a July 1984 letter to the editor published in the *Globe and Mail*, John Stroud wrote, "As a prisoner of war in Hong Kong with the Canadian Forces we came in contact with an Imperial Army interpreter named Inouye Kanao [*sic*]. Kanao, born and raised in Kamloops, BC, visited Japan prior to the Second World War and volunteered his services to the Imperial Japanese Army. He was sent to Hong Kong, where Canadian prisoners of war were held. He was a vicious, cunning devil and was responsible for the deaths of many Canadian POWs."[18] He was known to the prisoners as the Kamloops Kid, or Slap Happy Joe, or Brown Pig. Another writer used the analogy "one Japanese Canadian, one Japanese Canadian traitor. Multiply this figure by 20,000 and Canada could have a monumental problem. One would be naive to believe that, in the event of Japanese forces landing on the West Coast, Japanese Canadians would not have welcomed such a force, if not with open arms, at the very least with passive acceptance."[19] I would dispute that analogy, as most Japanese Canadians at the time were also Canadians either by birth or naturalization and would not have had allegiance to a country with which they had very little or no association.

This type of stereotyping was rebutted in several letters written by

17 Dane Sobat, "Internment Compensation Opposed," *Calgary Herald*, April 11, 1984, A6, www.newspapers.com/article/calgary-herald/128620010/.

18 John R. Stroud, "The Kamloops Kid," letter to the editor, *Globe and Mail*, July 24, 1984, 6, www.proquest.com/historical-newspapers/unfair-battleground/docview/1237547195 /se-2.

19 J.C. Davies, "No Apology," letter to the editor, *Winnipeg Free Press*, October 17, 1984, archives.winnipegfreepress.com/winnipeg-free-press/1984-10-17/page-1/.

other Canadians. The best response was from a woman in Winnipeg who wrote to me, "By this logic, are we to assume that all citizens of Scandinavian origin are potential rapists and murderers because [Canadian serial killer] Clifford Olson is?" This threat of fear and sabotage was politically induced and then used as justification for the measures the government took.

Not all veterans, however, opposed an apology or compensation to Japanese Canadians. One veteran from Winnipeg, who had been a prisoner of war of the Imperial Japanese Army in Hong Kong and Japan and subjected there to brutally inhumane treatment, saw the two issues as different. In his letter he stated that "First and foremost, those Japanese Canadians were citizens of Canada, not Japan, and had nothing whatsoever to do with the cruelty and insane brutality exercised by the Japanese army. The civilian population of Japan was also subject to their brutal treatment." He also cited a comparison that revealed the racism behind the Canadian government's actions, writing that "the assets and properties of German and Italian internees were kept in custody by the wartime custodian and were returned after the war ended. However, assets, properties, and real estate rightfully owned by Japanese Canadian citizens were not returned to them." He supported an apology and also compensation for the confiscation of their belongings and concluded by commenting, "But now, better late than never."[20]

In the early stages of the redress campaign, veterans' organizations were silent on the issue of an apology and compensation for Japanese Canadians. In April 1985, one of the largest divisions of the Royal Canadian Legion broke the silence. The administrative council of the Ontario Command of the Legion, which represented about 195,000 war veterans, endorsed a formal resolution asking the federal government not to make any financial settlement with Japanese Canadians. They did this without the approval of the national body. The Ontario Command, however, technically could not act without their sanction. James Forbes, assistant provincial secretary to the Ontario Command, said that Ontario's position was that "if Japanese Canadians are awarded money, then the Japanese government should be pressed to compensate Canadian veterans who were held in concentration camps." A letter was sent on behalf of the NAJC to James

---

20 John Pople, "Better Late," letter to the editor, *Winnipeg Free Press*, November 22, 1984, archives.winnipegfreepress.com/winnipeg-free-press/1984-11-22/page-1/.

Forbes indicating our dismay at the position taken by the Ontario Command. It was pointed out that in the United States, the American Legion had adopted a position of support for Japanese Americans who had suffered a similar injustice. Copies of the US Civil Liberties Act of 1988[21] and of the NAJC's *Democracy Betrayed* were sent as information to the Ontario Command.

It is interesting to note that shortly after that announcement by the Royal Canadian Legion's Ontario branch, Ben Bianchini, president of the fifty-thousand-member Army, Navy, and Air Force Veterans in Canada, personally *endorsed* compensation for Japanese Canadians. He said from his Winnipeg base, "[Japanese Canadians] were staunch Canadians when the war broke out and had no intention of being treasonous." He agreed with the NAJC's position that actions of the Japanese military had nothing to do with the Canadian government's treatment of Canadians of Japanese origin.

Clifford Chadderton, chief executive officer of the War Amputations of Canada (or War Amps) and a patron of the Hong Kong Veterans Commemorative Association of Canada, indicated that his organizations had refrained from commenting on the claims made by Japanese Canadians despite pressure from the media and veterans. They were not taking issue with the merits of the claim. However, Chadderton took offence at a comment made by Roger Obata during a television broadcast in Toronto on January 30, 1986. On the program, Chadderton outlined the basis of the Hong Kong Veterans' claim against the Japanese government for slave labour. Roger, speaking on behalf of Japanese Canadians, commented, "We're comparing apples and oranges. Our claim to the Canadian government is as citizens of our own country, whereas, in the case of the Hong Kong veterans, they are making a claim against a country with which they were at war. I feel that it's very unfortunate that veterans, in particular, confuse the issue. They don't recognize us as Canadian citizens. They still consider us as Japanese nationals because of our features and our racial background." Roger Obata's comments were interpreted by Chadderton to mean that the NAJC was the first to make a public statement of the veterans' claim while the Hong Kong Veterans Association had deliberately remained silent on the Japanese Canadian claim. Mr. Chadderton stated, "We are in a no-win

---

21   GovTrack.us, "H.R. 442 (100th): Civil Liberties Act of 1987," text, www.govtrack.us /congress/bills/100/hr442/text.

situation. If we don't reply, then the public may feel we agree with Mr. Obata." To avoid a backlash from veterans, he recommended to the Hong Kong Veterans Association that they oppose any payments to Japanese Canadians until such time as the Japanese government honoured the claim of the Hong Kong Veterans. Chadderton sent a letter to Otto Jelinek, then minister of multiculturalism, with copies to George Hees, minister of veteran affairs, stating that "We are not opposed to the Japanese Canadian claim on the basis of merit; but rather there is a priority question involved."

One individual who crusaded against compensation for Japanese Canadians was retired Air Commodore Leonard Birchall, who had spent three and a half years in a Japanese prison camp. He was determined to stop the federal government from proceeding with plans to negotiate compensation with the NAJC. When Otto Jelinek announced in January 1986 that the government had agreed on the wording of the acknowledgment and was moving ahead with a redress proposal to cabinet, Birchall was so angered that he resigned his *membership* from the Conservative Party and dumped a forty-page personal commentary on Flora MacDonald's desk (MacDonald was the MP representing Birchall's Kingston riding). That document indicated his intention "to travel everywhere, any time, to any forum or platform I can seek out, to denounce the government action." Leonard Birchall's action received substantial media coverage and support from veterans' organizations.

In November 1986, the Army, Navy and Air Force Veterans in Canada passed a resolution at their biennial national meeting in Winnipeg "absolving the current government of responsibility for actions taken by its wartime predecessor," thereby signifying that Japanese Canadians should not be compensated. We contacted the organizers of the conference to ask what discussion had taken place on the resolution. Apparently, a multitude of resolutions had been brought to the convention floor and there was no discussion, or minimal discussion, on any resolution. The motion regarding compensation for Japanese Canadians was presented and voted upon without any discussion. I suggested that a representative from the NAJC would have been willing to present the NAJC position so that a balanced perspective could have been given. The conference organizer indicated that this would not have been possible because of time constraints. I offered to meet with the organization's executive to discuss the NAJC's redress program, but they never responded to my invitation.

In July 1988, two years later, the same organization passed another resolution in Edmonton reaffirming their opposition to compensation for Japanese Canadians. A letter to the editor in the *Calgary Herald* from George T. Campbell, president of Army, Navy and Air Force Veterans in Canada, who attended the convention, suggested that an incomplete picture emerged on the compensation issue. He indicated that a further resolution was initiated from the floor and passed unanimously; it declared that the perceived danger of a threat "could not be an excuse for depriving these Japanese Canadians of their property and possessions, certainly at less than their fair value" and called for "compensation to these internees for their losses occasioned by the dispersal of their property."[22] The media, however, failed to report on the second resolution and gave only one side of the picture.

A *Calgary Herald* editorial criticized the first resolution, which implied that any funds available for compensating internees should first be used to meet the needs of the veterans. The editorial stated, "Compensation for Japanese Canadians interned during the war has no connection with funding for the vets. If they feel short-changed, they should take it up with the government. Some BC veterans, however, recognized the red herring when they saw one. About a quarter of the delegates disassociated themselves from the resolution saying it is unfair to link the two issues together."[23]

Despite their disagreement, NAJC representatives had an amicable meeting with Clifford Chadderton and Brian Forbes, the solicitor for the War Amputations of Canada, in Ottawa on March 10, 1987. The NAJC asked for assurances from Mr. Chadderton not to oppose any action that the Canadian government might wish to take concerning Japanese Canadian redress. We had a very productive discussion and gained a clearer understanding of the veterans' direction. Mr. Chadderton indicated that their claim on behalf of the Hong Kong Veterans was made before the United Nations and did not involve the Canadian government. In his view, there was no

---

22 George T. Campbell, "Compensation Justified," letter to the editor, *Calgary Herald*, August 16, 1988, A6, www.newspapers.com/article/calgary-herald/133660126/.

23 "Veterans Miss the Point," *Calgary Herald*, July 25, 1988, 4, www.newspapers.com/article/calgary-herald/133660293/.

relation between the two claims, but rather an issue of priority. Mr. Chadderton assured us that he would not speak out against redress for Japanese Canadians, but he could not take responsibility for individual veterans or other veteran organizations expressing their views publicly.

Ann Gomer Sunahara, author of *The Politics of Racism*, responded to claims that Japanese Canadians didn't deserve compensation because of the inhumane treatment Canadian soldiers had received at the hands of the Japanese Imperial Army. She explained that the experiences of the veterans of the Battle of Hong Kong "were acts of brutality perpetrated by captors on defenceless captives." What was done to Japanese Canadians, by contrast, was "the abuse of powerless dependants by the very authority figures who were supposed to have been protecting them. Japanese Canadians were abused by their own government, the Canadian government."[24] The crimes were different; the perpetrators were different. What is common is that in both cases, the victims were Canadians.

During the course of the Japanese Canadian redress campaign, I received letters from many Canadians expressing their personal views about redress and about the treatment of Japanese Canadians during the wartime period. Letters were a way of assessing public opinion and were useful in determining how the views on redress within our country were changing.

In the period from 1984 to September 22, 1988, three-quarters of letters we received from Canadians outside our community were supportive of the NAJC efforts in seeking redress. We received many requests from interested individuals, teachers, and students for information regarding the Japanese Canadian experiences or the redress movement. Fortunately, we were able to use the NAJC document *Democracy Betrayed* as our educational tool.

One letter that we received was extremely derogatory and vicious, containing threatening comments directed at the NAJC representatives. The letter was sent shortly after our press conference in Calgary in February 1985 giving the status of negotiations with the Canadian government. The message was scrawled on a sheet of lined paper and was difficult to read. It was sent to the Japanese consulate's office in Edmonton, possibly because the media coverage emanated out

---

24 Ann Gomer Sunahara, "Vets' Ruling Illogical," letter to the editor, *Edmonton Journal*, August 7, 1988, B4, nikkeimuseum.org/www.item_detail.php?art_id=A41865.

of Calgary and with the thought that the NAJC was part of Japan's foreign office.

Unfortunately, as a public figure, the reality is that you are open to criticism and disturbing comments. The following words are hateful and difficult to read, so feel free to ignore this section.

> You don't deserve money. You Japs are slave, servant. You no good. Your no fuckin good. Jap your sick. The prime minister has no time for you Pigs. The Jap woman that spoke on T.V. will get it soon.

> The Jap are watch all the time. So get out of the way. A group of men are watching all Japs in the city. Old Jap must be shot. Watch your step all the time. TNT under your hood. TNT inside the seat. TNT muffler. TNT trunk in spare tire under seat. There will be a truck in city ready for Jap women silencer rope.

Although some may have considered this letter a prank, I considered it the work of a sick mind expressing hostility and racism towards Japanese Canadians and using threats in an attempt to discourage the NAJC from pursuing redress. Unsurprisingly, by sending the letter to the Japanese consulate, the writer did not differentiate between the people of Japan and Canadians of Japanese ancestry.

I first heard about the letter when I received a concerned call from the Consul General of Japan in Edmonton. He called specifically to tell me about the letter and described the content of the disturbing note to me. The Consul General, whose role is to maintain amicable relations with Canada, asked whether the NAJC would consider abandoning the redress issue. He implied that the redress movement would have negative effects on Canada's present relationship with Japan. I explained that redress was a Canadian issue and that we were dealing with our own government. So often, this misunderstanding between being Japanese and being a Canadian of Japanese ancestry resulted in the misconception that redress had something to do with Japan. I had to bluntly tell the Consul General that the NAJC could not withdraw but would continue to pursue redress from the Canadian government, following our mandate from the Japanese Canadian community.

CHAPTER 8

False Hopes

Acknowledgment of an imperfect past is a prerequisite for a future in which people live together in mutual respect, and self-righteous racism does not take us by surprise again.

—BRUCE McLEOD
former Moderator of the United Church of Canada (1988)

The arrival of the third Conservative minister on the redress scene in June 1986 raised hopes and optimism in the Japanese Canadian community. The Honourable David Crombie, formerly the minister of Indian Affairs and Northern Development, had developed a positive relationship with Indigenous groups. As Indian affairs minister, Crombie had been bestowed the honorary title of Chief Soaring Eagle by Canadian Indigenous business leaders. The NAJC representatives from Toronto sang high praises for Crombie's appointment because, as a former mayor of Toronto, he was well respected and loved. Our thoughts were that the prime minister regarded Crombie as a top-notch negotiator who would be able to handle the touchy redress file.

In a December 1986 interview, Dan Turner of the *Ottawa Citizen* asked Crombie how he planned to handle the issue of Japanese Canadian redress that had flattened his two predecessors in the portfolio. Crombie indicated that he had insisted that he would be allowed to fall back from the rush and deal with the issue in his own way, at his own pace, before agreeing to take on the job. He announced at the beginning that "everything is on the table and nothing is on the table." Furthermore, Crombie indicated that he "hope[d] to take the issue to Mulroney before Christmas, and present him with both a recommended process and what he [saw] as the basic elements that will be needed for a successful solution."[1]

But Crombie's wishy-washy attitude became more evident as time went on. He claimed that he didn't rule out the idea of a monetary settlement based on proven loss of property, nor did he say it was the appropriate way of settling the issue. He was noncommittal despite saying he was looking for "not just a solution, but a solution that heals, a just and fair settlement that both heals the wounds in the community and is seen as just and fair by the rest of the Canadian community."[2] All this would require a miracle. He was dealing with a diversified and assimilated community, once divided over the question of compensation but much less so after the results of the national survey.

Following Crombie's appointment, I requested an initial meeting with him for August 6, 1986, through his chief of staff, Ron Doering. Doering responded that Crombie would be unable to meet until he was fully briefed, but that the Japanese Canadian redress matter was top priority with him. Because of the failure by the two previous ministers, Doering intimated that Crombie would be taking a completely different approach.

Finally, on October 4, 1986, the first meeting with Crombie and Doering was held in a private upstairs room at a quaint downtown Toronto restaurant just off Yonge Street. We had an informal open exchange of views on all aspects of the NAJC redress program. Crombie in his amiable manner informed Roger Obata, Roy Miki, and me that he would deal personally with redress negotiation in a serious effort to reach a mutually acceptable settlement. Once again, he said he was "prepared to take the time required to arrive at a solution that is fair and just." Crombie indicated that he wanted to fully immerse himself in the history and read as much material by Ken Adachi, Joy Kogawa, and Muriel Kitagawa on the Japanese Canadian experience as he could before he began to put the pieces of the redress package together. His interest in the subject was encouraging. It was such a

---

1   Dan Turner, "Crombie May Help Attain Japanese-Canadian Settlement," *Ottawa Citizen*, December 9, 1986, A9, www.newspapers.com/article/the-ottawa-citizen/133552565/.

2   Ibid.

contrast to how Jelinek had approached the issue. To ensure the flow of accurate information, Crombie suggested that the NAJC maintain a direct communication link with him on an ongoing basis. My initial impression was that he was willing to listen and that whatever he was going to do would be different from what we'd gone through to this point.

In our press release following the meeting, we stated that the NAJC was pleased by Crombie's assurances that he recognized the NAJC as the only legitimate organization representing the Japanese Canadian community. But then we received a follow-up letter from Doering stating that it was misleading to suggest this. He stated, "The Minister does not want to leave the impression that he has prejudged that there are no other legitimate organizations with an interest in this matter." We began to have suspicions about what message he was conveying. Was he being nice to get our attention, or did he have other motives he wasn't willing to share? Or, after thinking about it, did the minister realize that such a commitment would restrict him from considering other ideas that could arise out of his consultation meetings?

Crombie did indicate that he wanted to listen to other ethnic community organizations and to individual Japanese Canadians to gather what he called "a wide spectrum of views," but he intended to achieve a solution that would be acceptable to the NAJC. We did not resist Crombie's intent to meet with other people in the Japanese Canadian community, although we had reacted against such actions with the two previous ministers. The NAJC reminded Crombie that in any diverse community, there were bound to be diverse views, and reiterated that he had to deal with the elected representatives of the community for the final resolution. The analogy that I used was that other nations would not bypass the Canadian government on the grounds that there were Canadians who did not support government policy. Subsequent to the meeting with NAJC representatives, Crombie met with George Imai as well as with individuals such as Thomas Shoyama, former deputy minister of finance, Ken Adachi, author of *The Enemy That Never Was,* Joy Kogawa, author of the 1981 classic novel *Obasan,* and Raymond Moriyama, the renowned Japanese Canadian architect.

Although there was a lull in our communications with Crombie, the NAJC patiently gave him time, and he continued his fact-finding mission on what would be appropriate redress. Then in January 1987, Crombie met with the Greater Vancouver Japanese Canadian Citizens' Association, where he stated that he would be recommending a redress proposal to Cabinet by late February. When questioned about compensation to individuals, he was vague and sidestepped the issue.

The NAJC strategy committee met with Crombie and Doering on February 7, 1987, in Toronto. He indicated that he would be taking a proposal to Cabinet by mid-March and hoped that a decision would be reached by Cabinet by the end of March before moving on to phase two. "Phase two," according to Crombie, would be a period of discussions on the government's decision.

At this meeting, Crombie became irritated as we pursued the principle underlying individual compensation, and he began to talk about other people who suffered as a result of the war. In his mind, he had already ruled out individual compensation. In a letter dated February 12, 1987, we reminded Crombie that the NAJC was the legitimate organization to deal with for discussions and negotiations with the government and demanded that a meeting take place prior to any public announcement of Cabinet's decision. We wanted to avoid any perception that the government was imposing unilateral action. We also wanted assurances that the acknowledgment, civil-rights issues, and compensation would be kept as one package.

Concerned with Crombie's inaction, the NAJC representatives went to Ottawa in March 1987 to establish contacts with government officials and other groups. Through NAJC representative Don Rosenbloom, we were able to arrange a meeting with the Honourable John Fraser, Speaker of the House, whom we knew would be sympathetic to the Japanese Canadian experience. This was based on Don's knowledge that during the war, when Fraser was a young boy, his father had told him that what the government was doing to Japanese Canadians was not right. We had productive meetings with Fraser, who indicated that he would informally talk to other politicians in the House and to staffers supportive of the NAJC's efforts. He had his staff arrange a meeting for us with the Honourable Don Mazankowski, the deputy prime minister, and offered his staff to assist us if needed. This encouragement from the Speaker of the House was certainly heartwarming and gave us optimism.

Meeting with the deputy prime minister meant that we were in the company of some of the government's power influencers.

Art with the Honourable John Fraser, 1988
PHOTO: Gordon King

Mazankowski graciously listened to our concerns about the lack of action and the importance of the NAJC having support for a negotiated agreement. He said very little, asked some questions, and the meeting ended without an indication of where he stood on the matter. I found out later that Vera Holiad, advisor to Mazankowski, would play a significant role in making redress happen.

Finally, on March 27, 1987, I received a letter from Crombie outlining the government's response to the redress claim. The government of Canada, he said, was willing to give an official acknowledgment in the House of Commons and a commitment towards legislative measures to prevent the recurrence of injustices similar to the ones inflicted upon Canadians of Japanese ancestry. With regard to compensation for those Japanese Canadians directly affected, Crombie had reviewed various forms of individual compensation but was not comfortable with any approach. He rejected the lump sum per capita payment to individuals recommended in the NAJC proposal because "both the amount and the individual entitlement to such payments would be arbitrarily established [and] unconnected to either the actual loss or established need." We perceived that it would be difficult to relate the amount to "actual losses" and therefore we felt that the amount specified by the NAJC was a "symbolic gesture" to reflect the seriousness of the government's actions. In the end, Crombie proposed the establishment of a $12 million community foundation, under the banner of the NAJC, representing all Japanese Canadian communities. In a follow-up telephone conference with Crombie and the NAJC strategy team, he absolutely rejected the notion of individual compensation.

The NAJC's position that individual compensation had to be considered in the government's offer received support in the *Globe and Mail*'s editorial of November 19, 1985, titled "Redress on Hold." Because the government's final offer of a $6 million to $10 million educational foundation resulted in an impasse with the NAJC, the editorial stated that "The only decent outcome would be a direct compensation to individuals who suffered losses. The excuse that these are difficult to calculate four decades after the event is now evaporating with the newly gained access to 40-year-old government records and the engagement ... of the accounting firm Price Water-house Associates to study the losses."[3]

Surely, the clamour that arose for the prime minister to show some leadership on this issue after three of his ministers had failed also had some impact on Mr. Mulroney's increased investment of time and people in 1988. "Now that three ministers have stumbled," the *Toronto Star*'s editorial of May 21, 1987, contended, "it's up to the prime minister himself to step in and resolve this dispute before it causes further embarrassment for Canada."[4]

In a last-ditch effort to have the negotiation process reinstated, the NAJC strategy committee flew to Ottawa to meet with Crombie at his office on May 9. However, Crombie repeatedly insisted that the $12 million foundation was the final offer. When questioned how the government had determined the figure of $12 million, he flippantly replied, "We took the offer that Murta made and we doubled the amount." When a heated discussion ensued over the topic of indi-vidual compensation, Crombie became incensed, stating that other

3   "Redress on Hold," *Globe and Mail*, November 19, 1985, A6, www.proquest.com/historical
     -newspapers/redress-on-hold/docview/1222381574/se-2.

4   "The Continuing Blot," *Toronto Star*, May 21, 1987, A24, www.proquest.com/newspapers
     /continuing-blot/docview/435566931/se-2.

people had also suffered because of the war and they were as deserv-
ing as Japanese Canadians. He suggested that if the NAJC wanted
to divide the $12 million among the victims, he had no difficulty
with that. This would have resulted in a mere $850 for the fourteen
thousand surviving victims.

The NAJC council met in Vancouver from May 16 to 18, 1987,
and formally rejected Crombie's offer. At the NAJC press conference
on May 17, the letter from Crombie outlining the government's offer
and the letter of response from the NAJC were both released. The
NAJC's response to Crombie outlined his government's failure to
recognize the basic elements of the NAJC's submissions over the past
two and a half years, particularly the demand for individual compensation and a reasonable settlement:

> This organization has a commitment to Japanese Canadians to
> negotiate a redress settlement that includes individual compen-
> sation as a fundamental component. We maintain our position
> that a just settlement must acknowledge each affected person
> as an individual, not merely as a member of an ethnic group.
> Your proposal fails to acknowledge that individuals suffered
> the injustices, some 14,000 who are still alive. We are shocked
> to learn that after considering this issue for nine months, and
> being aware of the enormity of the losses involved, you could
> recommend to the government that an amount in the range of
> $12 million could represent a fair and just settlement of our
> claim. A settlement offer that amounts to approximately $50 per
> affected individual in 1945 dollars belittles the significance of
> the issue. You, like the Ministers before you, have failed to fulfill
> the promise made by Mr. Mulroney in May 1984, to compensate
> Japanese Canadians.

From the beginning, Crombie had stated that his objective was a
"fair and just" settlement. He underscored that his approach would
be different from that of his predecessors, but in the end the results
were the same. He bided his time and was given the opportunity to
study the issue thoroughly and talk to as many people as possible to
get ideas. Did Crombie actually intend to give serious consideration
to our request for individual compensation? As previously stated,
Crombie ruled out individual compensation on the grounds that

"both the amount of and the individual entitlement to such payments would be arbitrarily established, unconnected to either actual loss or established need." However, losses incurred by the internment had been estimated at $443 million in 1986 dollars by the Price Waterhouse study. Crombie said that a figure of $400 million was "just beyond question. It's not possible for me to make any recommendation to the government anywhere near those figures." If he was truly making a serious attempt to find a solution, there should have been some room to come closer to that figure than the $12 million that he offered.

Many times, Crombie told us that he had monetary limitations. He used analogies such as "the size of the footprint" to describe the amount of money available for redress or talked about "the length of his leash" to explain the amount of flexibility he had. However, we knew that one of the strengths that Crombie had as the multiculturalism minister was that he was part of the inner Cabinet, where he had indubitable influence – if he chose to use it.

Talks with Crombie degenerated into frustrating stalemates. On one particular occasion, a heated discussion between Roy Miki and Crombie erupted into a furious shouting match. I attempted to intervene, ending the meeting. Despite the disappointing progress with Crombie, we decided to continue to press for further discussions and to keep the dialogue open. On July 11, 1987, members of the NAJC strategy committee met in Winnipeg with Crombie and Doering to see if we could find some common ground in which to resolve the redress issue. The strategy team again found Crombie inflexible, basically telling us to "take it or leave it." We pressed for further dialogue on individual compensation, and he again suggested that we take the $12 million and divide it among the individual claimants. Audrey Kobayashi, member of the our strategy team, remembers thinking, "No, this is never going to happen. That was the lowest point. I was so angry and I don't ever remember being so angry, but I think that what I felt at the time was much more determination to fight." Roger Obata, another member, commented, "It looked almost hopeless, but I still felt that if the issue was brought before the Canadian public and if they were aware of what was involved that we would receive a better settlement than what he was offering." I felt some disillusionment at the time, but the situation also forced us to seriously re-examine our strategy.

One of our strengths was the simple power of saying no. We had said no to several proposals put forward by previous ministers that did not reflect adequate compensation for the gross injustices suffered by Japanese Canadians. The government used scare tactics to try to divide our community while pressuring us to abandon our position, especially on individual compensation. Each time we rejected the government's proposal, our movement gained strength. We said no to what David Crombie claimed was the government's final offer. He responded that by rejecting his proposal, the community would get nothing from the government and that the NAJC would be criticized. But unless the principle of individual compensation, which was the cornerstone of the redress proposal, was met, we had no alternative but to reject his final offer.

Gordon Hirabayashi was a nisei living in Washington State when the United States declared war on Japan. When the government issued curfew and exclusion orders on Japanese Americans, Gordon felt that it was an unconstitutional and racially motivated legislation. He planned to deliberately disobey the laws, and when the orders came he turned himself in to the FBI with the intent of creating a test case against the government's right to incarcerate Japanese Americans without due process. He lost the case and was sentenced to prison. In 1987, lawyers appealed his original sentence and courts ruled in his favour. Gordon's case has elevated him to a prominent place in civil rights history, and he was posthumously awarded the Presidential Medal of Freedom, highest civilian award in the US, by President Obama in 2012, the year of his death.

I credit Gordon, a member of the National Council, for his conviction that the principle of individual compensation must be the cornerstone for any meaningful and just resolution with any government, and for his persistence in pursuing that goal. With his example, it became for me a no-brainer to refuse Crombie's "final" proposal. I first met Gordon in 1983, just when the redress campaign was getting underway. He had moved to Canada from the United States in 1959 to join the University of Alberta as a sociology professor. In Edmonton, he was active with the local Japanese Canadian community organization and became one of the representatives to the NAJC's National Council during redress discussions. With his personal experiences and his strong belief in civil rights, I felt that

Gordon brought forth compelling arguments for recognizing the principle and necessity of individual compensation.

I responded to Crombie that the NAJC would not accept the government's final offer and made him aware that the US bill's adoption was imminent. If we were to accept the $12 million community fund, our decision certainly would come back to haunt us. I said to Crombie, "I have to live in the Japanese Canadian community. I would not want to be the one responsible for selling out the community. I would rather walk away from the table than to be coerced into thinking that we can sell this offer to Japanese Canadians." Crombie indicated that his sources in Washington didn't think the American Bill would receive acceptance and that we would have lost an opportunity. I was willing to take my chances that another opportunity would arise.

PERSONAL LETTERS FROM INTERNEES[5]

After negotiations with David Crombie came to an abrupt halt in July 1987, the NAJC chapters orchestrated a Japanese Canadian letter-writing campaign to Crombie and his ministry so that they could hear, directly from the victims, the narrative of their horrifying experiences and sad outcomes. These letters were intended to revive the need for closure on the part of government. The letters were dispatched to the minister of multiculturalism, the prime minister, and other politicians who might influence the government to renew the negotiation process. Letters were often forwarded to the NAJC office as well.

As I read through the letters, I was moved by the vivid description of each internee's experiences and the traumatic and devastating effect that the internment had on their lives. I would like to share here excerpts from their unique and honest recollections.

---

5   I have avoided using names in these excerpts. All the letters are in the National Association of Japanese Canadians fonds at UBC under the file "NAJC Letter Writing Campaign (1988, May–Dec), 1987," no. RBSC-ARC-1791-09-04. See University of British Columbia Library Rare Books and Special Collections, "Finding Aid – National Association of Japanese Canadians fonds (RBSC-ARC-1791)," July 2018, p. 29, rbscarchives.library.ubc .ca/downloads/national-association-of-japanese-canadians-fonds.pdf.

A woman from Manitoba related her story in a letter to the Honourable David Crombie after meeting him at a dinner.

I have always been aware of a sense of deprivation when admiring friends' family treasures passed on from the previous generation, rich in tradition and sentiment, if not in monetary value. Because Japanese Canadian families could not believe their treatment at the hands of their own government was anything but a mistake, soon to be rectified, all their treasures and best possessions were left behind, my own family's being secreted in the attic. Of course, with confiscation everything was lost to their owners.

My grandfather owned several large rooming houses in Vancouver and a flourishing seed farm in the Fraser Valley. He worked hard and expected no less from his family. We weren't allowed to go in the house after school. We had to throw our books in through the window and rush out to the fields, my mother would recall many years later.

After half a century of hard work, doing little other than working, Grandfather waited to hear what he would be awarded in compensation for the confiscation of his life's work.[6] *Trying to be brutally realistic, the very least he might receive, he reasoned, was $25,000. Notification arrived that he had been awarded $2,500.00, mercifully just months after his decease. He would have been truly heartbroken at the news.*

The mother was a young widow and her losses meant years of slaving in the sewing factory ghetto to bring up her young family at considerable cost to her health and psyche, for she felt racial discrimination, intensified by harsh conditions at

---

6   Author's note: Perhaps in reference to the compensations afforded by the Bird Commission, a Royal Commission established in April 1947 and a forerunner to redress efforts.

work. How well I remember her staying up late every Friday night counting up her week's wages – hundreds of pockets sewn at one half-cent apiece and collars at 2 cents each – thousands of tickets to be glued onto sheets of paper and their meagre value tabulated weekly.

There is much to relate of the hardships endured by the internees – the cattle-barn concentration camp, the disrupted and inferior schooling, the vermin-infested destinations which meant being trucked from ghost town to ghost town, the leaky, uninsulated three-room shacks shared by two families, the uninformed separation of family members, the frightening uncertainty of final disposition ...

An eighty-six-year-old issei widow who was naturalized as a Canadian citizen in the early 1900s wrote about her reaction to Crombie's offer of $12 million to the Japanese Canadian community:

Twelve million dollars in 1987 money is a laughable amount. It is insufficient to establish a single, decent old-age care facility that is urgently required in several parts of the country. After the war, many older people like my husband were too old to re-establish themselves and we had to rely on our sons and daughters to help us enjoy a reasonable standard of living. If we hadn't lost everything, which I conservatively estimate to have been worth at least $45,000–$50,000 in 1942, the situation would have been reversed because the two businesses we operated would now have been at least ten times as large and profitable. My family would have been able to inherit and carry on. In spite of this, I am not requesting or expecting the government to fully compensate me for the losses. What I am outraged about is the total disregard for the losses and the lack of compensation to the individual.

A gentleman from Vancouver Island revealed the tragedy that resulted from the actions of the government and wrote the following in his letter to Crombie:

My father was a naturalized Canadian citizen who forfeited his inheritance to extensive properties in Japan when he left to start a new life in Canada. In 1940, after more than 20 years of saving, my parents moved from Prince Rupert to Salt Spring Island, taking my younger sister and brother. There, they built a house and cleared land, hoping to do some market gardening in order to support themselves in their remaining years. After investing two years of hard work and their entire savings in this venture, the Canadian government gave them $500 for their entire estate and evacuated them to Slocan, BC, for two years. Subsequently, my sister, a missionary in the Anglican Church, and I managed to get them relocated to Toronto. My father was a proud and honourable man who was, thanks to the Canadian government, now totally dependent on his children. Rather than being a burden on us, my father took his own life.

This letter sent by a woman from Toronto to David Crombie in June 1987 describes the effect that the internment had on her parents:

My parents and my sister were uprooted from Vancouver Island on May 3, 1942, and sent to Hastings Park and then to Greenwood, Midway, and Grand Forks, where I was born. Being a child raised in ghost towns and a log cabin in the mountains, I feel I was directly affected as a result of the internment suffered by my family. During my early years, I experienced medical problems due to malnutrition, inadequate housing, and conditions of poverty brought on by the internment of peoples whose only "crime" was being of Japanese origin. Along with the indignity of being branded an enemy in one's own country, temporary housing in cattle stalls, losing possessions, income, and other intangible losses, my mother also lost her citizenship, although she was born in Prince Rupert, BC. We did not realize this until she tried to go for a visit to Japan in the 1960s and was advised that she should apply for Canadian citizenship as she would not be allowed to return to Canada. My father returned to Japan immediately after retirement, after 50 years of working in and for Canada. He never trusted the Canadian government again as a result of his wartime and postwar experiences and was totally disillusioned with his choice of a new land of opportunity that he thought Canada would be. He died a bitter old man in Japan, a place that must have seemed somewhat foreign to him after living his entire life in Canada. My mother died some years ago and now there is only my sister and myself left.

A sansei from Richmond, although not directly affected by the internment, supported individual compensation for the victims. In a letter to Mr. Crombie, she wrote:

Although it can be argued that some people lost their properties and others didn't, or some people lost more than others, or some didn't lose any property, as some were only children and didn't lose any property, I'll tell you what they did lose: 7 years of their youth or 7 years in the prime of their lives, in the case of adults, who lost everything in their 40s and 50s, too late to get financially re-established once again.

My own parents were 11 and 15 at the time. Mother worked the sugar beet fields of Alberta along with the rest of the family to make their annual quota. At harvest time they were often cheated in their due payment. She had to clean and cook for her family of 6 because her mother had been stranded in Japan when the war broke out. She was 11. In 1946 her family opted to go to Japan as repatriates for practical reasons. As a single parent with 5 kids to care for, my grandfather wanted to join my grandmother in Japan because she could not re-enter Canada. Once there, the Japanese were not kind to my mother and siblings, as they were regarded as "Canadians." Rather than finish a traumatic school year, she went to work for the American army at age 16. In 1950, at 20, she made her long journey back to Vancouver via San Francisco, alone. She was the first of her family to return to the BC coast. It was a very lonely existence, no family or friends; she was a child when she left Vancouver and now had to acquaint herself all over again. She worked at three jobs, saved enough money to send for her sisters and brothers, one by one, then her parents, until all were back in Vancouver. Then she hit middle age.

My father went up to grade 9 at Point Grey High in Vancouver. He lost both parents within 6 months of each other to TB and cancer. Then they were ordered to evacuate. He was 15 and had a sister, 13, and a brother, 10, to take care of. They went to stay with a kind family who took them to Greenwood, BC, for the duration of the internment. My father volunteered to go to road camp with the menfolk. His request was granted. He was 15; minimum age for road camp was 16. As a result of his life experience, his personal self-esteem was so low he worked for minimum wage until he was in his mid-40s. For over 20 years, he couldn't aspire to a better-paying job. Things are better now, but in my childhood in the 1950s and '60s we were so poor.

My maternal grandfather had a thriving hotel business on Hastings Street in 1942 that he had recently renovated – new wallpaper and paint, beds linens, and other items. The renovations cost more than what he paid for the business, which was almost paid up. He was 48 years old and had been in Canada for 29 years.

When the order to move came, he obediently and hastily placed all his personal effects in one room and locked the door. He followed that order to the letter. When they left, he and his 5 children carried only a small suitcase each, were given $2.00, and their effects were not documented.

His son did not go with the rest of the family to Japan. He was Canadian and wanted to stay in Canada. He was arrested for being Japanese and being in Vancouver in November 1948. When my mother came back in 1950, she had a hard time finding him. He served one year of hard labour and within a week was picked up again. The reason was his "criminal record." He was charged with vagrancy. He was 19. No relatives, no friends, no money, no place to stay, no one willing to give him a job because he was "Japanese." Back into jail. This happened so many times. Whenever he was out, he was relentlessly pursued by some officer who got him fired from every menial job he could find. Sounds like Les Misérables, doesn't it? Finally, he cracked up and was institutionalized.

In one of his better moments, he told my mother that he felt he'd been born in jail. The rest of the story is too painful to tell. He is still alive. I'll always remember him composing poems, singing every song by heart he heard once on the radio. Boy could he sing! He had high aspirations to be in show business. His future was in Canada. That he even dared to express his dreams and paid dearly with his life must not be forgotten. His treatment by the racist, insensitive, and opportunistic persons, especially after WW II, have resulted in untold suffering that continues to this day. His was an entire life wasted. Is this not dearer than the loss of real property?

An issei from Vancouver, a Japanese national at the time of the war, tells of his experiences in his letter of May 25, 1987, to David Crombie:

I am an issei Japanese Canadian, now 86 years of age. I came to Canada in 1926. My wife was born in Steveston, BC, never having seen Japan. During those times when the war broke out, many of us were not highly educated, so we had to work physically hard to get where we were able to have a house and furniture. Many, many years of physical, sweating and exhausting long hours of lifting heavy logs in the lumber mills I had done, and suddenly, just like that, with no explanation, I was taken away and put in jail!

While I was in jail, I found out Pearl Harbor had been bombed and the Japanese were being put in jail. We were shipped to the PNE [Pacific National Exhibition grounds in Hastings Park, Vancouver] and eventually to Slocan City. I worked on the railway building in Jasper and many of us became very sick with dysentery because we were not fed properly.

During this time my house and belongings were sold after they had promised to look after everything for us and we would be given our house back.

It took many, many years to recuperate after that. My kids grew up with almost nothing. It was a struggle to put food on the table. No one would hire me as a Japanese to work after the war, so eventually, I started my own business.

After so many years of silence but always remembering the helplessness of having no rights to do anything, [it] was so humiliating and degrading, for most of us, we tried to block that past out.

These personal letters, through their many unique stories, reveal the painful private feelings of suffering, hardships, and loss that Japanese Canadians endured, as does their plea to the minister, other politicians, and government officials for the relevance of redress – that it would give closure to this dark chapter in their lives and restore their dignity. Their suffering was immeasurable, and yet the government refused to acknowledge the gross miscarriage of justice inflicted upon these Canadian citizens.

With doors closed to further negotiations, we wrote a letter to the prime minister requesting his personal intervention, as well as a meeting with the NAJC for frank discussion on possible strategies for reaching a mutually agreeable settlement. The government and Crombie had steadfastly refused to move from the "community fund" position offered by the previous ministers. My letter to the prime minister stated, "We must question the political will of a Government that would tell us that if we do not accept a unilateral offer, the discussions are over. It has always been our position that a meaningful solution can be achieved only through a negotiated settlement. We have stated publicly that our position is flexible, but Crombie's position leaves no room for the process of negotiations."

I further reminded the prime minister that the NAJC had received overwhelming editorial and public support and that redress was viewed as an issue of fundamental justice. We pointed out that in the United States there was legislation before both Houses that would provide the sum of US$20,000 to all surviving Japanese Americans who had been incarcerated, plus a $5 million educational fund. However, no response to our request was received, so a telex was sent to the prime minister's office. His office finally indicated that the prime minister was waiting for Crombie's report before making a decision.

At long last, on September 17, 1987, the House of Representatives in the US Congress passed a redress bill, the Civil Liberties Act of 1988, acknowledging the past injustices and approving an apology and reparations for the forced internment of Japanese Americans during World War II in commemoration of the bicentennial of the American Constitution. (The bill would be signed into law by President Reagan on August 10, 1988.) The NAJC sent a telegram to Prime Minister Brian Mulroney, reminding him that Canadians of Japanese ancestry had been treated more harshly than their American counterparts – Japanese Americans had not been dispossessed in the same way Japanese Canadians had been and were allowed to return to the coast in 1944, compared to 1949 for Japanese Canadians – and urging the Canadian government to seriously reconsider opening negotiations with the NAJC. Still, the prime minister refused to meet with us.

In the spring of 1987, shortly after Crombie had issued the government's position and prior to our final meeting with Crombie, representatives from the Canadian Ethnocultural Council (CEC) had a meeting with Prime Minister Mulroney to discuss multicultural concerns. Andrew Cardoza, executive director of the CEC at the time, had a consultation meeting at Crombie's office prior to the meeting with the prime minister to determine the agenda and the topics for discussion. Andrew suggested several issues, including Japanese Canadian redress, and was strongly counselled by Crombie's advisors not to raise either the redress issue or the controversial Meech Lake Accord. Andrew felt that Crombie wanted the meeting to "look good," showing the prime minister that he had control of the interest groups. The CEC executive met and decided that as a matter of principle, redress was a priority for the Japanese Canadian community; they would raise it regardless of whether it would go well or not. Redress became the last item on the agenda.

Andrew Cardoza vividly recalls that part of the meeting. He said that the prime minister started off sanctimoniously and talked about how he had first raised the redress issue in the House, how Trudeau had not dealt with it, that it was the last question he had asked Trudeau, and how significant that was. During the conversation, Andrew recalls Mulroney saying, "Well, Mr. [Art] Miki now changes his mind. At the beginning he was not interested in individual compensation, now he wants individual compensation." Then he took off his small reading glasses and threw them on the desk. "Mr. Miki has changed his mind." He threw his glasses again on the desk. Andrew remembers looking at the glasses and thinking, "Boy, I wonder if he has a spare available." Over the course of the meeting, he threw down his glasses two or three times when showing his indignation at someone else. He was pretty upset about redress. He gave the impression that the NAJC and I were either pushing him too far or taking him for a ride. But the main thing that Andrew recalls was that Mulroney was upset because the NAJC had decided to press for individual compensation, and had we not done that, the matter would have been settled far sooner. It is true that the NAJC had not raise the issue of individual compensation because we feared a backlash from the general population, that is, until the internment experiences had been more publicized.

The main point that the CEC representatives tried to make at the meeting was that the NAJC was the legitimate representative of the Japanese Canadian community, and that they hoped that negotiations would continue with us. Mulroney said that discussions would be ongoing. He handled the meeting himself and said that he was willing to give an acknowledgment or apology in the House of Commons and a community fund. That is what they were prepared to do.

Unable to arrange a meeting with the prime minister, the NAJC strategy team began to explore alternatives. We looked into the possibility of hiring political consultants from Ottawa to identify key people in government to contact about the redress issue and to help determine the potential for a reversal of the government's present position. Included in the plan was the establishment of a National Coalition for Japanese Canadian Redress, inviting individual Canadians and organizations who represent mainstream Canada to express their support for a negotiated settlement and to make redress a Canadian human-rights issue. We also began to inquire into the possibility of taking legal action against the government of Canada.

The latter option was quickly discarded when we discovered the horrendous price of such a venture. One Vancouver law firm told us it would cost half a million dollars just to launch a suit against the government; of course, there was no guarantee that we would be successful at the end of this exorbitantly long and expensive road.

To our surprise, in August 1986 the prime minister appointed Conservative journalist Dalton Camp as senior advisor to the Cabinet. I personally believed that the decision for a redress settlement lay within the prime minister's office. A first meeting with the prime minister's office staff was established in the spring of 1987 with the influence of Speaker of the House John Fraser's staff. Prior to the meeting, I was contacted by Andy Stack, Dalton Camp's assistant, to supply him with information regarding the progress of the Japanese American reparations and the document on the wartime relocation,

Personal Justice Denied.[7] We met with Sharon Wolfe, our contact at the PMO during Crombie's term, Denise Cole, and Andy Stack. After we presented the rationale for seeking individual compensation, Wolfe reacted strongly against the idea and tried to refute our arguments. It was obvious that Wolfe, who did most of the talking, was not sympathetic and had strong personal views against individual compensation. Also, we had the opportunity to meet with Dalton Camp. Although he said very little, I thought that we had his ear as we explained how the government had terminated the negotiation process. I sensed by the tone of the meeting that Dalton Camp had an intuitive personality and showed sympathy for our concerns. We were not sure what impact this meeting would have. It's possible that Camp's previous articles may have influenced Prime Minister Mulroney and the eventual outcome of our efforts.

Alan Redway, Conservative MP and Cabinet minister from Toronto, spoke in the House on several occasions expressing his desire to see the redress issue resolved. During one of their visits to Ottawa, the strategy team members met with him to lobby for his support. As a member of the Standing Committee on Multiculturalism, he heard several presentations from other ethnic groups as well as from the NAJC and from individuals on the redress question. Redway remained in contact with Roger Obata and me throughout the campaign and had compassion for the community.

In the early part of 1988, I met Redway at a banquet in Toronto where the prime minister of Japan was being hosted by our prime minister. David Crombie had abandoned further talks with the NAJC, and so I asked Alan Redway what the government might do if the American Bill was passed. He said to me, "Our caucus is concerned that if that happened, they would have to change their present position." He meant that the government would have to rethink David Crombie's proposal of a community fund and consider the possibility of individual compensation (which was included in the

---

7   United States' Commission on Wartime Relocation and Internment of Civilians, *Personal Justice Denied: Report of the Commission on Wartime Relocation and Internment of Civilians* (Washington, DC, and San Francisco: Civil Liberties Public Education Fund; Seattle and London: University of Washington Press, [1997] 2012). Online: U.S. National Archives and Records Administration, "Justice Denied: Personal Justice Denied," www.archives. gov/research/japanese-americans/justice-denied.

American bill). His response gave us a sliver of hope that the issue of individual compensation might be resurrected.

In March 1988, the Honourable Gerry Weiner was appointed the minister of multiculturalism, replacing Crombie, who had failed to resolve the Japanese Canadian redress issue. Weiner became the fourth minister of multiculturalism in the Conservative's four years in power to handle the redress issue.

There was no optimism this time.

We didn't expect much to be different after fruitless encounters with Crombie. However, we had begun to mobilize the coalition, and support for Japanese Canadian redress was escalating.

Dennison Moore, Weiner's chief of staff, stated that the difficulty in moving the issue had been because of opposition from the PMO, especially from the bureaucracy: Derek Burney, chief of staff, and Denise Cole, who was not supportive of individual compensation. Somehow, the issue did not appear on the Planning and Priorities meeting agenda, and when the prime minister realized what was happening, he had asked Mazankowski and Wilson to look into it so they could get the issue moving. In May 1988, there was a change in the PMO when Vera Holiad was appointed senior advisor by Don Mazankowski and took over the redress file. George Corne, president of the CEC, suggested that I meet with her. So I requested a meeting with Holiad and sent her copies of *Democracy Betrayed* and Roy Miki and Cassandra Kobayashi's *Justice in Our Time.*[8] Surprisingly, she quickly responded to my request; she and I had a meeting to review the redress's progress to date and discuss the impasse we had reached with Crombie. She appeared interested and sensitive to our concerns, willing to listen rather than simply to react. Holiad's accepting attitude was refreshing, and I felt that we were finally making inroads into the PMO.

---

8   Roy Miki and Cassandra Kobayashi, *Justice in Our Time: The Japanese Canadian Redress Settlement* (Vancouver: Talonbooks; Winnipeg: National Association of Japanese Canadians, 1991).

CHAPTER 9

The Last Hope

What would finally ease the bitter memories and deep hurts that simmer inside of me is for the government in Ottawa to take the high road in producing a redress settlement. It should not satisfy Japanese Canadians but also assure all Canadians that, despite temporary aberrations, our country guarantees that the rights and privileges of citizenship cannot be taken away, for whatever reason.

—FRANK MORITSUGU
"The Japanese Expulsion," *Winnipeg Free Press*, August 2, 1987

After negotiations were terminated in July 1987 at the final meeting with David Crombie, the NAJC strategy committee met in Vancouver with its legal advisors and decided that a new direction was necessary. Up to now it had been the Japanese Canadian community represented by the NAJC against the government. In many ways the NAJC was at a disadvantage. Whereas the government had readily available legal advice, full-time staff, and communications personnel, the members of the NAJC leadership team were all volunteers with other full-time employment. In my case, I was an elementary school principal and had to spend most of my weekends attending meetings across the country. I commend the government officials for arranging with us to meet on the weekends so that our day jobs were not interrupted. Although it was most difficult for my wife Keiko and the children, Geoffrey, Tani, and Jonathan, because of my absence from their special activities and family get-togethers, they

supported the sacrifice of my time and effort because of the importance of redress for the Japanese Canadian community. The strategy
committee grappled with many questions: How can we have a greater
impact in moving redress forward with the government? What have
we done in the past that has not worked in our favour? What other
approaches do we need to explore? It was a time for sober reflection
and thinking "outside the box." What message would resonate with
the Canadian public in order to gain their support? No doubt, we
were too insular in our approach with the government. A decision
was made to expand our scope beyond the Japanese Canadian community and to engage other citizens by making redress a Canadian
human-rights issue.

We devised a plan to establish a National Coalition for Japanese
Canadian Redress and to solicit support from organizations and individuals across the country. Chief Justice Thomas Berger from British
Columbia agreed to be the honorary chair, and David Murata was
hired as the national coordinator. His role was to contact prominent,
influential individuals across the nation and a wide range of national,
provincial, local, and religious organizations. The *Toronto Star article*
of December 23, 1987, "Japanese Canadians Say Public Supports War
Compensation" stated that "organizations representing millions of
Canadians agreed to lend their names and power to the [redress]
cause."[1] The list included national labour unions, ethnic groups,
human-rights organizations, churches, authors, social activists, members of the public, and politicians. The Canadian Labour Congress,
for example, represented 2.3 million members. This approach of
involving other Canadians turned out to be a highly effective strategy. Coalition members sent letters of endorsement to the prime
minister and politicians and signed petitions and postcards urging
the government to negotiate a just and meaningful settlement with
the NAJC. To culminate the coalition's activities, a two-day redress
rally was planned for Ottawa, beginning with an informal gathering
of supporters in Hull, Québec, on the Friday evening, April 13, 1988.
On the following Saturday, former internees and supporters would
march on Parliament Hill and host a redress forum.

The key component of the new strategy was the framing of the

---

1   Tim Harper, "Japanese Canadians Say Public Supports War Compensation," *Toronto
     Star*, December 23, 1987, A1, www.proquest.com/newspapers/japanese-canadians-say
     -public-supports-war/docview/435694348/se-2.

redress message. Words such as "human rights" and "justice," easily understood by the Canadian public, were used repeatedly in press releases and dialogues to emphasize that redress was more than a Japanese Canadian problem, but a Canadian human-rights issue. To avoid negative public reactions, terms such as "negotiated settlement" were emphasized rather than "financial or individual compensation."

The government of Manitoba under Premier Gary Filmon also passed a resolution in support of the NAJC. At a rally of ethnic organizations held in Toronto in October 1987, leaders endorsed a resolution calling upon the prime minister to intervene personally to resolve this basic human- and civil-rights issue. The support we received from organizations, groups, and citizens throughout Canada helped push the government to recognize redress as a human-rights question. .

After David Crombie was removed, a senior official in Gerry Weiner's office told me that when a minister is assigned to a new portfolio, the prime minister issues a letter of mandate. In multiculturalism, the resolution of the Japanese Canadian redress issue was given top priority. The responsibility for how an issue is handled and resolved, however, lies in the hands of the minister in charge. Even if the prime minister wants a specific matter resolved, it is up to the minister to ensure that his staff is supportive of the initiative. In the cases of David Crombie and Otto Jelinek, the political staff and the bureaucracy weren't working together. This was part of the stalling process that we encountered: anyone in the system can find hundreds of ways of delaying an issue. To expect the prime minister to know exactly what is going on with a particular issue is unrealistic – especially when they hold responsibility for so many areas.

As the new minister for multiculturalism, Weiner was given very few guidelines. According to Dennison Moore, Weiner's first chief of staff, the prime minister didn't indicate what amount of money was available to negotiate with but signified that he was not satisfied with the progress made to date. Whatever solution the minister arrived at had to satisfy Cabinet. As a result, former ministers tended to bring forward redress proposals that were conservative (no pun intended!), and not to introduce a controversial concept such as individual compensation. Likely an intervention from the highest level – that is, from the prime minister – would be needed before that pattern would change.

Prior to his appointment to multiculturalism, Gerry Weiner had been a junior minister for immigration, and his move to multiculturalism was viewed as a promotion. When Weiner first arrived in his new department, Moore indicated that Crombie's redress file was unavailable to him. It may have been destroyed, so he received a briefing on the redress issue from the department's bureaucrats. When given the Japanese Canadian redress file, Weiner and Moore were told, "Good luck, guys," in a sarcastic tone. In spite of this seemingly inauspicious beginning, Moore later reflected, "When we came upon the scene, we had a minister with a Jewish Canadian background, and his first reaction to redress was that we had to move on this."

One of Weiner's first decisions as minister for multiculturalism was whether or not he should attend the redress rally that was planned by the NAJC for Parliament Hill on April 14, 1988. Weiner had been advised by his political staff not to attend and was forewarned that the three previous ministers had lost their portfolios because of the redress issue. What could Weiner offer that the others couldn't?

Although he did not have anything more to advance, Moore disclosed that Weiner had insisted on attending the rally. Unsure of how he would be received, he nonetheless was not intimidated. He wanted to meet the NAJC's leaders and the members of the Japanese Canadian community. He thought that this would be the best way to learn more about the redress issue and to hear the views of representatives of various non–Japanese Canadian groups. Given the mandate from the prime minister, Weiner wanted the redress issue resolved.

When I talked to Weiner after the redress settlement, he intimated to me that the rally had a significant impact on him, because he had made first-hand contact with the victims of the injustices. Although the stories of the victims were relayed second-hand during the negotiation meetings, the true impact of the experiences was not made known there.

There were a number of MPs who supported the NAJC's efforts to achieve redress. David Kilgour, a Conservative MP for Edmonton-Strathcona, raised the redress issue in the House a number of times and expressed his support at the pre–redress rally gathering on April 13, 1988. In his speech, Kilgour said, "We Canadians should be ashamed of this stain on our recent history, yet we have the tools at our disposal to alleviate some of the pain that Japanese Canadians have suffered at the hands of the rest of Canada." David Kilgour went on to publicly endorse the NAJC's redress proposal.

The rally and march on Parliament Hill presented a unique challenge, as this approach was unconventional for Japanese Canadians. The NAJC was able to bus in two to three hundred Japanese Canadians to Ottawa, mostly seniors and victims of the internment, from the Toronto, Hamilton, and Montréal areas, to join other Japanese Canadians from across Canada, which included my mother, my wife, and my son Jonathan. This was the first time such a large contingent of Japanese Canadians had ever marched on Ottawa and collectively expressed their feelings. We were warned by some Japanese community leaders that having the elderly march on Parliament Hill would be embarrassing. "It is not in keeping with the character of the Japanese way," we were told. We took a risk. Aren't demonstrations and marches the Canadian way of expressing frustration with the government?

I was amazed and delighted to witness this historic event where Japanese Canadians demonstrated their democratic rights by carrying placards and ribbons of hope displaying the names of people who were unable to attend and shouting "Redress Now!" vociferously. I wonder how many seniors ever thought that they would be doing this in their lifetime!

The marchers converged on the Confederation Hall in the Parliament Buildings' West Block for the redress forum. Roy Miki and Cassandra Kobayashi had the following to say in *Justice in Our Time*: "As the speeches began, it became clear the Japanese Canadians were no longer alone in the struggle for justice. The National Coalition for Japanese Canadian Redress reflected the conscience of Canadians who had come to realize the importance of redress as a major human rights issue."[2] The crowd, including many Japanese Canadian seniors who sat in the front, listened to the words of David Suzuki and speakers such as Lewis Chan, Archbishop Ted Scott, Ernie Epp, Gilles Tardif, Alan Borovoy, Sister Mary Jo Leddy, Sergio Marchi, and Roy Miki. These speakers, politicians, as well as representatives of ethnocultural, religious, and civil-rights organizations in support of the coalition, were eloquent on the importance of righting past wrongs. When Gerry Weiner spoke, I think many Japanese Canadians listened intently, perhaps expecting a different message. But the words that

---

2   Miki and Kobayashi, *Justice in Our Time*, 123.

TOP: Internees march on Parliament Hill, 1988

BOTTOM: David Suzuki, Art, and Mary Jo Leddy marching at the Ottawa redress rally, 1988

PHOTO: Gordon King

Weiner delivered to the estimated audience of five hundred that day were a disappointment. His speech seemed to reinforce the messages that they had heard from previous ministers. He mentioned the government's last offer of a $12 million community fund and indicated that legislative changes were forthcoming. He made reference to the prime minister's personal feelings of wanting to settle the redress matter – this despite the fact that the NAJC efforts to meet the prime minister to get him personally involved had been fruitless. As a gesture of goodwill to the gathered audience, Weiner announced that his "door was open" to meet with the NAJC and signified that Crombie's last offer was no longer the final position of the government.

The national media coverage put human faces to the stories of the elderly victims and their memories of hardships and alienation. Surely, seeing seventy- and eighty-year-olds demanding their democratic rights was a powerful message and hopefully would have a significant effect on politicians and the Canadian public. This was a first-hand opportunity for Gerry Weiner to come face to face with victims of the internment and to speak to them with a message of hope.

After the forum, as an expression of support, Weiner offered to accompany a group of internees carrying fifteen thousand postcards in large sacks signed by supporters to the prime minister's office. The postcards, addressed to the prime minister, had been distributed at public events asking supporters to sign. They stated, "Japanese Canadian Redress is a Canadian issue, it's a justice issue, it's a human rights issue."

When Gerry Weiner reported back to his Cabinet colleagues, he indicated that he was impressed by the dignified and respectful manner in which the demonstration had been carried out by Japanese Canadians. The mood of the rally helped dispel the illusion in Weiner's mind that the leaders of the NAJC were unreasonable radicals. The rally created optimism for our community and anticipation that support expressed by Canadians would persuade the government to reconsider its position.

The first substantive meeting with Mr. Weiner occurred on June 15, 1988, when members of the NAJC strategy committee gathered in Winnipeg at the Multiculturalism office to meet with Weiner, Dennison Moore, and advisor Rick Clippendale. As I recall, the first thing I said to Weiner was, "Look, if it's the same story that we heard from Crombie, there isn't much point in discussing the redress question." Weiner responded, "I come with an open mind. I come wanting to hear what you have to say. Nothing is closed." Dennison Moore recalled, "Everything was on the table. We were prepared to open the whole thing for discussion. We were willing to look at individual compensation, community fund, wiping out of criminal records, etc." The atmosphere of this meeting was very different from the meetings we'd had with previous ministers. In our earlier meetings, we had devoted a significant amount of time to basically giving the minister and his staff a history lesson and justifying the importance of redress for the community. Weiner, however, was well versed on the issue and ready to sit down and do business.

At the meeting, the NAJC stressed that monetary recognition for individual victims was essential if we were to break the deadlock. Because our community members were scattered across Canada, a community fund alone would not meaningfully acknowledge the hardships suffered or rectify the loss of dignity endured by individual Japanese Canadians. Weiner assured us that individual compensation was not out of the question.

When the NAJC representatives walked out of the meeting with Crombie in July 1987, signifying the end of the negotiation process, the government had to find a way to save face if negotiations were to reopen. How might the deadlock be broken to facilitate a redress decision? We explored processes that would yield a judgment for appropriate redress. An impartial, independent decision by an outside body might be an acceptable solution. How would the compensation figure be determined? As a possible face-saving approach for the government, we discussed "third-party involvement" such as establishing a mini-commission, or a committee of non-partisan people, or appointing a commissioner to recommend possible remedies. With the pending resolution in the United States, we stressed that any agreement with the government had to be comparable to the US resolution, and that individual compensation had to be included.

Weiner indicated that he would explore the various possibilities with his political staff and the prime minister's office. If a third-party intervention were acceptable to the prime minister, the NAJC would insist on participating in determining the parameters and must approve of the persons appointed to work on the committee or commission before endorsing the process. Weiner agreed to a follow-up meeting in early July.

During the latter part of June and in July 1988, I made numerous phone calls to Weiner's office to determine the promised meeting date, but to no avail. Suggestions that the government was stalling became more believable. In mid-July, I was in Ottawa to attend the Canadian Ethnocultural Council meeting, and I arranged to meet with several key government bureaucrats. I met with Vera Holiad, who was very much aware of our discussions with Weiner. She assured me that the prime minister considered the redress issue a high priority because of the promise he had made in 1984. Although Holiad was new in her role, she had considerable knowledge of the redress question and offered to assist us in any way. I also met with Andy Stack, executive assistant to Dalton Camp, who was also aware of our June discussions with Weiner and who asked for my impressions of a third-party intervention. I concurred that it had possibilities. My impressions after meeting with Holiad and Stark were that the PMO was directing the redress process through Weiner.

I was finally able to speak with Weiner on July 11 by phone to discuss a meeting date. However, he indicated that he needed to be present in the House for the third reading of the new Multicultural-ism Act and then would have to leave for London, UK, and would not return until the last week of July. Therefore, a meeting date could not be arranged.

In the NAJC press release of July 15, 1988, summarizing the details of the initial meeting we had with Weiner, I stated, "The NAJC remains ready to explore the Minister's offer to reopen discussion with the government in the last hours of their term. We will continue to meet in good faith, and remain flexible in our approach, without compromising the basic principles of justice in the NAJC position." This was done to assure the prime minister and government that the NAJC was open to further discussions.

In the meantime, Roy Miki and Cassandra Kobayashi consulted with lawyers Don Rosenbloom and Thomas Berger regarding the government proposal of third-party involvement. Both were skep-tical of the government's intentions but considered the change of attitude to be positive and encouraged us to arrange that meeting with Weiner.

On July 28, I was in Ottawa to attend a ceremony to celebrate the passage of the Multiculturalism Act, and I chatted briefly with the minister to see whether a meeting date could be determined. Weiner was unable to give me a commitment because he had been instructed by Mazankowski to visit every province during a two-week period to promote the new Multiculturalism Act. He suggested that we meet after he had completed his travels, which would take us into mid-August. During Weiner's visit to Winnipeg on August 2, I talked to him, expressing my concern with the delays because they were creating a perception in the Japanese Canadian community that the government was delaying until a federal election was called.

The US Civil Liberties Act, signed on August 10, 1988, would compensate Japanese American victims $20,000 each for a similar injustice as that experienced by Japanese Canadians. Clearly, the significance of the US agreement for the Japanese Canadian redress movement was the awarding of individual compensation. The NAJC sent a letter to the prime minister with a copy to Weiner on August 4 urging a meeting. Letters were sent to John Turner and Ed Broadbent asking the Opposition to raise the issue in the House and urge the government to take action in light of the American settlement. On August 6, 1988, the *Winnipeg Free Press* editorial regarded the American conclusion as "An Example for Canada" and urged that "because the US has reached a solution, the climate in Canada is more propitious. The Government should try again."[3] The *Globe and Mail* editorial called the American action "An Example to Shame Us."[4]

Around the same time, a debate heated up in the House of Commons when Liberal critic Sergio Marchi and NDP critic Ernie Epp both challenged the prime minister to keep his promise of 1984 and to reach a similar settlement with Japanese Canadians. Mulroney responded: "There are ongoing discussions with the representatives of the NAJC at this moment. I know my honourable friend will be happy to learn that negotiations are moving ahead and they are in the extremely capable hands of the minister for multiculturalism." And yet, at the same time, we were unable to arrange a meeting with the minister.

After hearing the prime minister's comment, I called the minister's

---

3   "An Example for Canada," *Winnipeg Free Press*, August 6, 1988, 6, archives.winnipegfree press.com/winnipeg-free-press/1988-08-06/page-6/.

4   "An Example to Shame Us," *Globe and Mail*, August 8, 1988, A6, www.proquest.com /historical-newspapers/example-shame-us/docview/1238338966/se-2.

office to set up a meeting. On the same day, I received a call from Vera Holiad from the PMO and expressed to her our frustration regarding the difficulty in arranging a meeting with Weiner. She said that she would call the minister's office to see what the problem was.

Meanwhile, I consulted with the NAJC strategy committee and Don Rosenbloom regarding the delays and decided that the NAJC strategy committee should go to Ottawa in an attempt to meet with Weiner and confer with Opposition MPs. The NAJC would plan to hold a press conference in Ottawa on Wednesday, August 24.

On August 18, I called Dennison Moore to express our concern that a meeting date had not been scheduled and to inform him that we would be in Ottawa on August 24 for a press conference. He explained that "things were beginning to move" and that we should wait until we were requested to go to Ottawa, possibly the following week. He further declared, "You will be pleased with what the government is willing to do." I asked whether the third-party intervention was still a possibility. Moore said no and indicated that the prime minister himself wanted to adopt a "fast-track" approach. I believe that his decision to move quickly on the issue was influenced by the signing of the American bill.

Moore also indicated that they were consulting other ethnic leaders to share the government's plan. Then the government proposal would be taken to the Finance Cabinet Committee on Monday, August 22, and from there to the powerful Planning and Priorities Cabinet Committee.

The following day, Moore called me again to inform me that there had been a change in plans and that the prime minister wanted to move even more quickly, bypassing the Finance Committee and going directly to the Planning and Priorities Committee on Tuesday morning, August 23. Moore promised that I would receive a call on Tuesday regarding the committee decision. My understanding in discussions with the minister was that there was some difficulty as to where the redress funds would come from if and when a settlement was reached. The normal procedure is that the request for funds would go to the Planning and Priorities or Finance Cabinet Committees. In post-redress interviews with Weiner's staff, they revealed that the prime minister was extremely concerned that if the matter of redress were brought before the Finance Committee, the information could possibly be leaked to the public. He was afraid that this might result in a backlash from Conservative members and from veterans' organizations. The whole of the Cabinet Committee had not been very supportive, especially of individual payments; Mulroney feared that certain Cabinet members might argue strongly against a redress settlement. Such dissension, if it were to become public, would create a potential for public and political backlash. It would take only one politician speaking against redress to create a negative chain reaction. If the prime minister had the support of the influential Planning and Priorities Committee members, then he could move the redress resolution through the House.

Gerry Weiner called me on Tuesday afternoon, August 23, to resume negotiations after approval was given by the Planning and Priorities Committee. The negotiation meetings were to begin the next evening, August 24. He stressed that the meeting was to be confidential and that no one was to know where we were meeting. On Tuesday evening, all of the NAJC strategy committee members and Don Rosenbloom were informed of the positive news and were asked to make arrangements to be in Montréal the following day.

CEC's Andrew Cardoza recalled that Dennison Moore had telephoned him two days before negotiations began. Andrew and I had a fairly close relationship, since I was a board member of the CEC. Andrew was surprised to hear from Moore, who told him that negotiation meetings with the NAJC were beginning and shared information with him that Andrew thought to be very confidential. Moore called Andrew again the next day and seemed to suggest to Andrew that he should pass the information on to me, although he never said so directly. Andrew was given the bottom line as to what the government was prepared to offer in terms of individual compensation. Moore told him that if the bottom line wasn't good enough, Weiner could call the Honourable Lucien Bouchard, secretary of state, and Bouchard would call Prime Minister Mulroney. Bouchard appeared to be pulling the strings. After the second call, Andrew realized that maybe Dennison Moore was suggesting that he pass the information to me, so Andrew said to him, "I suppose I should give Art a call and let him know." Moore replied, "Oh, he's probably left Winnipeg at this point." Although Moore wasn't saying, "Yes, go ahead," he was making a last-ditch effort to inform me indirectly of the possibilities.

Thinking that the information would be valuable for the negotiations meeting, Andrew decided to call me. He contacted me just before I left for Montréal and reported that the government was seriously interested in reaching an agreement. Andrew said that he had had an unusual conversation with Moore, who revealed that the government was supporting individual compensation to a significant amount, but he wasn't sure whether he should be telling me. Andrew wondered if Moore had called of his own volition, or if he had called on behalf of the minister. Regardless, the information certainly gave us some leverage as to how far we could push specific amounts.

On the evening of August 25, the NAJC strategy team, consisting of my brother Roy, Roger Obata, Maryka Omatsu, Cassandra Kobayashi, Audrey Kobayashi, legal advisor Don Rosenbloom, and me, were to meet at Montréal's Ritz-Carlton with the government team to begin the secret meetings. It was strange. The whole scene took on an aura of secrecy. As soon as we arrived at the Ritz-Carlton, we were quickly ushered via the back staircase adjacent to the kitchen area to an upstairs meeting room. Here we were met by Weiner, Moore, Rick Clippendale, Anne Scotton, and Alain Bisson, the legal advisor from the Department of Justice. To our surprise, Lucien Bouchard joined us at the beginning of the meeting. Weiner introduced Bouchard as the "man who has the prime minister's ear, and who can get things done."

As secretary of state, Bouchard was the senior minister. He had been appointed to Cabinet by Mulroney even though he had not been elected. Bouchard was considered a close friend to the prime minister and his right-hand man. The initiative to settle the long, drawn-out dispute between the NAJC and Ottawa came in April 1988 when Mulroney appointed Bouchard, a trusted classmate from the Faculté de droit de l'Université Laval (the Laval University Faculty of Law), to assume control of the redress negotiations. Weiner, who worked under Bouchard, was then given the mandate to settle the issue. One official told me that when Bouchard received the initial briefing on the Japanese Canadian redress issue, he listened intently without saying a word. When the briefing was completed, he stood up and said, "We must do something about this."

According to Moore, Bouchard was sensitive to the unjust treatment of Japanese Canadians as an episode of Canada's history that needed to be addressed. I wondered if his sympathy for Japanese Canadian redress is related to his involvement and militancy for the independence of the Québécois people. Did his fervent advocacy for sovereignty rights parallel his defence of minority rights? Whatever the case may be, there was no question in Bouchard's mind that the redress issue had to be settled quickly, and now. At no time did Bouchard endeavour to restrain Weiner in the negotiation process, but always gave him the full authority to go ahead within the parameters that had been established for the total package.

At the meeting, Bouchard expressed the desire to resolve the impasse and indicated that the government was willing to negotiate individual compensation. It was Bouchard who suggested an initial offer of $15,000 per person for individual compensation. His presence was strong evidence of the government's seriousness. We were elated that the government was finally going to recognize the individual victims. Bouchard assured us that he would be in contact with Weiner throughout the negotiation process and would be available if difficulties arose in trying to reach an amicable conclusion.

Following the first offer, the government officials implied that the NAJC proposal of $25,000 was too high. The NAJC strategy committee caucused to decide what position we would put forward. In the back of my mind, I was reminded of what Andrew Cardoza had told me. He thought the government might be willing to go as high as $25,000 for individual compensation if they were pushed hard. I shared this information with the committee members, but I felt that most of the members would be satisfied with $20,000, a figure similar to the one in the US redress agreement. After the years when consideration of individual compensation had been denied, the government's initial offer was a positive sign. Finally, we agreed on a counteroffer of $20,000. In hindsight, we likely should have stayed firm on the initial position to see whether Lucien Bouchard would be called in.

For the longest time, however, the government would not budge from $20,000. The US bill called for individual compensation of $20,000 for each Japanese American incarcerated in concentration camps at the same time as Japanese Canadians were being forcibly removed. But our strategy committee argued, for good reason, that the treatment in Canada was far worse and more severe than that of our counterparts in the United States and therefore it was important that the amount for individual compensation should symbolically reflect the difference. In a concession to this position, the minister agreed to pay $21,000 instead of $20,000 to each survivor – a symbolic victory for the negotiators and a meaningful gesture from the government. After he left the government, Moore told me that when Weiner was conferred the task to negotiate, he had been given the authority to go as high as $25,000 per individual.

The discussion regarding the community fund was interesting. The government team began by offering a $5 million fund that the government would administer. Much deliberation was held as to how the fund would be used to rebuild the Japanese Canadian community, and we provided concrete examples of how the fund might be allocated. We held firm on a community fund of $25 million. The final trade-off came when Weiner said that he would be willing to increase individual compensation to $21,000 per victim if we would accept a $12 million fund over which our community would have full jurisdiction. The NAJC negotiators caucused and weighed the pros and cons of this offer. We recognized that an increase of $1,000 per victim would cost the government between $17 million and $18 million dollars, while we were giving up $13 million in the community fund. In the end, we determined that the symbolic $21,000 per individual was of greater importance in reflecting the differences in the wartime treatment between the American and Canadian Japanese.

After seventeen hours of negotiations over two days, the NAJC reached a settlement we felt would be acceptable to our community. The various components outlined in the NAJC redress proposal, including individual compensation, were fulfilled. Furthermore, we discussed ways to involve the NAJC in the redress implementation process.

Weiner was extremely receptive to our suggestions and discussed ways in which the government might take the high road in the implementation process. The strategy team reminded the government negotiators that many of the survivors were advanced in age, and each delay saw more people pass away. Weiner shared this concern and agreed to adopt a fast-track approach in ensuring that qualified individuals would have their applications processed as soon as the forms were ready and would receive their redress payment shortly after.

I also indicated to the minister that the NAJC had an outstanding debt to Price Waterhouse for the *Economic Losses of Japanese Canadians* study that had been conducted in 1986. We had promised to pay the balance of the costs if redress was attained, and requested the government pay the balance as part of the settlement. Mr. Weiner agreed without hesitation and asked that Price Waterhouse bill the government. The other concession that was granted was the assurance that the NAJC would assist with the implementation process within the Japanese Canadian community. In 1941, Japanese Canadians had severe restrictions imposed upon them without any consultation with their community or its involvement. We insisted that as part of the healing process, the NAJC work co-operatively with the government in determining guidelines for application forms, the wording of the Order-in-Council, assisting with the application process, and developing objectives for the Canadian Race Relations Foundation.

The NAJC wanted to assist individuals in the community with their redress claims rather than having government employees hired for the job. This would make the application process less threatening, especially for seniors. Mr. Wiener also favoured the proposed partnership arrangement with the NAJC and allocated $3 million for that

Art shaking the hand of the Honourable Gerry Weiner, minister of state for multiculturalism, as the redress agreement is reached
PHOTO: Cassandra Kobayashi

GAMAN — PERSEVERANCE

purpose. Mr. Weiner admitted that this was a positive public-relations strategy. These two provisions – the payment of the Price Waterhouse bill and the inclusion of the NAJC in the redress-awarding process – made the Canadian redress settlement superior to its US counterpart.

After reaching an agreement on August 25, the strategy team members went out for a well-deserved tardy dinner. We were elated with the final outcome, and it was difficult to believe that the long struggle was finally at an end. Back at the hotel room, we sat around late into the evening reflecting on the past struggles, the meeting, and finally the successful conclusion, a result that exceeded our expectations. As I sat on the floor in the corner of the room, Roger Obata and I discussed the events unfolding before us. I could tell by Roger's reaction and facial expression that he was overwhelmed by the accomplishment and overcome with happiness. Finally, he said, "We did it. I knew we could do it. I have lived for this day."

Much of the following day was devoted to jointly drafting the wording of the agreement that would be presented in the House of Commons. Because I had to return to Winnipeg on August 26, NAJC Vice-President Obata and Minister of Multiculturalism Weiner signed in my absence the historic tentative document outlining the general terms of the redress agreement. When we left the meeting, all of us were sworn to secrecy until the official announcement could be made by the prime minister in the House of Commons at the appropriate time. What was amazing to me about the final negotiation process was that only four members of the Cabinet, the prime minister, the deputy prime minister, the secretary of state, and the minister of multiculturalism, knew that negotiation with the Japanese Canadian community was occurring in Montréal. The reason we could not reveal that there was an agreement was that the four key people needed time to convince their Cabinet colleagues to support the decision.

In the meantime, we had to keep this burning information to ourselves. The confidentiality of the agreement was extremely important. The information could not be shared with the rest of the strategy committee members who had not been involved in the Montréal meeting, nor with the NAJC National Council members. The government representatives were also bound by the secrecy obligation.

I remember being at home after the Montréal meetings, when my mother was complaining to me that nothing was happening with redress and said to me, "All you do is meet. When is something going to happen?" I wanted to tell her that it was all over and finally a settlement had been reached, but all I could tell her was that she needed to be patient and to have faith in us. I realized that if I told her the news, even if I asked her not to tell anyone, she wouldn't have been able to contain herself, and within a day the whole community would know. Roger Obata told me that he didn't even tell his wife, Mary, about our successful meeting. It was difficult for all of us to remain silent, but we had to keep that promise.

The prime minister was concerned that any leak to Cabinet before the terms of the redress agreement had been presented to key Cabinet members might result in a negative reaction against the agreement. Therefore, any premature release of information might jeopardize the agreement and prevent the prime minister from taking action. The other concern was that veterans' organizations might lead a massive campaign against the agreement, forcing the prime minister to delay the announcement or even to shelve it.

However, Dennison Moore felt that the veterans' organizations were no longer a threat. He had met with Clifford Chadderton of the War Amps to solicit their support, so that the organization would not publicly oppose the settlement. In our talks with Chadderton, it had been apparent that although he realized that the redress issue and the veterans' concerns were distinctly different, he wanted the government to put pressure on Japan to redress Hong Kong veterans. That request, according to Moore, was something the government could not address.

When I returned home from the negotiations meeting in Montréal, who should be waiting at my door but a CBC reporter. She had called my home on the day I left for Montréal to speak to me about our redress progress. Keiko, my wife, mentioned to the reporter that I was out of town and that I had gone to Montréal. I had neglected to tell her that our meeting was supposed to be a secret and not to let anyone know where I was. The reporter called Weiner's office and was told that he couldn't be reached because he was attending an important meeting. Our intrepid reporter surmised that we might be meeting over redress. When I met her at the door, she asked me whether I had had a meeting with Weiner in Montréal. I could not lie, and yet I was bound by the promise of secrecy. I finally replied that we had had a meeting and that we were still in negotiations.

I felt bad that I had revealed to the reporter that a meeting had taken place, and I wondered what information would appear in the media. Early next morning, I called Weiner in Montréal to alert him about my interview with the reporter. By nine o'clock in Montréal, he had already heard the news on the radio. I apologized for my comments, but Weiner assured me that what he heard was not damaging or jeopardizing to the redress agreement.

Before further steps could be taken, however, the prime minister indicated through Weiner that he, Deputy Prime Minister Don Mazankowski, and Secretary of State Lucien Bouchard would be talking to other Cabinet ministers individually to obtain their guarantee of support for the negotiated redress settlement. We were told that this would require some time, so we shouldn't anticipate the announcement in the House for several weeks.

There was some speculation that the announcement would be made on September 1, but Weiner called on August 30 to say that any announcement would not occur until after the House reconvened on September 13. By this time, the North American Free Trade Agreement (NAFTA) was a hot issue receiving enormous media coverage and publicity. The prime minister wanted to present the resolution in the House at a time when the historic redress announcement would receive full attention from the media.

Why had there been so many delays in the negotiation process during the period prior to August 1988 before the redress issue was finally addressed? I found out from a senior political staff member that there had been difficulty in moving the redress issue because the opposition to a settlement came from the PMO itself, particularly from Derek Burney, chief of staff for the prime minister, and Denise Cole, the multicultural advisor. Somehow, the redress issue had not appeared on the agenda for the Planning and Priorities meetings. When the prime minister finally realized what was happening, he asked Don Mazankowski and Michael Wilson, minister of finance, to look into the matter so they could settle the issue. When Vera Holiad became responsible for the redress issue in the PMO, this was a positive step. She was amenable to exploring possible solutions, so Dennison Moore was able to provide her with instructions on how to deal with the issue.

The other delaying factor was the opposition within the Conservative Party to moving ahead with negotiations. With the election date nearing, many party members were upset at Mulroney for proceeding. On the other hand, the prime minister had promised Japanese Canadians that he would conclude the issue; failure to do so would tarnish his credibility. The prime minister had to be cautious with how he moved on the issue. His decision was to limit the number of people who knew the "plan," and to quietly negotiate the agreement.

Right from the beginning of Weiner's appointment to multiculturalism, the department was very supportive of seeing the redress issue settled to the satisfaction of the Japanese Canadian community. People in the department such as Anne Scotton, Shirley Serafini, and Rick Clippendale were very sympathetic and reassuring, and they provided background information for Weiner and his staff. They were warned over and over by Justice officials not to proceed with negotiations. All they heard from Justice was, "Don't do this, don't do that; you'll set a precedent." This was in addition to what was being told to the heads in the Privy Council Office (the PCO advises the prime minister and, along with the PMO, determines the agenda for Cabinet meetings). There are many places in the bureaucracy where an issue can be stalled.

An important event that took place in the spring of 1988 was the resignation of Minister for Veteran Affairs George Hees from Cabinet. Whenever the redress matter was discussed in Cabinet, Hees showed himself to be a zealous adversary to making any amends to Japanese Canadians. As minister, Hees faced strong opposition from many veterans who expressed their indignation that the treatment they had received in Japanese prisoner-of-war camps was being overshadowed by the experiences of Japanese Canadians. Hees was a well-respected senior statesman and a powerful influence in Cabinet. Early in 1988, he had fallen ill; he was hospitalized and had to leave Cabinet. It wasn't until after Hees's resignation that Mulroney contemplated a change in direction and reconsidered the possibility of individual redress. This was a courageous move on his part. I was told by a government official that days before the redress agreement announcement, a staff member had gone to the hospital and had Hees sign a document stating that he would not oppose the agreement. How true this is I don't know, but it's plausible. I suspect that every effort was made by the prime minister to ensure that there would be no backlash from other Conservatives.

The government's original offer of a community fund would have been a modest expenditure, but including individual compensation increased the cost significantly, making it more difficult to sell the idea to Cabinet. Prime Minister Mulroney had these factors to consider when deciding to go ahead with the negotiation process.

Although I felt that the signing of the US redress bill influenced the change in attitude, Moore said that the prime minister, with Weiner, had consciously made the decision to go ahead with the resolution before the US bill was signed on August 10, 1988. However, there were clear signs in early 1988 that it was a matter of time before the US bill would be passed, and the prime minister might have anticipated this. In early July, the prime minister had given Weiner the full mandate to reach a settlement with the NAJC. With the Canadian public's increased awareness about the redress issue, the prime minister knew that there were many organizations rallying behind the NAJC's efforts and thought a settlement would be received positively. This would help his election campaign and retain votes from "ethnic communities." A national poll conducted shortly after the redress agreement was announced revealed results that were highly supportive of the government's action to compensate Japanese Canadians. This confirmed that Canadians endorsed the prime minister's decision to "right the wrongs of the past."

While I was waiting for the prime minister's notification of the announcement, I received a strange call on a Sunday evening in mid-September from a community member from the East. He accused me of doing nothing and ordered me to resign as president of the NAJC. I was startled by the tone of his comments, which suggested he was all-powerful, as he threatened to have me removed as president if I didn't resign. I couldn't understand how that might be possible, but I suggested that if that was what he wanted to do to go ahead and try. Two weeks later, the announcement of the agreement was made. I wondered whether the caller was embarrassed that he had made disparaging personal comments. Needless to say, I didn't receive a congratulatory note from the individual, nor have I heard from him since.

Surprisingly, for nearly a month, the news of the redress settlement was kept under wraps. Finally, on the morning of September 21,

1988, I received a call from Weiner indicating that the announcement of the Japanese Canadian redress settlement by the prime minister might be made the following day. He asked that all the members of the NAJC strategy committee arrange to come to Ottawa for the long-awaited announcement.

I immediately began to receive calls from reporters asking whether I knew that an announcement would be made. The government had obviously leaked the information that morning, but I had to plead ignorance and say that we were still negotiating.

When we arrived in Ottawa, we were taken to bed and breakfasts not far from downtown. I was placed in a quaint home near the University of Ottawa alone, likely to ensure that the media would not locate me. I couldn't sleep that evening, thinking about the next day.

For over forty-six years, this was the day Japanese Canadians had been waiting for.

CHAPTER 10

The Day of Celebration

Shitsuyo ni
Shinri wa magezu
Tatakaishi
Tsuini kaiketsu
Hosho mondai

Reaching for justice
In time's persistence,
Unwaveringly
At last –
Our redress resolution.

—Tanka by **HARUKO KOBAYAKAWA** (issei) composed on the occasion of our redress celebration, September 22, 1988 (reprinted with permission)

For every Japanese Canadian who had experienced the wartime trauma of forced removal, internment, and the deprival of their basic rights, September 22, 1988, was a day to remember. The dramatic statement by the Honourable Brian Mulroney in the House of Commons that a comprehensive redress agreement had been reached between the government of Canada and the National Association of Japanese Canadians came as a pleasant surprise and shock. Some were lost for words to express their feelings; others felt that a burden of guilt was lifted or that the stain of shame they felt from having been branded enemy alien was finally removed; while others just felt relieved that the struggle for redress was finally over.

When Roger Obata listened to Mulroney's statement in the House, he said, "After almost forty-seven years, I felt for the first time that I was being officially recognized as being equal to any other Canadian. At last I am a first-class citizen and not a person suspected of disloyalty." Whatever the emotions aroused in Japanese Canadians, the government's decision to admit that a wrong had been committed was a historic precedent. It was the day to celebrate!

That eventful day began for me at Weiner's office in Hull to meet with the minister, other members of the strategy committee, and government officials from the Department of Multiculturalism for a briefing on the day's agenda. First, we would be escorted to the visitors' gallery of the House of Commons to sit opposite the prime minister, so that we would have a full view of him delivering the historic proclamation. Following the announcement, I would be taken to the prime minister's office to meet him personally and then walk with him to the main floor's press room in the Centre Block, where the official signing of the agreement would take place. To celebrate this unprecedented achievement, we would then be invited to a reception attended by politicians and members of the Japanese Canadian community. Later, a press conference was scheduled at the Parliamentary Press Gallery's National Press Building, across from the Parliament Buildings' West Block, at which Weiner would review the terms of the agreement in more detail for the media. I would then have an opportunity to respond on behalf of the Japanese Canadian community.

While Rick Clippendale and Anne Scotton outlined the day's activities, Lucien Bouchard was meeting the Conservative caucus to explain that an announcement of the Japanese Canadian redress agreement would be made that morning. Dennison Moore was with Bouchard when he told caucus the news. One member was going to speak when Bouchard quickly shut him up and said, "This [the internment of Japanese Canadians] shouldn't have happened and we should be ashamed of ourselves that this happened. We have to put an end to this." He was very abrupt. "I'm informing you and not asking for opinions." Moore suspected that the members of the party may not have had respect for Bouchard but were in fact afraid of him. They knew that he was extremely close to the prime minister and had his support.

We were taken by taxis from Hull to the visitors' gallery in the Parliament Buildings for the announcement scheduled at 11:00 a.m. Other Japanese Canadians from various cities who were aware of this momentous occasion met us to join in the celebration. We took our places in the gallery as we waited for the prime minister's appearance. When he arrived, we stood and clapped for him. He began his speech:

> Mr. Speaker, nearly half a century ago, in the crisis of wartime, the Government of Canada wrongfully incarcerated, seized the property, and disenfranchised thousands of citizens of Japanese ancestry. We cannot change the past. But we must, as a nation, have the courage to face up to these historical facts.[1]

Those words began the acknowledgment we had so dearly wanted to hear from the government. As the prime minister continued with his speech, tears began to flow and it was difficult to contain my emotions as I struggled to listen to every word he said. It was hard for me to believe that we had finally achieved the goal we had pursued for so long. I had dreamed that we would succeed, but to personally witness this accomplishment was absolutely exhilarating.

A number of times during his speech, Prime Minister Mulroney gestured to us in the gallery as he made reference to the National Association of Japanese Canadians. When he finished his address, the prime minister received a standing ovation from his colleagues in the House and from the visitors in the gallery. It was a moment to behold as people cheered, congratulated each other, hugged, kissed, and shed tears of joy. For those of us who had struggled through the redress campaign, especially during the last four years, it was a dream come true. It was difficult for me to express in words the joy of triumph, except to say, "I can't believe that this has really happened!"

Hearing the words of Prime Minister Mulroney brought back flashes of the struggles we had confronted. We had faced many difficult situations within the Japanese Canadian community that were not only divisive but could have destroyed the redress movement. We had to reassess our direction many times but always kept our sight on the end goal: a just and honourable settlement. That day in Ottawa confirmed for me that we had made the right decisions

---

1   See Prime Minister Mulroney's full speech here: Library of Parliament, Canadian Parliamentary Historical Resources, House of Commons Debates, 33rd Parliament, 2nd session, vol. 15, "Japanese Canadians Interned during World War II – National Redress," September 22, 1988, 19499–19501, parl.canadiana.ca/view/oop.debates_HOC3302_15/1037.

in our strategies and taken the time necessary for Canadians to accept redress.

Members from the Opposition parties also expressed their support. Sergio Marchi spoke on behalf of John Turner, who was in Vancouver, and reminded us that the redress settlement would be a measure by which Canada recognized the rights of all Canadians. In his speech to the House, Sergio Marchi noted, "It is not a sign of weakness for a country to render this apology. Instead, it is a sure sign of strength and a sign of reflection of our country's commitment to try wherever and however to right our wrongs, not merely for the sake of correcting the history books but, more important perhaps, to establish important standards that will serve Canadians today and future generations of Canadians tomorrow." He also praised the NAJC and the Japanese Canadian community "for their never-ending determination and deep belief in the cause that they carried so well for so long. Today's resolution, no doubt, is a tribute to their sense of purpose, but it is also an appropriate response to those who continue to question the legitimacy and motivation of the leadership of the National Association of Japanese Canadians."[2]

The most moving speech that day was given by NDP Leader Ed Broadbent, who was visibly overcome by emotion while quoting from Joy Kogawa's novel *Obasan*. Kogawa was one of the many Japanese Canadian supporters in attendance for the announcement. Broadbent had a special interest in the redress movement because his first wife, Yvonne Yamaoka, had been interned as a child. He said tearfully:

> In the 1940s our Government, a democratically elected Government, did a great injustice to some 22,000 of our citizens, a permanent injustice to those who are no longer living. This was done, not because of what they had done, but because of who they were. These Japanese Canadians had their families broken up, their property confiscated, their businesses destroyed. They were forced to abandon their homes on the coast of British Columbia and they were forced to move to the interior and to elsewhere in Canada.
>
> They, as Canadian citizens, had done no wrong. They were the victims of intolerance and racism brought about, not because we were at war with them but because we were at war

---

2   Ibid., 19500.

with the land of their ancestors. They had done no wrong to any of their fellow citizens. It was an inglorious moment in our, on the whole, proud history.[3]

The prime minister in his speech acknowledged "the strong moral leadership"[4] that the Speaker John Fraser had provided on the redress issue. Sergio Marchi saluted the pivotal role played behind the scenes by Fraser, who "offered us a sense of encouragement in the day-to-day questions that we posed on the floor of the House of Commons over the last four years."[5]

Immediately after the orations, a member of the prime minister's staff escorted me directly to the prime minister's office. Waiting alone to meet with the prime minister, I wondered how I should greet him. Should I address him as "Mr. Prime Minister" or "Honourable Brian Mulroney"? While I was thinking about what to say, the prime minister walked into the room and said "Hello, Art" and came over to shake my hand. My quick response was "Hello, Brian, nice to meet you." All that formal protocol had vanished. I felt at ease with the prime minister as I thanked him for his passionate words.

As we walked downstairs to the room in which the official signing of the agreement would be taking place, I said to him, "It's taken a long time, but it was worth waiting for." His reply was, "Well, it's taken this long for me to convince some of my colleagues that it was the right thing to do." I sensed sincerity and honesty in his response. My impression of Brian Mulroney was that he had had a genuine interest in resolving the redress issue earlier, but that his party members did not share the same view.

It was an unbelievable feeling as we entered the small, crowded room of cameras and reporters for the signing ceremony that was to symbolize the settlement. Members of the NAJC's strategy committee Don Rosenbloom and Harold Hirose from Winnipeg and Ottawa supporters Mas Takahashi, Amy Yamazaki, Harry and Yoshi Ashimoto, along with Lucien Bouchard and Gerry Weiner, stood behind the table at which the prime minister and I sat. There were

---

3   Ibid., 19501.

4   Ibid., 19499.

5   Ibid., 19500.

TOP: Prime Minister Brian Mulroney and Art Miki signing the redress agreement, 1988

BOTTOM: Mulroney thanking the NAJC negotiation team after signing the redress agreement, 1988

PHOTOS: John Flanders

two sets of the same documents to sign, in English and in French. The prime minister signed the first document and then handed it to me to sign. Meanwhile, all I could hear were the constant clicks from the cameras in the background.

Once the documents were signed, we both stood. The prime minister then turned to me and said, "May I just say to you and the leaders of the community who are here, some who are eighty-six and eighty-seven years of age, who went through this personally, I say this is a moment of long coming, of tolerance and for justice for your community and for Canada. I just want to do this for you and for all of you who have believed in the basic fairness of Canada." Mr. Mulroney began to clap, and everyone joined him. I replied, "I must say, Mr. Prime Minister, we were very moved this morning by the comments that were made in the House. I know that today is a historic landmark not only for our community but for the human-rights issue." Indeed, for me, the importance of the redress settlement was not only what it did for the Japanese Canadian community but what it did for the recognition of minority rights in Canada.

The prime minister then shook the hands of the people who were standing behind us and quickly left the room to go back to his office. I was relieved that formality was over and joined a reception that was organized by the government in celebration of the redress settlement. John Fraser, Sergio Marchi, Ernie Epp, Ed Broadbent, Gerry Weiner, and other members of Parliament, as well as government bureaucrats, offered words of congratulation and talked and mingled with the many Japanese Canadians who had come to Ottawa for this special moment.

Following the reception we, as a group, walked across the grounds of Parliament Hill and across Wellington Avenue to the National Press Building for the joint press conference. Weiner indicated in his press statement that "This was a historic agreement. And it is an honourable and meaningful settlement." He explained the principles that guided and defined the negotiations:

> First, we sought to reach an agreement that would have the sup-port of the NAJC, on behalf of the Japanese Canadian community.
>
> Second, we wanted to ensure that this kind of injustice could never happen again in this country.

And third, we struggled to finalize an agreement now for compassionate reasons. We were mindful of those Japanese Canadians whose health and advancing age might deprive them of knowing that the shame on their honour, their dignity, their rights as Canadians is now removed forever.

The compensation package was structured on the principle that the rights of the individuals had been violated based on racism. Weiner outlined the specific details written in the terms of the agreement. As the agreement indicated, the $21,000 individual redress was not specific compensation for the loss of property, belongings, and so on, but represented symbolic compensation for the loss of basic rights, more specifically, the loss of freedom for seven years. Eligible recipients had to have been directly affected by the War Measures Act. The agreement also called for a community fund of $12 million to be administered by the NAJC for education and cultural or social activities, an additional $3 million to the NAJC to assist in the administration of the redress payment process, and $24 million to establish the Canadian Race Relations Foundation. A critical component in the deal was the formal acknowledgment that had been delivered in the House of Commons by the prime minister.

The creation of the Canadian Race Relations Foundation to foster racial harmony, encourage cross-cultural understanding, and fight racism was a key component in the agreement. Japanese Canadians contributed $12 million in commemoration of those who had suffered wartime injustices and had passed away, an amount which was matched by a further $12 million from the government of Canada.

The government also announced that it would clear the names of Japanese Canadians who had been convicted for defying the War Measures Act for such actions as breaking curfew or returning prematurely to the West Coast. Offers of Canadian citizenship would be granted to people who had been deported to Japan or had their citizenship revoked between 1941 and 1949.

In my press statement, I referred to September 22, 1988, as "a great day for justice and human rights – a historic day for Canadians of Japanese ancestry who have been struggling so long to resolve the injustices of the 1940s."[6] When asked by a reporter at the press conference how I felt, I remember saying, "I don't know how else to express it but jump up, shout, and yell."

After the press conference, the strategy committee members and Don Rosenbloom went to the Honourable Gerry Weiner's office in the Confederation Building, a half-block from the National Press Building. Moore opened bottles of wine as we continued celebrating and revelling in our success. Weiner was getting ready to fly to Toronto for a redress celebration event at Sutton Place and invited the members of the strategy committee to join him on his flight to Toronto. I was unable to go, as I had already made plans to return to Winnipeg for a celebration with members of the NAJC President's Committee and the Manitoba Japanese Canadian Redress Committee at my home that evening.

The editorial comments across Canada were certainly favourable to the government's announcement. The following day, the *Lethbridge Herald*'s editorial stated, "The Honour Belongs to Japanese Canadians," and the *Calgary Herald* declared, "Justice Is Finally Done." "A Nation Apologizes" was the headline of the *Toronto Star*'s editorial, while the *Montreal Gazette* announced, "Justice, 45 Years Later."[7] These headlines demonstrated a remarkable acceptance of finally recognizing the past injustices – the shame, humiliation, and suffering faced by Japanese Canadians – and a willingness of Canadians to be fair and just.

On the Saturday following the redress announcement, I was on my way to the Muskoka area, north of Toronto, to attend a Canadian Ethnocultural Council executive meeting at Past President George Corne's cottage. When I arrived, George informed me that there had been a call from the prime minister, and I was to call him as soon

---

6   Herbert H. Denton, "Ottawa to Pay Reparations for War Internees," *Washington Post*, September 23, 1988, www.washingtonpost.com/archive/politics/1988/09/23/ottawa -to-pay-reparations-for-war-internees/1e4c10d9-eb9e-4753-be2f-749c369a349a/.

7   "The Honour Belongs to Japanese Canadians," *Lethbridge Herald*, September 23, 1988, newspaperarchive.com/lethbridge-herald-sep-23-1988-p-1/; "Justice Is Finally Done," *Calgary Herald*, September 23, 1988, 4, www.newspapers.com/image/484484903; "A Nation Apologizes," *Toronto Star*, September 23, 1988, A26, www.proquest.com/news- papers/nation-apologizes/docview/435780382/se-2; "Justice, 45 Years Later," *Montreal Gazette*, September 23, 1988, 14, www.proquest.com/historical-newspapers/september -23-1988-page-14-56/docview/2197898332/se-2.

as I could. I called the prime minister's home, but he was out with his kids. I tried again and left a message indicating where I could be reached. I never heard from the prime minister and wondered why he had been trying to contact me. While I was at the Toronto airport on my way to the cottage, I read an article in the Saturday *Toronto Star* in which a Tory backbencher, Barrie MP Ronald Stewart (Simcoe South), harshly criticized the government's decision to provide compensation to Japanese Canadians interned during World War II. He stated, "Really, it's a windfall profit for them. I can't be very sympathetic."[8] I wondered whether the prime minister wanted to talk to me about that particular article. I'll never know.

In many ways, we were thrilled with the outcome of the negotiations. Each component of the NAJC's redress proposal that had been submitted in May 1986 had been satisfied and reflected in the agreement.

What does the settlement mean? It meant that the process of negotiations that we had stressed with the various ministers was finally honoured and had resulted in a final redress agreement. For Japanese Canadians, the agreement was an official acknowledgment by the present government of Canada that its predecessors had committed a grave injustice towards Canadian citizens of Japanese ancestry.

I recall David Suzuki's words at the Ottawa redress rally on April 13, 1988, when he expressed regret that his mother had died as an "enemy alien" without ever hearing the government's apology. With that burden of guilt lifted, Japanese Canadians could now continue with their lives as equal Canadians.

Seldom does a nation confront the errors of the past and try to make amends. It does so at the risk of setting a precedent that might result in further costly settlements, not to mention the potential tarnishing of the national self-image. For Canada, the government's gesture in recognition of past errors demonstrated its commitment to the preservation of human rights and justice and the protection of minority rights. It strengthened its Charter of Rights and Freedoms, Multiculturalism Act, and very Constitution.

A critical component of the redress proposal was a recommendation to either change the War Measures Act or to rescind it to

---

8   Quoted in William Walker, "Tory MP Condemns Deal for Japanese Canadians," *Toronto Star*, September 24, 1988, A3, www.proquest.com/newspapers/tory-mp-condemns -deal-japanese-canadians/docview/435774527/se-2.

ensure that what had been done to Japanese Canadians could not be perpetrated against any other minority groups and to protect citizens against future injustices. The process to revamp or revoke the Act was underway prior to the redress rally in Ottawa. The NAJC, represented by Audrey Kobayashi and me, appeared before the Parliamentary Committee reviewing the War Measures Act to offer a significant number of changes to the bill. Ann Gomer Sunahara, author of *Politics of Racism*, assisted the NAJC in drafting the amendments. On July 2, 1988, the government adopted the Emergencies Act and rescinded the War Measures Act. The new act authorized Parliament, rather than just Cabinet, to take temporary measures to ensure safety and security during national emergencies. The NAJC had played a prominent role in recommending significant changes to the original government draft of this act. I was fortunate to be in the House the day the bill was passed, when Minister Perrin Beatty acknowledged the efforts of the NAJC in assisting with the drafting of the new legislation. Although there were (and are still) some areas of the act that needed to be strengthened, it was a positive step forward. (Thirty-four years after the settlement, the Emergencies Act was invoked for the first time by Prime Minister Justin Trudeau on February 14, 2022, to deal with the so-called Freedom Convoy's illegal blockades and protests in Ottawa and other parts of Canada against the government's COVID-19 pandemic restrictions.)

All in all, the redress settlement was a historic gesture of reconciliation. Prime Minister Mulroney deserves commendation and respect for his courageous act in confronting the irresponsible actions of a past government.

On September 22, 1988, history was made. It was the first time the government of Canada had apologized to an entire community and given compensation to each individual who had been a victim of the government's wrongdoing. The significance of this momentous accomplishment was expressed by Roger Obata as we were sitting on his hotel room's rug, reminiscing about what had just transpired and marvelling at our unbelievable achievement, and repeated in the Redress Anniversary issue[9] of the Japanese Canadian national news-

---

9   See, for example, Kelly Fleck, "Redress 30 Years Later," Nikkei Voice (website), October 17, 2018, nikkeivoice.ca/redress-30-years-later/, and Frank Moritsugu, "Frankly Speaking: Redress 30th Anniversary – Almost Forgot It," Nikkei Voice, October 25, 2018, nikkeivoice. ca/frankly-speaking-redress-30th-anniversary-almost-forgot-it/.

paper *Nikkei Voice*: "The amazing thing to me is how a small group within a small community was able to achieve so much."

Japanese Canadian redress was a political and moral issue. Often the strength of the lobbying process is in direct proportion to the voting power of the group doing the lobbying. In the Japanese Canadian redress situation, this was not the case. With a total population of approximately sixty thousand, the Japanese Canadian community represents about one-fifth of 1 percent of the Canadian population, a numerically insignificant voice. Furthermore, Japanese Canadians were deliberately dispersed across the nation after World War II and have remained so, thus not constituting a voting power in any area of the country. However, by making the redress campaign a human-rights issue, we ensured that Canadians could understand the former government's action as unacceptable and undesirable, especially in comparison to today's standard of fair play and justice. Our collective voice convinced the government and the public that the time was ripe for the apology and compensation.

The question most often raised in press interviews following the redress settlement was what influenced the government to make a sudden reversal of its opposition to individual compensation and then arrive at a mutually acceptable agreement. I believe that the signing of the US redress bill by President Ronald Reagan in August 1988, which would pay $20,000 per person in individual compensation to Japanese Americans, was the turning point. This bill clearly established a precedent for individual compensation which our government would have difficulty dismissing, because of the similar wartime treatment in both countries of citizens of Japanese ancestry. Also, with the upcoming federal election, Mulroney may have wanted to fulfill his 1984 election promise to Japanese Canadians by "putting things right." Perhaps the resignation of the Honourable George Hees from Cabinet allowed Mulroney more latitude to reconsider the position taken by Crombie and other ministers. I heard suggestions that the redress settlement was the means of securing the "ethnic vote." Regardless, this did not diminish our satisfaction or praise for the government. All of the factors mentioned were, in some way, instrumental in the government's decision to redress past injustices against Japanese Canadians.

To commemorate the successful achievement of the redress settlement, associations of Japanese Canadians across Canada put together celebration dinners that were the beginning of the healing process for the internees. The first dinner was held in Montréal on October 8, 1988, with Gerry Weiner, the minister responsible for the settlement, as guest of honour. Attendance at the fourteen gatherings that were held was overwhelming, and in nearly every centre, organizers indicated it was the largest gathering of Japanese Canadians they had ever witnessed. During the seven months following the celebration in Montréal, Keiko and I, along with Anne Scotton or another staff member, attended every other celebration dinner taking place across the country. The atmosphere was exhilarating as people were happy to see each other and talk sentimentally about the past. It was an opportunity to hear details of the negotiation process, the settlement, and the already ambitious future plans for the community fund. A feeling of unity permeated the evening, with accolades bestowed on the NAJC leadership, its strategy team, and the local delegates who had spearheaded the redress campaign. As I left each dinner, I felt the jubilation among the victims for the apology and compensation, but more importantly, the feeling of revitalization rising in the hearts of a community that had once been oppressed. The internment, starting in 1942, had drastically altered the lives of Japanese Canadians, but the redress agreement of 1988 had now become an important milestone in Canadian history.

At the dinner to celebrate the tenth anniversary of the redress agreement in Toronto, the former prime minister was recognized for his role. His wife Mila and son Ben were in attendance to join in the celebration before an appreciative audience. I had the privilege of sitting between Brian and Mila Mulroney at the head table. In our discussion I asked how much he was influenced by the signing of the US bill. He responded without hesitation and said, "I had made up my mind earlier than that." One interesting question he asked me was, "How much did the redress settlement cost the Canadian government?" I was surprised to hear that, so I told him it was close to $450 million. After his comments, I began to think that when George Hees left Cabinet in April 1988, it gave Mulroney leeway to be more flexible in trying to reach a resolution that would include individual compensation. Another influential consideration is the role played by Lucien Bouchard, who came into Cabinet around the same time that Hees left and was supportive of redress and of Mulroney. At the final negotiations meeting, it was Bouchard who first proposed that the government would be willing to offer individual recognition.

In the fall of 1989, the consul general of Japan in Winnipeg Yuzuki Kaku invited Keiko and I, along with members of the president's committee, to a private celebration at his residence on Wellington Crescent. Mr. Kaku explained that he wanted to express his appreciation as he had followed the redress movement closely during his time in Winnipeg and was happy and pleased to see the issue successfully resolved. For me, this was a significant gesture on his part as it was the first time that a member of the Japanese government ever acknowledged the redress achievement.

The success of the redress campaign can be attributed to a number of influences. First, there were the politicians, especially the Opposition's multicultural critics Sergio Marchi (Liberal) and Ernie Epp (NDP), their respective leaders John Turner and Ed Broadbent, MPs such as David Kilgour and Alan Redway, and Senator Jerry Grafstein, who supported our cause and gave it a voice in parliament. The Standing Committee on Multiculturalism, which invited the NAJC to make a presentation, the Toronto Ad Hoc Committee for Japanese Canadian Redress, made up of interested supporters who undertook several public-relations projects, such as massive educational advertising campaigns, and our rallies – all of these elements highlighted redress as more than just a Japanese Canadian concern. The formation of the National Coalition for Japanese Canadian Redress by the NAJC effectively raised the profile of redress among the Canadian public.

In the Canadian political system, the prime minister, along with a few colleagues, can exercise enormous powers. For a volatile and controversial issue such as redress, not to mention a minority-group issue, leadership support from the top is essential. Again, it must be said that Prime Minister Brian Mulroney deserves much credit for taking the initiative to concede that a violation of the human rights of Canada's own citizens had occurred and to "right the wrong" of those past injustices.

September 22, 1988, aroused many emotions for me. First, I had to convince myself that the day was really happening – finally, a dream come true. I had difficulty in containing my joy at the moment that the prime minister acknowledged that Japanese Canadians had done no wrong. That statement alone relieved the burden of guilt that many of the victims carried throughout their lives. I thought of my grandparents and my father who, I'm sure, would have been so proud of our achievement but had not lived long enough to savour the celebration. I could see the joy on my mother's face in Winnipeg as she heard the apology. She had been such a strong supporter of Roy and me. I think it is so important that we remember September 22, 1988, as a glorious day, a day that Japanese Canadians commemorate annually, so that following generations will always keep in mind the campaign that triumphed over the pain and humiliation suffered by Japanese Canadians during and after World War II.

CHAPTER 11

Implementation

I know for many of us this is not the end. I must say, with the responsibilities bestowed upon us by the government, it is just the beginning, because there is much work to be done in rebuilding the Japanese Canadian community.

—ART MIKI

at the press conference following the announcement of the Japanese Canadian redress settlement on September 22, 1988

Following the redress announcement, the government moved quickly to implement the agreement by establishing the Japanese Canadian Redress Secretariat (JCRS). This government agency would be responsible for establishing the redress application procedures and making decisions regarding individual redress claims. Provisions were made in the terms of the redress agreement so that the NAJC would be involved in the implementation process at the community level. In its official 1988 "Acknowledgement," the government offered "to provide, through contractual arrangements, up to $3 million to the National Association of Japanese Canadians for their assistance, including community liaison, in administration of redress over the period of implementation."[1]

This was a very important symbolic gesture for us because, as part

---

1   Point (f) in "Terms of Agreement between the Government of Canada and the National Association of Japanese Canadians," quoted in Miki and Kobayashi, *Justice in Our Time*, 138–139.

of the process of healing the community, Japanese Canadians played a role in assisting the victims of the government's wartime measures with their redress claims. This unique arrangement was put forward by the NAJC during negotiation meetings as a means of involving the community in the decision-making process. The recognition that it was no longer the government acting unilaterally against the community, as in 1942, but that it was rather the government liaising with Japanese Canadians in a spirit of co-operation, was an important historical milestone.

The details of the agreement and the implementation process were shared with community representatives at the NAJC Annual General Meeting in October 1988 in Montréal. Following the signing of the redress agreement, the work of the NAJC strategy committee that had been empowered to negotiate a redress settlement came to an end. The NAJC National Council established the Settlement Advisory Committee (SAC) to implement the redress agreement. The committee was composed of the president, as the chair, two representatives from the west of Canada, two from the east, and two more appointed by the NAJC president. They were Cassandra Kobayashi (Vancouver), Henry Kojima (Winnipeg), Tony Tamayose (Vancouver), Roger Obata (Toronto), Aki Watanabe (Ottawa), Audrey Kobayashi (Montréal), and me (Winnipeg).

The SAC's role was to develop plans for the four major elements in the redress agreement: the administration fund of $3 million, individual compensation, the community fund of $12 million, and the Canadian Race Relations Foundation. The administration fund was assigned to the NAJC; funds were released by the Japanese Canadian Redress Secretariat's office on a contractual arrangement, whereby the use of the funds had to be clearly specified, budgeted, and approved. The funds were used to establish national, regional, and local liaison offices, to employ personnel for them, and to support various projects that would educate Canadians about the Japanese Canadian experience and the redress process.

Staff were hired under the direction of the SAC's first executive director, Anne Scotton. She had been in the public service for four years prior to becoming involved as a government representative in the initial negotiation process under Jack Murta in December 1984. Because of her interest in political science, she was aware of the historical importance of what had been done to Japanese Canadians during the war and of the politics of that period. Also, she was familiar with the redress agreement, having been a member of the government's negotiation team in August 1988. After the negotiation meeting, Anne Scotton was asked to coordinate the details of the agreement, prepare the acknowledgment (in English and French), establish the signing process, the signing ceremony, and guest list, and arrange the prime minister's speech and the press conference. According to Anne, "All this had to be prepared in less than a month and had to be done in secrecy because we didn't know what the timing would be until we had some word from the prime minister's office."

Sensitive to the suggestion offered by the NAJC during the final negotiation meeting that the settlement should go beyond the financial package, Anne Scotton recognized that it was also the beginning of the healing process for the victims. In establishing the office for the Japanese Canadian Redress Secretariat, Anne wanted a location that would give immediate access to the public and an open, friendly, accessible application process that would be appropriate to the culture of the community it was serving. As Anne said, "We didn't want to go through a bureaucratic and police-oriented kind of process which would bring back memories of what it was that happened long ago. We wanted to create the perception that [the] community was part of the process of implementation even at the secretariat level." Anne was personally committed to accurately portraying the community she was trying to serve: "Having Japanese Canadians working very closely with us would be more culturally appropriate and more sensitive to their needs and would undoubtedly be more successful." Anne went immediately to the Public Service Commission of Canada (PSC) and was told that looking for only Japanese Canadians to hire was discriminatory, despite the circumstances! How ironic it was that the government had discriminately targeted Japanese Canadians during the war but wouldn't target Japanese Canadians for government positions that required an intimate knowledge of the community and Japanese language because that was discriminatory. Anne's response was, "Fine, I will then look for visible-minority candidates who self-identify as such and I'll attempt to identify out of that group those who can speak or understand Japanese." This worked to a certain extent. With the help of contacts in the Ottawa Japanese Canadian community, several members were recruited, such as June Takahashi, Roy Kawamoto, and Lillian Lee (née Taguchi), for the secretariat office by December 5, 1988, just in time for the office opening on December 15. Joy Kamibayashi, a teacher by profession, hearing that the secretariat was looking for Japanese Canadians, sent in her résumé and was hired in January 1990 as a program officer. She was later involved with educational projects such as the first NAJC education conference in Toronto, which the secretariat supported. Having Japanese Canadians working at the secretariat, with their knowledge of the community and familiarity with the families, proved to be invaluable to the secretariat's work.

Roy Kawamoto, a nisei from Ottawa, was one of the first people hired, given his knowledge of Japanese and because he knew his way around government. His bilingual abilities were especially valuable when working with issei or people living in Japan. When Kawamoto was asked whether hiring Japanese Canadians in the office was a positive move, he related this story:

> One day I received a call from a Japanese Canadian applicant who was shouting obscenities because he hadn't received his cheque and was critical of the office for the delay. After patiently listening to the caller, I indicated that I would check into the progress of the file and asked for his name. When the caller spelt out his name, I commented that his name was very close to mine. Curious, the caller asked me, "What is your name?" I spelled my name very slowly. Surprised, the person said, "But you're Japanese." My quick response was: "Who did you think I was?" As soon as the irate caller realized that he was speaking to a fellow Japanese Canadian, I felt the tone of his voice change drastically, likely because of embarrassment. He thanked me for listening and assisting him. Most callers expressed appreciation that some Japanese Canadians were working in the office, and others were pleasantly surprised to hear that Japanese Canadian voices were hired specifically for the redress program.

The greatest personal challenge for Anne was helping the younger employees understand or have sympathy for the older Japanese Canadians with whom they were dealing, explaining to them the life-altering effect that the redress settlement would have on the victims who remained impacted by the government's actions. She said the stories they were collecting in the redress applications were so horrendous and tragic, and in some cases so debilitating, that it was difficult for people who had not lived through that period or hadn't known or hadn't heard people speak about it to accept that those things had happened. She thought the most difficult thing for staff was patiently and sensitively listening to stories which were so difficult to absorb, believe, or accept. Anne felt that the process of making a redress claim from the government should be painless and as positive as possible for the survivors who had waited so long.

There were forty-two employees at the peak of activity in the secretariat office. The establishment of the office was an intense process, as job descriptions needed to be developed and personnel hired on term and permanent contracts. Because it was a short-term project (five years), Scotton envisioned that much of the work would be completed within two years. By spring 1995, the secretariat office had processed 18,534 applications, in which 17,953 payments of $21,000 were issued and 581 applications were rejected. Many of those rejected came from Japanese Canadians who had been born in Canada but were living in Japan during wartime (often to attend school or for employment) and were therefore not directly impacted by the War Measures Act. In most cases, Japanese Canadians who had been trapped in Japan while visiting and unable to return were often granted redress on appeal. At the end of the redress program, in the spring of 1995, only Roy Kawamoto, Lillian Lee, June Takahashi, researcher Paul O'Donnell, and executive director Joanne Lamarre remained as secretariat employees. By this time, Anne Scotton had been promoted to a higher-level position.

I personally had a collegial relationship with Scotton. Whenever I was in Ottawa, I would visit the secretariat office to confer with her and meet the staff. At one of my visits, Scotton called me over to indicate that she'd been receiving calls from someone I knew complaining that he hadn't received his redress cheque. She showed me the name. It was someone who had been vehemently opposed to individual compensation and a strong supporter of George Imai. My first reaction was to think, "Such hypocrisy!" I understand now that whether they opposed individual compensation or not, they were entitled to apply because of their personal suffering.

The secretariat office's success in meeting the government's redress obligations should be attributed to Anne Scotton's efforts and the dedicated staff she recruited for this unique project. Scotton now feels that her experience as executive director of the secretariat was a highlight of her career because of what it was able to accomplish and because, with her understanding and ability, she could do something that she felt was right. "It was enormously fulfilling and a satisfying experience professionally," she said. Scotton and her staff members attended many of the orientation meetings in communities across Canada, introducing Japanese Canadians to the people who were processing their applications. I know Scotton enjoyed the visits, interacting with the internees and listening to their stories. She stated, "It allowed me an opening on life and on understanding human situations. I mean on both sides, the stories we heard about the kindness of Caucasian Canadians or about white people who worked with Japanese Canadians." People wrote in at the time of redress expressing views on both sides, but mainly in favour of redress. One individual, learning about the impact of the expulsion for the first time, stated, "I grew up beside somebody who was Japanese Canadian and they disappeared when they were ten years old and now I know what had happened"; another: "We had a Japanese Canadian maid when I lived in Toronto. I had no idea she had been sent from her family." Another person wrote, "My best friends were Japanese Canadians. I didn't know they had been interned" or "that they had worked on this horrible sugar beet farm." And then, of course, on the other side, Anne received critical comments such as, "Why would you do this for a group that together represents an enormous amount of money and influence"; or: "[The Japanese Canadians] are the most integrated and most adaptive. They've all integrated, why should you start focusing on them now?" Redress made a lot of people think through what was right and what was just, and not what was expedient or what was the best use of millions of dollars. Roy Kawamoto also had high praise for Anne Scotton and felt she was the best person for the job: "I don't think anyone else could have gotten the redress secretariat off the ground the way she did."

Joy Kamibayashi felt the office was like "one big family," much different from other departments she had worked in. Joy added, "It was due to Anne Scotton's leadership and personality. She involved everyone in the process. I think her sensitivity and caring made the difference. She really cares." She was most untypical of the majority of bureaucrats. "We were fortunate to have her." As national administrator, Tony Tamayose was required to work closely with Anne

Scotton, as he was accountable to the secretariat office; he refers to Anne as "not a typical bureaucrat, as she doesn't always tow the government line." Unlike in most government programs, Anne was able to have the office operational quickly, and the first survivor redress payment was made three months after the settlement was announced. This speady turnabout is untypical of how government operates, but it was due to Anne's persistence and ingenuity.

For the Japanese Canadian community, individual compensation was clearly the most urgent priority the SAC should deal with. One of the priorities that the minister gave the secretariat office was to expedite redress for the older recipients first, as agreed by the NAJC. Within two months of the announcement, members of the SAC had provided input to the redress secretariat staff in developing criteria for application and for the application form itself. This process required the enormous efforts of the whole government, including the monstrous machine of the Department of Supply and Services and the Ministry of Multiculturalism's finance department. Although the oldest recipients were the priority, many of them did not receive an application immediately, because the application forms had to be developed, prepared, and translated into Japanese and French. These application forms and the accompanying information developed in collaboration with the NAJC needed to be culturally sensitive and required a great deal of thought and reflection. In the end, the application form devised with the secretariat was only one page long, unlike the far lengthier and more cumbersome application form being used for residential school Survivors. The government was anxious to see the process get underway quickly and had the application forms ready for distribution by December 1988. In addition, forms were mailed out to individuals whose addresses were available to the NAJC. Forms were available at NAJC offices across Canada or could be ordered from the secretariat's office through a toll-free number. An information pamphlet was produced by the NAJC to assist individuals in filling out the application form. The SAC made arrangements to organize the process of handling application forms across the country and to assist applicants in filling out the forms.

To manage this enormous task in an efficient and expeditious manner, Tony Tamayose worked closely with me. In early December 1988, he was selected as national administrator from a list of well-qualified applicants. He had served as the manager of the Vancouver district office and was also their Pacific regional administrator responsible for finance and general administration. His more than thirty years' experience in the public service were invaluable in establishing the implementation's organizational structure for the NAJC, and his knowledge of governmental finances was an asset.

To assist eligible Japanese Canadians, regional offices were established in Vancouver, Toronto, and Winnipeg and staffed by regional coordinators Tatsuo Kage, Harry Yonekura, and Jim Suzuki, respectively. Tatsuo was a bilingual community worker for the settlement and employment services organization MOSAIC in Vancouver and a freelance writer and translator. He had been involved with various community groups, including Japanese Canadian organizations. As an accredited member of the Society of Translators and Interpreters of British Columbia, he was a valuable asset in his role as western regional bilingual coordinator.

Prior to the war, Harry Yonekura had been a fisherman. Before retiring in 1988, he owned his own construction business and had received the Shell Canada Limited Award in recognition for his quality of service. In 1986, he was the recipient of the Ontario government's Volunteer Service Award. His contribution to the Japanese Canadian community through his work with the Toronto Buddhist Church as well as with the NAJC at the regional and national levels was valued.

Jim Suzuki was an engineering graduate from the University of Manitoba. Through his broadcasting services and engineering and consulting work, he acquired a useful knowledge of the workings of the federal government's departments and agencies. He was involved in the community as president of the Manitoba Japanese Canadian Citizens' Association and a director of their cultural centre.

The regional coordinators were responsible for instituting field offices in temporary facilities such as community centres or churches in their region, especially in places where a substantial number of Japanese Canadians resided. In smaller centres where there were fewer than fifty families, assistance to individuals was done in private homes. Field workers ranged from voluntary helpers to part-time and full-time staff, depending on the need.

Once the administrative structure had been laid out, the implementation program took place in three phases. In the first phase, the field workers made contacts in their areas, providing applicants the necessary information, translation services, or help in filling out the claim forms. They supported community members by arranging information and assistance meetings, preparing advertisements, and taking phone calls. Because the application forms required a sworn statement by the applicants, the NAJC offices held attestation meetings providing the services of a lawyer, public notary, or commissioner of oaths.

The second phase involved locating and identifying applicants requiring special assistance, such as the elderly, the disabled, those confined to institutions, persons living in isolated areas, and others. The third phase involved the carrying out of projects through formal contracts with the NAJC that would promote awareness of redress nationally and internationally. The news spread rapidly, and within a few months of the application form being available, the Japanese Canadian Redress Secretariat's office was swamped with 9,500 requests. By June 1989, they had received fifteen thousand applications. The overwhelming response was due largely to the information program and the effectiveness of the local offices. Once the secretariat received an application, its information could readily be verified to see if the applicant qualified, as the government had kept meticulously detailed records on each family in Archives Canada. The first *ex gratia* redress cheque for $21,000, accompanied by a copy of the official acknowledgment, was received on December 23, 1988, only three months and a day after Mulroney's formal apology and announcement. The redress secretariat office reaped the benefit of the NAJC's involvement in the implementation contract.

By the end of April 1989, the NAJC team of twenty-six staff had held seventy-two public meetings with over eleven thousand people attending. At many of the meetings, a Japanese-speaking representative from the secretariat's office attended to answer questions from the audience. The local staff members provided phone services, handed out application forms, gave direct advice to claimants, and assisted individuals in completing the forms.

In order to accelerate the number of redress cheques issued, the Japanese Canadian Redress Secretariat's staff of forty-two worked overtime. By the end of September 1989, more than seven thousand cheques had been issued. The NAJC requested that the secretariat give priority to those applicants born before 1920 and those who had been identified as terminally ill or in financial need.

Apart from the files that did not meet the criteria, there were approximately eight hundred applications that fell within the "grey" area for eligibility. The secretariat had processed and made symbolic payments to the majority of applicants within two years. An amazing accomplishment! I would contrast this to the rate of payout to Japanese Americans in the United States, where the system used was different. Each year Congress had to approve a budget of a fixed amount for redress payments with distribution based on age, with the oldest first. As a result, it took nearly *twenty* years before the last Japanese American received their $20,000 payment.

One area of dispute was the government's interpretation of the Order-in-Council for redress payments, especially for children born in Japan during the period up to April 1, 1949, to parents who had either been sent to Japan or stranded there. In November 1988, sensing that the secretariat would reject those applications, the NAJC Council passed the following motion: "That NAJC Council supports compensation to the children who were born in Japan on or before March 31, 1949, to individuals of Japanese ancestry who were exiled or deported to Japan." The wording of the motion was conveyed to the Honourable Gerry Weiner. However, the government's legal advisors recommended against accepting the motion, indicating that it was not within the terms of the agreement.

In anticipation that some applications might fall within the grey area, provisions were made in the implementation parameters to establish an independent body consisting of NAJC and government appointees. Therefore, a Redress Advisory Committee (RAC) was established to review claims for individual compensation which did not clearly meet the eligibility criteria. Approval for this committee was given by the NAJC at the National Council meeting in Vancouver in January 1989, and interested individuals wishing to serve on the committee were asked to submit application letters to the NAJC.

The Redress Advisory Committee consisted of two representatives from the Secretary of State, two representatives from the NAJC, and a chair appointed by the government. The Committee's role was to review all cases that were not clearly included or excluded within the eligibility guidelines and to make recommendations for a decision to the minister of multiculturalism. The final decision in cases on which the committee could not reach consensus would be left to the minister's discretion.

At the Winnipeg National Council meeting held in May 1989, Roy Miki and Ann Gomer Sunahara were appointed as NAJC representatives to the RAC. Lizzy Fraikin and Catherine Lane represented the Secretary of State and Rick Clippendale, the assistant under the Secretary of State, was the chairperson. The two resource persons were Anne Scotton and Anne Daniel, a lawyer from the Department of Justice.

In accordance with the Privacy Act, the two NAJC representatives could not divulge information about individual cases. In fact, in reviewing a file, the RAC would not know the applicant's identity. They were given details of the individual's background and experiences during the period from 1941 to 1949 and the reason why the file had been held up. During the discussions, Anne Scotton provided additional information, if required.

In the early phases, the most controversial issue of the children born in Japan between 1945 and 1949 to repatriated or deported individuals was not dealt with. The eligibility criteria for individuals negotiated between the NAJC and the government in August 1988 seemed much broader than those of the government's Order-in-Council. The criteria applied to all individuals of Japanese ancestry regardless of citizenship "who were uprooted, interned, deported, or repatriated or otherwise deprived of their rights because of the government's action." It was the government that inserted a more restrictive qualification that the individual had to be "a British subject, Canadian citizen or landed immigrant during the period beginning December 7, 1941, and ending March 31, 1949." The legal advice from the Justice lawyers was that those individuals born in Japan during the designated period had not been deprived of their rights because they did not meet the standard, as they were in Japan and not in Canada. The NAJC argued that had the parents not been deported or repatriated to Japan, these children would have been born in Canada and, therefore, should be eligible.

Paul O'Donnell, a researcher with the JCRS, said that in dealing with people who weren't in the country at the time, the records in Archives Canada were of no use, and he had to use External Affairs and Immigration records. A lot of the individual case files there had been destroyed as part of routine record maintenance. The office did their best to fill in the details with the External Affairs records, resulting in delays for decisions. The NAJC attempted to meet with the Minister of Multiculturalism Gerry Weiner on several occasions. At a meeting with Mr. Weiner in Vancouver on June 10, 1989, he emphasized that if the matter was directed to the minister's office, he would have to disqualify the applicants based on his knowledge of the government's position. He indiscreetly implied that a more practical solution would be to use the Redress Advisory Committee under the direction of the undersecretary to consider these cases. Dr. Noël A. Kinsella, the undersecretary, who was present at the meeting and had the minister's confidence, appeared to respond positively and supported the approach suggested by the minister. This disagreement between the Japanese Canadian Redress Secretariat office and the NAJC, however, continued, as the RAC did not deal with the children born in Japan because these cases were not considered a priority. It wasn't until the federal election in 1993, when the Liberal government came into power, that the issue would finally be resolved.

While a member of RAC, Ann Gomer Sunahara was hired by the Department of Justice in Ottawa and had to resign because of conflict of interest. Paul Kariya, a civil servant in Ottawa, was appointed by the NAJC to succeed her.

As time went on, there were fewer and fewer meetings of the RAC, and the number of files needing a decision began to pile up. After Anne Scotton left the secretariat in September 1989, Rubin Friedman became the executive director. Directed by his superiors, he said that there was intense pressure to concentrate on processing the less complicated files and not be concerned with the files in the "grey area." When, in June 1990, Joanne Lamarre succeeded Friedman as executive director, she realized that there were inconsistencies with the decisions made by the RAC, because they looked at each anonymous file case by case (which was the original mandate of the committee as agreed by the minister). In an attempt to speed up the process, Joanne received advice from the government lawyers to establish rigid arbitrary categories with which to determine the eligibility of the files without going through the RAC. A meeting was held with Lamarre to discuss the outstanding applications. Government lawyers continued to argue that Japanese Canadians who had been stranded in Japan during World War II and until 1949 were not affected by the War Measures Act. Unable to resolve this difference in interpretation, a stalemate resulted, and the over seven hundred outstanding files were left in abeyance.

Lamarre gives an example of a difficult file that the secretariat had to deal with:

> A Japanese Canadian man applied for redress shortly after the settlement. However, while he was waiting for the file to be processed, he died and left his estate to his wife, a non–Japanese Canadian. The applicant didn't send in the necessary data, so the secretariat couldn't proceed. In the meantime, the wife passed away and left the estate to her housekeeper. The housekeeper then died, leaving her estate to her daughter. The daughter put in a request for the redress cheque to be put into her estate. Unfortunately, the information that was required for the original applicant was no longer accessible. The daughter had no way of getting the information. Her lawyers are still pursuing the redress payment.[2]

In October of 1993, the Liberal Party won a large majority and came to power. The Honourable Sheila Finestone was appointed secretary of state for multiculturalism and was now responsible for the Japanese Canadian redress file. In December 1993, I met with Finestone in Montréal to discuss the current state of the redress implementation process and our concerns regarding the outstanding files. She was apprised of the current impasse and developments within the Japanese Canadian community. Redress Action Committees in Vancouver and Toronto had begun to create profiles on applicants whose files had been rejected or not yet processed. I recommended that Finestone either adopt the process that had been agreed upon at the outset or meet face to face with the NAJC representatives to hear our rationale. A meeting was finally convened on March 22, 1994, in Finestone's office in Hull, Québec. Hearing the NAJC's and the Redress Action Committees' representatives, Finestone was so moved by the plights of the rejected victims that she agreed to accept the broadest interpretation for eligibility. Finally, many individual redress applications first considered ineligible were approved by the Redress Advisory Committee. Had the NAJC pressed Minister Weiner in 1989 to adopt a public position on those children born in Japan during World War II, he would not have qualified them. Thus by delaying the government decision, we were able to achieve more

---

2   From an interview with Joanne Lamarre on September 27, 1993, in Ottawa.

Canadian delegation to Japan. Front row, left to right: Roy Kawamoto, Art (NAJC), Anne Scotton, and Anne Daniel. Back row, left to right: Harry Yonekura (NAJC), Naomi Shikaze (NAJC), June Takahashi, Tatsuo Kage (NAJC), Masako Tsuchiya, and Lucy Sumi

PHOTO: Harry Yonekura

approvals. When the NAJC first negotiated the agreement, it had been impossible to anticipate the variety of situations that would not be included within the defined eligibility criteria and yet merited consideration.

The approximately four thousand Japanese Canadians exiled to Japan were eligible for individual compensation under the redress agreement of September 22, 1988, since they had been interned and deprived of their basic rights. The government agreed to send a joint delegation of four NAJC representatives and six government officials from the secretariat office to Japan to promote the redress agreement, explain the application procedure, and assist individuals in filling out the application form. The delegation, including NAJC representatives Tatsuo Kage, Harry Yonekura, Naomi Shikaze, and myself with Anne

Scotton and the secretariat staff, visited nine cities in sixteen days, starting in Tokyo and moving on to major cities across Japan.

I was surprised by the interest shown by the Japanese media, especially NHK, the country's public broadcaster.[3] What impressed them the most was the action of the Canadian government in actually sending a delegation to Japan to seek out applicants eligible for redress. When the Canadian delegation arrived at Narita International Airport, a television crew was waiting at the gate to interview members of the group. There was a large group of Japanese travellers, curious to know which important personality was arriving in Japan. I'm sure they anticipated some celebrities. Anne Scotton was quickly approached for statements from the reporters. We were overwhelmed by the reception we received.

The Japanese media wanted to know why the Canadian government would send a delegation to give money to people living in another country. NHK had a crew follow us from one city to another for four days, filming our meetings with potential applicants and reporting our progress on the nightly news. During interviews, Japanese reporters had difficulty understanding why any government would admit to making a mistake and provide compensation. This seemed an inconceivable concept for the reporters, who wondered how redress came about. In Japan, racist government policies exist, especially towards Koreans who have lived for several generations in Japan and yet are denied citizenship. Perhaps the differences in government policies towards minority rights is a result of Japan being "ethnically homogeneous," as it is often described (whether accurately or not), whereas Canada is undoubtedly a country with a diversity of cultures.

At the first meeting in Tokyo, nearly a hundred people attended; many internees were meeting each other for the first time since repatriation and had not realized that other people they had known had been living in Japan all this time. In fact, one woman was so excited to reunite with people from her past in Canada that she followed us to other cities to see who else she might discover. During the nine meetings, nearly seven hundred people attended, all grateful that Canadians had taken the time to visit Japan and facilitate the applications for individual redress. At each meeting, Anne Scotton

---

3   The acronym stands for Nippon Hōsō Kyōkai 日本放送協会 (the Japan Broadcasting Corporation).

opened with Prime Minister Mulroney's acknowledgment and an explanation of the spirit and content of the redress agreement. I provided an overview of the struggle of Japanese Canadians for redress and the role of the NAJC in achieving redress and in its implementation. The trust relationship and co-operation between the NAJC and government representatives were for us a clear demonstration of a unique partnership.

When we met with Japan's External Affairs officials during the visit in Tokyo to discuss how redress evolved, they were taken aback by the fact that the Canadian government was publicly acknowledging its past mistakes and sending bureaucrats to Japan to facilitate individuals' applications for compensation. After one of the top officials heard our story, he surmised that the Japanese government would not be able to admit to a mistake the way Canada had or be willing to compensate victims. He stated sincerely, "You know, it takes a mature country to do what Canada did." I was moved by his astute comments and was really proud at that moment to be Canadian, because of Canada's conscious actions to "right the wrong." However, what was not discussed at the time was the inadequate progress in both our countries in our relationships with Indigenous Peoples, whose unresolved Land claims, social needs, and poverty still exist today.[4]

Roy Kawamoto felt that the trip was a positive move because "it gave the perception that Canada was doing something no other country would ever dream of doing." At one of the meetings, he met a woman who remembered him from the Greenwood internment centre. She said to Roy, "I never dreamt that I would ever see you again." It was a nostalgic trip, and Roy commented that the positive feelings it aroused made it worthwhile.

A highlight of the trip for me personally was my encounter with Hank J. Nakamura, who had been sent to Japan as a "repatriate." Hank travelled from the city of Sasebo in Nagasaki Prefecture to attend a redress meeting in Fukuoka. Hank's father had been interned in the Angler POW camp in Ontario while the rest of the family was

---

4   Japan is also the modern home of Indigenous Peoples, most notably the Ainu アイヌ and the Okinawans/Ryūkyūans 琉球民族, whose Ancestral Territories and languages have been severely impacted by historical Japanese governments and reigns. See, for example, International Work Group for Indigenous Affairs (IWGIA), "The Indigenous Peoples in Japan," April 1, 2022, www.iwgia.org/en/japan/4651-iw-2022-japan.html.

The Honourable Gerry Weiner signing the Community Contribution
Agreement, March 1989
PHOTO: Courtesy of the Government of Canada

in another camp. At the end of the war, his father decided that the
family should go to Japan, so Hank, at the age of fourteen, reluc-
tantly went. His father was so angered by the treatment he and his
family received from the Canadian government that he gave up all of
their Canadian citizenship rights. Later, when Hank realized that his
citizenship had been revoked, he wrote letters to the Canadian government asking for a reinstatement. He was refused. He was told that
his father had signed away his citizenship when he stepped aboard
the boat to go to Japan. Hank told me that he never really felt at home
in Japan but more like an outsider, so his biggest wish was to regain
his Canadian citizenship. When hearing that one of the terms of the
agreement was reinstatement of lost citizenship, the first thing he
asked for at the meeting was the citizenship form. Hank Nakamura
filled out the form and indicated to me that he would inform me
when and if his citizenship was approved. Canadian citizenship was
what he cherished the most from the redress settlement.

Finally, I received a letter from Hank with the marvellous news. He wrote: "I am happy to report that the government has decided to grant me citizenship. I, of course, am gratified for the redress payment that I have received. But more importantly, the reinstatement of my Canadian citizenship was something that had a greater impact on me than anything else for I have been fighting a losing battle since 1952 in attempting to retrieve it." On November 19, 1990, Hank Nakamura was finally reinstated as a Canadian citizen following the oath-taking ceremony held at the Canadian Embassy in Tokyo. He further states in the letter, "I shall pay homage to my parent's grave to advise Dad of my reinstatement. I hold him blameless for the bitterness of Angler, but he died a sad man and broken-hearted as he held himself responsible for causing his children the anguish and humiliation we were compelled to experience in the early days of repatriation. Presently, I have a much better understanding as a grown man, only to wish that my parents were here today to see what has been accomplished." For me, Hank's story highlights one of the successes and some of the emotional impact of the redress agreement.

The implementation phase of the redress settlement was a significant milestone in the development of the Japanese Canadian community. Community infrastructure was strengthened as local NAJC chapters played a vital role in organizing gatherings and assisting applicants, thereby elevating the profile of the NAJC nationally.

The government's decision to disperse Japanese Canadians across the country after the war had been a deliberate move to assimilate them. The psychological damage and the loss of language resulted in cultural disintegration that had a permanent effect upon Japanese Canadians. Having faced racism and discrimination, they turned their backs on their language, culture, and heritage, as many nisei parents encouraged their children to assimilate into mainstream society. If Canada had had a multicultural policy in the 1940s encouraging the promotion and retention of one's own culture and language, perhaps the cultural disintegration would have been minimal. Today, the reality of Canada's ethnic and cultural diversity is recognized as a positive asset, especially as countries around the world become more interconnected in their economies and relations with each other.

The Canadian government's policy of forced relocation from the West Coast destroyed the existence of a vibrant Japanese Canadian

Japanese Canadian Redress Foundation, September 2001. Front row, left to right: Art, Tony Tamayose (executive director), Connie Sugiyama, Henry Shimizu (chair), Irene Nemeth, Lucy Yamashita, and Keiko Miki

Back row, left to right: Fred Kamibayashi, Marcia Matsui, Roger Obata, Fred Yada, Roy Inouye, and Dick Nakamura

community. Unlike the United States, where Japanese enclaves exist with their own "Japantowns," no such centre exists in any city in Canada. The NAJC strategy committee, realizing that it was impossible to recreate Japanese Canadian communities as they had been in the past, felt that endeavours to generate interest in Japanese Canadian community activities and culture were an essential part of the healing process. As part of the settlement, the Canadian government's $12 million community fund, designated at the request of the NAJC, assisted in the revitalization and rejuvenation of a community torn apart by the government's own actions. This fund is unique to the Canadian settlement. In the United States, a $5 million Education Fund was allotted for research and education, although not for community development. The Canadian government gave the NAJC the responsibility of putting in place an organizational structure that would be accountable for administering the community fund. At the January 1989 meeting in Vancouver, the National Council approved the formation of the Japanese Canadian Redress Foundation (JCRF). The purpose of the foundation was "to preserve our history, rebuild and develop our community on a local, regional, and national basis, and heal, unite and assist in establishing the future direction of community development" in accordance with the redress agreement.

The Settlement Advisory Committee, through their legal advisor, Cassandra Kobayashi, asked Blake Bromley, a Vancouver lawyer with expertise on foundations and charitable or not-for-profit organizations, to draft up the constitution and bylaws for the new foundation based on discussions with the NAJC. The JCRF was incorporated and registered with the federal Department of Consumer and Corporate Affairs in 1989.

In order to expedite the transfer of funds before the end of the government's fiscal year, $12 million was turned over to the NAJC on March 28, 1989. On that day I met with the Honourable Gerry Weiner to sign the Community Contribution Agreement with the government. Once the process was completed and pictures taken of this historic event, Mr. Weiner handed me a cheque in my name for $12 million. For at least half an hour, I was a "multimillionaire." Anne Scotton then escorted me by car to a prearranged bank in Ottawa so the money could be transferred over to the JCRF bank account in Vancouver.

The $12 million and the potential accumulation of interest were entrusted to the JCRF that was officially confirmed by the NAJC in March 1989. The term of the foundation was initially set for five years. A community survey was conducted by the *Nikkei Voice* and the *Vancouver Bulletin* after a number of community meetings were held across Canada to provide feedback on community's projects and program priorities. Based on opinions expressed at meetings and the results of the survey, it was clear that seniors placed community cultural facilities and the future of the community as their utmost concerns, whereas nisei and sansei indicated health-care and housing facilities for seniors as their priorities.

According to the mandate specified in the Memorandum of Agreement between the NAJC, the Foundation, and the government of

Canada, the use of the funds was based on the following criteria: no less than $8 million would be used for capital projects; no more than $4 million to undertake educational, social, and cultural activities and programs that contribute to the well-being of the community or that promote human rights; and a maximum of $500,000 to the NAJC for community outreach.

The board of directors of the JCRF consisted of three representatives from the NAJC, five people elected from the designated regions, and up to three people who might be appointed by the board for their specific skills or the needs of the foundation. The first board of directors consisted of Charles Kadota, Harold Hirose, and me, representing the NAJC, the elected regional directors Roy Inouye (Western), Fred Yada (Greater Vancouver), Henry Shimizu (Central), Roger Obata (Toronto), and Fred Kamibayashi (Eastern). After the second meeting of the Foundation, Irene Nemeth, Lucy Yamashita, and Connie Sugiyama were appointed to the board to improve its gender representation.

The first meeting of the foundation was held on July 17, 1989, in Winnipeg. During the initial phase, directors concentrated on the establishment of policies and programs, regional allocation guidelines, and the guidelines and standard practices for processing applications for capital projects. Every care was taken to ensure fairness and responsibility in the process. With the assistance of Connie Sugiyama's expertise, we developed conflict-of-interest guidelines. Once the parameters had been determined, the foundation was ready to take applications and begin the funding process.

Recognizing that the JCRF had to expend the community fund within the time frame established by the government, we requested that the minister of multiculturalism extend the agreement until 2001. The concern was that once the funds had been expended, the Japanese Canadian community would not have the financial resources to support the kinds of projects that would sustain it in the future. I drafted proposals for two different funds, SEAD (Sports, Education, Arts Development) and a Cultural Development Fund, and then requested that the JCRF establish endowments. These endowment funds were structured so that only the interest would be distributed annually as grants to recipients and the original capital would remain intact in perpetuity. In order to ensure its future existence, the NAJC was given the responsibility of administering funds, advertising programs to the Japanese Canadian community, and adjudicating grant applications. Once the process had been established, the JCRF requested and received approval from the minister of multiculturalism to revise the original Memorandum of Agreement to include provision for the endowment funds.

In 1990, following approval from the JCRF, the NAJC established the two endowments. The SEAD Fund, with an endowment base of $250,000, would assist young Japanese Canadians to explore areas of interest in sports, education, and the arts. Although academic scholarships were available, there was very little support for Japanese Canadians who are engaged seriously in these fields. The SEAD Fund would help to cover training expenses and special program costs that would facilitate the development of successful applicants' skills and talents. The Cultural Development Fund was established to support cultural and artistic groups within the Japanese Canadian community in the promotion of Japanese and Japanese Canadian culture. The JCRF awarded the NAJC $350,000 towards this endowment fund, but with the restructuring of the funds in 1999 it was increased to $550,000.

The Endowment Funds Committee (EFC) consisted of four members elected for a two-year term from the Japanese Canadian community based on regional distribution and chaired by the NAJC president. The first committee, under direction from the JCRF, developed the criteria for eligibility, the application process, and the application forms. The committee's role is to review applications to the SEAD or Cultural Development funds and recommend grant recipients to the NAJC Executive Committee.

Before the JCRF ceased operations and all expenditures were completed, the board decided that the remaining funds of approximately $1 million would be transferred to the NAJC for project funding. The NAJC now has prime responsibility for the management of the funds used for undertakings as determined at the discretion of the board. This will ensure that the NAJC will have the financial support to deliver activities in the future.

During the life of the JCRF, 152 projects were assisted financially with awards totalling nearly $17.5 million. Because the foundation provided funds on a cost-sharing basis, more than $80 million was raised through other sources, including generous contributions from community members. These projects involved thousands of volunteers who contributed many hours of valuable time. This tremendous effort reflects the energy and enthusiasm that abound in our community and that with stimulus will continue in the future. Surveys showed that 60 percent of respondents felt that the projects created more activity in the community, and 50 percent indicated that they had increased their participation after the redress settlement. The work of the foundation ceased on June 30, 2001, after three extensions to the original Memorandum of Agreement had been negotiated with the government.

One of the terms of agreement was the establishment of the Canadian Race Relations Foundation (CRRF), an institution for all Canadians. Bill C-63 was first tabled on January 31, 1990, and was later passed by the House of Commons after hearings by the Legislative Committee. However, for reasons unknown, the Conservatives refused to proclaim the bill that would make the foundation a reality.

Dr. Audrey Kobayashi and I worked closely with Anne Scotton to help develop the mandate and objectives for the foundation. Its role would be to serve as a national clearinghouse of data, provide resources to further understand racism and racial discrimination in Canadian society for community groups, researchers, and the general public, and develop effective race-relations policies and programs.

In commemoration of those Japanese Canadians who suffered injustices during and after World War II and sadly passed away before the settlement day, the Japanese Canadian community contributed $12 million, matched by the government, to establish an endowment fund of $24 million for the Canadian Race Relations Foundation. Sachiko Okuda, Dr. Audrey Kobayashi, and I appeared before the Parliamentary Committee on June 14, 1990, to present the NAJC brief, which outlined a number of recommended amendments to the bill, including the physical location of the foundation and its name. The NAJC representatives strongly urged that the term "race" be removed from the name. These two issues were not addressed to our satisfaction. Minister Weiner refused the suggestion to remove "race" because he felt that the term "race relations" was generally understood by the public and was an accepted convention in Canadian society.

Despite consistent lobbying by the NAJC, the Conservative government never proclaimed Bill C-63 during their term of office and the foundation did not become a reality. During the 1993 federal election campaign, Jean Chrétien attended a rally in the riding where

I was a candidate for the Liberal Party and announced that the establishment of the CRRF was one of the commitments written in the famous Liberal Party's Red Book (officially, *Creating Opportunity: The Liberal Plan for Canada*).[5] When the Liberal government came into power in October 1993, although I was not elected, we anticipated that the government would immediately proclaim Bill C-63. However, Sheila Finestone, secretary of state for multiculturalism, did not take any action to establish the long-awaited Race Relations Foundation. The NAJC implored Finestone to enact the bill. With each contact, the minister indicated that action would be taken once the appointments of the directors to the board had been finalized. Although many ethnic organizations expressed concern that racism was on the increase and the need for the foundation was even more crucial, the government failed to act. It seems that the Reform Party's opposition to the concept of a race relations foundation had compelled the government to take a cautious approach. After persistent lobbying by the NAJC and other Canadians, Bill C-63 was finally proclaimed in October 1996, thus giving birth to the long-awaited Race Relations Foundation.

On October 29, 1996, the CRRF was formally launched in Toronto by the Honourable Hedy Fry, secretary of state for multiculturalism. Dr. Fry indicated that the CRRF was in keeping with the Red Book promise but seemed to downplay the fact that the foundation was one of the terms of the Japanese Canadian redress settlement. Dr. Fry said, "The Foundation will be an important asset to build an inclusive society based on social harmony." The foundation, located in Toronto, operates at arm's length from the government with its primary role being "to work at the forefront of efforts to combat racism and all forms of racial discrimination." I was invited by the minister to participate in the press conference and met the Honourable Lincoln Alexander, the newly appointed chairperson of the CRRF, and Moy Tam, its executive director. I was impressed by Lincoln Alexander's down-to-earth attitude; his friendly manner made me feel comfortable immediately. He had impressive credentials and was an excellent role model and mentor for minority leaders. He was the first Black member of Parliament for

---

5   Liberal Party of Canada, *Creating Opportunity: The Liberal Plan for Canada* (Ottawa: Liberal Party of Canada, 1993). See archive.org/details/creating-opportunity-the-liberal -plan-for-canada.

Lincoln Alexander receiving the Canadian Race Relations Foundation
Lifetime Achievement Award from Karen Mock and Art, 2003

the Conservative government, the first Black cabinet minister, and
had been the first Black Lieutenant-Governor of Ontario in 1985.
Despite being seventy-five years of age when appointed as chair and
having undergone lung-cancer surgery, this distinguished gentleman
served on many boards and had been chancellor of the University of
Guelph. He was a person who had lived through racism and knew
how damaging it could be. His involvement in the greater Canadian
community and his breadth of knowledge and experiences represented the embodiment of the foundation.

Mr. Alexander was born in Toronto to a father from Saint Vincent
who was a railroad porter and a mother from Jamaica who cleaned
homes. After serving in the air force during World War II, he enrolled
at McMaster University in Hamilton and received his Bachelor of
Arts degree. When he applied for a sales position with a large manu-
facturer, he was turned down because "he was not right for the job."
Instead, he was offered a job on the factory floor, which he refused.
Unable to find a job suited to his education, he decided to go into law,

where he could be his own boss. He went on to distinguish himself as a leader in the political field.

I was appointed to the CRRF's initial board of directors and was elected vice-chair. My introduction to the board was through a teleconference arranged the day before the official announcement of the CRRF. I was with Lincoln Alexander, Moy Tam, and Dr. Fry, who welcomed the new board members and briefed them on their role. Mr. Alexander asked me to share why the foundation was an important part of the redress settlement and the crucial role it would play in assisting other minority groups encountering racism.

When asked by Prime Minister Jean Chrétien to chair the Foundation, Mr. Alexander said he accepted because he recognized the important role that it could play in addressing the many problems related to racism in our society. "Racism, and all it entails in terms of impact on society, should be a concern to all of us as Canadians. I think that more than anyone, our young people recognize that racism is real and frightening, and that it will not go away on its own," he stated at the press conference.

The establishment of the CRRF, an institution for all Canadians, has finally brought resolution to the redress agreement. The board of directors represents various ethnic backgrounds and various regions of Canada. Since its inception, the foundation has undertaken a number of programs, such as research funding, grants for initiatives, being a national clearinghouse of information on racism, awards recognition, sponsorship of conferences, training of educators, and public education. In 1999, the CRRF launched the largest anti-racism campaign in Canadian history, using television networks to deliver messages through creative video productions. In addition, the CRRF conveys to all people of Canada the promise to work towards the creation of a society that ensures equality and justice for all, regardless of "race," colour, or ethnic origin. In 2017, the CRRF celebrated its twentieth anniversary, and it continues to play an important role as "Canada's leading agency dedicated to the elimination of racism and all forms of racial discrimination in Canada."[6] In 2021, the CRRF received significant funding to educate and promote intercultural support concerning anti-Asian racism, Black Lives Matter, the discovery of thousand of unmarked graves of Indigenous students at

---

6   See the foundation's website at crrf-fcrr.ca.

the sites of former Canadian residential schools, and other disputes of Indigenous relevance that are yet to be resolved.

The implementation phase of the redress agreement was crucial for the Japanese Canadian community's maturation. Given that Japanese Canadians took responsibility for the implementation process and were deeply involved with it, this partnership with the government assisted in facilitating the healing process for the victims of the injustices. The positive impact of the redress closure is evidenced in the Japanese Canadian community by the growth of interest and involvement in community activities and the feelings of self-worth and acceptance that it has generated.

On reflection, I think that the redress settlement and acknowledgment were meaningful not only for the victims of the injustice but for all Japanese Canadians in the implementation and revitalization phases of community development.

CHAPTER 12

Reaching Out

As victims of a great injustice, I also believe that Japanese assume an extra burden. We, the victims, know from experience the effects of racism and bigotry. And so ours must be the first voices raised whenever we see prejudice rear up.

—DAVID SUZUKI
Ottawa redress rally, April 14, 1988

David Suzuki's message has had a tremendous impact on how the NAJC deals with past and present injustices faced by minority groups. And when it comes to Indigenous issues, the NAJC has continued to play a role as an ally over the years.

The first intervention on Indigenous matters was the NAJC's public statement on September 27, 1990, regarding the Kanehsatà:ke Resistance (a.k.a. the Oka Crisis), the famous confrontation between the Kanien'kehá:ka (Mohawk) Nation and the federal and provincial governments during the summer of 1990. The Kanien'kehá:ka were rightfully upset by a proposal to expand a golf course and build condominiums on their Traditional burial grounds. Barricades were set up, preventing access, and tensions arose between the Kanien'kehá:ka and the Québec police to the point where one officer was killed. One Kanien'kehá:ka Elder was also killed, and hundreds of civilians were injured. We were critical of the government's handling of the situation, which had deteriorated to a point where the threat of violence was the only means to end the stalemate. The NAJC urged government leaders to clearly demonstrate a genuine willingness to negotiate and settle the Indigenous claims and urged the prime minister to intervene, if necessary, before further violence erupted. After seventy-eight days, the protesters surrendered on September 27 because of the extreme pressure brought to bear by military intervention, requested by Québec Premier Robert Bourassa. The golf course and condominiums were never built.

I was contacted by members of the Stony Point First Nation (Wiiwkwedong Anishinaabek) in Southern Ontario requesting a meeting with the NAJC while I was in Toronto in the spring of 1990. We discovered that the government wanted to build an army training camp on the Stony Point Reserve along the shores of Lake Huron (Gichi-aazhoogami-gichigami in the Ojibwe language) and had confiscated the property under the War Measures Act during World War II. Lacking resources and recognizing the NAJC's success in achieving redress, the Stony Point First Nations leaders requested our help in getting their Land back. They had been promised its return once there was no longer a need for the base. However, the Department of National Defence continued to use the land, which they called Camp Ipperwash, for only six weeks each year for teenage cadets. With the expertise of lawyer Ann Gomer Sunahara, the NAJC provided research and wrote the submission which was sent to the government by the band.

In their press release, the NAJC urged all Canadians to support the call by Indigenous communities for the return of their Land to its rightful owners. "The injustice suffered by the Stony Point First Nations members parallels injustices suffered by Japanese Canadians during the same period," I stated as president of the NAJC. "Both the Indigenous people and Japanese Canadians were uprooted from their homes, stripped of their property, and dispersed. They were both victims of the War Measures Act." Sachiko Okuda, chair of the NAJC Human Rights Committee, added: "Our research suggests that the motivation for taking the Stony Point Reserve was the same motivation for abusing Japanese Canadians: a mixture of racism and administrative convenience … Taking the Stony Point Reserve appears to have been a cheap and easy way to acquire a training camp without expropriating white-owned farms or recreational land."

Letters were sent on November 19, 1991, to the prime minister, the minister of Indian Affairs and Northern Development, the minister of National Defence, and the Standing Committee on Aboriginal Affairs, which would be discussing the issue on December 12, 1991. In my letters, I stated, "The NAJC is of the view that the wrongs done to the Stony Point [First Nation] in 1942 are wrongs as grave as, and of the same kind as, the wrongs done to Japanese Canadians during the Second World War. There are, however, two important differences. The exile for Japanese Canadians ended on April 1, 1949, while the exile of the Stony Point [First Nations members] continues to the present. The wrongs done to Japanese Canadians have been redressed, while the wrongs done to the [First Nations members] continue." The letter urged the government to return the land and pay appropriate compensation.

In 1994, the government announced that the camp would be closed and the Indigenous Land returned. However, there was no action on the part of the government, so band protesters occupied Camp Ipperwash. A confrontation erupted with the Ontario Provincial Police, and Dudley George, a band member, was killed. This news received national attention, as had the Kanehsatà:ke Resistance. After many promises, in September 2015, the reserve land was returned to the Stony Point First Nation, with compensation. During the struggle for justice, members of the Toronto chapter of the NAJC participated in demonstrations that were held to publicize the issue. It was rewarding for us to hear that finally the matter had been resolved and that the NAJC had contributed to aiding the Stony Point First Nations regain their rightful Land.

The NAJC publicly supported the Lubicon Lake Nation (ᒪᐢᑯᑌᐤ ᓴᑭᐦᐃᑲᐣ Muskotew Sakahikan Enowuk) in their dispute with the Daishowa Paper Manufacturing Company from Japan. The First Nation occupied a fairly remote area in Northern Alberta along the British Columbia border. They were rightfully displeased when in 1989 the Alberta government gave Daishowa timber rights on their Traditional Territories. There was strong disagreement over land rights as Daishowa began clear-cutting trees in the fall of 1990. In an attempt to force the company to cease cutting, in 1991 the Friends of the Lubicon launched a major boycott of Daishowa's products, endorsed and supported by the NAJC.

This conflict resulted in an uncomfortable situation for the

NAJC, because the chief spokespeople for Daishowa were Japanese Canadians. One of them, Henry Wakabayashi, had been a strong advocate for the NAJC during the redress struggle and had assisted the NAJC in eventually convincing Price Waterhouse to undertake the economic losses study. They met with the NAJC executive to clarify Daishowa's position and wanted the NAJC to reconsider their action. For the NAJC, here "caught between a rock and a hard place," this was one situation that required diplomacy, but the NAJC's commitment to protect the rights of Indigenous Peoples prevailed. The NAJC refused to back down. In 2004, an agreement was reached between the Friends of the Lubicon and Daishowa that they would not log Lubicon Lake First Nation Lands until the land claim was settled with the governments.

In January 1989, the NAJC established a Task Force on Native Peoples. This committee, based in Toronto, met with Indigenous leaders to discuss ways to support them in their struggles. The committee felt that a project involving both Japanese Canadian and Indigenous communities in planning and organizing co-operatively would be the best way to enhance our understanding and appreciation for each other. Thus the concept for the Earth Spirit Festival was born.

On August 7, 1990, I attended a get-acquainted event at Toronto's Church of the Holy Trinity that brought Indigenous people and Japanese Canadians together for the first time to publicize the purpose and range of activities to be held at Toronto's Harbourfront in a three-day festival. Abe Kabayama, chair of the task force and planning committee, felt that the festival of sharing would be the most appropriate vehicle to facilitate open communications. A fundraising event held at the Japanese Canadian Cultural Centre was attended by over four hundred people. The two keynote speakers were Grand Chief Gordon Peters and well-known broadcaster and scientist David Suzuki. Indigenous Elder Cliff Solomon noted in his closing prayer that Suzuki was the first non-Indigenous person he had heard who "expressed what [Indigenous people] have been trying to tell Canadians for years."

Over one hundred thousand people attended the Earth Spirit Festival, held under sunny skies on between July 5 and 7, 1991. It brought together various Indigenous Nations (including First Nations, Inuit, and Métis) and the Japanese Canadian community to celebrate their rich and varied cultures. The sharing of history

The Gateway to Understanding, a stone cairn created by Inuk artist David Ruben Piqtoukun ᑎᐊᑎ ᐱᑐᑦ ᑭᐱᐃᐦ, the Earth Spirit Festival, 1994

and traditions occurred through genres such as music, theatre, book readings, arts and crafts, and food. Japanese Canadian participants included David Suzuki, Joy Kogawa, Eiko Suzuki, Denise Fujiwara, and Jay Hirabayashi. The list of performers was impressive, with names such as the Innu duo Kashtin (Claude McKenzie and Florent Vollant), one of the most successful groups in First Nations music history; the Tabo Duo (Takeo Yamashiro and Teresa Kobayashi), playing the traditional Japanese instruments shakuhachi and koto; and drum groups from both communities. In the theatre section, *Dear Wes/Love Muriel*, an adaptation for the stage by Terry Watada of the late Muriel Kitagawa's book *This Is Our Own*,[1] was performed by Brenda Kamino. An inukshuk-like stone cairn created by Inuvialuk artist David Ruben Piqtoukun ᑎᐊᑎ ᐱᑐᑦ ᑭᐱᐃᐦ entitled *The Gateway to Understanding*, a permanent fixture at Harbourfront's Queens

---

1   Muriel Kitagawa, *This Is My Own: Letters to Wes and Other Writings on Japanese Canadians, 1941–1948*, ed. Roy Miki (Vancouver: Talonbooks, 1985).

Quay, is a lasting legacy of the festival. This stone gateway is similar in style to a torii gate found at temples in Japan.[2]

I first met Ovide Mercredi, who had just been elected Grand Chief of the Assembly of First Nations (AFN), in 1991 on an airplane to Ottawa. We started chatting, and he told me that he followed the redress issue closely and indicated that he was impressed by the non-confrontational approaches we had employed in reaching a successful conclusion. I invited Ovide to address Japanese Canadian delegates at the NAJC Annual General Meeting in Toronto to speak on Indigenous issues and concerns. Speaking with him on several occasions, I was impressed by his astuteness with constitutional law, Indigenous constitutional rights, and his clear vision for their future. He advocates non-violence and the forging of links with other people, such as the dispossessed and disadvantaged in the dominant society, in order to maximize the efforts of Indigenous Peoples.

On January 25, 1992, I was invited to Ottawa by the AFN to share our successful redress strategy and how we had been able to mobilize the community with the AFN's Residential School Committee. This committee was mandated to uncover the detrimental and lasting effects of residential schools upon Indigenous Peoples and to propose a strategic redress plan in condemning the actions taken by the governments and churches. I heard emotional and heartbreaking testimonials from committee members, who elaborated on the various forms of abuse inflicted upon the Indigenous youth at the hands of the Catholic and Anglican priests, nuns, and workers. These disclosures revealed that emotional and cultural trauma had permanently affected their lives, as demonstrated by the frustrations and disillusionment among some Indigenous youth today.

I reiterated that Japanese Canadians had initially been extremely reluctant to support redress and had to undergo a process of learning that "if a right as a citizen is violated, the citizen has the right to speak out." This was the philosophy that the NAJC adopted to combat those who wanted us to leave the past behind. There are many parallels between Japanese Canadian internment and the residential school experiences of Indigenous students when it comes to the loss of language, culture, and self-esteem. Our community's forced

---

2   See, online, Toronto Sculpture, "The Gateway to Understanding," www.dittwald.com /torontosculpture/image.php?Artist=Piqtoukun&Title=The%20Gateway%20to%20 Understanding.

removal from the West Coast was somewhat analogous to the forced relocation of students into residential schools. However, in the case of Indigenous Peoples, taking children away from their parents and inflicting sexual and physical abuses had more severe consequences to the community than those experienced by Japanese Canadians. Many Indigenous Elders and parents did not want the residential school issue raised. "Let the past be the past; let it go," the committee members were often told. There was fear that revealing the past would result in a backlash and antagonism from the churches and from government. Respect for authority is strong in many Elders. One committee member expressed that she was fearful of returning to the reserve, where she would be confronted with threats to her life because some band members were afraid of what might be revealed through the process of disclosure. The physical and sexual abuses and the cultural disintegration that occurred over several generations have been ingrained in many Indigenous people's psyches and require extensive healing processes.

I was invited again in March 1992 to Edmonton, where the AFN strategy group and legal advisors met to discuss possible actions that the committee would recommend to its parent body. However, one committee member claimed that there were hostile reactions from some communities about pursuing redress, especially from the Elders who respected the work of religious organizations and were reluctant to speak against the church. I sensed a similar response of division and resistance to moving ahead that I encountered in the Japanese Canadian community during the early stages of our campaign. The diversion of views within the Indigenous communities temporarily halted further action.

The Kanehsatà:ke Resistance and the failure of the 1987 Meech Lake Accord raised such concerns about the livelihoods of Indigenous Peoples that a Royal Commission on Aboriginal Peoples (RCAP) was established by the government in August 1991 to assess the relationship between Indigenous people and non-Indigenous Canadians. The commission, consisting of several high-profile Indigenous leaders, travelled to numerous communities and issued a five-volume, four-thousand-page-long report in November 1996 that included

440 recommendations.[3] One of the outcomes of the report was a statement of reconciliation for unchecked abuses experienced by Indigenous children in residential schools. Georges Erasmus, one of the chairs, denounced the role of the Catholic Church in the forced integration of Indigenous Peoples. As a result, the Aboriginal Healing Foundation was founded in 1997 by the federal government to assist those affected by the negative impact of residential schools.

As another example of communication with the Indigenous community, I share this experience, which gave me a different insight about Indigenous Peoples. In the spring of 1992, I was in my office at Joseph Teres School when my assistant, Ann Hruda, said she'd received a call from Stony Mountain Institution, a maximum-security penitentiary a short drive from Winnipeg, and did I want to take it? I had no idea why anyone would be calling me from there, but I accepted the call. The person at the other end introduced himself, and I recalled him as someone I knew growing up in the core area of Winnipeg. He then told me he was a counsellor at the penal institution working with Indigenous inmates and asked whether I would come out to talk about the Japanese Canadian experiences and redress. I accepted and headed out to visit a classroom within the prison, where I spoke to thirty or more Indigenous inmates. After the presentation, one inmate asked me when I thought that their concerns would be addressed by the government and resolved to the satisfaction of Indigenous Peoples. I indicated that, in my opinion, within ten years we would see many successful resolutions of their demands. I explained that the strong stand by Indigenous leaders on the Meech Lake Accord, the summer of unrest at Oka over Indigenous Land Rights, the Royal Commission on Aboriginal Peoples, and the power demonstrated by Indigenous communities in support were all indications that major changes were occurring. Little did I realize at the time that I would be involved indirectly with the residential-school resolution. A short time later I was approached by the Manitoba Indian Brotherhood (later reconfigured as the

---

3   The five volumes can be found online here: Library and Archives Canada, "Report of the Royal Commission on Aboriginal Peoples," www.bac-lac.gc.ca/eng/discover/aboriginal -heritage/royal-commission-aboriginal-peoples/Pages/final-report.aspx. A 1997 fifty-page summary by the Institute on Governance is made available here: *Summary of the Final Report of the Royal Commission on Aboriginal Peoples*, April 1997, www.metisportals.ca /cons/wp-content/uploads/2009/02/rcap-final-report.pdf.

Assembly of Manitoba Chiefs) to talk to all the Indigenous inmates at the same institution about the Japanese Canadian experience. It was an enlightening exposure for me to see that Indigenous traditions were practised inside the walls of the Stony Mountain Institution; so was their interest in the experiences of racism and discrimination that Japanese Canadians faced in the early years. Getting to know one another is the key for greater understanding and respect for each other's history and culture. There was continued interest from Indigenous communities concerning redress. I was invited on March 25, 1996, to Vancouver by the Union of British Columbia Indian Chiefs to address their conference and outline the NAJC's strategies in achieving a successful resolution.

In 1993, Keiko and I met with representatives of an Indigenous veterans' organization in Saskatoon to share redress strategies and to listen to their stories. The veterans had been deprived of soldiers' benefits after serving Canada during World War II, an experience similar to that of the experiences of Japanese Canadian veterans. Following the meeting, the organization lodged a legal redress claim through the federal courts in Saskatoon. However, before legal proceedings began, the Honourable Rey Pagtakhan, Liberal minister of Veterans Affairs, recognized existing precedents and offered individual compensation of $20,000 to each living Indigenous veteran based on the model of Japanese Canadian redress.

In June 2001, the office of Indian Residential Schools Resolution Canada became an independent government department responsible for the evaluation of abuses experienced at residential schools. In 2003, an alternative dispute resolution (ADR) process was introduced as a way of resolving claims of sexual abuse, physical abuse, and forcible confinement without going through the courts. This was proposed without consultation with Indigenous communities or former school students. I was invited by Grand Chief Phil Fontaine from the AFN, who was sponsoring a conference on March 13, 2003, in conjunction with the University of Calgary, to discuss alternative dispute resolutions related to the abuses in residential schools. I found the comments from government officials restrictive as to what the government was proposing. Their suggestion was to limit the awarding of compensation to those Indigenous students who had been either sexually or physically abused. The AFN was very critical of the proposed approach, as they should be, because of the government's failure to consider the recognition of all Survivors. Speaking to participants, I outlined the Japanese Canadian experiences and the strategies that led to a successful resolution for our community. In response to the government's position, the AFN under Grand Chief Phil Fontaine launched a class-action lawsuit in 2005 against the federal government. However, the issue was resolved before any legal action had progressed.

Subsequent to this meeting, Phil Fontaine and Kathleen Mahoney, negotiator for the AFN, invited me to Vancouver's Bayshore Inn in January 2006 to address a large gathering of residential school Survivors. In my presentation, I emphasized how we had arrived at an individual compensation figure. We recognized that individuals had encountered various degrees of suffering and loss, but the common element among all victims was that each person had been deprived of their basic rights regardless of age, livelihood, or economic status. The experiences of residential school students has parallels with the Japanese Canadian experience. The NAJC agreed on a symbolic individual compensation of $21,000 for every person who had been affected by the powers of the War Measures Act. I compared this to the residential school Survivors who were forcibly deprived of their languages and cultures and faced various forms of abuse; I argued all surviving residential school Survivors should be entitled to individual compensation. This message resonated with the gathering and gave the AFN clearer direction to propose a more acceptable approach to the alternative-dispute-resolution model.

The AFN adopted the position of seeking individual compensation for all victims based on the amount of time spent in residential school and put forth an argument to the federal government. To settle the case, the government of Canada signed the Indian Residential Schools Settlement Agreement on May 8, 2006. I was pleased to hear that a compensation package recognizing all Survivors of residential schools had finally been achieved. This agreement included funding for communities, health support, and the Truth and Reconciliation Commission. On June 11, 2008, Prime Minister Stephen Harper issued a formal apology in the House of Commons, on behalf of the government of Canada, to residential school Survivors, their families and their communities, for the abuse, suffering, family dislocation, and cultural disintegration resulting from the government-sanctioned system, and to educate Canadians in the history and legacy of the residential school system. The commission organized seven meetings across Canada where residential school Survivors had an opportunity to share their stories. The first of these meetings was held in Winnipeg[4] between June 15 and 19, 2015.

On June 18 of that year, I was invited as a speaker as we gathered in a large tent on the grounds of the Forks National Historic Site located at the junction of the Red and Assiniboine Rivers. The Forks is situated on Treaty 1 Territory, concluded between the British Crown and the Anishinaabe ᐊᓂᔑᓈᐯᐗᐠ and Néhinaw (Swampy Cree) Nations, whose Traditional Territories are located on the Land. In my session, I spoke about the Japanese Canadian community's experience with racism, the forced removal, internment, and finally the redress settlement. One of the Indigenous presenters was Elder Tobasonakwut Peter Kinew, an Anishinaabe and a residential school Survivor who devoted his efforts to reconciliation between Indigenous and non-Indigenous peoples, and the father of Wab Kinew, leader of the New Democratic Party in the Manitoba government and first First Nations person to be elected a provincial premier in Canadian history. At the conclusion of the speeches, an Indigenous Survivor named Alvin Dixon from British Columbia rose and thanked me for sharing the story of Japanese Canadians, which he could relate to from his experience in residential school. He pointed out that both peoples were deprived of their freedoms and cultures and suffered abuses and humiliation. He recalled that when he was an Indigenous fisher with the Native Fishing Association in the late 1940s, a government official asked his organization and members of different fishing groups whether Japanese fishers should be granted fishing licences after their return to the West Coast in 1949. He said that the only group to support the Japanese Canadians at that time was the Indigenous fishers. I assume that the racism endured by Japanese Canadian fishers, who were so successful before the war, would have influenced their decision. I also reconnected with Chief Dr. Robert Joseph, a Hereditary Chief of the Gwawa'enuxw First Nation, a residential school Survivor from Vancouver, and Ambassador for Reconciliation Canada, who was one of the keynote speakers for this meeting. I had met Chief Joseph earlier, when I participated at a

---

4   Like so many place names used in Canada, the name Winnipeg is of Indigenous origin and is from a Nêhinawêwin ᐅᑉᐋᐊᐳᐋᔭ (Swampy Cree) and Anishinaabemowin ᐊᓂᑉᔑᐋᐳᒉᐊᐣ (Ojibwe) term meaning "muddy waters."

Truth and Reconciliation meeting in Winnipeg. To the right of Art is Chief Dr. Robert Joseph, Hereditary Chief of the Gwawa'enux̱w (Gwawaenuk) First Nation. They are accompanied by two residential school Survivors.

National Reconciliation Gathering organized by Reconciliation Canada on March 11, 2015, at the University of Manitoba. This gathering had brought together Indigenous and non-Indigenous delegates to learn and share ways for Indigenous and non-Indigenous peoples to interact economically and socially in a respectful and fruitful way.

A January 2015 *Maclean's* article by Nancy Macdonald entitled "Welcome to Winnipeg: Where Canada's Racism Problem Is at Its Worst"[5] raised anger in Winnipeg citizens. In reaction to the article's harsh criticism of our city, Mayor Brian Bowman, who is of Métis descent, and City Council adopted an Indigenous Accord as

---

5   Nancy Macdonald, "Welcome to Winnipeg: Where Canada's Racism Problem Is at Its Worst," *Maclean's*, January 22, 2015, macleans.ca/news/canada/welcome-to-winnipeg -where-canadas-racism-problem-is-at-its-worst/.

Art signing Winnipeg's Indigenous Accord, 2017

an important step towards the city's Journey of Reconciliation and to demonstrate that the city was taking action to combat racism. Organizations and individuals were invited to establish their own goals towards achieving the ninety-four Calls to Action outlined in the report of the Truth and Reconciliation Commission.[6] The intent of this process is to create understanding between Indigenous and non-Indigenous peoples by creating partnership initiatives that recognize and respect Indigenous Rights.

On June 20, 2017, I signed Winnipeg's Indigenous Accord as president of the Japanese Cultural Association of Manitoba (JCAM), pledging to further reconciliation and to report our progress annually to the city. More than eighty groups gathered around the fire in Oodena Celebration Circle at the Forks in downtown Winnipeg

6   See, for example, CBC News' web page "Beyond 94: Truth and Reconciliation in Canada," last updated June 22, 2023, www.cbc.ca/newsinteractives/beyond-94.

for the signing ceremony. Mayor Bowman eloquently expressed the Accord's purpose: "It is the voice of our community, not one voice, but a chorus of diverse voices from across Winnipeg ... saying yes, we want to listen. Yes, we want to understand and respect each other. Yes, we want to work together."[7] Signatories including government officials, church groups, health organizations, educational institutions, school boards, universities and colleges, museums, arts organizations such as the Winnipeg Symphony Orchestra and the Royal Winnipeg Ballet, media, sports groups, businesses, and cultural organizations demonstrated that "we want to work together." Surprisingly, the JCAM was the only ethnocultural organization represented. As part of the JCAM's commitment, a Circle of Reconciliation was held in March 2018 at the Japanese Cultural Centre, where members of the Japanese Canadian and Indigenous communities learned about each other's histories, shared in personal and at times emotional dialogue, and were then nourished on dishes prepared by chefs from our respective cultures. The participants were mindful of the commonality that existed between the imposition of residential schools and the internment of Japanese Canadians. It was an invaluable learning for all involved, and both communities wanted to follow with further encounters. Since then, I have been involved in several Sharing Circles with Indigenous people as a facilitator and participant. I believe in the words of Governor General Mary Simon ᒣᐊᕐ ᓴᐃᒪᐣ: "Reconciliation is getting to know one another."

I believe that the NAJC and Japanese Canadians have had a long history of collaboration with Indigenous groups and have developed and strengthened our relationships with Indigenous leaders. But within the Japanese Canadian community, there still is a need to create a closer understanding and appreciation of our respective cultures and experiences. Face-to-face dialogues between Japanese Canadians and Indigenous Peoples would be an important process and needs to be promoted.

Collaborating, supporting, and sharing our redress experiences with disadvantaged communities have become important mandates for the NAJC. In the past, the association has supported Ukrainian Canadians, Chinese Canadians, Italian Canadians, and others in their quest for redress by sharing our negotiation strategies. Letters from

---

7   National Association of Japanese Canadians, "JCAM Signs the Indigenous Accord," n.d., najc.ca/jcam-signs-the-indigenous-accord/.

the NAJC have been sent to the prime minister and the minister of multiculturalism stressing the importance of a negotiated conclusion to the past injustices faced by minority groups. In the early days of the redress campaign, we met with Lubomyr Luciuk, head of the Ukrainian Canadian Civil Liberties Association, established in 1986 to champion the cause of recognition of the internment of Ukrainian Canadians during World War I. He proposed at that time that the NAJC join forces with his group to seek justice. The NAJC decided that with our mandate already established, we would pursue it alone. However, we maintained contact with Lubomyr and the Ukrainian Association over the years to share strategies, and we invited him as a speaker for the In Justice Conference in 1992 in Vancouver (as I describe below).

In March 1991, I spoke at the Challenge for Chinese Canadians in the '90s Conference in Winnipeg, sharing the strategies and processes that the NAJC employed during the redress campaign and in support of the Head Tax redress issue. The Chinese Canadian National Council (CCNC) held a rally in support of Chinese Head Tax redress at Parliament Hill on Victoria Day, May 19, 1992. Head-tax payers, their spouses, descendants, and supporters came from Toronto and Montréal by bus to express support for the CCNC. I was invited as one of the speakers and reminded the audience of the Japanese Canadian rally held in 1988, stressing the importance of these events to educate other Canadians about historical injustices. As we marched on the Hill, a Chinese Canadian veteran thanked me for taking part in the rally and expressed his happiness that I was there to promote their pursuit for justice. Little did I realize at the time that he must have been reflecting on the past animosity between China and Japan. In talking with leaders of Ukrainian Canadian and Chinese Canadian organizations, it was interesting to note that they not only encountered resistance from their community members, but divisions were created as to the form of redress, and power struggles for leadership happened, similar to what we faced in our own community. These internal community disputes made it easy for the government to defer taking action, as exemplified by the long delay of nearly twenty years before apologies for the Ukrainian internment and Chinese Head Tax were forthcoming.

With financial support from the Japanese Canadian Redress Foundation, two major projects were undertaken to reach out to other Canadians through educational initiatives. As an organization that stood for human rights, the NAJC has an obligation not only to assist communities whose rights have been violated, but to educate all Canadians on the perils of racism and importance of learning from these mistakes.

First, a conference, "In Justice: Canada, Minorities and Human Rights," was held at Simon Fraser University (SFU) at Harbour Centre in Vancouver from April 30 to May 2, 1992. The conference was designed for ethnic-minority organizations, human-rights commissions, civil-liberties associations, government policy-makers, educators, journalists, and scholars and was sponsored by the NAJC and the SFU's Centre for Canadian Studies with financial support from the Japanese Canadian Redress Foundation. For the first time, minority groups who had endured injustices as a result of government policies shared their experiences and collaborated together to suggest positive legislative and policy safeguards to prevent future injustices. To open the conference, writers Joy Kogawa, Myrna Kostash, Fred Wah, Sadhu Binning, and Marie Annharte Baker participated in literary readings to celebrate the rich body of literature and poetry based on their personal experiences.

The conference focused on three main themes: Historic Injustices in Canada, Legislative Causes, and Future Protection of Human Rights for Minorities. Personal testimonials were given by representatives from Ukrainian Canadian, Chinese Canadian, Indo-Canadian, Jewish Canadian, Italian Canadian, First Nations, Inuit, Black Canadian, and Japanese Canadian communities that contributed to open discussions and support for resolutions of past wrongs. A special session was devoted to learning more about Canada's Indian residential school system (still effective at the time). I was especially shaken by the emotional disclosure by Bev Sellars, Chief of the Xatśūll First Nation (formerly the Soda Creek Indian Band) at Williams Lake, BC, who recalled watching her brother Bobby being dragged back to the school by the RCMP after he had run away. It was only after the "angry young man" fell or jumped off the cliff that it was discovered he had been among the boys who had been sexually abused at "the Mission" (Saint Joseph's Indian Residential School at Williams Lake). "The saddest part," Bev said as her voice cracked, "is that stories like this are a dime a dozen." A tragic outcome of the residential school experience, in addition to the high suicide rate, is that some

Indigenous people have lost their parenting skills and find it difficult to break the cycle of violence, abuse, and low self-esteem with their children. Hearing first-hand stories such as Bev Sellars's[8] and heart-wrenching accounts from Japanese Canadians across the country reinforced for me the importance of recognizing past wrongs.

The delegates heard presenters talk about the use and abuse of the War Measures Act, immigration law and policies, and the Indian Act. In discussing future protections of human rights, the participants addressed three main issues: past treatment of minorities during national crises; the use and abuse of emergency laws and powers and their impact on the rights of minority groups; and proposals for legislative and operational safeguards to maintain the rights of minority Canadians during periods of national crisis. What was thought-provoking was that representatives from various minority groups recounted for the first time their past injustices in a public forum. There was a strong desire from the affected groups to reclaim their histories. It was through this venue that frank and open dialogue on the need for acknowledging past wrongs and strengthening protections against future injustices were offered as advice to the government officials present. A request for an apology and redress from the groups was presented to the Liberal government. What was so special was the informal get-togethers in the evening at my brother Roy's home, where we sat around sharing our thoughts and experiences and learning about each other, thus strengthening that bond of friendship and understanding.

In 1995, the concerned organizations received a letter from Sheila Finestone, Secretary of State for Multiculturalism, expressing regret for past injustices but rejecting any settlement. Since then, there has been some success in getting recognition for past violations. On June 22, 2006, Prime Minister Stephen Harper apologized to head-tax payers, their families, and the Chinese Canadian community. Symbolic payments were made to living payers and living spouses of deceased payers, and a fund of up to $5 million was created for community projects aimed at acknowledging the impact of the wartime measures and immigration restrictions imposed on the Chinese Canadian community. With the Ukrainian Canadian community, the Internment of Persons of Ukrainian Origin Recognition

---

8   For more such stories, see Bev Sellars's award-winning memoir *They Called Me Number One: Secrets and Survival at an Indian Residential School* (Vancouver: Talonbooks, 2012).

Act was passed in November 2005, opening room for negotiating an agreement.[9] In May 2008, an agreement was reached between the representatives from the Ukrainian Canadian community and the government of Canada to create the Canadian First World War Internment Recognition Fund to support commemorative, educational, scholarly, and cultural projects as a reminder of this history.[10]

As a result of the redress settlement, the history and experiences of Japanese Canadians have become a topic of study in school curricula and have also kindled public interest. At the negotiation table, NAJC representatives had stressed the importance of educating Canadians about Japanese Canadian experiences and helping the general public understand the significance of the redress settlement. Many of us were invited to schools to talk to students and teachers to share our knowledge of what our parents and grandparents had faced living in Canada and the effect that this hardship has had on our community. The NAJC office is often deluged with requests for materials and has developed a list of suggested books to provide teachers with background information.[11]

A comment I have heard from many Canadians is that they were not aware of Japanese Canadian history and internment or taught about it. To assist teachers, the NAJC hosted two educators conferences shortly after the redress settlement; the first conference focused on resources available within the community, and the second concentrated on teaching strategies for the subject matter. In order to create greater exposure, a third conference, "Designing the Japanese Canadian Curriculum," was held in Toronto on May 22 and 23, 1992. This conference brought together educators from across Canada interested in teaching about the Japanese Canadian experience in their classrooms, school districts, and provinces. The Japanese Canadian story and internment are rarely taught in schools because of a lack of resources and a lack of teachers with adequate background on the topic. Workshops were designed to provide educators with teaching strategies and more knowledge of the subject. A number of Japanese Canadian educators served as workshop leaders and were

---

9   See the government of Canada's Justice Laws Website at laws.justice.gc.ca/eng/acts/i-20.8/page-1.html.

10 See the fund's website at www.internmentcanada.ca.

11 For a good start, see the NAJC's "Resources" online: najc.ca/resources/.

GAMAN — PERSEVERANCE

willing to share their expertise. The keynote speakers were Ted Aoki, a curriculum specialist, Roy Hardie, superintendent of student and community services for the North York Board of Education, and me, president of the NAJC and school administrator.

From my experience as a Faculty of Education teacher in recent years, I have found that education students have little or no exposure to past injustices faced by minorities. It is obvious that these topics received minimal attention when they went through the school system. When I taught a multiculturalism course, which is mandatory in the University of Winnipeg's education program, and asked how many students in my class of thirty knew anything about the internment of Japanese Canadians and Ukrainian Canadians, the Chinese head tax, and the *Komagata Maru* and *St. Louis* incidents, less than 10 percent had any knowledge, while more students had some knowledge of the Indian residential school experiences. This is understandable, as there were several Indigenous students in the class. But generally speaking, teachers are reluctant to teach Japanese Canadian history as an optional topic unless they are comfortable with the issues. Therefore, exposing students to these areas early in their academic path will then have a positive effect on their interest and knowledge as teachers in the future.

Unfortunately, we have not made much progress in having Japanese Canadian experiences taught in schools. We do have the resources, including lesson plans, videos, and printed materials prepared by dedicated teachers, but the difficulty is finding teachers who are willing to include them as part of their social-studies, history, or language-arts programs. This can be attributed to the lack of exposure on the subject of Japanese Canadians or the lack of training or professional development opportunities for interested teachers.

The present provincial curricula have sufficient flexibility for teachers to incorporate topics such as the internment of Japanese Canadians, the Chinese head tax, the Ukrainian Canadian internment, and other injustices into their program. We need to find ways to convince the school system through provincial education departments to offer teacher-development training sessions to show that the experiences of Japanese Canadians would be an excellent model for teaching about human rights, citizenship, and social justice. Right now, these topics are optional and it is left to the interest of the teacher whether topics that relate to injustices in Canada are presented.

However, in the last few years, some progress has been made in the production of curricular resources. The Landscapes of Injustice, a seven-year research and public-history project, explored the dispossession of Japanese Canadians as part of the forced displacement and internment in the 1940s. The project is housed at the University of Victoria and received significant funding from the Social Sciences and Humanities Research Council under the leadership of Associate Professor Jordan Stanger-Ross. I was involved in this exciting endeavour as a member of the Japanese Community Council, providing advice and insights about the Japanese Canadian community. An important component of the project was the development of learning materials for teachers willing to teach about the Japanese Canadian experience. A searchable digital archive of curricular materials was developed for the project by teachers experienced in Japanese Canadian history. It provides an Elementary Teacher Resources website (loi.uvic.ca/elementary/) and Secondary Teacher Resources website (loi.uvic.ca/secondary/), which include lesson plans and supplemental teaching strategies that can easily be easily accessed and utilized by classroom teachers.[12]

Another educational component of the project is the field school for practising teachers to receive training in teaching Japanese Canadian history. In a 2019 pilot project, ten university students and ten classroom teachers from across Canada embarked on a five-day tour of the former internment sites in interior British Columbia, followed by a one-week intensive university course at the University of Victoria. I was one of the guest lecturers for the course and had informal discussions with the learners and shared first-hand experiences. This innovative and interactive approach to learning about the forced uprooting and dispossession of Japanese Canadians exposed the participants to powerful recollections from community members who had lived through the experience. Landscapes of Injustices hopes this pilot approach might become a template or model for teacher-training workshops in the future for pedagogues who wish to teach Japanese Canadian history, including the deprivation of rights during wartime. More attention needs to be given by ministries of education

---

12 Other first-rate materials are readily available on the Landscapes of Injustice website; see www.landscapesofinjustice.com/teacher-resources/.

to teach those areas in Canada's history that are often ignored in the school books. We have the necessary tools to make inroads into the public-school systems, but we will need commitment from educational bodies to ensure the availability of professional development and workshop opportunities in order to develop a cadre of teachers enthusiastic to teach Japanese Canadian history.

Other organizations and projects besides Landscapes of Injustice are using the internet to create student awareness about human rights. I participated in an online project called Speak Truth to Power Canada, Defenders of Human Rights (sttpcanada.ctf-fce.ca), a collaboration between five partners: the Canadian Teachers' Federation, the Canadian Museum for Human Rights, Robert F. Kennedy Human Rights, the Assembly of First Nations, and Inuit Tapiriit Kanatami ᐃᓄᐃᑦ ᑕᐱᕇᑦ ᑲᓇᑕᒥ. The project, launched in March 2015, is an online educational resource for Canadians, especially school students, presenting role models who are making a difference in the world today as defenders of human rights. The online lesson plan "Arthur Miki: Equality and Redress"[13] focuses on the Japanese Canadian experience and consists of an interview, a biography, and student activities for students in grades seven to twelve. The aim is for participants to gain greater understanding of the physical, emotional, and economic hardships encountered by Japanese Canadians stripped of their human rights during and after World War II, of the impacts of racist and discriminatory laws, to develop empathy and a sense of justice, and to acknowledge that governments can and do make mistakes. It was an honour for me to participate in such a project among other Canadian defenders of human rights.

It is clear that the National Association of Japanese Canadians, in the interest of keeping Japanese Canadian history alive, can play a vital role in offering resources to people with a background in Japanese Canadian history so that they can conduct workshops for teachers. The NAJC could provide support for teachers by adopting initiatives such as collaborating with teacher-training institutions to offer a teacher-education course on Japanese Canadian history, offering scholarships for teachers to take courses, compiling a "Best

---

13   Under "Lessons Plans": sttpcanada.ctf-fce.ca/lessons/arthur-miki/. Other defenders and creators of lesson plans include Louise Arbour ("Crimes against Humanity"), Jeremy Dias ("Gender and Sexual Diversity"), Rosemary Sadlier ("Human Dignity"), and Karihwakè:ron Tim Thompson ("Equitable Education for All").

Practices"-style handbook for teachers, organizing tours for teachers to visit internment centres, and using cultural centres and museums as centres of learning.

The Japanese Canadian redress settlement has also become a precedent for other class-action suits –whether civil or criminal cases. Prior to the redress settlement, there were no clear examples of group-action or class-action suits in Canada where groups of people received compensation for wrongs committed against them by their own government. The government's legal advisors, namely their lawyers, warned the ministers of multiculturalism that giving individual compensation to Japanese Canadians would be a costly precedent for future governments. In a *Globe and Mail* article entitled "Deal with Japanese Canadians Not a Precedent, Minister Warns," Minister Jerry Weiner denied that it would be a model for other groups, saying that what Japanese Canadians suffered between 1942 and 1949 was "unique and unparalleled."[14] He was quickly criticized for his statement by Lubomyr Luciuk, who pointed out that Ukrainian Canadians had been interned during World War I. Furthermore, Luciuk said that the settlement is "a moral and legal precedent that Ukrainian Canadians can use to press for redress of wrongs between 1914 and 1920."[15] Ed Lam from the Chinese Canadian National Council felt that the settlement would renew their campaign for compensation and an apology for the head tax charged to the Chinese who wanted to settle in Canada prior to 1923, after which time they were banned from Canada.

It was, indeed, the precedent that government bureaucrats feared. In the 1990s, the federal government distributed lump-sum payments of between $52,000 and $82,000 to 109 thalidomide survivors. Pregnant women who had taken this drug between the late 1950s and early 1960s gave birth to babies with severe physical disabilities. However, the amount was insufficient to cover their children's medical needs, and in 2015, the survivors were awarded an additional lump-sum payment. The same applied to hepatitis C and HIV tainted-blood survivors who received varying degrees of compensation for their misfortune resulting from the Canadian government's

14 Richard Cleroux, "Deal with Japanese Canadians Not a Precedent, Minister Warns," *Globe and Mail*, September 23, 1988, A8, www.proquest.com/historical-newspapers/deal-with-japanese-canadians-not-precedent/docview/1238588240/se-2.

15 Ibid.

neglect during the 1980s tainted-blood disaster. Furthermore, the Honourable Thomas Berger commented to me that he used the Japanese Canadian redress model to gain compensation for victims who had been sexually and physically abused during the 1980s and 1990s at the Jericho Hill Provincial School for the Deaf in Vancouver. Despite Gerry Weiner's comments, all of these settlements were based on the example established by the Japanese Canadian redress agreement, which has become a clear precedent for class-action lawsuits in Canada.

Finally, in reaching out, we must remind ourselves that it is important to educate the Japanese Canadian community about the obligation we have accepted regarding racism, discrimination, and human rights. Today, most Japanese Canadians will tell you that they rarely encounter racism or discrimination, but we know that it exists, especially towards people of Middle Eastern backgrounds and Muslims – and more recently, starting in early 2022, towards Russian Canadians who have faced harassment and hate speech because of Russia's invasion of Ukraine. A Russian Community Centre in the Kitsilano neighbourhood of Vancouver had its doors vandalized with yellow and blue paint, the colours of the Ukrainian flag. As a member of a minority group that has been stereotyped and discriminated against in the past, I insist that we must be prepared to speak out whenever discrimination or racism occurs. However, we need to realize that we, Japanese Canadians, are also prejudiced and hold inaccurate assumptions about other groups. I recall hearing disturbing discriminatory comments made by Japanese Canadians towards other groups, especially Indigenous communities. As victims of racism, we need to be more aware of racism directed against other groups and sensitive about it. One of the priorities for the NAJC is to be vigilant; when human-rights violations occur in our country or in our communities, the NAJC must be one of the first to raise their voice.

CHAPTER 13

Revitalization

The emergence
of its self
is a reminder of renewal.

—SALLY ITO
"Crocus"

The community fund was a vital component of the redress agreement and a reminder that an important nucleus of the Japanese Canadian community had been decimated by the forced removal from the West Coast. Before the war, the area around Powell Street in the East End of Vancouver was home to a thriving business and residential enclave where the economic, social, and spiritual life of Japanese Canadians flourished and prospered. During negotiations, the government asked the strategy committee to provide suggestions of ways the Japanese Canadian community could be energized and examples of actions that might assist with its revitalization.

How could the redress settlement be an instrument for the NAJC to revitalize and reenergize a community that had been destroyed and dispersed? The concept that we envisioned in utilizing the community fund was to subsidize capital projects and programs that would benefit Japanese Canadians and help extend the Japanese Canadian community's existence. The year 1999 marked the tenth anniversary of the Japanese Canadian Redress Foundation (JCRF) and was a time to reflect on the achievements resulting from the financial assistance given to groups and individuals. This had been the most exciting period in our history. It was a time of rejoicing, of celebrating, of dreaming a vision for the community, of testing our talents, of working together, and in the end of realizing that we had gained much more than we had hoped.

Essential to the revitalization process was the development of community facilities for seniors. In the NAJC survey on the use of the funds, housing for seniors and health-care facilities ranked as the top two priorities. Without the community fund, I doubt if Momiji's Seniors Active Living Centre (SALC), with apartments and a recreational centre for more than 133 seniors in Scarborough, Ontario, or the renovation of the Nipponia Home, a minimal-care facility for Japanese Canadians in Beamsville, Ontario, would have been established as quickly as they did. In Burnaby, BC, the fund was used to purchase the property on which Sakura-so, a thirty-four-unit affordable seniors' residence, was first built; it set the stage for the development of Nikkei Place (which combines three organizations: the Nikkei Place Foundation, the Nikkei National Museum and Cultural Centre, and the Nikkei Seniors Health Care and Housing Society), followed by the Nikkei Home, an assisted-living residence.

Of all these, Momiji's Seniors Active Living Centre has a special place in my heart. My aunt, Kome Nagasaki, was one of its early residents and enjoyed the company of other Japanese Canadians. Whenever I was in Toronto, I made a special effort to see her. She would take me, or sometimes Keiko and me, for lunch at the Japanese restaurant in the facility. I saw first-hand the benefits of this facility, where my aunt felt safe and secure – she left her doors unlocked, as friends dropped in freely – and where she enjoyed a variety of activities. She enjoyed fraternizing with the residents and was very popular. I adored her and marvelled at her smartness and memory. I learned about my father's family from her. She was the last of my dad's siblings. My aunt was in her ninety-ninth year when I last visited her at Momiji. She was still living independently and cooking for herself. I kidded her that she would live past a hundred, and so I requested that the PMO send Kome Nagasaki a congratulatory certificate for her hundredth birthday.[1]

In September 2002, I received a call from my cousin in Toronto,

---

1   For those interested, see the Prime Minister of Canada's official website, "Request Greetings for a Special Occasion," www.pm.gc.ca/en/connect/greetings.

Carolyne Miki, to let me know that Auntie Kome was in the hospital. I called my aunt to let her know that I wanted to visit her. She insisted that she was okay and I need not visit. Somehow it didn't feel right not to go, so I booked a flight to Toronto. Carolyne picked me up at the airport and I stayed at her place overnight. The next day we visited Scarborough's Centenary Hospital to see Kome. She was in good spirits as we talked about our families and how she was doing. I was uplifted by her attitude and her sense of humour. The following day we visited again, and she was as bubbly as ever and enjoying our conversations. I was going back to Winnipeg that day, so at three o'clock we left the hospital for the airport. Carolyne and I waited in the lounge for the flight. Around five o'clock on September 24, 2002, Carolyne received a call from the hospital informing her that Kome had just passed away. I was shocked. It was unbelievable, because two hours earlier we had been laughing and joking, and she seemed so happy. I said to Carolyne that maybe we should go back to the hospital. She said, "There isn't anything you can do. You should go home." I had difficulty making sense of what had happened. When I shared the story with someone, the comment that made sense to me was that she waited to see me, and once I left she finally let go. I'm so glad that I saw her before she passed away.

Just shortly after her death, the special certificate arrived from the minister. She had passed away just shy of her hundredth birthday. At the funeral, the congratulatory certificate was displayed. In her eulogy, Joanne Leier, Kome's granddaughter, said, "To survive persecution by the Canadian government during the internment of Japanese Canadians, to survive the death of her husband and her son, and to live to her hundredth year with dignity and grace makes her one of the most amazing women I have ever crossed paths with." Those words expressed my feelings about Kome. She was an amazing aunt. For Kome and many others, moving from a close-knit Japanese community as a youngster to a close-knit life at Momiji was "coming full circle."

The emergence of cultural centres is critical for the Japanese Canadian community's future. They are places for young and old Japanese Canadians to gather, preserve their identity, and promote culture through activities. The neighbourhood of Steveston, BC, was one of the first to receive funds from the JCRF for a cultural centre. In Winnipeg, I was on the search committee of the Manitoba Japanese

Art with his aunt Kome Nagasaki

Canadian Citizens' Association (MJCCA), which had purchased a building in 1987, prior to the redress agreement, because of pressures exerted by seniors who wanted a place to meet and a community centre for their children. Within a short time, the small facility outgrew its ability to provide space and activities for its members. The MJCCA received significant funding from the JCRF, which aided the organization in purchasing a much larger building that allowed for expansion of programs. In Toronto, the Japanese Canadian Cultural Centre was relocated to a newly renovated facility much larger than its previous location. In Vancouver, the new Nikkei National Museum and Cultural Centre (NNMCC) in Burnaby was officially opened in September 2000. Other cultural centres exist in Kamloops, Vernon, Calgary, Edmonton, Thunder Bay, Hamilton, Ottawa, and Montréal.

Following the redress settlement, the National Council overwhelmingly endorsed the establishment of a permanent head office in Winnipeg because of its central location in Canada. I was tasked with the challenge of finding an appropriate location in town for the office. Fortunately, Jim Yamashita, a sansei architect, offered to assist me, as he was familiar with the North Portage Development complex located in the heart of downtown Winnipeg, and was aware of some possibilities. One location that appealed to us was a free-standing building of approximately twenty-four thousand square feet, originally designed as a day-care centre, that remained empty. Izzy

Koop, president of the North Portage Development Corporation, challenged us to put forward a proposal for a long-term lease. In July 1991, the NAJC signed an agreement with a one-time payment of $135,000 for a twenty-year lease. The NAJC agreed to renovate the building and pay the annual property taxes and maintenance costs. With financial assistance from the foundation, the NAJC finally had permanent headquarters at 404 Webb Place; it was officially opened on May 31, 1992, by Mayor Bill Norrie.

Films and videos are a powerful tool for raising consciousness among Canadians. Jesse Hideo Nishihata was a Japanese Canadian pioneer in documentary filmmaking. I first met Jesse in Toronto during the redress campaign, and the first film I saw about Japanese Canadians was his CBC creation *Watari Dori: Bird of Passage*, produced in 1973. In his quiet, meticulous manner, he captured the Japanese Canadian fight for redress in his film *Justice in Our Time: How Redress Was Won* (1989). He created another wonderful film in 1991, *Catch the Spirit!*, which documents the Earth Spirit Festival.[2]

The JCRF provided financial support for several notable film projects, including *The Last Harvest*, written and produced by sansei Linda Ohama. It tells of her family's plight in Southern Alberta after having been forcibly removed from British Columbia during World War II. She has produced other documentaries; one is *Obachan's Garden*, the story of Linda's grandmother, Asayo Murakami, who came to Canada as a picture bride and settled in Steveston, BC.[3] In the early Canada, the Japanese population was predominantly male, with very little opportunity to find a partner. The common practice was to ask relatives back in Japan to arrange a marriage through an exchange of photographs of potential brides. I met Asayo in Calgary and was impressed by her tenacity, enthusiasm, and pride at the thought of her story was being told. *Minoru*, produced by Michael Fukushima with assistance from the National Film Board, tells the story of his father, who was exiled to Japan in 1946, and his eventual return to Canada. These films complement the stories about Japanese Canadians in a vivid and captivating manner and are a great vehicle for educating Canadians about our history. A number of other films produced by Japanese Canadian filmmakers such as Meiko Ouchi, Midi Onedera and Nancy Tatebe, Mitch Miyagawa, Greg Masuda,

2   See Nishihata's website at jessenishihata.wixsite.com/home.

3   See Ohama's website at www.ohamalinda.com/films.

Jeff Chiba Stearns, and Warren P. Soroda have added to the collection of films that provide historical and contemporary perspectives. The emergence of so many talented filmmakers from within the Japanese Canadian community is phenomenal; they continue to produce films and documentaries that portray various aspects of Japanese Canadian life and influences.

The tremendous development of the artistic community is a credit to the foundation's efforts to promote their talents. Writers, artists, dancers, actors, and other performers have benefitted from grants given by the foundation. One interesting story is about a young author who had difficulty in sustaining her writing project but received encouragement from the foundation to persist. She finally completed her first novel, which has received literary recognition. Kerri Sakamoto, a sansei born and raised in Toronto, was awarded the 1999 Commonwealth Writers' Prize for Best First Book for *The Electrical Field*. Her latest novel, *Floating City*, was published in 2018.

Many books have been written on various aspects of our history: personal accounts of individuals during the redress campaign, the story of the redress movement in Toronto, stories of Japanese Canadian internees, of life in a POW camp and of teachers in ghost towns, the history of the famous Asahi baseball team, and other interesting events and subjects. There is now a wealth of reading materials available reflecting the history and experiences of Japanese Canadians. Local Japanese Canadian histories have been written on Manitoba, Kelowna, Québec, and the Niagara Peninsula. I believe redress was an inspiration for many Japanese Canadians filmmakers, writers, and other creative artists, and with funding support from the foundation, they have deepened the understanding of Japanese Canadian culture and history. More recently, several publications of memoirs influenced by the redress settlement have emerged which add to the collection of stories that gives substance to what Japanese Canadians experienced. In 2018, Mark Sakamoto's book *Forgiveness* was selected as the winner of the CBC *Canada Reads* program. Published as a family memoir in 2014, his book details his grandparents' real-life experiences, their two divergent lives, and their respectful admiration for each other. Another notable memoir, Sally Ito's 2018 *The Emperor's Orphans*, traces the journey of family members who were among the four thousand Japanese Canadians exiled to Japan during and after the war. Another autobiographical text, *Chiru Sakura—Falling*

Cherry Blossoms, by Grace Eiko Thomson, is based on her mother's diary and their relationship. A book that may have appeal for the younger generation is a graphic novel, *On Being Yukiko*, created by Jeff Chiba Stearns and Lillian Michiko Blakey. In this story, twelve-year-old Emma learns about her heritage and identity through her great-great-grandmother Maki's recollections of wartime horrors. It is important that these stories be conveyed to the younger generations, so that these real-life experiences can be remembered, understood, and appreciated by all.

Our history is an important legacy to maintain. The JCRF provided assistance to local museums and archival groups to collect and preserve historical documents, artifacts, photographs, and personal papers. The Japanese Canadian National Museum (JCNM), located at the Nikkei National Museum and Cultural Centre in Burnaby, BC, is building a national database of information. For the opening of the centre in September 2000, the museum prepared its inaugural exhibit, *Re-Shaping Memory, Owning History: Through the Lens of the Japanese Canadian Redress*. This exhibit chronicled the early struggle for Japanese Canadian citizens' rights, the blatant acts of racism at the hands of their own government, the pursuit of redress, and the acknowledgment and redress.[4] Preparation of other historical exhibits on Japanese Canadians is an ongoing role for the national museum. A recent exhibit entitled *Broken Promises*, based on the extensive research from the Landscapes of Injustice project, explored the dispossession of Japanese Canadians in the 1940s. Testimonials from Japanese Canadian voices conveyed their life stories, the loss of their homes, and the struggle for justice. The travelling exhibition, exposing this unique chapter in Canadian history to national audiences, has been shown at the Japanese Canadian Cultural Centre in Toronto, the Museum of Surrey, the Royal BC Museum in Victoria, the Canadian Museum of Immigration at Pier 21 in Halifax, the Galt Museum in Lethbridge, the Cowichan Valley Museum in Duncan, and will be shown in 2024 at the Nanaimo Museum.[5]

---

4   See the exhibition catalogue: Roy Miki, Yuko Shibata, and Michiko Ayukawa, with the Japanese Canadian National Museum, *Re-Shaping Memory, Owning History: Through the Lens of Japanese Canadian Redress*, ed. Grace E. Thomson (Burnaby, BC: Japanese Canadian National Museum, 2002).

5   For more information, see the Nikkei National Museum and Cultural Centre's website at centre.nikkeiplace.org/exhibits/broken-promises/.

Museum projects in other British Columbia centres such as Kaslo and Mission have received funding from the JCRF. New Denver's Nikkei Internment Memorial Centre is located on the "the Orchard" internment site along the shores of Slocan Lake, where the original shacks are displayed and used for the exhibit. I attended the official opening in July 1994, and some of the comments from speakers described the project along the lines of "magnificent," "powerful," and "historical legacy." Sakaye Hashimoto, president of the Kyowakai Society, initiated the concept of the historical site and with the support of the village of New Denver turned a vision into reality. The Memorial Centre is now a designated National Historic Site and is run by the village of New Denver.

As part of the West Coast Communities display at the Canadian Museum of Civilization in Ottawa, the NAJC and the JCNM, with support from the JCRF, contributed funds to restore the *Nishga Girl*, an old gill-netter fishing boat. This vessel, designed and built by a Japanese Canadian shipwright, Judo "Jack" Tasaka, and donated by Nisga'a Heredity Chief Harry Nyce (Sim'oogit Naaws) in 1967, was a model typically used by Japanese Canadian fishers before the war. The Canadian War Museum in Ottawa has created an exhibit on the lives of Japanese Canadians during World War II. The Canadian Museum for Human Rights, opened in Winnipeg in 2014, prominently displays material on the early history, internment, and redress in the Japanese Canadian alcove located in the Canadian Journeys gallery. I'm happy to see that exposure of our past is now part of mainstream facilities such as national museums and is being acknowledged as important part of Canada's heritage.

Following the redress settlement, the NAJC, with support from the JCRF, organized many conferences and emotional gatherings, attracting large numbers of Japanese Canadians. I was fortunate to participate in these projects as a keynote speaker or an active participant. The Homecoming conference in Vancouver in 1992 and The Best Years conference in Calgary in 1989 were well attended by Japanese Canadians, especially seniors from across Canada. These two events brought together the largest numbers of former internees in one location. The atmosphere was unbelievable. People saw friends from internment days or even before the war for the first time in decades. The enthusiasm, happiness, and tears evident among the participants made plain to me how the once close-knit community had been dismantled by the government's inhuman actions. These gatherings were the beginning of a healing and revitalization process for Japanese Canadians.

The Intergenerational conference in Ottawa in 1994 brought delegates from the three generations together to have frank and open discussions on issues that affect our community, while the Gender Sensitivity gathering in Toronto in 1994 looked at attitudes towards gender within the community. The Social Change conference in 1995 was held in collaboration with the David Suzuki Foundation to look at strategies to affect social change. These major gatherings have been a tremendous source of learning on current and past issues faced within the Japanese Canadian community and have facilitated enriching social interactions for their participants.

How do we ensure that we will maintain a strong national organization? In 1992, the NAJC organized regional leadership conferences in Toronto and Calgary to provide potential leaders with practical organizational skills. Leadership training resulted in a number of participants becoming involved with their local organizations or at the national level. Other training workshops were held in subsequent years to generate future leaders. I encourage the NAJC to revive leadership opportunities by hosting national gatherings and conferences, so the younger generation can understand the need to keep the NAJC active and relevant, especially in the area of human rights.

Recognizing that the community fund would soon be expended, the NAJC requested support from the JCRF in 1989 to establish endowments whose earned interest would be awarded as grants, while the initial capital would remain intact in perpetuity. This action was necessary, as the community financial resources would diminish in the future and weaken our ability to support a variety of projects. I see the NAJC's role as helping in developing and maintaining community organizations, providing a communications network, and being a forceful voice for human rights. The NAJC will continue to be the national voice for Japanese Canadians with its specific mandates, including the management of the endowment funds.

The overwhelming joy of the redress announcement displaced the feelings of guilt and inferiority and of being considered "second-class citizens" as many issei and nisei have had to deal with. Likely the pain, suffering, and humiliation experienced during the wartime years contributed to these feelings. It was important for Japanese Canadians to have reaffirmation from their government that they had not committed any wrong. As we've seen and learned, during times of national crisis, citizenship rights are fragile and can be taken away swiftly.

Our success in achieving redress is living proof that the power of minorities should not be underestimated; perhaps this is the benefit of living in a multicultural milieu. A small Japanese Canadian community, insignificant in population but with support from others, overcame tremendous odds to accomplish what seemed to many to be an "an impossible task" and has altered the way that we, Japanese Canadians, perceive ourselves. The redress settlement had a powerful personal influence on the survivors and gave them a feeling of revival. A nisei from Hamilton remarked, "I felt that the redress settlement was something of a closure for me." "I think that redress was important because it had a psychological effect and helped our elders to open up and gain peace of mind," commented another nisei. For others, the redress announcement meant that a tremendous burden was lifted, a feeling of guilt, since so many Japanese Canadians felt (undeservingly) responsible for what had happened to them during the war. One woman said, "Since redress, my awareness has grown and also my sense of myself. I feel that it's easier to walk tall and talk about my culture." One gentleman, feeling a sense of acceptance, commented, "I finally feel as if I'm a true Canadian." For me, the announcement brought closure to the prolonged struggle to achieve justice.

The settlement was a result of persistence and faith shown by the people who were involved in the redress movement, either directly or on the periphery. It would have been so easy to succumb to the government's offer of a $12 million community fund in July 1987, especially when David Crombie had emphasized that it was the final "take it or leave it" offer. By accepting, we might have put our frustrations behind us. But we persisted, believing that it was better not to accept what was not just and fair, but to seek a solution that encompassed the principles and objectives to which we were committed.

I have been asked many times during the campaign, "Do you believe that the government will ever redress Japanese Canadians for the wrongs and compensate them?" During the four and a half years that I was totally engrossed in the struggle, I never considered giving up or quitting when it appeared hopeless. Despite people telling me that redress was futile, I always maintained a solemn belief that we would somehow succeed. Regardless of the outcome, I believed that Canadians were benefactors, because through the public discourse, they gained a clearer understanding of the history and experiences of Japanese Canadians. We had not failed in our mission to expose the government's actions towards the community during wartime. When the redress settlement was finally announced by Prime Minister Brian Mulroney, it was a realization of a dream for me. The redress settlement of 1988 has had tremendous repercussions on the Japanese Canadian community and Canadian society as a whole. A voice of justice and a voice of equality have been created through the NAJC Human Rights Committee, which is ready to speak out on injustice and inequality issues affecting other groups. As a legacy of the redress settlement, Japanese Canadians will continue to demonstrate leadership and be a positive role model when speaking out against violations of human rights.

What is the future for the Japanese Canadian community? Consideration must be given to its changing nature. Factors that will influence the future are the effects of the high intermarriage rate, the degree of involvement by postwar and more recent immigrants from Japan, and efforts of present organizations to be more inclusive in their membership and to offer relevant activities.

The dispersal policy implemented after the war by the government had tremendous consequences on the sociological and cultural dimensions of the Japanese Canadian community. Following internment, Japanese Canadians were encouraged not to form ghettos but to assimilate into the mainstream Canadian milieu, resulting in isolation and a lack of contact with other Japanese Canadians apart from near relatives. Many sansei grew up in primarily white communities with little or no contact with other Japanese Canadians. This resulted in a high rate of intermarriage among sansei and yonsei (third and fourth generations) because of their close associations with people in the immediate community and lack of opportunities to meet other Japanese Canadians. In my family, I'm the only one who is married to another person of Japanese ancestry and all the grandchildren, nephews, and nieces are products of mixed marriages. This is the reality. I think this has hastened assimilation, which in a positive way is becoming a defining characteristic of Canadian identity. Eventually, most Canadians will be a mixture of not only two cultures but of multiple ones.

Dr. Audrey Kobayashi, a geography professor at Queens University and a member of the NAJC's strategy team, suggests in her study *A Demographic Profile of Japanese-Canadians and Social Implications for the Future* that the rate of intermarriage of Japanese Canadians with people from other ethnic backgrounds is around 95 percent.[6] This startling rate is the highest among all ethnic groups in Canada and the highest among all countries in the Americas with nikkei populations. The high rate of intermarriage will drastically alter what the Japanese Canadian community will look like in the future. Prior to the relocation from the West Coast, mixed marriages among nisei were extremely rare. Nisei were generally brought up in close-knit Japanese communities where the possibility of meeting non-Japanese was limited. In addition, because of racism towards Asian Canadians in British Columbia, interracial marriages were frowned upon and discouraged. Those who chose to intermarry experienced extreme prejudice, and not only from outside forces. They were also ostracized within the community, often being cut off by their families.

Today, attitudes towards mixed marriages involving Japanese Canadians have changed almost completely. Japanese Canadians have become integrated into mainstream society. If a sansei or yonsei falls in love with a non-Japanese or non–Japanese Canadian companion, they can marry regardless of their parents' wishes. This was not the case before the war for nisei, who would more often be influenced by the desires of their issei parents or have to participate in arranged marriages.

The challenge for partners of mixed marriages is to determine whether retaining their cultural background is important, and if so, what they will do about it. From my perspective, it seems that in mixed marriages, non–Japanese Canadian partners are often more interested in Japanese culture than their spouses are. This is understandable, because a non-Japanese who marries a Japanese Canadian will likely have made a commitment to accept the differences associated with Japanese culture, whereas the Japanese Canadian spouse may view the marriage as a process of assimilation or move into the majority culture. The other possibility is that both partners may not have any interest in retaining either cultural background. This means

---

6   Audrey Kobayashi, *A Demographic Profile of Japanese-Canadians and Social Implications for the Future* (Ottawa: Department of the Secretary of State, 1989). See also Natsuko Chubachi, "Gender and Construction of the Life Course of Japanese Immigrant Women in Canada" (Ph.D. diss., Queen's University, 2009), hdl.handle.net/1974/1779.

that children from mixed marriages will choose whether or not to identify or associate with the Japanese Canadian community. Their decision may be a result of their desire to know more about Japanese Canadian identity and heritage or influenced by the involvement of their parents in community activities. Young people who have gone to Japan on programs such as Japan Exchange and Teaching (JET) may identify more closely with their Japanese Canadian heritage after having lived in Japan.

The future of the Japanese Canadian community is unpredictable, because much will depend on how the children of mixed marriages view themselves culturally. The number of people of mixed background with one partner being Japanese constitutes 53 percent of the Japanese Canadian population, according to the 2016 Canadian census. This number will continue to rise. Will they want to maintain interest in the Japanese side of their identity? Some have become leaders in the Japanese Canadian community. With the next generation, children from mixed marriages must be encouraged to participate and take leadership responsibilities at the local and national levels. One of the expectations of the redress settlement was to revitalize interest in the Japanese Canadian community. The future strength of Japanese Canadian organizations which are responsible for community, cultural, and history-preservation activities will be determined by the degree of interest shown by its community members.

Another important factor to consider is the role of postwar and more recent immigrants from Japan. Presently, many immigrants have established their own organizations rather than associate with Japanese Canadian groups that may be less relevant to them because of language and cultural barriers. On the other hand, Japanese Canadians often see themselves as different from the immigrant population because of their unique internment and wartime experiences. Some immigrants, especially those married to non–Japanese Canadians, may have no desire to associate with any community groups, while others may take an active role with local or national Japanese Canadian organizations. The involvement of new immigrants and their children is paramount if our Japanese Canadian identity is to survive in this new millennium. No doubt some children, as they get older, will want to satisfy their identity needs, learn more about their Japanese Canadian background, and take interest in the Japanese Canadian community.

Cultural centres do provide a community focal point and can be a vehicle for attracting younger Japanese Canadians, new immigrants, and children from intermarriages to participate in social and cultural activities. The greatest challenge for cultural centres and local organizations is to find how to be relevant to the present and future generations and to consciously develop strategies that will promote the importance of being Japanese Canadian. This means adapting programs and activities that will entice the young nikkei, especially ones from mixed marriages, to participate. Organizations will need to provide workshops and programs that deal with issues such as intermarriage and identity, but also openly solicit suggestions that would enhance services and programs. Having sincere dialogues among various target audiences is vital in order for local organizations to be in tune with their current needs and develop collaborative programs and activities that will inspire greater participation. Parents play a pivotal role in exposing their children to cultural activities, language classes, and community events. This may provide the stimuli for continued participation in activities and programs as children get older.

Organizations will also need to become more flexible, open, and creative in their attempts to attract people. The present leadership of most organizations is still mostly nisei and sansei. Very few members of mixed Japanese background are involved at the leadership level. Leadership training is essential for groups to sustain themselves in the future.

The increasing interest and participation at local levels stimulated by the support given by the JCRF and local organizations are positive signs that the Japanese Canadian community has a chance for survival in this millennium. The future of the Japanese Canadian community will depend on the development of a new generation of leaders and the relevance of the activities available to people of mixed Japanese backgrounds and new immigrants. I'm optimistic that interest in Japanese culture and heritage will survive but recognize that the faces of this community in the future will certainly not resemble those of today.

CHAPTER 14

Opening New Horizons

My involvement in Japanese Canadian community organizations in a leadership capacity and being immersed in the redress campaign during the 1980s not only altered me as a person but energized me. Our success with redress elevated my confidence in my ability to seek different experiences and challenges, opening new horizons I would not have considered before.

ASPIRING POLITICIAN

My exposure to the Canadian political system during the struggle for redress gave me a more comprehensive perspective on the role of government, politicians, and the political process and spurred a desire to seriously consider running as a candidate in a federal election. I noticed there were no Japanese Canadian politicians to champion the redress cause, unlike in the United States. Unless Japanese Canadians participate in the political process, we will continue to have a void in the decision-making process at the national level. Although there have been Japanese Canadians in the county for over 145 years, the first Japanese Canadian elected as a Member of Parliament was Bev Oda in 2004. In 1992, I decided to run as a Liberal candidate in the 1993 federal election because of my conviction that we needed

Japanese Canadians as full participants, especially in the political process. What follows is the story of my journey into politics.

Having planned to retire from education in June 1993, here was an opportunity for me to consider running for political office. I felt that my experience gained through the redress campaign gave me an in-depth insight into government workings and the role of politicians. This exposure had piqued my interest. Prior to the 1993 federal election, there was great anticipation in the Canadian public that the Conservatives might be dethroned and the Liberals under Jean Chrétien become the next government. I was tempted to run as a candidate, as there never had been a person of Japanese ancestry elected to the Canadian Parliament.

There were several factors that motivated me to consider going into politics. First, I had served at the provincial level as chairperson of the education committee for the Manitoba Intercultural Council, an advisory body to the Manitoba government. We were a lobby group for ethnocultural communities on educational policies and worked closely with the minister of education. This experience thought me something about the government's decision-making process and made me wonder what it would be like to be on the decision-making side. I also served two terms on the advisory body for the minister of multiculturalism in the federal government.

Secondly, during the redress campaign I had the chance to interact with government leaders, politicians, caucuses, and parliamentary committees, recognizing that the people I met were not extraordinary but people with knowledge and skills similar to the ones I possessed. This made me think that I could do their job adequately if given the opportunity. Looking at the US political scene reminded me of the importance of having politicians from our own background. I'm thinking of Japanese Americans such as Congressman Norman Mineta from California or Senator Daniel Inouye from Hawai'i, whose personal testimonies had a tremendous influence on the government establishing the Commission on Wartime Relocation and Internment of Civilians in 1980, and who were later to lobby other politicians in the House of Representatives and the Senate before President Reagan signed the Civil Liberties Act in 1988.

Finally, I had been approached in 1990 by Gary Doer, leader of the Manitoba New Democratic Party (NDP), to run provincially; I declined because in principle I was more inclined towards the Liberal philosophy. He must have recognized some political potential in my abilities. Had I run, I would most likely have been elected, as it was a landslide victory for the NDP. The NDP's interest, coupled with the experiences I had gained politically through the redress campaign and its successful conclusion, aroused my desire to run. When you enter politics, you take with you the question "How will I make a difference?" That was the motivation for me, as I believed that I could have an impact at the highest decision-making level.

In 1992, certain that a federal election would be announced, I contacted Sergio Marchi, who was responsible for recruiting federal Liberal candidates. Because of our acquaintance through the redress campaign, I felt at ease calling him. Sergio then contacted Richard Good in Winnipeg, who was responsible for recruiting Manitoba candidates. Good suggested three possible ridings in which to run: Winnipeg South, Winnipeg–Transcona, and Selkirk–Red River. I thought Winnipeg–Transcona would be my best choice, since I had been a school principal in Transcona for twenty-five years and had strong name recognition there. But the challenge was that the incumbent, Bill Blaikie, had been the NDP Member of Parliament for the past fourteen years. He had grown up in the area and his family was well established there. In determining whether to run, I consulted with three close friends who had a strong connection with the riding: Henry Kojima, a teacher, principal, and later a superintendent in the River East Transcona School division, which was part of the riding; Paul Moreau; and Laurie Sodomlak, both colleagues who were long-time residents in the area. All three gave me their thumbs-up, but warned that it would be a tough battle to unseat the incumbent. The next step was to meet the Winnipeg–Transcona Riding Association executives and inform them of my decision. Their attitude was not promising, as one of them asked me, "Why would you even consider running when it's a waste of time?" I sensed that they had already conceded the riding to the NDP and that I could not rely on their support. Although my campaign team lacked hands-on practical experience, as political neophytes we were willing to learn, so we established our own team and recruited a strong cadre of enthusiastic volunteers.

In the fall of 1992, my campaign team was established, with Paul Moreau as campaign manager and Richard Kozak, a former provincial politician, as official agent. Building a campaign team was a

Art, Aline Chrétien, and Jean Chrétien at a campaign rally during a bus tour of Manitoba Liberal candidates in Transcona, Winnipeg, 1993

phenomenal experience. School colleagues, former students from Harold Hatcher School, community members, interested volunteers, and friends offered their support in organizing campaign activities, door-to-door canvassing, and phoning. Although most had never been involved in a campaign, their eagerness, commitment, and willingness to learn helped us develop into a cohesive team. A number of Japanese Canadians who came to canvass had never been involved politically but commented on how they enjoyed the campaign process and experience.

The nomination meeting, held on March 17, 1993, was attended by nearly two hundred supporters after recruiting over three hundred paying members to the Liberal Party. My nomination, moved by Paul Moreau and seconded by Birgit Hartle, was acclaimed, as it turned out that I was the lone candidate. The exuberance at the meeting was elevated by a dynamic motivational speech by Sharon Carstairs, former provincial Liberal leader and senator. The next day, Richard Good was quoted in a press release as saying, "Art Miki is respected nationwide, as well as at the local level in Transcona. The people in the area have been backing the same horse for a long time. I think they might be ready to give Art Miki and Jean Chrétien a chance."

The next step was to develop an election strategy. We took advantage of people who had gained experience during other campaigns and could give advice and conduct workshops on various facets, such as organizing polls, volunteer recruitment, fundraising, establishing a budget, developing media releases and information brochures, and most importantly, how to run an effective election day. A strong group of spirited volunteers was assembled, with every one being committed to the task of getting me elected. What our group lacked in experience we more than made up for in determination and passion.

Poll organization is important in order to plan the critical door-to-door canvassing to meet potential supporters and create name recognition. We carefully crafted a profile brochure, recognizing that, as I was a visible minority, some people might have assumed that I was an immigrant. That has been my experience when I meet people who don't know me well. Anticipating that there might be racist views towards me, the first line of my profile stressed that "Art was born in Vancouver, BC." Our plan was to canvass fifty thousand households in the riding using blitz teams of three to six volunteers. I didn't realize the enormity of the riding, and even after six months of campaigning we were unable to get to every home. Nevertheless, by the end we had identified fifteen thousand supporters. MPs Lloyd Axworthy, Ron Duhamel, and their workers came out on several occasions to canvas. Sharon Carstairs spent one Saturday with me in front of Safeway talking to customers and went door-to-door on several other occasions. Also, several city councillors, including Terry Duguid, now an MP, several hundred volunteers, Japanese Canadian constituents, and friends spent varying amounts of time canvassing, putting up signs, phoning, and doing clerical work. It was an exciting time for us all. Our enthusiasm and hopefulness carried on to election day to see if our efforts would be rewarded with a victory.

Fundraising is a crucial part of a campaign, as the expense of running an effective campaign can be enormous, running to around $50,000. The campaign team hosted a fundraising event on June 22, 1993, at the Forks, where Paul Martin was the guest of honour. We received donations from prominent individuals, but the largest amount came from direct mailing to Japanese Canadians across Canada. Here I had high name recognition. Their support was overwhelming, as they wanted to see a Japanese Canadian elected to Parliament.

The exciting part of the campaign was the support I received from the Federal Liberal Party. They had targeted Winnipeg–Transcona as a potentially winning riding. Jean Chrétien and his wife, Aline, officially opened our riding office before embarking on a two-day pre-election provincial bus tour to which all Manitoba candidates and their spouses were invited. Dressed in casual clothes, we visited the New Rosedale Hutterite Colony near Portage la Prairie, two high schools at which Chrétien responded to provocative questions, a barbecue party in Virden, a breakfast gathering in Neepawa, and the city of Dauphin before returning to Winnipeg. Throughout the tour, Manitoba candidates were introduced and Chrétien captivated the attention of media and voters with his humour, down-to-earth language, and platform, as articulated in the famous Liberal Red Book. Each candidate had an informal chat with the leader, talking about their family, experiences, and aspirations. I found Chrétien to be warm, sincere, and honest and I valued his willingness to listen. He recalled his admiration of Thomas Shoyama and praised him for his role as the most powerful public servant as deputy minister of finance. Born in Kamloops, BC, Shoyama had been the editor of the

New Canadian newspaper during the internment period. He had been instrumental in designing social services in Canada, especially Medicare. Chrétien's love for Canada and emotional attachment to it were evident in his comments and his willingness to make sacrifices to serve the country. He was adored and loved by the people who came into contact with him. Keiko and I cherished our time with Jean and Aline Chrétien and enjoyed their warm friendship.

A highlight was the second visit by Jean Chrétien to the Winnipeg–Transcona riding rally on September 19, 1993, a week before the election, in anticipation of a possible upset. His usual dynamic speech excited the overflow crowd jammed into St. Michael's Ukrainian Catholic Church in the heart of Transcona. In his speech, Chrétien made reference to my involvement with the Japanese Canadian redress settlement and announced that the Liberal government would proclaim the bill to establish the Canadian Race Relations Foundation, as outlined in the Red Book. The Conservative government had negated proclaiming the bill.

The night before the election, I was sitting at the campaign office, recollecting my thoughts on what we had accomplished. It was over a year since I had first considered the possibility of running. I realized that a group of political greenhorns had just completed a major campaign. I was satisfied that we had run a solid campaign, although I had no way of comparing mine to others'. The outsiders who assisted us commended our team for what we had achieved. Now it was up to the voters to determine my fate.

September 25, 1993, election day, was an anxious time for all of us. All we could do was wait. As the results came in after the polls closed, we sensed that it would be a close race. The lead see-sawed back and forth all evening between Bill Blaikie and me, never more than a few hundred votes apart. At the end of the evening, our tally indicated we were nineteen votes behind, but with no official confirmation from Elections Canada. Assuming that our numbers were correct, Campaign Chair Paul Moreau announced to our supporters gathered at election headquarters that I had lost by a mere nineteen votes. I addressed the gathering, expressing my deep disappointment but acknowledging and praising the energetic effort of the team and volunteers and thanking them for their confidence in me.

After most people left, a few who were recording the results stayed behind to double-check the data. However, the results were the same.

Thinking I had lost, Keiko and I went to the central Liberal Party celebration to offer congratulations to the elected MPs from Winnipeg. Eventually, we went home, not knowing the final count. My brother Roy and sister Joan both called from Vancouver wondering what was happening. They said the BC results were already in, yet they had not heard anything about Winnipeg–Transcona. It seemed that this was the last riding to be decided.

At about three o'clock in the morning, I received an anonymous call from someone working in the Elections Canada office in the Winnipeg–Transcona riding. He would not identify himself but told me that I was in the lead with only one poll to be counted. He gave me the poll number and so I checked our results and found the difference was not large enough to affect the lead. Now thinking I had won, I went to bed.

At 5 a.m., a CBC reporter called after talking to Elections Canada, confirming I had won. The *Globe and Mail* published election results in the morning, including my victory. Then later that morning, I received a call from the Elections Canada returning officer indicating that there would be a recount. The Elections Canada spokesperson, Valerie McPherson, told the media that the problem began when it was realized that one of the tally sheet had been inadvertently sealed inside the ballot box instead of being forwarded to the Returning Office. Opening the ballot boxes required permission from Ottawa. It wasn't until 4 p.m. the next day that the recount was completed. My legal counsel, John Stefaniuk, who was present for the recount, notified me that I had now lost by 219 votes. What a harrowing experience for my first attempt at politics!

To further aggravate the situation, a number of our scrutineers at the polls complained of questionable procedures and possible improprieties. To confirm concerns about the election process, I received an anonymous call from a constituent who wanted to meet with me secretly to share her observations while working at the polls. She told me that the NDP used deceitful tactics and that she knew this from past experiences. She showed me examples where the same name appeared on two different polling lists, so the same person could vote twice. She pointed out the name of a deceased person on the list. I don't know whether double or substitute voting occurred, but the possibility certainly existed. Skeptical of the election process, we asked the Liberal Party to share in the cost of a recount. John Stefaniuk filed for a recount through a court hearing.

Later in the week, a court hearing was held with Justice John Scollin of the Provincial Courts. The NDP lawyers argued vehemently against holding a recount, while we argued that the fiasco resulting from election night was sufficient reason to have a recount. Judge Scollin decided for starters that ten polling boxes be opened for a recount. We selected the ten based on feedback from the scrutineers. After the ten polls were counted, I had gained two more votes. The judge decided that the change was not sufficiently large enough to continue the process. I was disappointed that we had not looked at the rest of the boxes, even if only to satisfy myself and my supporters who had worked so hard on the campaign. I sent a letter to Elections Canada in Ottawa outlining our concerns about the process at the polls, along with written declarations from individuals who had observed inappropriate actions. I received a detailed response a year later agreeing that there might have been improprieties, but stating that the examples cited would not have sufficiently altered the final result.

My failure to get elected was a tremendous letdown. I sensed that many in the riding were looking for a change and a Liberal victory would have been promising because of the positive momentum for the party, especially with the growing negativism towards the Conservatives. I felt badly for the workers who had contributed so much of their time and effort during the campaign, and I felt remorse that I had let down the many Japanese Canadians from across Canada who had given their moral and financial support. For the longest time, I had difficulty accepting the loss because the race was so close. I wondered what we, as a campaign team, could have done differently. If I had lost by a larger margin, it would have been easier to accept the outcome. In analyzing the results, I wondered whether my Japanese ancestry played a role. During my visits door to door, some told me that they didn't agree with the redress settlement that Japanese Canadians had received and that they would not support me. Winnipeg–Transcona is predominantly white, and I sensed there was some prejudice towards Asian Canadian peoples, and especially towards having one as an MP. This feeling was reinforced by an encounter that one of the campaign workers had experienced. She had gone to her hairdresser and when they started talking about the upcoming elections and candidates, the hairdresser, without prompting, blurted out, "Well for sure I'm not voting for that immigrant." I'm sure she was referring to me, because I was the only visible minority on the slate. Personally, I admit that I have encountered feelings of racism at different stages. When I first expressed my intent to the Riding Association's executive, I met with resistance and discouragement. Was it because I was a visible minority? Would they have responded differently had I been white? Going door to door, I also encountered prejudice. I could feel malice directed towards me by facial expressions or body language without any words being expressed. Having grown up in an era where I encountered subtle racism, I can intuitively sense it. I felt empathy for what my grandparents and parents must have encountered in the early days in British Columbia.

During one of our blitzes in a middle-class housing development, one of the teacher volunteers handed a brochure to a young white man who had just gotten out of his car with his wife and small child. He looked at the pamphlet, crumpled it, and threw it on the ground. I happened to walk right past him but ignored him and went towards the next house. Halfway up the walk I could hear him yelling, "Why don't you go back to where you came from?" I'm sure his comment was directed towards me. Two of the campaign workers, both teachers on my staff where I was principal, overheard the comments and came running towards me expressing their disbelief. They couldn't believe the racist comment and were embarrassed for me. To put them at ease, I said to them, "Don't feel bad for me. I expected that this might happen so it's not surprising. The best thing to do is not to react to such comments." That experience was an eye-opener for my two colleagues who had never encountered racism quite like this.

How much did racist attitudes affect the outcome? With over forty thousand votes cast and losing by around two hundred votes, I couldn't help but wonder, "How many of those people made their choice based on my ethnicity and photo?" I now realize that being a visible minority is an extra challenge in a predominantly white area. In planning the brochure, we highlighted that I was born in Canada, but I think most often people look at the candidate's photo and make assumptions. Canadians need to overcome the perception that being a visible minority means being an immigrant. The Japanese Canadians have been in Canada now for five generations – issei, nisei, sansei, yonsei, and gosei – and yet we are still trying to overcome that perception.

I remember an article by Bill Blaikie in the *Transcona Herald*, a local newspaper distributed to eleven thousand households, criticizing me for not living in the riding for which I had been running as candidate. He said that by electing me, Winnipeg–Transcona would become a "colony" represented by an "outsider." He further mentioned, "Mr. Miki is not one of us."[1] For me that statement contained a double insinuation, an obvious one about the fact that I did not reside in the riding, but another with deeper, not-so-subtle racial overtones. It implied that being different ethnically conjured an image of "not belonging" in the minds of some constituents.

I do not regret running for political office; I have gained enormous appreciation for people who do. The election of David Tsubouchi to the Ontario Legislature in 1995 was an important milestone for the Japanese Canadian community. Ontario Premier Mike Harris, elected that year, appointed Tsubouchi as minister of social services. But what disturbed me was a comment in the press following his appointment to cabinet as the only visible minority that suggested Tsubouchi's nomination might have been motivated by tokenism.

Almost a decade later, in 2004, Bev Oda became the first Japanese Canadian sansei to be elected to the Canadian Parliament. For me, this signified that we, Japanese Canadians, had made inroads into decision-making at the highest level. Later, Prime Minister Stephen Harper appointed her as the first Japanese Canadian cabinet minister. Following some public controversy, Bev Oda resigned from the government in July 2012.

The challenge for the Japanese Canadian community is how to engage our strong leaders to actively participate in the political process as candidates at every level of government. First we need to encourage the younger nikkei to assist candidates in their respective areas or join political parties to become more familiar with policy development and the election process. That is my wish.

---

1   Bill Blaikie, *Transcona Herald*, 1993. Quoted from memory.

Feeling sorry about the election loss and thinking how close I came to achieving my goal, a friend pointed out that it wasn't meant to be, but there was something better in store for me. I had become used to chance happenings in my life and during redress and thought that I should look upon the loss as an omen. It is surreal when one of those unexpected events occurs. In February 1998, I was assisting the consul general of Japan's office, who was conducting interviews at the Cultural Centre in Winnipeg for the Japan Education and Training (JET) program applicants, when someone called me out of the meeting to take an urgent call. I took the unanticipated call to find out that it was from the Privy Council's office in Ottawa. I wondered why they would be calling me. The woman on the other end indicated that I had been appointed a Canadian citizenship judge. Hearing my shocked reaction, she quickly asked if I knew anything about this. I admitted that it was a complete surprise and that I had no knowledge that I was being considered. After getting over the news, she asked whether I would accept the appointment. How could I refuse? I considered it a privilege and honour and accepted to become the citizenship judge for Manitoba and Saskatchewan.

Once on the job, I asked one of the staff members at the Immigration and Citizenship office in Winnipeg if she knew how my name had been put forward for the position. I remembered that when I received the Order of Canada in 1991, I had been asked if I would be willing to volunteer in presiding over citizenship ceremonies. I filled in on a number of occasions when the previous citizenship judge, Elizabeth Willcock, was busy with other functions and was not available on the day the ceremony was scheduled. This was the same Elizabeth Willcock who had called me from Jack Murta's office during the redress campaign. Being retired, I had time to take on this ceremonial function. I conducted a Canada Day ceremony at Lower Fort Garry with the Lieutenant-Governor and became closely acquainted with the staff, who appreciated my involvement. My understanding was that when Elizabeth Willcock resigned as judge, the office manager was asked to suggest names for her temporary replacement to the minister of immigration's office and possibly recommended me because of my volunteering. I have never received confirmation that

that was the way it happened; however it transpired, it was a pleasant surprise. After my initial term was over, my contract was renewed based on a recommendation from the Honourable Lloyd Axworthy, a cabinet minister and my MP. The renewal occurred on three occasions, and I eventually spent ten years as a citizenship judge.

As citizenship judge, I was to review citizenship applications that had gone through the review process in Sydney, Nova Scotia, and through a criminal background check and other details before being received in Winnipeg. After the citizenship officer was satisfied with the review of the individual's form for mandatory information, the applicant would be invited to write a test in English or French on their thorough understanding of Canada's history, political system, and geography. If successful, and having met the basic residency requirement, they would be invited to a citizenship ceremony at which the judge would preside. If the applicant was unsuccessful with the test, or if the officer was concerned about them not meeting the residency requirements or having possible criminal records, the judge would conduct a face-to-face interview with the individual, who would be given an oral test or questioned about their requirements. It was possible for the applicant to have a translator if they needed one. The judge has the sole discretion to approve or reject the application. Before the applicant is invited to the citizenship ceremony, the judge has to sign off on each application.

The Canadian system of granting citizenship is very personal and requires the applicant to meet the judge, whereas in the United Kingdom, the certificates are mailed out after citizenship has been approved. However, there are areas I would like changed. When I was presiding over the courts in Toronto, I encountered a number of older Portuguese Canadians who had been living in Canada for thirty years or more and were only now becoming citizens. At sixty years of age, applicants are no longer required to take the test of their knowledge about Canada. I asked one of them why they had waited so long. He said that most of the Portuguese Canadians who work in the construction industry have weak English language skills and are reluctant to write the test for fear of failing. I think that if a person has lived in Canada for a long time, worked hard, and paid their taxes, they have already demonstrated that they are a valuable citizen without having to write a formal test. There should be provision made in the approval process to recognize people who have resided in Canada for a

TOP LEFT: Art with grandchildren Jesse and Alex at his retirement
TOP RIGHT: Art as citizen judge posing for a fun photo
BOTTOM: Citizenship photo with Governor General Michaëlle Jean

significant period of time and their contributions to Canada. The other area that needs to be considered is that women, especially women refugees, are at a disadvantage when it comes to citizenship approval. Many have spent years in a refugee camp raising children but have no formal education. When women come to Canada, many are expected to be at home with their children and have very little opportunity to learn English or French to meet the language requirement for citizenship. This anomaly needs to be rectified and women given alternative ways and means to become Canadian citizens.

The most rewarding and memorable part of my role as judge was presiding over the Citizenship Courts that were held in the court room at Union Station court and other locations such as schools, community centres, historic sites, the Lieutenant-Governor's residence, legislative buildings, and other public facilities. A memorable ceremony was one I shared with the Governor General Michaëlle Jean in 2005 at the residence of the Lieutenant-Governor. Before presenting citizenship certificates to the new citizens, I would address the gathering by sharing my thoughts on becoming a new citizen and their rights and responsibilities and relate the experiences of my family, who were not allowed to vote from 1885 until 1949, even though they were born in Canada, because racist provincial legislation in British Columbia forbid anyone of Japanese, Chinese, or Indian ancestry to be placed on the voters' list. I explained that Canada adopted its first Citizenship Act in 1947, setting out parameters on who could become a Canadian citizen, especially people born in Canada. After my mother passed away in 2002, I discovered my father's citizenship certificate stored away in her personal documents. It showed that he was born in 1906 in Tynehead, BC. He lived his entire life in Canada and only officially became a Canadian citizen on December 3, 1948.

The other message that I imparted to new citizens, especially parents, is that they were the pioneers for their family; I applauded them for making sacrifices so that subsequent generations will be the beneficiaries of their hard work, perseverance, and decision to find a new life in a new country. I think about my grandparents, who faced the challenges of language and cultural barriers and made sacrifices to give me the life I have today.

The most intriguing, heart-wrenching, and wonderful part of my role was to hear the hardships and struggles but also the optimism

Art's father's citizenship certificate, December 3, 1948

that these immigrants looked for in Canada for themselves and their children. I met a family from England who now owned a dairy farm in the Interlake region of Manitoba. The reason they immigrated to Canada was so that they could own their own farm, which they said would have been impossible if they had remained in England. The father said he was grateful to Canada for accepting his family. Now, his children were involved in running the farming business and would continue to do so. I felt sad for refugees from the Middle East who had spent most of their growing-up years in camps without any formal education and yet were expected to learn English sufficiently to write the citizenship test. For them, it would be a real hardship to become a Canadian citizen. Without citizenship, these refugees would have no status from the country they came from, no passport, and would not be able to leave Canada. I met young Asian immigrants who held several minimum wage jobs at one time in order to save enough money to pay for an education. There were the parents who sacrificed, leaving good lives but unsure about the stability and possibility of war in their own country. They immigrated to Canada in the hope of giving their children more opportunities and the freedom to pursue their dreams. Others came from countries that were not democracies and looked forward to voting for the first time. I heard stories where families banded together to work long and hard hours to save enough to have their own home. Despite the struggles, sufferings, and harrowing experiences these immigrants and refugees had encountered, I was amazed at the appreciative attitude they had about Canada and how this country had given them hope for a better life. I could see the happiness in their faces as they came before me to accept the citizenship certificate and finally belong to a country.

I would like to share some citizenship stories that have inspired me and given me greater insight into what it means to be a Canadian. The first story is about Molly Boland, who had immigrated from Scotland in 2001 because her only living sibling lived in Winnipeg. In the spring of 2005, her sister, Anne Boland, came to the office to ask if something could be done for Molly to receive her citizenship, because she was in the hospital and unable to attend a ceremony. The government policy is that in order to become a Canadian citizen, the individual must attend the ceremony. When I received the request, I indicated to the citizenship officers that I would be willing to conduct a special ceremony at the hospital. In October 2005, the officers and I went to the palliative care area at Riverview Health Centre where Molly was a terminal patient. When we arrived at the patients' lounge, there was a large crowd of family, doctors, nurses, and friends waiting to celebrate Molly's big day. Before the ceremony, I had met with Molly in her room to describe the process, and when she spoke I noticed that she held one finger over her tracheal tube, struggling to respond as a result of the effects of cancer on her tongue. We gathered in the lounge for the ceremony. When Molly was wheeled in, she was greeted by her friends, who were there to celebrate with her. Because Molly might have difficulty repeating the oath, I invited all the guests in the room to help Molly recite the oath as she mouthed the words. After everyone had affirmed their loyalty and sung "O Canada," friends from the two choirs that Molly belonged to sang Woody Guthrie's "This Land Is Your Land." It was probably the first time many of her friends had ever said the oath. Molly was so elated and thrilled that, as though unaware of her condition, she stood up and hugged a dear friend and then collapsed back into her wheelchair. In an article by Lindor Reynolds in the *Winnipeg Free Press* in October 2005, Dr. Jeanne Young, Molly's family physician, had this to say about her: "What struck me most about Molly was how truly blessed she felt to become a Canadian. What I take for granted every day of my life, and probably most of us do, she felt was the ultimate accomplishment. She feels this is the best country in the world and wanted to be part of that citizenship, regardless of how long she would enjoy that privilege."[2] I sometimes related Molly's story in my ceremony to get new citizens to ponder the question, "What does Canadian citizenship mean to you?" There are generic answers that you often hear, but I believe that each person values their citizenship in their own way. Two months later, I read Molly's obituary in the *Winnipeg Free Press*. What struck me most was this statement: "The happiest day in Molly's life was the day when she became a Canadian citizen." For me, the fulfillment of a dream that exhilarated Molly was my greatest reward.

One event that brings back fond memories for me was a private ceremony I conducted for Valdan, a young man originally from Croatia. He was anxious to get his Canadian citizenship so he could get a passport to compete in a marathon in the United States. Unfortunately, his citizenship ceremony had been delayed because of a water-main break in the court building. I agreed to hold a private ceremony at the office and set a specific date. When Valdan arrived at the office, he had about twenty-five people with him, so the staff had to locate a room large enough to accommodate his friends. These were all the caring people he met in Winnipeg after initially knowing only one person. After my brief commentary about citizenship rights and responsibilities, I asked Valda to repeat the words to the oath of citizenship after me.[3] I could see that Valdan was emotionally moved when he said the distinctive words; I could see tears running down his cheeks. After completing the oath in English and French he asked to say a few words. He told us his story of how in Croatia there were two ethnic groups in armed conflict. He said he was unwilling to take up arms because he had relatives on both sides. Valdan vowed not to remain to fight, and so he took refuge in Germany. There he met a Canadian from Winnipeg, who suggested that he should consider

---

2   "She'll Proudly End Her Days a Canadian," *Winnipeg Free Press*, October 15, 2005, archives. winnipegfreepress.com/winnipeg-free-press/2005-10-15/page-1/.

3   To read or hear the Canadian Oath of Citizenship, see "Discover Canada – The Oath of Citizenship / Le serment de citoyenneté," Immigration, Refugees and Citizenship Canada (website), last modified January 30, 2023, www.canada.ca/en/immigration-refugees-citizenship/corporate/publications-manuals/discover-canada/read-online/oath-citizenship.html.

immigrating to Canada. He was told that it was a great, peaceful country. After this friend left, Valdan thought about the suggestion and decided to go to the Canadian embassy in Bonn, Germany, to apply for landed immigrant status. Once approved, Valdan was asked by the immigration official where in Canada he wished to land. He said he didn't know any places in Canada but remembered his friend from Winnipeg, so he said, "Winnipeg." When he arrived in Winnipeg, he made contact with his friend, who introduced him to the joys of running. On the day that he was sworn in, all his friends from Winnipeg's Running Room, a fitness club where he was a member, came to celebrate with him. He was so happy and proud that he promised that wherever he ran in marathons, he would always have a Canadian flag with him. But the story doesn't end here.

The day after the Manitoba Marathon on June 18, 2001, I looked on the front page of the *Winnipeg Free Press* and was surprised to see a picture of Valdan draped in a Canadian flag. The article was an unforgettable story about this young man getting married to his Canadian-born girlfriend in front of four thousand people at the University of Manitoba stadium.[4] When asked about the flag, Valdan told the reporter that as he entered the stadium, his friend had handed him the Canadian flag, which he had draped around his shoulders as he completed the final lap. He wanted to show people how proud he was to be a Canadian. His heartwarming story captured media attention. I saw him again a few years later and he told me that he continues to run in major marathons in North America. Valdan is a great ambassador for Canada and someone I'm proud to have known.

During the period before I retired in 2008, I had the opportunity to swear in over forty thousand new Canadians and preside over one thousand citizenship ceremonies. It has taken me to all provinces except Québec and Newfoundland and Labrador; and I even held a small ceremony in Nunavut's Rankin Inlet (which is called Kangiqliniq ᖃᖏᕐᖠᓂᖅ in Inuktitut). Wherever I go in Winnipeg, people whom I have sworn in as citizens will approach to let me know that I was their judge and thank me. I continue to get similar reactions of happiness, thankfulness, and appreciation from our newest citizens whenever I meet them. Even this year, in 2023, my friends, including Keiko, were eating at a noodle restaurant and the woman at the next

---

4   "Runners Wed at Finish Line: Now Real Marathon Begins," *Winnipeg Free Press*, June 18, 2001, 2, archives.winnipegfreepress.com/winnipeg-free-press/2001-06-18/page-2/.

table kept looking at us. Finally, she came over and asked if I was Judge Miki. I acknowledged that I was. She went on to tell us that she became a citizen twenty years ago and remembered that exciting day. Then she took a selfie with me to put on social media for her friends to see. Occasionally I run into a Handi-Transit driver whom I had sworn in many years ago, dropping off passengers at the Reh-Fit fitness centre where I work out. Each time I see him, he thanks me and reminds me that he sees me every day, because the citizenship photo of him with me sits on the mantle in his living room. These situations are frequent, even fifteen years later.

When I reflect on my role as citizenship judge, I relate it to my daughter's teaching experience, where the concept of completeness or full circle is meaningful. I recall a trip that Keiko and I took to Japan in the late '90s to visit our daughter Tani, who was teaching English with the JET program. (JET is a joint initiative between Japan and Canada, a teaching exchange program run by Japan for students who have graduated from university. Each year Canada sends young people to work in schools as a native language assistant or work with the board of education.)

We were invited by the principal at the Mikazuki Junior High School in the prefecture of Saga to visit the school and meet the teachers. Later that evening, we joined the staff in a social gathering at a restaurant for a welcoming dinner. As an educator, what intrigued me most were the differences in school operations and atmosphere as compared to Canadian schools. When the principal entered the staff room to introduce me, all the staff stood as a sign of respect and then sat down when he explained about our visit. I shared this experience with my Canadian staff at my school, who responded by saying, "Don't expect that from us!" I noticed that the school didn't have a custodian, but rather the cleanup of the school and classrooms was left to the teacher and students. During lunch, it was the students who delivered the prepared food to the classrooms and cleaned up. As students and staff entered the school, everyone changed into their inside shoes. The care of the building was the responsibility of staff and students. I was impressed and envious of the students' dedicated effort and commitment to caring for the school environment.

The same day, Keiko and I accompanied Tani to the elementary school where she was teaching a grade-five English class. The students worked in teams to record answers on the blackboard to mathematics problems that she presented. At the end of the activity, the responses were reviewed by the teacher, who put a circle around answers that were *correct* and a check mark beside answers that were *wrong*. I asked her after class for the explanation of this difference in comparison to what teachers do in North America. Her response was very logical: "In Japan, a check mark is a sign the answer is incorrect and the student should check the answer again. On the other hand, a circle around the correct answer is a symbol for completeness."

For me, the symbol of coming full circle is powerfully represented by the fact that my parents were first denied citizenship, waited later in life to become citizens, and today, a generation later, their son is granting Canadian citizenship to others. This is a reflection of Canada's progress in social development.

What has intrigued me was how motivated these soon-to-be Canadian immigrants and refugees are to become citizens and belong to a country where they hope for a better life for their families, educational opportunities, and to have rights and freedoms as spelled out in Canada's Charter of Rights and Freedoms. I have met so many wonderful people across our large country and am grateful for the opportunity to have served it. Being a Canadian citizenship judge has been the most rewarding gift I could ever have hoped for.

CHAPTER 15

Reflections and Exploits

Being president of the NAJC was an exhilarating exposure to the complexities of the Japanese Canadian community and the generational differences within it, but one that has strengthened my appreciation for what the organization has accomplished. I recognize that battles are not won alone; our success required cohesiveness among strong, committed individuals and collaborative community representatives from across Canada. Keiko and I had the good fortune to be actively engaged in the genesis of the Canadian Museum for Human Rights and to participate on a number of occasions in the Pan American Nikkei Association (PANA) conventions that were held in various locations across the Americas. More recently the NAJC undertook a redress campaign with the British Columbia government, and I was asked to be an advisor to the negotiation team because of my past redress experience. At the community level, I maintained active engagement in a leadership capacity as president of the Japanese Cultural Association of Manitoba (JCAM) and initiated projects that celebrated our past.

In closing this book, I share my personal thoughts about fate or destiny, the unfailing support of my family, and the accolades that I have received. I'm wonderstruck at my good fortune and to have played a significant role in making Canadian history.

The first national Japanese Canadian organization, the National Japanese Canadian Citizens' Association (NJCCA), was formed in Toronto in 1947 as the voice for Japanese Canadians scattered across Canada. Harold Hirose, from Winnipeg, was one of its founding members and would later play a significant role in the 1980s redress campaign. The NJCCA's main mandate was to seek the franchise and rights of citizenship that had been denied. They also facilitated the implementation of the Bird Commission's awards for properties confiscated by the government. The process was unsatisfactory and the resulting settlement was far below the value of the property, which created division and dissension within the Japanese Canadian community.

The Bird Commission quandary was the forerunner to the redress campaign in the 1980s. In 1980, the national organization was renamed the National Association of Japanese Canadians and was designed to be more inclusive than the NJCCA with its chapter system.

When I became president of the NAJC in 1984, the headquarters moved to Ash Street in Winnipeg, my home. We established a President's Committee of volunteer members from Winnipeg's Japanese Canadian community to assist with the day-to-day operations, organize council meetings, maintain records of meetings, and provide input and advice. The dedicated volunteers Harold Hirose, Henry Kojima, Alan Yoshino, Fred Kaita, Lucy Yamashita, Carol Matsumoto, and Joy Ooto spent countless hours ensuring that the NAJC's headquarters was maintained over the four years until redress was finally achieved. Their commitment, dependability, and contributions were invaluable support for me. Harold's long history and experience in the Japanese Canadian community in Manitoba and nationally was a tremendous benefit for us. Unfortunately, Harold and Alan are no longer with us. My wife Keiko often willingly gave up our living room to become the NAJC's headquarters, as the table became cluttered with NAJC documents. She was a charming host, especially when council meetings were held in Winnipeg and out-of-town visitors dropped over for a relaxing social evening. As described, the NAJC was a localized organization with a minimal budget run by hard-working volunteers, but the impression from the outside, especially for reporters and other organizations, was that the NAJC was a large operation with a full office and paid staff. This façade was an advantage, as long as the NAJC was looked upon as a powerful entity. I had the wonderful opportunity of working with NAJC council members, who were dedicated and committed to pursuing redress on behalf of the community. We spent many weekends and late hours congregated at meetings across the country to discuss ways of reaching a consensus for the redress proposal, involving the communities in the process and developing strategies for negotiation meetings with the government. Many hot and open dialogues were held on how to counteract the government's insistence that we accept their offers, which the NAJC rejected on several occasions. Even through rejections and frustrations over the lack of progress and impediments from some members within the council over positions taken, the spirit of camaraderie and overwhelming support among the national council members for our strategy committee was an influential factor in the final outcome. I appreciated the strengths and dedication of council members in sustaining their focus throughout the four years before the settlement was reached.

The tenacity of the strategy committee needs to be further acknowledged; their commitment to the principle of individual compensation in the last two years before September 22, 1988, was unwavering. The committee struggled during the low, dark periods but was rewarded when we achieved our ultimate goal. What made this group unique were the individuals who contributed their expert skills and passion to steadfastly remain on task. Roy Miki and Cassandra Kobayashi were the scribes who prepared letters to government officials, wrote the NAJC's press releases, and co-authored the important book *Justice in Our Time: The Japanese Canadian Redress Settlement* (Talonbooks, 1991).

Maryka Omatsu and Cassandra Kobayashi, both lawyers, provided legal advice and perspectives along with Don Rosenbloom. Don's contacts with Thomas Berger and John Fraser were an invaluable asset in the negotiations process, and his knowledge of government inner workings helped strengthen our political strategy. Audrey Kobayashi, geographer from Queen's University, had readily available historical and community data that was irreplaceable in formulating the redress proposal and negotiation plans. Roger Obata, the senior statesperson, was our link to the past, especially with the Bird Commission's findings and the establishment of the national organization back in 1947. Roger's unwavering view was that redress was inevitable because, as he said, "When Canadians learn about what happened to Japanese Canadians, they will know that redress is the right thing to do." He held this view throughout the struggle. Roy Inouye from Kamloops and Bryce Kanbara from Hamilton provided local perspectives and an invaluable link to smaller communities. Generationally, Roger Obata and Roy Inouye were nisei and the rest of us were sansei. With the passing of time, we have lost these two dedicated leaders.

CANADIAN MUSEUM FOR HUMAN RIGHTS

In 2000, Keiko and I received a request from Israel Asper, president of the Asper Foundation and former leader of the Manitoba Liberal Party, to meet with him and Moe Levy, executive director, about his idea of establishing a human-rights museum in Winnipeg. We knew Israel Asper, known as Izzy, and his wife Babs from hockey, as our son Geoffrey played on the same team as Izzy's son Leonard for a number of years. Izzy would have been aware of my involvement in the redress movement. He was a strong proponent of human-rights education, especially in relation to the Holocaust. Each year, his foundation sent high-school students to the United States Holocaust Memorial Museum in Washington, DC. Rather than sending students to the US, he wondered whether it would be possible to have a museum in Canada where students could learn about human rights. He showed us a video of the students' visit to Washington and pitched his idea to Keiko and me. Realizing the importance of students being enlightened about human-rights violations, including the Japanese Canadian history and internment, we both saw the benefits of having such an institution here. We informed Izzy and Moe that the Japanese Canadian community would strongly endorse the concept. Later, Moe told us that this had been Izzy's first meeting to share his idea, and he was so elated with our enthusiasm and endorsement that he decided to go ahead and promote the creation of a human-rights museum to other groups in Winnipeg. We were invited to share in the concept development with museum designer Ralph Appelbaum, and Keiko was asked to be on the advisory body that promoted Izzy's concept. We attended the federal government's official announcement that the Winnipeg museum of human rights would be the first national museum outside of Ottawa; naturally, we also attended the museum's official opening on September 20, 2014. Although the exhibit space allotted to the Japanese Canadian experience isn't as large as I wanted, at least there is adequate information and photos, so that visitors can gain vivid knowledge of the Japanese Canadian internment and history.

I was shocked in June 2020 to hear allegations of pervasive racism, sexism, and homophobia at the Canadian Museum for Human Rights. This controversy brought into question its leadership and policies. The accusations were investigated, and a report by mediator Laurelle Harris confirmed that systemic racism existed and that employees who were Black, Indigenous, or People of Colour had been negatively impacted. Under the new chief executive officer Isha Khan, the museum has now adopted strong measures to deal with issues of inclusion and equity.

PAN AMERICAN NIKKEI ASSOCIATION

As president of the NAJC, I attended the Japanese American Citizens League's 1985 annual general meeting in Chicago with Keiko and Lucy Yamashita to update our US counterparts on the progress of the Japanese Canadian redress campaign. This is when I discovered that very few Americans realized that the Canadian government had taken similar actions against its citizens of Japanese ancestry as those undertaken by the US government. Although I was familiar with the US experience, its similarities and differences to the Canadian one, I wondered what other Japanese populations had experienced during the war in Central and South American countries.

In the early 1990s, Mark and Shag Ando, long-time supporters from Canada, asked me as the NAJC's president whether we would host the Pan American Nikkei Association (PANA) convention in Canada for the first time. At the time, the NAJC was extremely active in organizing national events across Canada, and we thought that hosting the 1993 PANA convention would add international perspective and connections. The NAJC, with financial support from the JCRF, chose Vancouver, a city known for its beauty and vibrancy, as the site, thinking it would be impressive for visitors from North, Central, and South America who had never been to Canada. Vancouver's large number of Japanese Canadian volunteers to help organize and assist was another factor in its choice.

What intrigued me most was meeting and getting to know people of Japanese ancestry from all over the Americas. Keiko and I met Alberto H. and his parents from Chile at a PANA convention and we became good friends, meeting up with him and his family at other PANAs. A special guest was Susana Higuchi, Peru's First Lady and Honorary Chair of the Convention. At the opening ceremonies, I sat with Mrs. Higuchi and had interesting conversations about Canada and Peru. She asked where my family came from in Japan. I told her that my grandparents came from Fukuoka. Right away her face lit up and she blurted out that her family came from Fukuoka as well. I felt that sense of intimate connection with her that emanates when you're from the same ken or region. One of the traditions I discovered at the PANA conventions was that there is a close relationship with Japan through the offices of the ambassador or consul general of Japan everywhere PANA is held. In Vancouver, the large delegation was invited to the residence of Consul General Yasuhide Hayashi for a marvellous reception and an opportunity to interact with visitors and consular staff.

In 1995, I was one of the speakers at the PANA convention in Lima, Peru, where there are about eighty thousand Japanese Peruvians, the majority in Lima. My speech was on the Japanese Canadian experience and the redress agreement with the Canadian government. Sharing our story and then hearing what had happened in Peru gave me a scope of the wartime atrocities directed at peoples of Japanese ancestry overseas. In Peru, Japanese Peruvians are prominent in business. There is a large Japanese cultural centre and school in Lima where Japanese is taught, with a recreational area including a large swimming pool. What is noticeable is that all these facilities are surrounded by high walls for security and protection.

At the cultural centre, there is an exhibit documenting the story of about eighteen hundred Japanese Peruvians who, during World War II, were kidnapped or rounded up by the Peruvian police and turned over to US troops. This was financed by the US government. The Japanese Peruvians were taken by transport ships to a US concentration camp in Crystal City, Texas, where they were labelled "enemy aliens" and remained incarcerated until the camp's closure in February 1948. The United States utilized these victims as exchange for US civilians stranded in Japan after Pearl Harbor. About eight hundred were sent to Japan as part of the exchange. Others were deported to Japan because Peru did not want the Japanese Peruvians back. After legal battles, a number of them were able to remain in the US after the war. Unfortunately, the victims who remained did not qualify for compensation, because they were not US citizens at the time of their incarceration. The group launched a class-action suit against the US government, and ten years after the US reparations, these victims were offered $5,000 each. This story of the plight of Japanese Peruvians was new to me, and I wondered what had happened in other South American countries.

In Lima, the PANA delegates visited the palace of President Alberto Fujimori, where we were welcomed by the president's sister and given a tour of the magnificent building. This was followed by a dinner hosted by the minister's office. We also visited the residence of the ambassador of Japan for Peru, a well-secured compound surrounded by high walls, where a reception was held for the delegates. This was the same place that in December 1996 received worldwide media attention when diplomats, government officials, and business leaders were held captive there by terrorists during the Japanese embassy hostage crisis.

A memorable PANA convention was the one held in 1999 in Santiago, Chile. Keiko, I, our friend Alberto, and Alex Yanoshita from Windsor were having lunch in a small restaurant in Santiago when the stand-up heater began to shake violently; Alberto was quick enough to stop it from tipping over. I could see shock and fear in Alex's face. Meanwhile, Alberto calmly commented, "That was an earthquake." Apparently, this happens quite often, so the local residents take it for granted. Alberto grew up on a farm north of Santiago in a more temperate area. His mother is Japanese Chilean and was a school teacher and his father was a native Chilean. They have eight wonderful children, and we met most of them on our visit to Santiago. All of the children are professionals: doctors, dentists, other health-care workers, and an accountant. Alberto owns two medical clinics and is extremely busy. In Chile, there is no universal health care per se, so in order to provide accessible care, professionals are restricted by the government as to what they can charge for services. As a result, doctors are poorly paid; this applies to other areas of health care as well. Alberto was astounded to hear what doctors earn in Canada. Chile has a small population of Japanese Chileans, only about two thousand. Apparently, a few Japanese Chileans were removed from sensitive areas during the war, but nothing to the scale of other countries.

A highlight of the 2013 PANA convention in Bolivia was the delegates' visit to one of the several so-called Okinawa colonies located in the rural parts of Bolivia. A group of Okinawan immigrants settled in the interior of Bolivia on the invitation of the Bolivian and United States governments in the 1950s and were given free land to develop. An Okinawa colony operates in a similar way to Hutterite colonies in Canada. On the farm, crops such as soy, rice, and other grains are grown, animals are raised; they've introduced macadamia nuts to Bolivia. The settlement has its own school, funded partly by the Japanese government, where Japanese is taught and cultural activities such as the Bon Odori are held at a large community centre. *Bon* 盆 is a traditional Buddhist holiday and festival and *odori* 踊り means "dance," so Bon Odori refers to a festival dance. We visited a first-class medical facility in the town built by the Japanese government with the latest technology. The hospital is open to all residents in the area, including non-Japanese. These Okinawa Colonies face difficult futures, as the younger generation are not interested in working locally and most leave for the city. Thanks to their Japanese ancestry, many younger Japanese Bolivians are able to go to Japan for employment.

Our last trip to South America was the PANA convention in 2007 in São Paulo. Brazil has the largest number of nikkei living outside of Japan, with a population of over 1.5 million. The Japanese and Okinawans first arrived in Brazil in 1908 from Okinawa and other parts of Japan and were given land by the government to establish their homes and farms. After Brazil declared war on Japan in 1942, travel restrictions were placed upon Japanese Brazilians and Okinawan Brazilians, newspapers were censored, Japanese schools closed, and goods belonging to companies confiscated. Some were arrested or expelled on allegations of espionage and others were placed in concentration camps. Unlike in Canada or the United States, not all

Japanese Brazilians and Okinawan Brazilians were placed in internment or concentration camps. Recently, there have been attempts by Japanese Brazilians and Okinawan Brazilians to have their government apologize for wartime actions, but so far to no avail.

At one time, São Paulo had a thriving Japantown, but today, with a few exceptions, the Japanese Brazilians and Okinawan Brazilians no longer operate businesses, and most shops have been taken over by more recently arrived Asian immigrants. The Japanese and Okinawans in Brazil are highly successful in politics and business. Keiko and I met a family that owns a shoyu (soya sauce) factory that provides shoyu to all of South America. We visited a large, successful tea farm owned by Japanese Brazilians. We enjoyed the three-day Japan Festival held annually in São Paulo in July. The attendance at this festival is over a hundred thousand; Japanese culture and food are the main attractions. You can visit over a hundred food stalls representing every ken in Japan and highlighting foods that are unique to that ken. Performances include taiko drumming, odori dances, and other activities that are familiar at Japanese festivals in Canada.

PANA has been an incredible learning experience, especially in meeting so many wonderful people and appreciating the hospitality of the tireless organizers and volunteers. PANA is a biennial event and conventions alternate between North and South American cities. What seems strange to me is to be in a room where delegates of Japanese ancestry are speaking only, say, Spanish, as in Chile or Bolivia, or Portuguese, as in Brazil. I would imagine they feel the same way when we Japanese Canadians speak English or French.

BC REDRESS

In May 2012, the BC Legislative Assembly passed a motion unanimously acknowledging and apologizing for the BC government's involvement in the federal government's decision to intern Japanese Canadians. This motion was introduced by the minister of advanced education, Naomi Yamamoto, whose family had been victims of the internment during World War II. The reaction of the Japanese Canadian community to the announcement was muted; the motion was a surprise to most of us. A group of Japanese Canadians had supported this initiative, but the BC government had not contacted representatives of Japanese Canadian organizations, including the NAJC, which had no knowledge of the forthcoming apology. I had sent a letter to Premier Christy Clark in June 2012 to express my view regarding the surprising gesture, saying: "If the apology was meant to be directed towards the Japanese [Canadian] victims of the internment, perhaps a more suitable overture such as a formal apology and expression of regret could be given by the premier at a public ceremony at a community venue with invitations to the Japanese Canadian victims, families, and friends."

In 2017, the NAJC launched action to advocate for meaningful support for the Japanese Canadian community to complement the apology issued by the BC government. NAJC President Lorene Oikawa, with members of the advisory committee, initially met with officials in the NDP government expressing the NAJC's intent to seek concrete remediation. The BC government was sensitive to the NAJC's request and provided funding to organize community consultation meetings to solicit suggestions and ideas for revitalizing and restoring our communities. This feedback reflecting the needs of the community would later form the basis for the government's report. Maryka Omatsu and I, members of the NAJC's 1988 strategy team, joined the NAJC's steering committee that was engaged in community consultation meetings. After much vetting and inputs from skilled professionals and community volunteers, a set of recommendations were formulated into a report. I was impressed with the intensity and dedication of the people involved in this process and developing a negotiation strategy. Angus McAllister's professional skills helped augment a dynamic communications process. Susanne Tabata and Paul Noble were instrumental in crafting the report *Recommendations for Redressing Historical Wrongs against Japanese Canadians in BC* that was submitted to the Honourable Lisa Beare, minister of tourism, arts, and culture.[1] A key factor in creating a polished, comprehensive report was the engagement of the Institute of Fiscal Studies and Democracies in Ottawa, whose analysis on the main thematic pillars of the proposal were quantified and legitimized. The report was

---

1   National Association of Japanese Canadians, *Recommendations for Redressing Historical Wrongs against Japanese Canadians in BC: Community Consultation Report*, October 2019, najc.ca/wp/wp-content/uploads/2019/11/NAJC_BC_Redress_report_only20191031.1421.pdf.

formally presented to the minister by Susanne Tabata in the presence of community members, including internment survivors.

The negotiation team, led by Susanne Tabata with Paul Kariya and Lorene Oikawa, worked tirelessly meeting with government officials, ministers, and anyone else of influence. Paul brought to the table his knowledge and government experience from working for an Indigenous organization (Coastal First Nations) as a senior policy advisor and lobbying government officials. Susanne's impassioned communication skills and Paul's political astuteness resulted in a formidable team. Both of them have dedicated enormous amounts of time and energy to the cause, and their efforts resulted in the positive outcome of the negotiation process. Maryka and I, as honorary advisors to the negotiation team, have marvelled at the accomplishments of Susanne, Paul, and Lorene. Despite the distractions of the COVID-19 pandemic and the extreme devastation caused by the 2021 and 2023 fires in the BC Interior, they have managed to maintain productive communications with the principal officials, including the premier and his office.

A pleasant surprise was the announcement of a $2 million grant by the BC government in May 2021 for funding towards the social well-being of Japanese Canadian survivors, marking the initial stage of ongoing negotiations by the NAJC. The purpose of the fund is to support the health and wellness of the estimated 6,600 survivors living today. The Nikkei Seniors Health Care and Housing Society was tasked with the administration of the fund, and the project office, managed by Eiko Eby and assistant Linda Reid, developed an application process for funding individual survivors' needs and the organizations that service survivors. This project was communicated nationally through online presentations. The massive funding process was completed in a short time due to the efficiency of the staff and volunteers. The project assisted over eighteen hundred underserved individuals, fifty organizational projects, and eighteen small group activities. I feel that the effective and expeditious manner in which the funds were dispersed reflects positively on the community's ability to manage funds.

The most important day for Japanese Canadians in British Columbia was perhaps May 21, 2022, a beautiful day at the Steveston Martial Arts Centre, located in what had been a thriving Japanese Canadian fishing village before the war. In his address to the many survivors present, Premier John Horgan stated, "Today, we are further building on [our] apology by making an historic investment honouring the Japanese Canadian community with lasting recognition of the traumatic internment of Japanese Canadians during the Second World War. The government of British Columbia is contributing $100 million in funding to support the legacy initiatives recommended by the National Association of Japanese Canadians."[2] The Japanese Canadian Legacy Society was created in July 2022 to oversee the implementation of the initiatives and funding for projects and activities directed towards Japanese Canadian education, heritage, community, culture, and seniors' health and wellness. To memorialize the unjust treatment of Japanese Canadians, a national monument will be erected on the grounds of St. Ann's Academy in downtown Victoria, with the names of all Japanese Canadians who had been uprooted, dispossessed, interned, and displaced.[3] Finally, eighty years after the internment, the recognition by governments, nationally and provincially, of the past wrongdoings brings closure to the long outstanding human-rights violations.

JAPANESE CULTURAL ASSOCIATION OF MANITOBA

The redress experience has strengthened my confidence in my abilities; I now believe anything is possible if you have the desire to chase your goal. Sometimes it is necessary to undertake projects for the betterment of your organization and community, despite opposition or contrary views around you. With two existing organizations, the Manitoba Japanese Canadian Citizens' Association and the Manitoba Japanese Canadian Cultural Centre, there appeared to be ongoing

2   John Horgan, "Acknowledgment of Internment and Japanese Canadian Legacies in BC," under "BC Redress," Japanese Canadian Legacies (website), jclegacies.com/bc-redress/.

3   See the NAJC's web page "Monument" (bcredress.ca/the-six-pillars/monument /) and the Japanese Canadian Legacies' page "Monument + Database" (jclegacies .com/monument-database/) for more information. The Japanese Canadian Legacies Monument Names Database is accessible here: University of Victoria's Humanities Computing and Media Centre, "Uprooted Japanese Canadians," hcmc.uvic.ca/project /monument/.

differences and competition for donations and recruitment of volunteers for their respective boards. With declining involvement, it seemed prudent to amalgamate the two groups and create cohesion in Winnipeg's small Japanese Canadian community. Both organizations agreed to have one organization represent the Japanese community. In 2013, I became president of the newly formed organization, the Japanese Cultural Association of Manitoba (JCAM).

As president, I thought that amalgamation would be an opportune time to set in motion a renewed momentum, including modifications to our building in order to create a new image. In 2015, I contacted an architectural firm to draw up several different plans for a vestibule adjacent to the main hall, with a new entranceway that would be wheelchair-accessible and easier to access for seniors. The initial projection of costs went between $125,000 to $150,000. The new JCAM board was divided on this project, with concerns of "Who will pay for it? It costs too much. We don't have the money." Although I assured the board that I would see that funds were raised, some remained skeptical and claimed that it was not a viable plan. One evening a board member, concerned about the organization's finances, spent several hours urging me to forget about the project. We might not have had the financial resources, but I refused to abandon the plan because we needed to take drastic action to have a different perspective now, rather than to continue to live in the past. For me, backing down was not an option. Desperate for the board's support, I said that I would personally raise the funds. The board finally approved, but the vocal opposition began to undermine the decision; some spoke to others about opposing the expansion. What I couldn't understand was why there was such adamant effort to discredit the project. I wasn't asking them to contribute money. How could change scare people so much? I had encountered similar situations as a principal or during the redress movement, when certain people had rejected changes or new initiatives without being able to provide any realistic alternatives or viable suggestions. For them, the only option was inertia. The problem is that if we adopt that attitude, no progress will ever be made, and yet we live in a world that is constantly changing.

I submitted a number of applications for capital grants to government bodies and private foundations and organizations. By chance, a close friend of mine in Toronto, Sid Ikeda, mentioned that there was a Japanese Canadian foundation I should contact. I wrote to the Frank

H. Hori Charitable Foundation in the fall of 2015 requesting $50,000 towards the renovation project, providing limited details but focusing on creating a renewed vibrancy for the centre. Two months later, I received a reply that the Hori Charitable Foundation had approved a grant in the full amount requested. I was shocked to receive the wonderful news and extremely grateful for the financial support, which came at the right time. Being a foundation administered by Japanese Canadians, its mandate is to assist in the safeguarding of Japanese culture and heritage, create opportunities for young people, and assist community organizations with programs that preserve history and identity. Many community organizations have benefitted from their generosity. I suspected the directors were aware of my involvement with the redress movement and settlement and that this was a factor in their quick decision. With other applications, the processing time takes much longer and the requirement for details can be overwhelming. For government or corporate funding, the process of evaluation and delivery of the decision can take nine months or more. After applying to the provincial and federal governments, the Winnipeg Foundation, and the NAJC's Renewal Fund, JCAM received another $105,000 in grants for the vestibule project.

The initial grant from the Hori Foundation was a catalyst for me to initiate a community fundraising campaign. I had previously been involved with two major campaigns. The Prairie Theatre Exchange, a theatre group, decided to move their theatre; as a board member, I attended a workshop on fundraising. There were two principles that stood out for me. First, as a board member, you must be the first to contribute to the campaign before you ask others to do so. It's difficult to convince a potential donor to contribute if you haven't personally. Second, you shouldn't be afraid to ask for a significant amount. For large campaigns, such as for Winnipeg's Reh-Fit expansion of their facility, fundraisers asked up front for $50,000 to $100,000 from corporations. I worked on the membership campaign for Reh-Fit and asked for $1,000 as a starter. The point is that if you ask for a little, you get a little, but if you ask for a large amount, there is a possibility that you will get a lot more.

I designed the JCAM fundraising campaign that began in the spring of 2016 by setting the categories of giving at $10,000, then $5,000, $2,500, $1,000, $500, and $250. Contributors of these sums would have their names acknowledged on a donor board. The key is: before you advertise the donation levels, find people who will commit to the top categories, so that when the campaign goes public there are already donors listed under each level. This is where the board's commitment to contribute is important. I received a lot of criticism for this approach. I was told that "we don't do it that way." But this process works – $170,000 was raised from the community.

The total raised was significantly over the amount that was needed. We were able to use the excess funds for a second phase of the renovation plans. The automatic sliding doors now allow for wheelchair accessibility and improved ease of entry for all. The addition of a vestibule and the interior renovation has made the facility more open, roomier, more functional, and inviting. The official opening of the JCAM's new vestibule and the unveiling of the donor plaque took place on December 4, 2016.

On November 9, 2017, on behalf of the JCAM, I accepted the 2017 Accessibility Award from the City of Winnipeg for the vestibule addition in recognition of "excellence in universal design and accessibility." This project required a lot of work and time, but the benefits now allow the centre to have larger events and attract more people. For the naysayers, all I can say is: anything is possible. Sometimes we have to dream before it becomes a reality.

FACING INJUSTICE

Most references to the forced removal from the West Coast are made to those who were sent to internment camps in the BC Interior or in Ontario. I was fortunate to meet filmmaker Aaron Floresco through his partner Rhonda Hinther, who was organizing a conference on the topic of internment. I was approached to be one of the many presenters who talked about various experiences of internment suffered by other groups in Canada. Aaron pointed out that there was no documented film on the Japanese Canadian sugar-beet farmers and wanted to create a documentary film with my assistance. Without hesitation, I agreed to help, contact potential interviewees, and provide photos and other resources. The documentary *Facing Injustice: The Relocation of Japanese Canadians to Manitoba*, completed in 2018 and narrated by David Suzuki, has twice been aired nationally on

CBC Television.[4] I was pleased with the production, as this story gives an excellent perspective into the contributions made by Manitoba's Japanese Canadians.

HISTORY AND PRESERVATION

Although I have always been deeply interested in the history of Japanese Canadians and the preservation of family experiences and stories, I have not taken the time to generate resources that would add to the collection of stories, especially those of Japanese Canadians who settled in Manitoba and especially in Winnipeg after World War II. Many Manitobans are unaware of the reason Japanese Canadians came to Manitoba in 1942 and know very little of the Japanese Canadian community and its contributions. During the COVID-19 pandemic, I explored filmmaking by creating historical and cultural resources using the computer and film-editing software to create interesting projects.

One question I grappled with over the years is: How can community organizations create and maintain the interest of the younger generations in their history? A board member who had come from Japan commented that he found it strange that in the Japanese Canadian Cultural Centre in Winnipeg there was no historical or cultural information anywhere to be seen except for a display of Japanese dolls. He was right; the building was devoid of content that would give visitors a reason for its existence. I think it is important for any Japanese Canadian cultural centre to have the ability to share, promote, and preserve the history of the Japanese experience in Canada. I believe it is essential to appreciate one's Japanese Canadian identity and understand the past.

To pursue my passion for preserving history, I examined creative ways to add historical meaning to our Japanese Canadian Cultural Centre. As a result, I personally undertook projects, as a board member, using the Japanese Cultural Association of Manitoba as a conduit to create historical resources that the centre would display or

---

4   See McIntyre Media, "Facing Injustice: The Relocation of Japanese Canadians," www .mcintyre.ca/titles/PPP000.

Art in front of the *Japanese in Manitoba* mural designed by Cindy Mochizuki.
PHOTO: Keiko Miki and courtesy of the Japanese Cultural Association of
Manitoba

have available on the website for anyone, members or non-members,
to access.

A large wall from a recent renovation at the centre struck me as an
ideal location to showcase a mural depicting the history of Japanese
Canadians in Manitoba. I thought that this would be an attractive
addition. I received approval from the board to go ahead with the
concept, provided that I find funding from outside sources to pay
for the costs. I was fortunate that the directors of the Frank H. Hori
Charitable Foundation in Toronto were so enthusiastic about the
mural proposal that they agreed to fund the entire project. Using
an approach similar to a graphic novel would have appeal with
the younger generation, especially students. I contracted Cindy
Mochizuki, a well-known Japanese Canadian artist from Vancouver,
to design and create the mural. We prepared a schematic outline of
the history of Japanese Canadians in Manitoba from 1942 to the
present to help her illustrate the mural's sections. The story is told in
five large panels mounted on the wall, showing the initial relocation
to the sugar-beet farms from the West Coast, movement into Winnipeg, the redress settlement, and the establishment of the Cultural
Centre and its present activities. Due to the COVID-19 pandemic,
the official unveiling took place online on September 27, 2020, with

a limited number of people attending physically at the centre. We have received many positive comments about the mural from outsiders who thought its colourful, simple technique was a great way to convey knowledge and information.[5]

The second project I embarked upon was to interest younger Japanese Canadians to explore their past through dialogue with parents, grandparents, and relatives and through old family photos. Parents often had not readily shared with their children the experiences they had endured as internees, and so many in the subsequent generations had little or no knowledge of their history. I was able to secure a grant from the Manitoba government's Ethnocultural Community Support Program to financially support applicants to create a family-history film. This Japanese Cultural Association of Manitoba project, entitled "Family History Videos: Through a Generational Lens," invited five young Japanese Canadians to research their families' past and produce a short video, whether it be about their grandparents, parents, or another significant individual. Throughout the process of development, mentorship was provided by an experienced filmmaker. The five completed family-history films produced by Ainsley Chester, Nina Dubik, Alex Miki, Kaoru Ryan Suzuki, and Danica Swire were premiered in front of family members, relatives, and friends in October 2021. In talking with the filmmakers, they said they learned a lot about their families, as they had known very little of the struggles in coming to Manitoba.[6]

The final initiative that I share here is "Manitoba Moments: Glimpse into the Lives of Japanese Canadians," a project I coordinated that was completed in 2022. As families moved away from the sugar-beet farms or left the internment camps for Winnipeg, a thriving, close-knit Japanese Canadian community evolved. The purpose of this project was to expose viewers to a glimpse into the Manitoba Japanese Canadian community by familiarizing them with events and activities that are unique to it. The nuances

---

5   You can have a preview of *Mural: Japanese in Manitoba* on the JCAM's website: www .jcamwpg.ca/mural-japanese-in-manitoba/. A YouTube video of the unveiling is also available: "Mural Japanese in Manitoba Unveiling," youtu.be/AlQUhlvqcm8.

6   For more information, see the JCAM's web page "History Preservation" (www.jcamwpg. ca/history-preservation/) or, on YouTube, the playlist "Family History Videos: Through a Generational Lens" (youtube.com/playlist?list=PLRtToDd7aRsEu2ltWLeqO7oY WUkPgNoGy).

of Japanese Canadians' lives and personalities are captured through short vignettes using photos, videos, documents, and interviews. With support from the Winnipeg Foundation's Centennial Institute Grant Program, twelve short vignettes of approximately two minutes were produced by the History Preservation Committee members. Members of the committee knowledgeable about the history and activities of Japanese Canadians researched the topics, gathered the resources, and prepared the scripts. An editor reviewed all of the scripts before the narration was professionally recorded. With the assistance of three film editors, the final vignettes production was completed.[7]

Also, five interviews with internee survivors who shared their personal experiences and stories were produced by Hue Productions and made publically available on the JCAM website and YouTube. The short vignettes can also be used as teaching tools by school teachers interested in having students learn about Japanese and Japanese Canadian culture, arts, and history. They will be an invaluable resource for events such as Folklorama, conferences, and community occasions.[8] It is through such projects that efforts are being made to reach out to the general community.

FATE OR DESTINY

Although I'm not a strong believer in fate or destiny, I can't help wondering whether there were forces that helped guide me throughout my life in surprising and mysterious ways. I mentioned earlier the serious accident I had as a four-year-old, and how by good fortune I was able to get to the hospital in time. As a result, I have carried a noticeable scar on my face which I become self-conscious about when people notice it, but which for me is a reminder of how lucky I am to be alive. I think this has motivated me to look at things with a

---

7   See the JCAM's web page "History Preservation," (www.jcamwpg.ca/jcam-history
    -preservation/) or, on YouTube, the playlist "Manitoba Moments" (youtube.com/playlist?
    list=PLRtToDd7aRsFkopbdq-JHYEtBOnHmvkFr).

8   See the JCAM's web page "History Preservation" (www.jcamwpg.ca/jcam-history
    -preservation/) or, on YouTube, "Japanese Manitoban Retrospective" (youtube.com
    /playlist?list=PLRtToDd7aRsHIJ5nXlDWCFPJZG0_lbsE8).

positive outlook and be willing to embrace challenges and take risks. I don't fear failure but look at it as a learning opportunity. This is the doctrine by which I have approached life and living.

On a personal note, I recall that shortly after the 1988 Ottawa rally, my family went for supper at our favourite Chinese restaurant, Shaing-Bo, in Winnipeg's west end. After supper, as is the practice, the waitress brought the bill and a handful of Chinese fortune cookies. I took one and opened it. My fortune read, "Your struggle will soon be over and you will succeed." When I read it over again, I wondered whether this was an omen. A few nights later, I had a dream that I was in the House of Commons listening to the minister apologizing to the Japanese Canadian community. It was so vivid. It was so real. When I awoke, I thought that it had really happened, only to realize that it had been but a dream. Was this a way of letting me know that things were changing? A month later, I received the call from Gerry Weiner's office about reopening the negotiation process.

As to whether the success I have had was based on destiny or chance, I happened to come across a Japanese zodiac on the internet. This is based on the ancient Chinese concept, with a different animal representing each of the twelve-year cycles and describing the personality for each year's animal. I happen to be a Rat or nezumi. It said that people who were born in the year of the Rat are "charming, honest, ambitious, and have tremendous capacity for pursuing a course to its end. They will work hard for their goals."[9] I believe that this perseverance was an important factor in our success.

I feel that the saying "being in the right place at the right time" applied to us and led to the memorable redress settlement. There were a number of happenings, some unforeseen, that speak to the importance of timing. Mulroney hinted that there was a possibility of a fall election coming. We continued to remind Mulroney of his promise to "compensate Japanese Canadians" during his term in office and press him to fulfill his obligation. The US Reparations Bill's inclusion of individual compensation for Japanese Americans incarcerated during World War II established a precedent for the Canadian government, as the Canadian wartime experience had been similar to that of the United States. The national opinion polls

---

9   Namiko Abe, "The Twelve Signs of the Japanese Zodiac: Does Your Zodiac Sign Fit Your Personality?," ThoughtCo, updated October 16, 2019, www.thoughtco.com/japanese -zodiac-overview-2028019.

showed very favourable support for redress and that Canadians were more enlightened about past injustices. Politically, there were some changes with the inclusion of Lucien Bouchard in Cabinet and in 1988 the appointment of Dalton Camp as chief of staff for the minister, both supporters of redress, and also the removal of George Hees, a strong opponent, from Cabinet due to illness. All of these factors symbolized to us that "the time was right."

FAMILY

It would be remiss of me not to acknowledge the importance of the family support that allowed me the latitude and freedom to pursue my passion, especially during the time-consuming redress campaign. My wife Keiko was extremely supportive and was actively involved with the Manitoba committee organizing local events to promote redress. I appreciated that Keiko had the interests of the community in mind as she raised questions and shared her perspectives during the campaign; this made discussions interesting and sometimes contentious, but in a productive manner. After I left the NAJC, Keiko became more actively involved at the national level, chairing the NAJC Human Rights Committee for a number of years; she was vice-president and became the first woman president of the NAJC in 1998. In Indigenous communities, Elders are sometimes referred to as Knowledge Keepers. Keiko's knowledge of the past and community experiences at both the local and national levels qualifies her as a Japanese Canadian knowledge keeper, a role that best describes her contributions today as she remains engaged with NAJC committees. As mentioned earlier, Keiko, my mother Shizuko Miki, and my youngest son Jonathan joined me at the Ottawa rally in April 1988 to march on Parliament Hill with other Japanese Canadians from across Canada. We thought it would be a great learning experience for Jonathan to attend the march. On Monday, after we returned from Ottawa, his school principal stopped him in the hallway and commented that he knew where he had been on the Friday he was absent. Apparently, the principal saw the media coverage on the national news and must have spotted Jonathan walking up the steps at the Parliament Building carrying a placard. My children were understanding and

Family photo taken during the redress campaign, 1985

never put demands on me when I was busy travelling and attending meetings. Even though most meetings were held on the weekend, we were able to attend most of Geoffrey and Jonathan's hockey games and Tani's ringette games. During the time I was involved in redress, I continued to play hockey for the River Heights Old Timers team, as I did for thirty-five years. Unfortunately, our games began at 11 p.m. on Mondays and getting home after midnight with an adrenaline rush made it difficult to get up the next day. I made a point not to miss any games, as physical activity is important to me. Today, I still attend Reh-Fit, a fitness facility in Winnipeg, at least four to five times weekly, as I have for nearly thirty years. After the federal election in 1993, I joined Reh-Fit by taking aerobic classes as a way to maintain the fitness I had developed over the nine months of campaigning.

Redress brought me closer to my brother Roy, who lives in Vancouver, with whom I often conferred throughout the campaign and who became an active member of our strategy team. I recall that when our mother was interviewed on CBC on the day of the redress announcement, she said with tears in her eyes, "I'm extremely proud of my boys, Roy and Art, who worked so closely to get redress."

RECOGNITION AND AWARDS

If it wasn't for my involvement with the successful redress settlement, I would not have gained the recognition that I received over the years from various institutions and the Japanese Canadian community. The achievement of the historic Japanese Canadian redress settlement has influenced Canadian society in many ways. It symbolizes that, in a democratic country, the majority doesn't necessarily rule, but that minority groups can use the system to influence the majority's views. It further emphasizes that human-rights principles are an integral part of the Canadian psyche and the determination of Canadians to prevent injustices similar to those from the past from happening again.

One of the greatest honours that a Canadian can receive is the Order of Canada, given to those who exemplify the highest qualities of citizenship and whose contributions have enriched the lives of Canadians. I was extremely fortunate to receive that honour on October 30, 1991, at Rideau Hall, the residence of the Governor General. The ceremony took place in the ballroom where the investment of various levels of membership – Companion, Officer, or Member – is made to outstanding Canadians. I was awed to be in the presence of dignitaries that I read about or saw on television. Among the list were Ken Read, Olympic skier, Barbara Ann Scott-King, Olympic figure skater, Karen Kain, one of Canada's greatest ballerinas, and Leonard Cohen, the internationally known poet, singer-songwriter, and novelist.

Following the official ceremony, Keiko and I were escorted to the dining area, where I had a chance to talk to Karen Kain, who I heard was from Winnipeg. She and her husband, Ross Petty, a well-known Canadian actor and theatre producer, wanted to catch up on the Winnipeg news. They often visited relatives, because Ross had been born there. We also met Lily Schreyer, wife of Ed Schreyer, the previous Governor General, who was assisting the staff. Lily told me that she had a close friend from Winnipeg, Amy Yamazaki, who now lived in Ottawa and would spend sleepovers at Rideau Hall with Lily

Art shaking hands with the Governor General the Right Honourable Ray Hnatyshyn after receiving the Order of Canada, November 1991

and the family. Amy was one of the strong redress supporters from the Ottawa community and attended a meeting we had in January 1984 with Ed Broadbent and the New Democratic caucus. Amy, a long-time supporter of the NDP, was privileged to be in their company. In meetings with politicians, it was customary for the strategy team to invite internment survivors from the community to provide anecdotes of their sufferings and add credibility to our demands.

While Keiko and I were enjoying the buffet dinner, Leonard Cohen asked whether he could join us at our table. He sat down and began telling me how he liked the way I bowed when I went

GAMAN — PERSEVERANCE

up to receive the Order of Canada from the Right Honourable Ray Hnatyshyn. I'm not sure how I bowed, but Leonard Cohen was so impressed that he mentioned it several times. I found him to be a down-to-earth, easy-to-talk-to person with interesting stories. He shared his experiences of going quite frequently or annually to a Zen monastery in the mountains in California to meditate. No words were spoken all day. When he was telling us about this experience, I wondered how much of his writings and songs were inspired there. When our children learned that we had had supper with Leonard Cohen, they were awed and asked whether we had taken a photo with him. Unfortunately, we hadn't – no cellphones with cameras then. When we heard that Leonard Cohen was coming to Winnipeg to perform at the arena, Keiko and I decided to attend. It was an astounding, mesmerizing concert, in which he captivated the audience with his well-known songs. Midway through the performance, Leonard took time to introduce his musicians. After he introduced each one with complimentary words, he then bowed to them in such a respectful manner. It was a moving, kindly gesture and I wondered whether our discussion about bowing had some influence on what we were seeing. I was impressed by Leonard Cohen and have a greater appreciation and respect for his talent and music since our encounter. I admit that I am one of his fans now.

On May 11, 2012, I was inducted along with eleven other recipients into the Order of Manitoba by Lieutenant-Governor Philip Lee at the Legislative Building. I was recognized for helping achieve the historic redress settlement for Japanese Canadians. I was the first Japanese Canadian to receive this honour, which was introduced in 1999. The induction was followed by a wonderful reception for recipients and their families at Government House, the Lieutenant-Governor's residence, hosted by Philip and Anita Lee. My family and I met Heather Bishop, a well-known folk singer and songwriter, who was a member of the nomination committee for the Order of Manitoba. Heather is recognized for her social-justice advocacy. We had an interesting dialogue with Order of Manitoba recipient Al Simmons, a children's performer who had toured nationally with Fred Penner. I had known Philip and Anita for many years and served with Philip on the board of the Winnipeg Chinese Cultural Centre for three years. I was honoured and delighted to receive the Order of Manitoba from him.

Art receiving the Order of Manitoba from Lieutenant-Governor the Honourable Philip Lee, July 2012

On March 2, 2017, the consul general of Japan in Calgary, Kunihiko Tanabe, presented me with the Order of the Rising Sun, Gold Rays with Neck Ribbon, before an audience of government officials, friends, and relatives at the Calgary Japanese Community Centre. This award is equivalent to Canada's Order of Canada. Over the years, I have been asked by consuls general in Vancouver, Toronto, and Calgary and by the ambassador of Japan to share my comments on the redress movement and agreement or on issues such as "comfort women" when these are raised in Canada. Receiving recognition from my country, province, and ancestral government was an unusual and unforgettable achievement and one that I will always treasure. For me, it was important that governments recognized the historic importance of the redress settlement and reinforced human-rights values. I was fortunate that the success of redress accorded me other recognitions as well, such as the Lifetime Achievement Award from the Canadian Race Relations Foundation and the NAJC and other awards from community service organizations over the years. The University of Winnipeg, from which I graduated in 1968, presented me with the Distinguished Alumni Award in 1997 and Chancellor Carol Shields conferred on me an Honorary Doctorate of Laws in 2001. On November 6, 2022, I received an Honorary Doctorate of

Art receiving the Order of the Rising Sun, Gold Rays with Neck Ribbon from Consul General of Japan Kunihiko Tanabe, March 2017

Canon Law at the convocation held at St. John's College, University of Manitoba, in recognition of my work as an educator and also for the Japanese Canadian redress campaign and agreement. The presentation was made by Bishop Geoffrey Woodcroft, chancellor of St. John's College. I had the privilege to give the convocation address. I am honoured to have been accorded various recognitions resulting from my prolonged engagement in the historic redress accomplishment. But the credit for my success goes to the unwavering support and confidence displayed by individuals and organizations that believed in the cause for justice.

Today, the rights of citizens are protected in the Canadian Charter of Rights and Freedoms, which gives us assurances that the extent of violations inflicted upon Japanese Canadians will not reoccur. However, for many of us, the struggle for justice will continue. In view of the events of 2020 and 2021, we who are spokespeople in the Japanese Canadian community must continue to remind politicians and Canadians that racism and discrimination are obstacles society must contend with. The murder of George Floyd in the United States, the Black Lives Matter movement, the Stop Asian Hate protests and rallies, and the discovery of thousands of unmarked graves of Indigenous children at the sites of former residential schools have captured

Art receiving his Honorary Doctorate from the University of Winnipeg with Chancellor Carol Shields, October 2001

national and international headlines for months on end. Now, with Russia's attack on Ukraine, we are faced with the catastrophic effects of the unprovoked attack upon Ukrainian civilians. We tend to forget, though, that there are victims on both sides. There is overwhelming support for Ukraine from the Canadian government and Ukrainian Canadians in general. Will this translate into indiscriminate actions against Russian Canadians? No doubt there will be acts of racism and harassment directed towards innocent Russian Canadians, who may become easy targets and scapegoats for what Russia is doing to Ukraine. As a related example, Chinese Canadians became victims of racism after the first known case of COVID-19 was identified as having occurred in China. As a result, anyone who "looked Asian" became a target for verbal abuse and other types of violence.

The attainment of redress is a testimonial to the Japanese Canadians who have overcome adversity and have come to terms with their identity and heritage. It gave us the fortitude to advance the cause of human rights for others who are victims of systemic racism at the hands of government and corporations or of racist attacks and hatred.

Thinking back on my involvement with the successful redress achievement, collaborations with Indigenous communities, foray into politics, role as a Canadian citizenship judge, and many other opportunities, I can truly say that I have been blessed with wonderful, unforgettable experiences in my journey of life. I had the good fortune to have had many opportunities to use my creative and exploratory skills in my endeavours.

I realize that over my many years, I have impacted the lives of many people. Whenever I visit a Japanese Canadian community or function, I am reminded of my redress involvement, as people want to thank me or remind me that they appreciate the work that the NAJC did on their behalf. Sometimes, children express thanks on behalf of their parents. It is very rewarding to hear these expressions of gratitude from the younger generations. If I'm at a shopping mall or store or walking on Winnipeg streets, if I hear someone calling "Mr. Miki, Mr. Miki," I know that it must be a former student or a parent from one of my schools. If someone passes me and says, "Hi Judge," or approaches me with "Judge," I know that they must be one of the many newcomers I had the privilege of swearing in as a Canadian citizen. It is heartwarming and amazing how my life has impacted people from different segments of Canadian society – my community, my students, and new Canadians. All I can say is that I have enjoyed a wonderful, fulfilling life and will always be proud that I'm a Canadian.

EPILOGUE

I was thinking of this book last night as I was going to sleep. I had the strangest dream. I dreamed that I was standing on a street when this young man who seemed to be lost approached me. He indicated that he didn't have a job and was just wandering. I gave him some money and my card, telling him to contact me if he needed help. He took the money and card and said, "Maybe I'll see you again." The next part of the dream was really odd. I seemed to have been driving around in a taxi and didn't know where I was going, so I asked the cab driver to let me out. I found myself on the same street as before and ran into the same young man that I had met earlier. This time, he had wads of money in both hands. He said to me, "If you give me a dollar for each handful of money, you can have it all." I thought that was a good deal and gave him the two dollars. He gave me all the money he had in his hands. He reminded me that he had my card and would contact me if he needed help. As I walked away, I could feel the bills in my pocket and wondered what I should do. I didn't need the money. That is when I woke up. The dream was so vivid that I wondered if there was a message. After thinking about it, it occurred to me that the message was "Pay it forward. If I have this knowledge, I should pass it to the next person. Hopefully, that person will pass on the same knowledge to someone else." For me, that analogy seems to fit the intent of this memoir. I hope that some of the knowledge that you might have gained from this book will be shared with others, fulfilling my dream's prophecy.

ACKNOWLEDGMENTS

I wish to thank the Japanese Canadian Redress Foundation, whose initial generous support assisted me at the beginning of this writing venture. Although the main emphasis was on the gruelling years related to redress for the Japanese Canadian community, its impact on me personally helped shape this book as my memoir. Kei Ebata was especially helpful in editing much of my early writings. Her devotion to the task was much appreciated. The office of the NAJC had organized the newspaper articles and minutes of the meetings in binders that made the task of researching easier. I want to thank Cheryl Miki and Tani Miki for the earlier editing and Terry McLeod for his thoughts and encouragement to complete the book. I need to acknowledge the support of my family, especially Keiko, who has given me constructive criticism throughout my writing journey. I apologize to Keiko for the many years of keeping parts of the manuscript lying around and unattended. It was the time at home in 2020 during the COVID-19 pandemic that finally motivated me to complete the manuscript that has taken me over twenty-five years to write.

I wish to acknowledge the use of quotes from Frank Moritsugu, Bruce McLeod, and David Suzuki, and from the poetry of Roy Miki, Sally Ito, and the late Haruko Kobayakawa.

Finally, my appreciation goes to Talonbooks and Kevin Williams, president and publisher, for their willingness to publish my memoir and to editor Catriona Strang for her supportive and constructive comments. I enjoyed meeting Erin Kirsh, who made tour arrangements and inserted photographs. Thanks to the book's cover designer, Les Smith, for incorporating the family logo. I am grateful to Phinder Dulai, substantive editor for the memoir, for his constructive suggestions, his instinctive feeling about how to make the stories come to life, and his openness and positive rapport. I enjoyed working with Phinder over the past few months and really cherish the discussions we had. My deepest appreciation goes to Charles Simard, editor at Talonbooks, who made the final touches to the manuscript. I am indebted to Charles for his suggestions, for his thoughtful and clarifying questions, for locating important citations, and for his patience as I struggled in creating a book that readers will find interesting.

BIBLIOGRAPHY

References of particular interest are preceded by an asterisk.

URLs for articles are provided in this bibliography whenever they could be located. However, some web pages may require a paid subscription or institutional membership to be consulted in full.

BOOKS

*Adachi, Ken. *The Enemy That Never Was: A History of the Japanese Canadians.* Toronto: McClelland and Stewart, 1991.

Government of Canada, House of Commons, Special Committee on the Participation of Visible Minorities in Canadian Society / Comité spécial sur la participation des minorités visibles à la société canadienne. *Equality Now! Report of the Special Committee on Visible Minorities in Canadian Society.* Report. Ottawa: Queen's Printer for Canada, 1984. Online: Library of Parliament, Canadian Parliamentary Historical Resources, parl.canadiana.ca /view/oop.com_HOC_3202_15_2.

Ito, Sally. *The Emperor's Orphans.* Winnipeg: Turnstone Press, 2018.

*———. *We Went to War: The Story of the Japanese Canadians Who Served during the First and Second World Wars.* Stittsville, ON: Canada Wings, 1984.

*Japanese Canadian Centennial Project. *A Dream of Riches: The Japanese Canadians, 1877–1977* / 千金の夢：日系カナダ人百年史 / *Un rêve de richesses: Les Japonais au Canada, 1877–1977.* Vancouver: Japanese Canadian Centennial Project, 1978.

Kobayashi, Audrey. *A Demographic Profile of Japanese Canadians and Social Implications for the Future.* Ottawa: Department of the Secretary of State, Canada, 1989.

*Manitoba Japanese Canadian Citizens' Association. *The History of Japanese Canadians in Manitoba.* Winnipeg: Manitoba Japanese Canadian Citizens' Association, 1996.

McIntosh, Dave. *Hell on Earth: Aging Faster, Dying Sooner; Canadian Prisoners of the Japanese during World War II.* Whitby, ON: McGraw-Hill Ryerson, 1997.

*Miki, Arthur K. *The Japanese Canadian Redress Legacy: A Community Revitalized.* Winnipeg: National Association of Japanese Canadians, 2003.

*Miki, Roy, and Cassandra Kobayashi. *Justice in Our Time: The Japanese Canadian*

Redress Settlement. Vancouver: Talonbooks; Winnipeg: National Association of Japanese Canadians, 1991.

*Miki, Roy, Yuko Shibata, and Michiko Ayukawa, with the Japanese Canadian National Museum. *Re-Shaping Memory, Owning History: Through the Lens of Japanese Canadian Redress*. Edited by Grace E. Thomson. Burnaby, BC: Japanese Canadian National Museum, 2002.

*National Association of Japanese Canadians. *Democracy Betrayed: The Case for Redress*. Winnipeg: National Association of Japanese Canadians, 1985.

*National Association of Japanese Canadians with Price Waterhouse. *Economic Losses of Japanese Canadians after 1941: A Study*. Winnipeg: National Association of Japanese Canadians, 1986. landscapesofinjustice.uvic.ca/archive/media/TINA/facsimile/ubc-rbsc_roy_miki_box_65_file_7.pdf.

Ohki, Takashi. *Demographic Characteristics of Japanese Canadians in 2016: From 2016 Census of Population*. Report. Winnipeg: National Association of Japanese Canadians. November 15, 2017. najc.ca/wp/wp-content/uploads/2018/05/2016-Census-Japanese-Canadians-Eng-Final.pdf.

Robertson, David A. *Black Water: Family, Legacy, and Blood Memory*. Toronto: HarperCollins Publishers, 2020.

*Robertson, Heather, with Clark Hopper and Verna Neufeld. *Sugar Farmers of Manitoba: The Manitoba Sugar Beet Industry in Story and Picture*. Winnipeg: Manitoba Sugar Beet Growers Association, 1968.

*Sakamoto, Mark. *Forgiveness: A Gift from My Grandparents*. Toronto: HarperCollins Publishers, 2014.

*Stearns, Jeff Chiba, and Lillian Michiko Blakey. *On Being Yukiko*. Vancouver: Meditating Bunny Studios, 2001.

*Sugiman, Momoye, ed., with the Ad Hoc Committee for Japanese Canadian Redress: The Toronto Story. *Japanese Canadian Redress: The Toronto Story*. Toronto: HpF Press (Hasting Park Foundation), 2000.

Sunahara, Ann Gomer. *The Politics of Racism: The Uprooting of Japanese Canadians during the Second World War*. Toronto: James Lorimer & Company, 1981. Online: Japanese Canadian History, japanesecanadianhistory.ca.

Takata, Toyo. *Nikkei Legacy: The Story of Japanese Canadians from Settlement to Today*. Toronto: NC Press, 1983.

Thomson, Grace Eiko. *Chiru Sakura – Falling Cherry Blossoms: A Mother and Daughter's Journey through Racism, Internment and Oppression*. Halfmoon Bay [xwilkway], BC: Caitlin Press, 2021.

United States' Commission on Wartime Relocation and Internment of Civilians. *Personal Justice Denied: Report of the Commission on Wartime Relocation and Internment of Civilians.* 2 vols. Washington, DC: U.S. Government Printing Office, 1982 and 1983. Online: U.S. National Archives and Records Administration, "Justice Denied: *Personal Justice Denied*," www.archives.gov / research / japanese-americans / justice-denied.

ARTICLES

WITH NAMED AUTHOR(S)

Camp, Dalton. "The PM's Honor Is at Stake." *Toronto Star*, May 27, 1986. A15. www.proquest.com /newspapers /pms-honor-is-at-stake /docview /435429885 /se-2.

———. "Time for the Apology." *Toronto Star*, January 16, 1986. A19. www.newspapers.com /article /the-toronto-star /133499630 /.

Cleroux, Richard. "Comments by Jelinek Are Found Baffling," *Globe and Mail*, January 29, 1986, A5, www.proquest.com /historical-newspapers /comments -jelinek-are-found-baffling /docview /1143871914 /se-2.

———. "Compensate Internees for Unfair Treatment, Mulroney Urges PM." *Globe and Mail*, May 16, 1984. 5. www.proquest.com /newspapers /compensate -internees-unfair-treatment-mulroney /docview /386447108 /se-2.

———. "Deal with Japanese Canadians Not a Precedent, Minister Warns." *Globe and Mail*, September 23, 1988. A8. www.proquest.com /historical-newspapers /deal-with-japanese-canadians-not-precedent /docview /1238588240 /se-2.

———. "Japanese Canadians Get Deadline." *Globe and Mail*, January 28, 1986. A4. www.proquest.com /historical-newspapers /japanese-canadians-get-deadline / docview /1151419670 /se-2.

———. "No Money, Just Apology, Jelinek Says." *Globe and Mail*, March 7, 1986. A1. www.proquest.com /historical-newspapers /no-money-just-apology-jelinek -says /docview /1151428817 /se-2.

Graham, Heidi. "PM Lashed for 'Ignorant' View." *Winnipeg Sun*, April 4, 1984. 8. www.newspapers.com /article /the-winnipeg-sun /133497158 /.

Granatstein, J.L. "The Enemy Within?" *Saturday Night* 101, no. 11 (November 1986). 32–34 and 39–42. www.proquest.com /magazines /enemy-within -expulsion-japanese-bc /docview /222411251 /se-2.

Harper, Tim. "Japanese Canadians Say Public Supports War Compensation." *Toronto Star*, December 23, 1987. A1. www.proquest.com /newspapers /japanese-canadians-say-public-supports-war /docview /435694348 /se-2.

Lynch, Charles. "Maybe Japan Should Help." *Ottawa Citizen*, January 26, 1985. 24. www.newspapers.com /article /the-ottawa-citizen /133552406 /.

Macdonald, Nancy. "Welcome to Winnipeg: Where Canada's Racism Problem Is at

Its Worse." *Maclean's*, January 22, 2015. macleans.ca/news/canada/welcome-to-winnipeg-where-canadas-racism-problem-is-at-its-worst/.

MacGregor, Roy. "Jelinek Acting like Rambo in Compensation Wrangle," *Ottawa Citizen*, January 30, 1986. A3. www.proquest.com/newspapers/jelinek-acting-like-rambo-compensation-wrangle/docview/238906939/se-2.

Melosky, Louis C., Orest Rudzik, and Peter McCreath. "Ottawa Plan for Redress for War Victims Praised." *Globe and Mail*, February 19, 1986. A7. www.proquest.com/historical-newspapers/ottawa-plan-redress-war-victims-praised/docview/1143806426/se-2.

Moritsugu, Frank. "The Japanese Expulsion." *Winnipeg Free Press*, August 2, 1987. 7. archives.winnipegfreepress.com/winnipeg-free-press/1987-08-02/page-7/.

Miki, Roy, and Cassandra Kobayashi. "Compensating Victims." *Globe and Mail*, March 20, 1986. A6. www.proquest.com/historical-newspapers/compensating-victims/docview/1151441839/se-2.

Silversides, Ann. "Japanese Canadians Disturbed over Refusal to Apologize." *Globe and Mail*, June 29, 1984. M4. www.proquest.com/historical-newspapers/japanese-canadians-disturbed-over-refusal/docview/1237540871/se-2.

Sobat, Dane. "Internment Compensation Opposed." *Calgary Herald*, April 11, 1984. A6. www.newspapers.com/article/calgary-herald/128620010/.

Spicer, Keith. "An Old Injustice Offers Opportunity." *Vancouver Sun*, June 28, 1984. 5. www.newspapers.com/article/the-vancouver-sun/133500036/.

———. "Victims of a Vengeful Paranoia." *Vancouver Sun*, August 4, 1982. 5. www.newspapers.com/article/the-vancouver-sun/133553106/.

Turner, Dan. "Crombie May Help Attain Japanese-Canadian Settlement." *Ottawa Citizen*, December 9, 1986. A9. www.newspapers.com/article/the-ottawa-citizen/133552565/.

———. "Talks with Japanese Canadians Deadlocked." *Ottawa Citizen*, January 21, 1985. 1. www.newspapers.com/article/the-ottawa-citizen/133498855/.

———. "Turner Opposes Government's Offer of Redress to Japanese Canadians." *Ottawa Citizen*, January 29, 1985. A3. www.newspapers.com/article/the-ottawa-citizen/133499010/.

Walker, William. "Tory MP Condemns Deal for Japanese Canadians." *Toronto Star*, September 24, 1988. A3. www.proquest.com/newspapers/tory-mp-condemns-deal-japanese-canadians/docview/435774527/se-2.

Wilson, Deborah. "Compensation for Japanese Canadians: Poll Indicates Ottawa, Public at Odds." *Globe and Mail*, April 11, 1986. 14. www.proquest.com/historical-newspapers/poll-indicates-ottawa-public-at-odds/docview/1151455816/se-2.

ANONYMOUS

"An Anti-Russian Wave Sweeps over Canada." *Toronto Star*, March 29, 2022. www.thestar.com /news /canada /an-anti-russian-wave-sweeps-over-canada /article_d56d157f-b1bb-54e1-b8a2-e7707f4a70e2.html.

"Canada's Shame." *Province*, August 3, 1982. 9. www.newspapers.com /article /the -province /133552737 /.

"The Continuing Blot." *Toronto Star*, May 21, 1987. A24. www.proquest.com /newspapers /continuing-blot /docview /435566931 /se-2.

"Don't Impose the Deal." *Montreal Gazette*, January 30, 1986. B2. www.proquest .com /newspapers /dont-impose-deal /docview /431296162 /se-2.

"Erase the Black Mark." *Vancouver Sun*, September 22, 1983. A4. www.newspapers .com /article /the-vancouver-sun /133552834 /.

"Ex-PoW Opposes Compensation for Interned Japanese Canadians." *Ottawa Citizen*, February 4, 1986. A3. www.proquest.com /newspapers /ex-pow -opposes-compensation-interned-japanese /docview /238909716 /se-2.

"An Example for Canada." *Winnipeg Free Press*, August 6, 1988. 6. archives. winnipegfreepress.com /winnipeg-free-press /1988-08-06 /page-6 /.

"An Example to Shame Us." *Globe and Mail*, August 8, 1988. A6. www.proquest. com /historical-newspapers /example-shame-us /docview /1238338966 /se-2.

"The Honour Belongs to Japanese Canadians." *Lethbridge Herald*, September 23, 1988. newspaperarchive.com /lethbridge-herald-sep-23-1988-p-1 /.

"In 1942 Canada sent a lot of kids to camp." Advertisement. *Globe and Mail*, March 6, 1986. 3. www.proquest.com /historical-newspapers /classified-ad-1 -no-title /docview /1143879755 /se-2.

"Japanese-Canadians May Get Compensation." *Toronto Star*, June 1, 1983. A1. www.proquest.com /newspapers /japanese-canadians-may-get-compensation /docview /435772090 /se-2.

"Japanese-Canadians Seek Relocation Redress." *Globe and Mail*, July 30, 1982. 8. www.proquest.com /historical-newspapers /japanese-canadians-seek-relocation -redress /docview /1238748403 /se-2.

"JC in Japan Regains Canadian Citizenship Thanks to Redress." *Nikkei Voice*, February 1991.

"Jelinek Rejects Report on Internees' Losses." *Globe and Mail*, May 14, 1986. A11. www.proquest.com /historical-newspapers /jelinek-rejects-report-on-internees -losses /docview /1143879163 /se-2.

"Justice Delayed, but No Longer Denied." *Ottawa Citizen*, January 21, 1985. A8. www.newspapers.com /article /the-ottawa-citizen /133573456 /.

"Legion Unit Faults Japanese Payment." *Globe and Mail*, April 12, 1985. 1. www. proquest.com /historical-newspapers /legion-unit-faults-japanese-payment /docview /1400714813 /se-2.

"Looking Back." *Vancouver Sun*, September 11, 1981. 4. www.newspapers.com /article /the-vancouver-sun /133552973 /.

"Masumi Mitsui Has a Right to Be Angry: Canadian Hero at Vimy Ridge, an Internee in World War II." *Toronto Star*, April 11, 1984. A17. www.proquest.com /newspapers /masumi-mitsui-has-right-be-angry-canadian-hero-at /docview /752381980 /se-2.

"Mennonites Apologize to Japanese Canadians." *Manitoba NDP*, November 1984.

"Mr. Jelinek's Haste." *Globe and Mail*, January 29, 1986. A6. www.proquest.com /newspapers /mr-jelineks-haste /docview /386213914 /se-2.

"Mulroney Prodded on Internment Issue." *Winnipeg Free Press*, May 29, 1986. 26. archives.winnipegfreepress.com /winnipeg-free-press /1986-05-29 /page-26 /.

"Ottawa to Defer Wartime Apology." *Winnipeg Free Press*, March 29, 1984. 37. archives.winnipegfreepress.com /winnipeg-free-press /1984-03-29 /page-37 /.

"Pay War Internees for Property Losses." *Toronto Star*, June 3, 1986. A14. www .newspapers.com /article /the-toronto-star /133575149 /.

"Redress for Internment Set at $25,000 Each by Japanese Group." *Globe and Mail*, May 20, 1986. A5. www.proquest.com /historical-newspapers /redress -internment-set-at-25-000-each-japanese /docview /1143874390 /se-2.

"Redress on Hold." *Globe and Mail*, November 19, 1985. A6. www.proquest.com /historical-newspapers /redress-on-hold /docview /1222381574 /se-2.

"Redress Should Be Made." *Winnipeg Free Press*, April 4, 1984. 9. archives. winnipegfreepress.com /winnipeg-free-press /1984-04-04 /page-9 /.

"Runners Wed at Finish Line: Now Real Marathon Begins." *Winnipeg Free Press*, June 18, 2001. 2. archives.winnipegfreepress.com /winnipeg-free-press /2001 -06-18 /page-2 /.

"She'll Proudly End Her Days a Canadian." *Winnipeg Free Press*, October 15, 2005. archives.winnipegfreepress.com /winnipeg-free-press /2005-10-15 /page-1 /.

"St. Boniface Would Ban Jap Workers [...]" *Winnipeg Free Press*, April 20, 1944. 3. archives.winnipegfreepress.com /winnipeg-free-press /1944-04-20 /page-3 /.

"Still Unenlightened." *Globe and Mail*, June 26, 1984. 6. www.proquest.com /historical-newspapers /still-unenlightened /docview /1313818135 /se-2.

"Talks Move Slowly." *Winnipeg Free Press*, January 14, 1985. 15. archives. winnipegfreepress.com /winnipeg-free-press /1985-01-14 /page-15 /.

"To Offset a Wrong." *Globe and Mail,* May 26, 1986. A6. www.proquest.com /newspapers/offset-wrong/docview/386129151/se-2.

"Top Veteran Favors War Compensation." *Winnipeg Free Press,* April 28, 1985. 2. archives.winnipegfreepress.com/winnipeg-free-press/1985-04-28/page-2/.

"Veterans Miss the Point." *Calgary Herald,* July 25, 1988. 4. www.newspapers.com /article/calgary-herald/133660293/.

"Wartime Wrongs Need Airing." *Toronto Star,* February 4, 1985. A10. www .newspapers.com/article/the-toronto-star/133553282/.

"Where's the Fire?" *Vancouver Sun,* January 30, 1986. A4. www.newspapers.com /article/the-vancouver-sun/133662208/.

"Wholesome Redress." *Globe and Mail,* January 22, 1986. A6. www.proquest.com /newspapers/wholesome-redress/docview/386199338/se-2.

LETTERS TO THE EDITOR

Campbell, George T. "Compensation Justified." *Calgary Herald,* August 16, 1988. A6. www.newspapers.com/article/calgary-herald/133660126/.

———. "Disagreement." *Winnipeg Free Press,* October 4, 1984. archives .winnipegfreepress.com/winnipeg-free-press/1984-10-04/page-1/.

Davies, J.C. "No Apology." *Winnipeg Free Press,* October 17, 1984. archives .winnipegfreepress.com/winnipeg-free-press/1984-10-17/page-1/.

"Let Japanese Bygones Be Bygones, Reader Says." *Globe and Mail,* May 22, 1984. 7. www.proquest.com/historical-newspapers/let-japanese-bygones-be-reader -says/docview/1237564338/se-2.

Parekh, Navin M. [No title.] *Globe and Mail,* March 20, 1986. A6. www .proquest.com /historical-newspapers /letter-editor-1-no-title /docview /1151430178/se-2.

Pople, John. "Better Late." *Winnipeg Free Press,* November 22, 1984. archives. winnipegfreepress.com/winnipeg-free-press/1984-11-22/page-1/.

Stroud, John R. "The Kamloops Kid." *Globe and Mail,* July 24, 1984. 6. www .proquest.com /historical-newspapers /unfair-battleground /docview /1237547195/se-2.

Sunahara, Ann Gomer. "Vets' Ruling Illogical." *Edmonton Journal,* August 7, 1988. B4. nikkeimuseum.org/www/item_detail.php?art_id=A41865.

INTERVIEWS

Andrew Cardoza. By Art Miki. August 23, 1988.

———. By Art Miki. May 12, 1994.

Anne Scotton, Japanese Canadian Redress Secretariat (JCRS). By Art Miki. Ottawa, September 27, 1995.

Audrey Kobayashi. By Art Miki. Montréal, June 29, 1994.

Dennison Moore, chief of staff for the Honourable Gerry Weiner. By Art Miki. Ottawa, May 27, 1984.

John Stroud. By CBC. N.d.

Joy Kamibayashi. By Art Miki. Ottawa, September 26, 1995.

Larry Hill. By Art Miki. Winnipeg, October 1, 2015.

Paul O'Donnell and Joanne Lamarre. By Art Miki. Ottawa, September 27, 1995.

Pierre Berton. By Art Miki. Vancouver Island, January 1985.

Roy Kawamoto. By Art Miki. Ottawa, September 26, 1995.

Sergio Marchi. By Art Miki. Ottawa, December 10, 1993.

Shizuko Miki. By Roy Miki. Winnipeg, August 11, 1989.

LETTERS

Art Miki to the Honourable Jack Murta, minister of multiculturalism. January 18, 1985.

Imperial Order Daughters of the Empire and Children to the Honourable Erick Willis, Premier of Manitoba. May 18, 1942.

Individual Japanese Canadians to the Honourable David Crombie. 1987.

NAJC to the Honourable David Crombie. May 1986.

Penny Simpson from Tatla Lake, BC, to Art Miki. September 1985.

Ramsay Cook, York University, to the Honourable David Crombie. May 1986.

Shirley Yamada to Art Miki. April 26, 1984.

WEBSITES

Abe, Namiko. "The Twelve Signs of the Japanese Zodiac: Does Your Zodiac Sign Fit Your Personality?" ThoughtCo. Updated October 16, 2019. www.thoughtco .com/japanese-zodiac-overview-2028019.

Canadian Teachers' Federation / Fédération canadienne des enseignantes et des enseignants (CTF/FCE). "Arthur Miki: Equality and Redress." Speak Truth to Power Canada. Accessed July 2023. sttpcanada.ctf-fce.ca/lessons/arthur-miki /interview/.

Horgan, John. "Acknowledgement of Internment and Japanese Canadian Legacies in BC." BC Redress. May 21, 2022. bcredress.ca.

"Japanese and Okinawan Bolivians." Wikipedia. Accessed July 2023. en.wikipedia. org/wiki/Japanese_and_Okinawan_Bolivians.

"Japanese Brazilians." Wikipedia. Accessed July 2023. en.wikipedia.org/wiki /Japanese_Brazilians.

FILMS

Masuda, Greg, dir. *Children of Redress*. 2014. movingimages.ca /fr /products /children-of-redress.

Miyagawa, Mitch, dir. *A Sorry State*. 2012. vimeo.com/43128341.

Onodera, Midi, dir. *The Displaced View*. 1988. midionodera.com /film /the -displaced-view/.

———. *Skin Deep*. 1995. midionodera.com/film/skin-deep/.

Ouchi, Mieko, dir. *Saiki: Regeneration*. 1998. centre.nikkeiplace.org/events/redress -film-night/.

Sonoda, Warren P., dir. *Things I Do for Money*. 2019. www.imdb.com /title /tt8932756/.

Stearns, Jeff Chiba, dir. *One Big Hapa Family*. 2010. www.imdb.com /title /tt1588374/.

Tatebe, Nancy, dir. *Momiji: Japanese Maple*. 1994. prod-www.tcm.com /tcmdb /title /516927/momiji-japanese-maple/#overview.

INDEX OF PROPER NAMES

GAMAN — PERSEVERANCE

ART (ARTHUR) KAZUMINI MIKI, CM, OM is an active leader in the Japanese Canadian community, having served as president of the National Association of Japanese Canadians from 1984 to 1992. He led the negotiations to achieve a just redress settlement for Japanese Canadians interned during World War II. He and his family were forcibly relocated to Manitoba sugar-beet farms in 1942.

For his efforts nationally, provincially, and locally, he has received this country's highest recognition, the Order of Canada, as well as the Order of Manitoba, and recently the Order of the Rising Sun from the government of Japan. He received an Honorary Doctorate from the University of Winnipeg and from St. John's College, University of Manitoba.

Art is past-president of the Japanese Cultural Association of Manitoba and of the Asian Heritage Society of Manitoba. With the Asian Heritage Society, Art has organized high-school symposiums on Asian heritage and is involved with activities fighting racism. He is a former teacher and principal, advisor to the Canadian Race Relations Foundation, a Canadian citizenship judge, and a lecturer at the University of Winnipeg.

PHOTO: Alex Miki